Streets in Motion

The book studies the social production of motion in a capitalist urban context. In the city of capital, motion refers to a fetish. The bourgeois order posits motion as a metaphor for energy, positivity, and progress—a norm—and obstruction (motion's dialectical opposite) as delinquency. The book uncovers the social tectonics of spatial mobilization and thus demystifies motion. Who and what set spaces on the move? How did various classes of city dwellers activate, experience, and negotiate motion?

Streets in Motion develops an approach to urban history by theorizing and historicizing the 'street' as an apparatus of city-making and subject formation. It works at two registers—a local history of Calcutta in colonial and post-colonial periods, and a theorizing of the logistical and political-cultural centrality of the street within this rubric. It is argued that the street is politics inasmuch as politics is the production of space.

Ritajyoti Bandyopadhyay teaches History and Political Economy at the Indian Institute of Science Education and Research, Mohali. He is also a permanent module fellow of the M.S. Merian–R. Tagore International Centre of Advanced Studies 'Metamorphoses of the Political'. Currently, he is a guest professor at the Centre for Modern Indian Studies, Universität Göttingen.

METAMORPHOSES OF THE POLITICAL: MULTIDISCIPLINARY APPROACHES

The Series is a publishing collaboration of Cambridge University Press with The M. S. Merian–R. Tagore International Centre of Advanced Studies 'Metamorphoses of the Political' (ICAS:MP). It seeks to publish new books that both expand and de-centre current perspectives on politics and the 'political' in the contemporary world. It examines, from a wide array of disciplinary and methodological approaches, how the 'political' has been conceptualized, articulated and transformed in specific arenas of contestation during the 'long twentieth century'. Though primarily located in India and the Global South, the Series seeks to interrogate and contribute to wider debates about global processes and politics. It is in this sense that the Series is imagined as one that is regionally focused but globally engaged, providing a context for interrogations of universalized theories of self, society and politics.

Series Editors:
- Niraja Gopal Jayal, King's College, London
- Shail Mayaram, formerly at Centre for the Study of Developing Societies, Delhi
- Samita Sen, University of Cambridge, Cambridge
- Awadhendra Sharan, Centre for the Study of Developing Societies, Delhi
- Sanjay Srivastava, SOAS, University of London, London
- Ravi Vasudevan, Centre for the Study of Developing Societies, Delhi
- Sebastian Vollmer, University of Göttingen, Germany

ICAS:MP is an Indo-German research collaboration of six Indian and German institutions funded by the German Federal Ministry of Education and Research (BMBF). It combines the benefits of an open, interdisciplinary forum for intellectual exchange with the advantages of a cutting-edge research centre. Located in New Delhi, ICAS:MP critically intervenes in global debates in the social sciences and humanities.

Other Titles in the Series
- *The Secret Life of AnOther Indian Nationalism: Transitions from the Pax Britannica to the Pax Americana* • Shail Mayaram
- *Debt, Trust, and Reputation: Extra-legal Finance in Northern India* • Sebastian Schwecke
- *Saffron Republic: Hindu Nationalism and State Power in India* • Edited by Thomas Blom Hansen and Srirupa Roy
- *Women, Gender and Religious Nationalism* • Edited by Amrita Basu and Tanika Sarkar

Streets in Motion
The Making of Infrastructure, Property, and
Political Culture in Twentieth-century Calcutta

Ritajyoti Bandyopadhyay

CAMBRIDGE
UNIVERSITY PRESS

Shaftesbury Road, Cambridge CB2 8EA, United Kingdom

One Liberty Plaza, 20th Floor, New York, NY 10006, USA

477 Williamstown Road, Port Melbourne, VIC 3207, Australia

314 to 321, 3rd Floor, Plot No. 3, Splendor Forum, Jasola District Centre, New Delhi 110025, India

103 Penang Road, #05–06/07, Visioncrest Commercial, Singapore 238467

Cambridge University Press is part of the University of Cambridge.

It furthers the University's mission by disseminating knowledge in the pursuit of education, learning and research at the highest international levels of excellence.

www.cambridge.org
Information on this title: www.cambridge.org/9781009100113

© Ritajyoti Bandyopadhyay 2022

This publication is in copyright. Subject to statutory exception and to the provisions of relevant collective licensing agreements, no reproduction of any part may take place without the written permission of Cambridge University Press.

First published 2022
Reprint 2024

Printed in India by Avantika Printers Pvt. Ltd.

A catalogue record for this publication is available from the British Library

ISBN 978-1-009-10011-3 Hardback

Cambridge University Press has no responsibility for the persistence or accuracy of URLs for external or third-party internet websites referred to in this publication, and does not guarantee that any content on such websites is, or will remain, accurate or appropriate.

Contents

List of Maps, Tables, Appendices, and Images	vii
List of Abbreviations	ix
Acknowledgements	xi
Introduction	1
1 The Making of the Modern Street: Engineers, Commoners, Agitators	36
2 The Regime of the Streets: Renewal and Riots, 1910–1926	73
3 City as Territory: Institutionalizing Majoritarianism	119
4 Frontier Urbanization	158
5 Durable Obstructions, Spatializing Motion: The History of Footpath Hawking in Calcutta	204
Epilogue	254
Glossary	268
Bibliography	271
Index	289

Maps, Tables, Appendices, and Images

Maps

1.1	The work of the Calcutta Improvement Trust between 1912 and 1947	41
2.1	The planned layout of Central Avenue in 1916	91
3.1	1946 Riot Map-1: 'North Calcutta'	128
3.2	1946 Riot Map-2: 'Central Calcutta'	129
3.3	1946 Riot Map-3: 'South Calcutta'	130

Tables

2.1	'The cost of this scheme, based upon the "assessed" value of the houses and lands through which it passes increased 15 percent' (between 1884 and 1888)	80
2.2	'[A]nd the corresponding cost of widening Cotton Street and Machooa Bazaar Street to 70 feet'	81
2.3	Objections raised by property owners of Bhawani Charan Dutt Lane and their status in 1918	94
2.4	Suits and tribunal decisions between 1922 and 1928	101
2.5	Resettlement of the displaced *bhadralok* owners from various scheme areas in central Calcutta	104
2.6	'War prices and house rents: statistics showing (1) wholesale and retail prices, and (2) house rents, at the end of December, 1917, as compared with the pre-War level (July, 1914), August, 1915, 1916, and 1917'	108
2.7	Increase in land prices per *cottah* between May–June 1919 and January 1920	112
3.1	Names of local clubs, *akharas*, associations, and their addresses in 1927	142

3.2	Fifty-year trend of Hindu–Muslim population ratio in Calcutta	145
4.1	Holdings along Russa Road between 1796 and 1939	162
4.2	Refugee encroachment of properties in south Calcutta	180
5.1	Pedestrian survey on 'Do hawkers cause obstruction to your passage?'	240
5.2	Pedestrian survey on 'Should hawkers be evicted for your passage?'	240

Appendices

| 4A.1 | Rice mills in the vicinity of Scheme IV | 195 |
| 4A.2 | Contractors and the Trust's operations, 1916–1928 | 198 |

Images

5.1	Demolition drive in Gariahat, 1996	246
5.2	Post–Operation Sunshine look of Sealdah	247
5.3	An image of a demolished stall, 1996	247
5.4	Having lost his stall due to demolition, a hawker trying to find his belongings among rubble being aided by a co-worker and a sympathetic policeman, 1996	248
5.5	Hawkers marked their stall locations after demolition with emotive appeals written in placards; this one was by one Badal Debnath who wrote, 'We want to live'	249
5.6	Hawkers and activists put a police traffic post on fire, 1996	249
5.7	A protest scene: a child hawker expresses his dissent, 1996	250
5.8	Hawkers trying to dismantle their shops before being bulldozed by the authorities, 1996	251
5.9	Opposition leader Mamata Banerjee (now Chief Minister of West Bengal) addressing citizens in a protest rally	251
5.10	A poster proclaiming how Bulu Poddar committed suicide having lost his job after Operation Sunshine, 1996	252
5.11	Hawkers trying to rescue their wares while the municipal payloader is about to demolish their stalls, 1996	252
5.12	Mamata Banerjee and her colleagues in the opposition selling garments in Gariahat while encouraging hawkers to reclaim their spaces	253

Abbreviations

CIT	Calcutta Improvement Trust
CMDA	Calcutta Metropolitan Development Authority
CSSSC	Centre for Studies in Social Sciences, Calcutta
HSC	Hawker Sangram Committee
NAI	National Archives of India, New Delhi
NHF	National Hawker Federation
SVA	Street Vendors (Protection of Livelihood and Regulation of Street Vending) Act, 2014
WBSA	West Bengal State Archives, Kolkata

Acknowledgements

This is a book about the mobilization of space in twentieth-century Calcutta and its social outcomes. Like many books of historical materialism, this book, too, is a product of political mobilizations that informed contemporary public debates about our cities. I thank all my interlocutors, especially the footpath hawkers of Kolkata, for including me in their struggles over the last two decades. I extend my gratitude to all those human rights activists who are literally on the streets to protect India's Constitution. I am also obliged to the tax-paying publics of two countries—India and Germany—for ensuring my livelihood during the last decade when this book gradually took shape.

I am indebted to many institutions for providing research, logistical, and livelihood support during this journey. This study began at the National Institute of Advanced Studies (NIAS), Bangalore, where I was employed immediately after my PhD. Subsequently, I pursued this line of inquiry while at the Centre for Modern Indian Studies (CeMIS) in the University of Göttingen, Centre for Studies in Social Sciences, Calcutta (CSSSC), and the Indian Institute of Science Education and Research (IISER), Mohali. I am thankful to various libraries and archives from where I collected the research materials for this book.

Many friends and comrades in South Asian History and Urban Studies actively contributed to the making of this book. They are too many, spreading across three continents. I am especially grateful to Saeed Ahmad, Debarati Bagchi, Trina Nileena Banerjee, Deepasri Baul, Akash Bhattacharya, Samata Biswas, Lisa Björkman, Devika Bordia, Camille Buat, Upal Chakrabarti, Humadri Chatterjee, Neha Chatterji, Sumandro Chattopadhyay, Priyankar Dey, Curt Gambetta, Rajarshi Ghose, Anwesha Ghosh, Nabaparna Ghosh, Ujaan Ghosh, Bodhisattva Kar, Iman Mitra, Uponita Mukherjee, Pratyay Nath, Rajan Pandey, Sushmita Pati, Ritwik Ranjan, Srimoy Roy Chaudhury, Sanam Roohi, Anu Sabhlok, Anna Sailer, Aditya Sarkar, Parnisha Sarkar, Sebastian Schwecke, Anwesha Sengupta, Aviroop Sengupta, Kaustubh Mani Sengupta, and Shivali Tukdeo for constant intellectual and emotional support. Many of them read some of the chapters and gave detailed comments. Debarati read the first-ever draft of the introduction and cautioned me about its shortcomings.

I continued to receive valuable advice and encouragements from senior academics, mentors, and colleagues such as Ravi Ahuja, Sibaji Bandyopadhyay, Amita Baviskar, Solomon Benjamin, Dwaipayan Bhattacharyya, Rajesh Bhattacharya, Swapan Chakravorty, Anuradha Chanda, Partha Chatterjee, Shibashis Chatterjee, Rosinka Choudhuri, Soumyabrata Choudhury, Supriya Chaudhuri, Anirban Das, Keya Dasgupta, Rajarshi Dasgupta, Partho Datta, Prachi Deshpande, Satish Deshpande, Curt Gambetta, Tapati Guha-Thakurta, Niraja Gopal Jayal, Bodhisattva Kar, Manabi Majumdar, Prabhu Mohapatra, Manas Ray, Raka Ray, Nate Roberts, Ananya Roy, Joyashree Roy, Srirupa Roy, Ranabir Samaddar, Priya Sangameswaran, Aditya Sarkar, Tanika Sarkar, Samita Sen, Sanjay Srivastava, Lakshmi Subramanian, Carol Upadhya, Lalit Vachani, and Rupa Viswanath. Several long academic sessions with many of them, particularly Dwaipayan Bhattacharyya, Partha Chatterjee, Rajarshi Dasgupta, Prachi Deshpande, Tapati Guha-Thakurta, Bodhisattva Kar, Srirupa Roy, Ranabir Samaddar, Aditya Sarkar, and Samita Sen over the last decade have been absolutely formative in my growth as an academic. Bodhi *da* insisted me repeatedly to move away from my PhD thesis and write a new book on Calcutta's streets. Here it is! I thank my teachers from university days—Sudeshna Banerjee, Anuradha Chanda, Jayanta Sengupta, Nupur Dasgupta, Rila Mukherkee, Kunal Chattopadhyay, Ranabir Samaddar, and Samita Sen—for nurturing my interest in history. Anuradha *di* was my first-ever thesis supervisor. She is the reason why I pursued research.

Deepasri Baul, Partho Datta, Ranabir Samaddar, and Samita Sen were kind enough to read various drafts of the whole book and provide important comments that enriched the project in many ways. Deepasri remained a key interlocutor during the final stage of this project. Arpita Das of Yoda Press agreed to professionally edit this book thoroughly. She did a fantastic job in making me realize the difference between a PhD dissertation and a book.

I am thankful to Lekha Adavi, Parag Banerjee, Abhishek Chaudhuri, Saktiman Ghosh, Subhadip Ghosh, Shreya Ghosh, Murad Hussain, Manjari Jain, Kanupriya, Ramaswami, Partho Sarothi Ray, Anu Sablok, Neeraja Sahasrabudhe, Ranbir Sharma, Vinay Srinivasa, and Vaibhav Vaish for being my mentors and comrades in many battles on the streets. Saktiman Ghosh has been a living archive for me on various urban matters. This project would not have been possible without his critical support.

This project would not have been possible without the intellectual and logistical support of the M.S. Merian – R. Tagore International Centre of Advanced Studies 'Metamorphoses of the Political' (ICAS:MP). This collaboration gave me the right environment to pursue research with an office space in Delhi, financial support for archival research, and consultation with the Indian and German academic world through workshops and conferences. I am thankful to Laila Abu-Er-Rub,

Rohan R. Seth, and other colleagues at the ICAS:MP and the Max Weber Stiftung for their support. Debjani Mazumder was crucial in making me write this book. Much of my final writing happened in the ICAS:MP office. My collaboration with the ICAS:MP researchers gave me two opportunities to spend time at the CeMIS in the University of Göttingen. I started writing this book at the CeMIS and finished the project at the CeMIS. Lalit and Srirupa frequently invited me to dinner and took care of me when I was writing intensely. I am thankful to Karin Klenke and her team for necessary administrative support. Karin is also a great friend and a warm host besides being an anthropologist. The Hawker Sangram Committee allowed me to reproduce some of the rare images from their archives. I was told that some journalists and activists had taken those pictures during a brutal eviction drive in 1996–1997. I am thankful to all those citizens of Calcutta who documented the drive meticulously. I tried my best to find those images in contemporary newspapers and periodicals. I shall be happy to acknowledge and further cite the sources if somebody can identify their photographers.

I am thankful to the staff and archivists of the Centre for Studies in Social Sciences, Calcutta, the Hawker Sangram Committee and the Kolkata Improvement Trust for their unconditional support.

Many students, who worked with me in the last ten years, shaped my sensibilities. Some of them worked directly with me, while others maintained a deep intellectual engagement with my work. To name a few, I am deeply indebted to Amartyajyoti Basu, Biboswan Bose, Mayukh Chakrabarty, Pintu Das, Soumita Mazumder, Ashirbad Mishra, Vikas Kumar Moola, Ritam Sengupta, and Mihir Singh for illuminating discussions on my project. Brainstorming with some of my remarkable undergraduate students at IISER Mohali such as Nandan Malhotra, Kavir Manali, Lakshmi Ramesh, Swaparjith, and Aishwarya Viswamitra has been deeply enriching. The members of the 'Infrastructure Studies Research Group'—Rashid Ali, Amartyajyoti Basu, Deepasri Baul, Navdeep Bora, Himadri Chatterjee, Manisha K, Jonayed Roushan Mandal, Vikas Kumar Moola, Rajan Pandey, Ashirbad Mishra, Shriya Raina, Nikita Singh, and Subham Amarendra Singh—kept me intellectually engaged. I have benefited from conversations with all the PhD students at the Department of Humanities and Social Sciences.

I have learned a lot from my departmental colleagues and thank all of them for developing a cordial academic environment in the department. I am a regular guest in the drawing rooms of Abhishek, Anu, Manjari, Neeraja, and Prasad. They are comrades in many battles in the past five years. I thank them and their families for their care and friendship. Shobha Madan has been a true friend and a warm host. She gave away many of her valuable books along with three bookshelves, while leaving Mohali. Those books made my leisure at home colourful. Somdatta Sinha encouraged me to keep singing in all these years, braving all kinds of pressure in professional life. I am thankful to Devika, Kavita *ji*, Prema *ji*, Saraswati *di*, and Suresh *ji* for keeping our household in order.

I hope the next generation will read this book and come to know about a century that they had not experienced. Their representatives made this expedition enjoyable. I shall keep my thoughts in the safest custody of Ananda, Anushka, Darshan, Dimpu, Laila, Jhinuk, Kuhu, Oishi, Pudlu, Rai, Riti, Rukai, Toya, Umang, and all the 'campus kids' of IISER Mohali.

Besides my family, I grew up under the care of some remarkable teachers of a small-town college. They gave me a reading habit, a taste for deep learning, and a dream to work from a great reference library. They have been my earliest mentors.

Some of my well-wishers have passed away over the last few years. I shall miss Kalyan Bhattacharyya, Pradip Bose, Swapan Chakravorty, Amaresh Das, Prasanta Dhar, Hemanta Mukhopadhyay, Shrimoy Roy Chaudhury, and Hari Vasudevan.

Dimu passed away peacefully at my home in Mohali during the lockdown. She would have been the happiest person in the world to see the book's publication. She became part of my life more intensely in the last decade. Debarati, Dimu, and I shared an unalloyed emotional bonding which kept us going even during the most difficult phase of our life. I shall not mention Debarati's contribution to prolong this acknowledgement. Some acknowledgements are bound to remain private.

I am thankful to Qudsiya Ahmed, Priyanka Das, Aniruddha De, and Anwesha Rana of Cambridge University Press for their support and encouragement. Three anonymous reviewers played a very significant role in helping me give this book its current shape.

Introduction

… the scandalous alleys disappear to the accompaniment of lavish self-praise by the bourgeoisie on account of this tremendous success, but they appear again immediately somewhere else…. The breeding places of disease, the infamous holes and cellars in which the capitalist mode of production confines our workers night after night, are not abolished; they are merely shifted elsewhere! The same economic necessity that produced them in the first place, produces them in the next place.

—Friedrich Engels[1]

> O what a dream of dreams I had one night!
> I could hear Binu crying out in fright,
> 'Come quickly and you'll see a startling sight:
> Our city's rushing in a headlong flight!' …
>
> Rolls on the Howrah Bridge
> Like a giant centipede
> Chased by Harrison Road
> Breaking the traffic code …

—Rabindranath Tagore[2]

When I entered the dusty 'record room' of the Calcutta Improvement Trust[3] for the first time in 2011—exactly a century since its inception—and began to

---

[1] Friedrich Engels, 'The Housing Question' (1872), published (and re-published) as a pamphlet, reprinted by the Co-operative Publishing Society of Foreign Workers, transcribed: Zodiac, June 1995: https://www.marxists.org/archive/marx/works/1872/housing-question/index.htm, accessed 3 October 2021.

[2] Rabindranath Tagore, 'The Runaway City', in *Rabindranath Tagore: Selected Writings for Children*, ed. Sukanta Chaudhuri, trans. Sukhendu Ray (New Delhi: Oxford University Press, 2002), 25.

[3] For an understanding of the genesis of the Calcutta Improvement Trust and the debates around it in 1910–1911, see Partho Datta, *Planning the City: Urbanization and Reform in Calcutta, c. 1800–c. 1940* (New Delhi: Tulika Books, 2012).

discover Calcutta in the early-twentieth-century planning documents, land acquisition records, and files of property disputes, these two quoted texts gave me a perspective: a study of the city is a study of the social production of 'motion'.

In mechanics, motion refers to the phenomenon by which matter changes position over time. It marks displacement and distance, change and acceleration of objects along the coordinates of time and space. In a historical materialist enquiry—on the other hand—motion stands for 'impersonal' forces operating within a mode of production in a given time and space that enact social change, movements of bodies, capital, migration, and displacement.

People's relationship with motion is marked by differential access based on class, caste, gender, ethnicity, race, and generational hierarchies. Therefore, a critique of motion must track its politics in generating 'mobile subjectivities' and differential mobilities. More importantly, it ought to identify how one social group's access to motion may actively exclude or disable that of others.[4] In my story, the 'modern' urban street is a central actor and a key mediator between such mobilities and materialities.[5]

The quote by Engels that opens this book situates the modern avenue-style urban streets in the context of the capitalist mode of production that consolidated itself in space during the second half of the nineteenth century after many decades of urban insurrections in Europe and in the colonial world. The second quote, by Tagore, reveals the anxiety of a city dweller in grasping the spaces already inserted in capital's creative destruction. It represents the moment of transition to a new regime of motion that came as a revolution—when the located and 'sunk' infrastructures appeared unstable, rootless, and on the move.

The discourse of motion creates its own contexts and effects under the capitalist mode of production. This is a book to uncover the social tectonics of spatial mobilization and thus demystify motion.[6] Who and what set spaces on the move? How did various classes of city dwellers activate, experience, and negotiate it? What meanings, sensibilities, and values did they attach

---

[4] Doreen Massey, 'A Global Sense of Place', in *Exploring Human Geography*, ed. Stephen Daniels and Roger Lee (London: Routledge, 1996), 237–245; Kevin Hannam, Mimi Sheller, and John Urry, 'Editorial: Mobilities, Immobilities and Moorings', *Mobilities* 1, no. 1 (2006): 1–22.

[5] Peter Adey, 'If Mobility Is Everything Then It Is Nothing: Towards a Relational Politics of (Im)mobilities', *Mobilities* 1, no. 1 (2006): 75–94.

[6] Motion can be viewed as a 'bourgeois masculine subjectivity' that projects itself as 'cosmopolitan'. Skeggs Beverley, *Class, Self, Culture* (London: Routledge, 2004).

with motion, and what were the implications of spatial motion for the city as a 'settlement'? Every human 're-action' to spatial mobilization was also a new action. City dwellers acted and did something and did not merely react. What did they act upon and act towards? How did they form and transform spaces through labour and action? Conversely, what mobilized them to action? Did a distinctly twentieth-century vision of urbanism emerge in Calcutta as a result of these encounters? If so, how did it proceed through a century?

Tagore was a resident of a central Calcutta neighbourhood which witnessed a momentous transformation in the early twentieth century at the behest of the Improvement Trust.[7] Several new thoroughfares came to cause a considerable demographic and spatial reorganization of the central quarters of Calcutta. Jorasanko, where the poet resided, witnessed the destruction of old dwellings, gardens, ponds, and *bustee*s,[8] as land entered the whirlwind of speculation in the post–First World War years. The new north–south Central Avenue—built between 1914 and 1928—divided central Calcutta into two halves and swallowed neighbourhoods, houses, and lanes that dotted the place in the nineteenth century. The Tagore family and other already decaying rentier Bengali families lost control over the city as many of the *bustee*s, houses, bazaars, and shops they once possessed and circulated in the rental market gave way to compulsory land acquisition and real estate developments, and were passed on to the city's upwardly mobile Marwari trading community.[9]

---

[7] The rise of nationalist movements since the late nineteenth century and their gradual penetration in civic governments elicited a strong response from the colonial state. These developments coincided with the rise of an expert-managed, urban reform state culminating in the founding of the Improvement Trusts in Bombay (1898), Calcutta (1911), and Delhi (1936). These Improvement Trusts were deliberately kept out of the fast nationalizing and democratizing municipal corporations, and they were given enormous power of demolition and enclosure. Prashant Kidambi, 'Housing the Poor in a Colonial City: The Bombay Improvement Trust', *Studies in History* 17, no. 1 (2001): 57–79.

[8] In Calcutta, a *bustee* (slum) in the early twentieth century referred to a collection of hutments with a three-layer class structure. At the top of it was the owner (*zamindar*) of the land with rent-collecting rights from the *thika* (leasehold) tenants. The latter were often a group of non-resident hut owners (some might have lived in the huts themselves as well) who took land lease from the owner and rented out huts to the working-class dwellers (*bharatiyas*).

[9] In Rajasthan, Marwari refers to anybody who resides in or traces his or her homeland in the Marwar region (formerly the princely state of Jodhpur). In the rest of India, especially in Calcutta, the term applies to whoever has migrated

The new automobile-friendly avenue-style streets unsettled the old Bengali rentier class. They also cast out a large section of the lower-middle-class and working-class populations as they brought the hitherto 'locked up' spaces into the circuits of capital accumulation. This recycling of the inner city was accompanied by several schemes aimed at the phased dispersal of residents into Calcutta's frontier suburbs. But in the frontiers, planned urbanization ensured large-scale enclosure, land use transformation, and dispossession. Furthermore, a large section of those evicted due to inner-city gentrification could not find resettlement in these new suburbs due to already high land prices. These changes intensified social tensions in the city sharply in the interwar decades.

The new streets and public spaces, which emerged as a result of this urban revolution, became entangled with the distinctly twentieth-century developments of mass communalism, trade unionism, popular sovereignty,[10] mass democracy, and the collective encroachment of vital urban infrastructures by the dispossessed. How did the city embrace and evolve with this new political climate? How did the production of space and the production of political culture condition each other over the twentieth century?

In this book, I propose to develop an approach to urban history by theorizing and historicizing the 'street' that emerged in the context of the nineteenth-century urban insurrections and evolved with the twentieth-century automobile revolution and mass political culture. I work at two registers—a local history of Calcutta in

---

from Rajasthan. By the nineteenth century, this community became one of the wealthiest trading communities of the British Empire. When jute industry began in Calcutta in the mid-nineteenth century, hundreds of Marwari traders migrated to Calcutta and settled in Burrabazaar. Most of the notable Marwari houses in Calcutta's Burrabazaar came from Sikar, Bikaner, and Jhunjhunu. Anne Hardgrove, *Community and Public Culture: The Marwaris in Calcutta* (New Delhi: Oxford University Press, 2004); Ritu Birla, *Stages of Capital: Law, Culture, and Market Governance in Late Colonial India* (Durham: Duke University Press, 2009).

[10] During the middle of this century, the colonial world transitioned from imperial-colonial to (putatively) popular sovereignty. In the Indian context, popular sovereignty coincided with the age of mass democracy. Universal adult franchise contributed immensely to mass political formations, which fundamentally transformed the relation between the municipal government and the governed. Gradually, the Left and other smaller political parties emerged as important political constituencies that offered this new post-colonial electorate the choice to advance pressing issues such as housing crisis and unemployment into the forefront of political debate.

colonial and post-colonial periods, and a theorizing of the logistical and political-cultural centrality of the street within this rubric.[11] The book discusses the street as an apparatus of city-making and moves on to various kinds of subject formation over the twentieth century. It is also about the ways in which various social groups accessed, inhabited, and attached meanings to the street, imagined the city, and how the street shaped and moulded social relations, cooperation, and conflicts in twentieth-century Calcutta. In so doing, I study institutions, conventions, policies, power, and politics that contributed to the making and the governing of the street. As an instrument of politics, the street was central to the execution of state power, class power, communal authority, and their contestations.

I have three central objectives. First, I wish to study the production of urban space in colonial and post-colonial contexts through the life of the streets. I deploy the triad—property, territory, accumulation—as the template of urban history. My desire is to unravel the colonial and post-colonial imports of the relationship between urbanization and accumulation in Calcutta—a city that moved from the Empire's 'second city' to India's 'dying metropolis' in the twentieth-century autobiography of capital. *Streets in Motion* contests this hegemonic representation of Calcutta by documenting how a 'people's economy' kept the city vibrant in all these decades of apparent decadence and disorder.

Second, I probe into the relation between space (infrastructure) and polity (superstructure) and describe the materialities of political culture. I show how popular sovereignty materialized in space in the twentieth-century city. I argue that popular and collective actions on the streets were not merely the

---

[11] Studying colonial Calcutta from its streets is not a new thing. There are at least four volumes that had done so in the past. The first volume about the streets was by Harisadhan Mukhopadhyaya, *Kolikata: Sekaler O Ekaler* (Calcutta: P. M. Bagchi, 1915, reprint in 1985). This book contains a long discussion about Calcutta's old streets. Ajit Kumar Basu, *Kolikatar Rajpath: Samaje O Sanskritite* (Calcutta: Ananda Publishers, 1996). The author was an employee of the Municipal Corporation. This volume contains histories of the streets from primary materials. P. T. Nair, *A History of Calcutta's Streets* (Calcutta: Firma KLM, 1987). This book is known for its encyclopaedic qualities. These books helped me in tracking colonial documents in the archives and the National Library, Kolkata. My use and interpretation of those documents were, however, very different. A more recent and academically sophisticated account of Calcutta's history through its streets is by Sumanta Banerjee, *The Memoirs of the Roads: Calcutta from Colonial Urbanization to Global Modernization* (Delhi: Oxford University Press, 2016).

epiphenomenon of property relations; it was in fact the indeterminacy of popular politics on the streets that reframed the contours of the city's political economy and infrastructure through the twentieth century. Thus, in tracing the dialectic between planning and dwelling, physical space, and social practice, I consider political economy not just within its usual domain of the government, the law, and the planner's apparatus but also parallelly within the unlikely domain of public action on the street. In this sense, the crowd is not simply the dialectical antithesis of the planner. It performs, in some instances, the groundwork for the plan. For instance, *jabardakhal*, or the forcible collective occupation of space by people, in the context of a refugee influx and mass democracy (as discussed in Chapter 4), rebuilt the city and its frontiers and designed new calculative rationalities by reversing the order of planning and practice.

Third, this is also a book about the twentieth-century urban experience. In the extant South Asian urban historiography, the twentieth century has been treated rather unevenly. For instance, Douglas E. Haynes and Nikhil Rao have identified the five decades between 1920 and 1970 as particularly impoverished of historical attention.[12] These decades are sandwiched between the 'long nineteenth century' and what might be called the equally long twenty-first century, which is deemed to have started in India since the liberalization of the economy in 1991. However, the decades between 1920 and 1970 were some of the most formidable ones when automobility, mass politics, and organized appropriation of the street came together to give rise to a new urban political and material culture. The absence of an adequate urban historiography related to the mid-twentieth-century decades has resulted in what Haynes and Rao call a 'radical disjuncture' between historical works and contemporary urban studies.[13]

---

[12] Douglas E. Haynes and Nikhil Rao, 'Beyond the Colonial City: Re-Evaluating the Urban History of India: 1920–1970', *South Asia: Journal of South Asian Studies* 36, no. 3 (2013): 317–335. Nikhil Rao makes an admirable attempt to bring the early twentieth century in conversation with the Nehruvian era after Independence. In many ways, Rao's book has remained a silent reference-point for the current work. Nikhil Rao, *House, But No Garden: Apartment Living in Bombay's Suburbs, 1898–1964* (Minneapolis: University of Minnesota Press, 2013).

[13] It is only in Janaki Nair's monumental work on Bangalore that one sees a robust venture to link the developments until 1920 with post-colonial processes. Even in her work, however, there is a lack of attention to the three intervening decades of the 1920s, 1930s, and 1940s, and their significance in the making of this premier south Indian city. Janaki Nair, *The Promise of the Metropolis: Bangalore's Twentieth Century* (New Delhi: Oxford University Press, 2005). Some more recent works on

Perhaps, Calcutta is the only city to have some literature on the mid-twentieth-century decades. A variety of factors affecting the popular life of the city in these decades—the rise of mass nationalism in the realm of civic politics, the Second World War and the Bengal Famine in 1943, intermittent communal riots, and finally the refugee influx after the Partition of British India—kept historians occupied.[14] While these works have enriched our understanding of Calcutta in the twentieth century, they are not urban histories. The city is in

---

Delhi after the transfer of the capital from Calcutta have underscored the necessity for more discussions on the decades between 1911 and 1947. Awadhendra Sharan's brilliant historical work on an environmental history of Delhi's 'congestion' remains one of the rare works that takes the discussion through the colonial to the current neoliberal conjuncture. Awadhendra Sharan, *In the City, Out of Place: Nuisance, Pollution and Dwelling in Delhi, 1850–2000* (Delhi: Oxford University Press, 2014). This is also a work that situates the Delhi Improvement Trust in historical perspective. Most of the other historical works on Delhi rarely breached the great wall of 1947.

[14] Indivar Kamtekar, 'The Shiver of 1942', *Studies in History* 18, no. 1 (2002): 81–102; Janam Mukherjee, *Hungry Bengal: War, Famine and the End of Empire* (Noida: HarperCollins, 2015); Tanika Sarkar and Sekhar Bandyopadhyay (eds.), *Calcutta: The Stormy Decades* (London: Routledge, 2015); Suranjan Das, *Communal Riots in Bengal, 1905–1947* (Delhi: Oxford University Press, 1993). Calcutta's social, spatial, and political developments in the 1950s and the 1960s have been covered by the Partition historians. They discussed the meaning of Partition among the refugees, their everyday struggles after they flocked into Calcutta, their rehabilitation, and agitation by squatter groups, which resulted in the expansion of citizenship in Calcutta. Some of these works provide rich narratives of Calcutta's urban life in the early post-colonial years. Prafulla Chakrabarti, *The Marginal Men: The Refugees and the Left Political Syndrome in West Bengal* (Calcutta: Naya Udyog Edition, 1999); Nilanjana Chatterjee, 'Midnight's Unwanted Children: East Bengali Refugees and the Politics of Rehabilitation' (PhD dissertation, Brown University, 1994); Sandip Bandyopadhyay, 'The Riddles of Partition: Memories of the Bengali Hindus', in *Reflections of the Partition in the East*, ed. Ranabir Samaddar (Delhi: Vikas, 1997), 59–72; Joya Chatterji, *The Spoils of Partition: Bengal and India, 1947–67* (Cambridge: Cambridge University Press, 2007); Uditi Sen, *Citizen Refugee: Forging the Indian Nation after Partition* (Cambridge: Cambridge University Press, 2018); Romola Sanyal, 'Contesting Refugeehood: Squatting as Survival in Post-Partition Calcutta', *Social Identities* 15, no. 1 (2009): 67–84; Romola Sanyal, 'Hindu Space: Urban Dislocations in Post-Partition Calcutta', *Transactions of the British Institute of Geographers* 39, no. 1 (2014): 38–49; Anwesha Sengupta, 'The Railway Refugees: Sealdah, the 1950s–1960s', IDSK Working Paper Series: https://ideas.repec.org/p/ess/wpaper/id11759.html, accessed 12 August 2020.

the background as a stage. *Streets in Motion* belongs to contemporary urban history drawing insights from social history, historical anthropology, and labour history. Because of its complex life histories, a focus on the street of Calcutta has compelled a threading together of seemingly diverse historical processes that unfolded over the twentieth century into a narrative whole.

As a means and an outcome of these objectives, I develop a 'thick description' of how Calcutta's streets witnessed the unfolding of the twentieth century. The street is the framing device of our story, which is also a metaphor. The streets of Calcutta were imbricated with rich histories of political struggles and livelihood, turning it into a metaphorical space where human rights, equality, and dignity could be asserted. I harness this narrative power of the street as I weave stories of property, rent, communalism, and livelihood in twentieth-century Calcutta. In reading the street in this way, we come to a deeper understanding of the social production of (its) motion.

The Twentieth-century Street

The street is a space immediately outside privately controlled spaces—a space shared by a group more substantial than a single household, a passage that must be navigated before one can access other private or public spaces. It is a shared intermediate space between buildings, dwellings, parks, and other sites, which may or may not be public. As an interstitial space, the street plays a vital role in determining urban form and social life.

Our language recognizes the power of the word 'street'. An examination of this word and its etymological migration reveals that 'street' is indeed a playful word. The *Cambridge Dictionary* definition is worth considering: 'a road in a city or town that has buildings that are usually close together along one or both sides'. A couple of associations are integral to the very lexical definition of the street. First, streets must inhabit an urban world ('a city or town') and, second, streets must share boundaries with a dense assemblage of buildings 'along one or both sides', that is, the street by definition is three dimensional, involving not just the surface and sidewalks but also vertical projections for which it provides a baseline. In short, the street is urban, and it refers to an ensemble of spaces—a 'spatial complex'.

The street is etymologically unique. Even its closest synonym—the road—does not necessarily convey the same social and literary connotations of the street. Roads are corridors that connect points in space. Streets, on the other hand, presuppose and result in density, congestion, conviviality, and neighbourliness of urban life.[15] In spatial practices such as urban design and planning, the street is often imagined as a stage on which public life is performed—a backdrop to activities that are designed within its boundaries. Consequently, regulations ranging from land use and zoning, restrictions on hawking and dwelling, and traffic lights attempt to circumscribe its trajectories of use and movement.[16] Streets, therefore, refer to a lifeworld.

An ensemble of spaces, which hosts 'life' as it were, streets perform a social function wherein various kinds of boundary crossings occur. Unsurprisingly, then, streets have been the object of anxieties about social intercourse and forms of collective belonging and exchange that are unpredictable but vital forces in the life of a city. Regularly, urban life unsettles the social, economic, vehicular, and hygienic functions that are assigned to the street. This not only creates many alternative meanings in space but also influences urban planning. Thus, the tension between planning and practice, 'intended' use and 'actual' use, remains alive in the street.

The messy relations of the street were increasingly scrutinized since the late nineteenth century by discourses of sanitation and colonial-era improvement schemes and often managed through techniques of segregation between black and white towns in colonial India.[17] The street was evaluated through what Anthony Vidler calls a 'pathology of urban form', where urban processes were understood as living organisms whose 'ills' and 'dysfunctionalities' could be 'diagnosed'.[18] Unfolding in the shadow of the Enlightenment, industrialization in Europe, and colonization, reformers/administrators of the colonial and post-colonial cities indexed the health of the city through the perceived health of the street, stirring up socialist critiques of industrial capitalism by thinkers such as Friedrich Engels, as well as provided the seed for the demolition drives of Baron Haussmann in Paris. Either way, it was supposed that to improve the street was to improve the city at large, assuring a healthy and productive urban society.[19]

[15] Lata Mani, 'Urban Triptych', *Seminar* 636 (August 2012): https://www.india-seminar.com/2012/636/636_lata_mani.htm, accessed 12 October 2021.

[16] Curt Gambetta and Ritajyoti Bandyopadhyay, 'The Problem', in Curt Gambetta and Ritajyoti Bandyopadhyay (eds.), *Streetscapes: A Symposium on the Future of the Street*, *Seminar* 636 (August 2012): https://www.india-seminar.com/2012/636/636_the_problem.htm, accessed 12 October 2021. This co-authored editorial piece has served as a constant reference-point for this book. The idea of this book emerged out of this exercise.

[17] Ibid.

[18] Anthony Vidler, *The Scenes of the Street and Other Essays* (New York: The Monacelli Press, 2011).

[19] Gambetta and Bandyopadhyay, 'The Problem'. For a historiographical account of the streets in Indian cities, see Ritajyoti Bandyopadhyay, 'Negotiating Informality:

The twentieth-century street emerged in Europe, in the crucible of revolutions and insurrections that took place in the eighteenth and the nineteenth centuries. In Paris, we know, the Revolution of 1848 thrived on strategically placed barricades in the early-modern architectural layout of the city. Riots and rebellions found their home in densely populated and closely built-up streets where life and labour, production, and reproduction, came into close interface. The authoritarian state that followed the Revolution of 1848 destroyed the early-modern riotous Paris streets and replaced them with a series of intersecting and parallel avenue-style streets, along with diagonal thoroughfares. Unobstructed straight lines 'through the closely-built workers' quarters' made the city spatially legible. Paris in the hands of Haussmann became a template of authoritarian urban reform for the rest of the world.

While commenting on the spatial contexts of the 1848 Revolution and the 1871 Commune, Engels wrote in 1895: 'Rebellion in the old style, the street fight with barricades, which up to 1848 gave everywhere the final decision, was to a considerable extent obsolete [in 1871].' The Revolution of 1848 exposed the spatially beleaguered state of the authority in the city, which called for major avenue-building initiatives. As Engels writes in 1872:

> By 'Haussmann' I mean the practice which has now become general of making breaches in the working class quarters of our big towns,

---

Changing Faces of Kolkata's Footpaths, 1975–2005' (PhD dissertation, Faculty of Arts, Jadavpur University, 2010): http://hdl.handle.net/10603/146584, accessed 24 February 2022; Jonathan Anjaria, 'Is There a Culture of the Indian Street?', *Seminar* 636 (2012): https://www.india-seminar.com/2012/636/636_jonathan_s_anjaria.htm, accessed 24 February 2022. In this essay, Anjaria classifies writings on the Indian streets into three categories: The first sees the street as a space of *difference* (I would rather say *deviation* from the *ideal* western model). These writings see the streets as reflective of 'the exotic orient', a 'premature metropolis' (Nirmal Kumar Bose, 'Calcutta: A Premature Metropolis', *Scientific American* 213, no. 3 [1965]: 90–102), or 'underdeveloped' (Sidney Low, *A Vision of India* [New York: E. P. Dutton and Company, 1907]). The second group (of a more recent origin) sees streets as 'manifestations of power, arenas on which forces of global capital and ideologies of neo-liberalism unfold' (Arvind Rajagopal, 'The Violence of Commodity Aesthetics: Hawkers, Demolition Raids, and a New Regime of Consumption', *Social Text* 19, no. 3 [2001]: 91–113). The third perspective—a 'culturalist' approach—observes the street in terms of 'their unique rhythms and logic of practice' (Arjun Appadurai, 'Street Culture', *The India Magazine* 8, no. 1 [December 1987]: 12–22; Sarayu Ahuja, *Where the Streets Lead* [New Delhi: Penguin, 1997]).

and particularly in those which are centrally situated, quite apart from whether this is done from considerations of public health and for beautifying the town, or owing to the demand for big centrally situated business premises, or owing to traffic requirements, such as the laying down of railways, streets, etc.[20]

In another place, he adds:

> The newly built quarters of the large cities, erected since 1848, have been laid out in long, straight, wide streets, as if made for the effective use of the cannon and rifles. The revolutionary would be mad who would of himself select the new working class districts of the north and east of Berlin for barricade struggle.[21]

Similarly, some cities in colonial South Asia, like Delhi and Lucknow, also underwent a major recycling of urban space in the post-1857 rebellion reconstruction. According to an estimate, one-third of Delhi was demolished after the rebellion to make way for new kinds of racial segregation of space. Roads and railway lines were deliberately run through the densely populated native neighbourhoods. A railway station and associated roads were positioned in such a manner as to demarcate the native quarters from the European areas of the Civil Lines.[22] Recycling is valorizing.

In Calcutta, colonial authorities set up an expert-managed Improvement Trust in 1911, whose 'street schemes' in the central city were deliberately run through the *bustee*s and the 'street-less' neighbourhoods to produce a more legible and automobile friendly urbanscape—free of insurrections and riots.[23] The central city where this renewal took place was not yet fully motorized and small enough for someone to traverse it on foot. The whole city was still centripetal in the early twentieth century. All other parts had to converge in this tiny area for trade and commerce, livelihood, and education. Its lanes and alleyways acquired notoriety during the Swadeshi Movement for clandestine

---

[20] Engels, 'The Housing Question'.
[21] Friedrich Engels, 'Introduction to Karl Marx's *Class Struggle in France, 1848–1850*', in *Selected Works of Karl Marx and Friedrich Engels*, vol. 1 (Moscow: Progress Publishers, 1969), 1–14.
[22] Anish Vanaik, *Possessing the City: Property and Politics in Delhi, 1911–1947* (Oxford: Oxford University Press, 2020).
[23] Datta, *Planning the City*.

revolutionary activity. For instance, the Alipore Bomb Trial of 1909 revealed deep connections that local clubs, *akharas* (gymnasiums), and volunteer associations had with various underground revolutionary societies. During interrogation, several houses, boarding houses, and shops on Harrison Road, Bhawani Charan Datta Lane, Mirzapore Street, Mechuabazaar Street, Raja Dinendra Street, Grey Street, and many other localities were found to be part of an underground revolutionary network. Several police officials and informants had been trapped and killed in these lanes in the recent past.[24]

The Improvement Trust was to break all these established features of the insurgent city through rental reorientation, class-based population dispersal, suburbanization, automobilization, and road electrification. In the interwar years, Calcutta embraced avenue-style streets with sidewalks and boulevards, massive intersections, and public parks. These new spaces, however, did not put an end to protest. Instead, they became sites of a new kind of protest politics involving large public demonstrations, mass gatherings, agitation,[25] communal warfare, and organized encroachments of sidewalks—nothing clandestine about these. If the nineteenth-century streets prompted insurgency in a clandestine way, the new streets of the twentieth century enabled a politicized mass culture of protest and encroachment to flourish. This does not, however, mean that the new streets replaced the lanes everywhere and exhaustively. The lanes reappeared elsewhere as Engels' opening quote suggests. The coexistence of wide, open streets and narrow alleys resulted in a complex coevolution.

Apart from security, military, and surveillance functions, the new streets fulfilled three more purposes. First, these streets were supposed to facilitate trade and commerce, and capital accumulation *in* and *through* the city by ensuring the mobility of labour, commodities, and space. Second, they were made to ensure better circulation of air and fluids in the city to minimize the chance of the outbreak of an epidemic. Third, one of the objectives and implications of street-building as a centralized 'public work' was to claim monopoly state control over the pathways and circulation of large-scale civic utilities such as drinking water, drainage, gas, and electricity that facilitated and followed the streets and lanes to reach a destination. Thus,

---

[24] Biboswan Bose, 'On Death and Early Revolutionary Terror in Bengal, 1902–1916' (M. Phil dissertation, Centre for Studies in Social Sciences, Calcutta and Jadavpur University, 2016).

[25] Colonial officials used the term 'agitation' to mark any kind of collective action that could also be termed as 'protest'. The term 'protest' seems to have attained currency in Calcutta only in the second half of the twentieth century.

late-nineteenth-century street-building was entangled and coeval with the emergence of modern urban government, whose key objective was to facilitate and regulate motion.

The Urban Dialectics of Motion and Obstruction

In *The Arcades Project*, Walter Benjamin gives us a 'small methodological suggestion' regarding the 'dialectics of cultural history' which is equally applicable to the dialectics of urban history. He writes:

> It is very easy to devise ways of dividing up the various 'areas' of any given period between, on the one hand, the 'fruitful', 'forward-looking', 'living', 'positive' part and, on the other hand, the futile, backward, dead part. The contours of this positive part can, indeed, be brought into clear relief only when set against its negative counterpart. Conversely, every negation has value only as the backdrop for the living, positive aspects. It is, therefore, crucially important that the excluded negative part be divided up in turn so that with every shift in perspective (but not standards!) another positive aspect emerges that differs from what was established thus far.[26]

I consider this supplication of the positive from what has been jettisoned and marginalized to be a prime task of an urban dialectician. In my case, 'obstruction' is such a term, much vilified by the bourgeois sensibilities of motion. In the bourgeois autobiography of capital, motion is a painstakingly constructed ideology in the backdrop of imagined and real obstructions, while obstruction stands for capital's discursive 'other'. I show that urban histories can be written through the dialectics of motion and obstruction. I deploy these two words as 'concepts'—two bricks that build the city as a process.

As a process, the city—like most landscapes—is a constant interplay of both conditioning and human agency. The city allows us to see this process in intense relief because of the unique concentration and proximity of people, activities, and spaces. By conditioning, I mean impersonal (and hence interpersonal) structural forces in society and economy that affect human action. I posit motion[27] as a

---

[26] Cited in Irving Wohlfarth, 'Et Cetra? The Historian as Chiffonnier', in *Walter Benjamin and The Arcades Project*, ed. Beatrice Hanssen (London and New York: Continuum, 2006), 12–32, quoted from 23–24.

[27] In western liberalism ever since Thomas Hobbes, motion substituted order and became entangled with the positive notion of individual freedom from the 'Chain

modular form of the operation of conditioning in the urban context. By agency, I mean the history that people make.²⁸ The physical environment of a city is the outcome of how people dwell or make space, which in turn constitutes who they are or become. In our story, human agency appears as obstruction in its modular form in relation to the structural forces of urban motion. The city as process—the dialectic of motion and obstruction—that plays out in time (and space) can hardly be anything but historical. Paraphrasing E. P. Thompson, we may say a city does not 'rise like the sun at an appointed time. It is present at its own making'.²⁹

In this book, motion stands for two kinds of conditioning: first, the 'involuntary social relationship' that humans get into, in producing and reproducing their existence within a mode of production, and, second, the forces of the 'self-propelled movement of capital'.³⁰ In short, motion—in

---

of Being' of the enclosed feudal era. Hobbes' notion of 'freedom-as-motion' gave rise to a powerful liberal metaphor—'race of life'—which is the kernel of the American notion of freedom. Hobbes defined motion as the 'absence of opposition'. At the heart of the liberal concepts of individualism, reason, and enterprise lies this image of life as nothing but a race. Hobbes compares individuals with runners in a competition who strive to 'outdo others and stay foremost'. In a similar vein, Adam Smith describes enterprise as a runner who runs 'as hard as he can and strain every move and every muscle in order to outstrip all his competitors'. Leslie D. Feldman, 'Freedom as Motion: Thomas Hobbes and the Images of Liberalism', *Journal of Philosophical Research* 22 (1997): 229–243, quoted from 231. Hobbes and Smith self-consciously avoided obstruction. It can be said that this omission has been common in much of social and political thought.

28 In *The Eighteenth Brumaire of Louis Bonaparte*, Marx writes: 'Men make their own history, but they do not make it as they please; they do not make it under self-selected circumstances, but under circumstances existing already, given and transmitted from the past. The tradition of all dead generations weighs like a nightmare on the brains of the living.' In this, one can see the dialectic between agency ('men make their own history') and conditioning ('but they do not make it as they please....'): https://www.marxists.org/archive/marx/works/1852/18th-brumaire/ch01.htm, accessed 12 October 2021.

29 E. P. Thompson, *The Making of the English Working Class* (New York: Vintage Books, 1963), 9.

30 For Marx, motion stands for the 'self-propelled movement' of capital—a motion which is activated because of its internal contradictions. Motion reconciles these contradictions. In Chapter 3 of *Capital*, vol. 1, Marx compares capital's law of motion with that of Earth's elliptical motion:

this book—refers to the involuntary tendential aspects of society and the economy.³¹

At the same time, in the city of capital, motion also refers to a fetish. Much like commodities, motion is a form of appearance by which 'social relations between men' manifest as unending 'relation between things'—exchange value. As a fetish, motion appears as a self-evident, natural, and inevitable force that stands outside history. The bourgeois order posits motion as a metaphor for energy, positivity, and progress—a norm—and obstruction as delinquency. The motion narrative posits 'delay', 'disconnection', and 'blockade' as matters to be conquered by the street's spatial exploits. Each spatial conquest must result in the reduction of delay in the circulation of bodies and objects. This continual improvement in the rate of circulation is aimed at enhancing the prospects

---

> We saw in a former chapter that the exchange of commodities implies contradictory and mutually exclusive conditions. The differentiation of commodities into commodities and money does not sweep away these inconsistencies, but develops a modus vivendi, a form in which they can exist side by side. This is generally the way in which real contradictions are reconciled. For instance, it is a contradiction to depict one body as constantly falling towards another, and as, at the same time, constantly flying away from it. The ellipse is a form of motion which, while allowing this contradiction to go on, at the same time reconciles it. (Karl Marx, *Das Capital*, vol. 1 [Moscow, Progress Publishers, 1887], 71)

Marx's notion of capital's motion came from Epicurus via Johannes Kepler's elliptical planetary orbits and G. W. Friedrich Hegel, who found in Kepler's explanation the essence of the dialectics of space and time. There are reasons to believe that Marx did not borrow the idea of motion from Isaac Newton, as it is often believed. For Newton, motion in a matter happens only when it is acted upon by an external force. He sees Kepler's elliptical motion of planetary orbits as a special case of inverse square law of gravitation. John P. Brukett, 'Marx's Concept of an Economic Law of Motion', *History of Political Economy* 32, no. 2 (2000): 381–394. For a book-length treatment of the genealogy of motion in Marx, see Thomas Nail, *Marx in Motion: A New Materialist Marxism* (Oxford: Oxford University Press, 2020). For Marx, motion is not coterminous with circulation. In capital's motion, Marx mentions, one has to consider the entire process of the metamorphosis of commodity. Circulation is just a constituent element in commodity's metamorphosis.

31 I arrive at this composite formulation of motion by combining Marx's notion of qualified human agency in historical change in *The Eighteenth Brumaire* and his 'law of the motion of capital' in *Capital*.

for capital accumulation in the city. It influences the valuation of the city as a site of production, circulation, and exchange. Furthermore, streets mobilize adjoining urban spaces into the real estate market and thus play a key role in the 'production of space'.[32]

This narrative of ceaseless motion and smoothness posits obstruction as its negation, which it must eventually overcome. I examine this powerful common sense of the motion-driven modern city and show how obstructions are internal to and constitutive of urban motion. Obstruction—as a domain of human subjectivity and diversity—continuously modifies motion. Accessing motion through obstruction unmasks and hence de-naturalizes motion and unravels social relations in it. Thus, obstructions give us access to 'more effective narratives of human belonging'.[33]

In this book, I describe how the wheels of motion come to encounter the 'real' world through its dialectical opposite—obstruction. Obstructions are momentary, unstable, and creative, which attune motion and add an element of randomness to its course, making it a historically specific force operative in a particular space–time coordinate. In other words, through obstructions, the universality of motion acquires historical contingencies and meanings. Motion ceases to be the same everywhere because of the contingencies of obstruction. It can be said that obstruction renders motion a subject of historical enquiry—obstruction offers 'grip' to motion, as Anna Tsing would tell us.[34] Obstruction

---

[32] Henri Lefebvre, *The Production of Space*, trans. Donald Nicholson-Smith (Oxford: Basil Blackwell, 1991).

[33] Dipesh Chakrabarty, 'Two Histories of Capital', in Dipesh Chakrabarty, *Provincializing Europe: Postcolonial Thought and Historical Difference* (Princeton: Princeton University Press, 2000), 47–71, quoted from 71.

[34] Anna Tsing, *Friction: An Ethnography of Global Connection* (Princeton: Princeton University Press, 2005). While theorizing mobility in the context of the twenty-first-century age of global connection and finance capital, Kevin Hannam, Mimi Sheller, and John Urry—in their manifesto of a new mobility paradigm—assert: 'There is no linear increase in fluidity without extensive systems of immobilities.' Hannam, Sheller, and Urry, 'Editorial', 3. Also see John Urry, *Global Complexity* (Cambridge: Polity, 2003). Mobility becomes possible, writes Urry, through 'material worlds that involve new and distinct moorings that enable, produce and presuppose extensive new mobilities'. Ibid., 138. In referring to the mobility paradigm, it is, however, important to maintain its conceptual difference keeping in mind my conceptualization of obstructed motion. Hannam et al. define mobility purely in 'movement' terms: 'The concept of mobilities encompasses both the large-scale movements of people, objects, capital and information across the world, as well as

is static 'relative' to motion, but obstruction, too, generates motion. Obstruction inheres in motion while actively interrupting and punctuating its course. While waging a constant battle against obstruction, the city of motion also retains and at times even creates forms of obstruction that do not belong to the logic of capitalist accumulation. A historical analysis of obstruction, on the other hand, shows how ordinary people negotiate and come to terms with capital's law of motion. These human negotiations produce motion as a social phenomenon.

Thus, obstruction is not external to motion. Nor is it 'subsumed' in motion. Its relationship with motion is multiple, 'ranging from opposition to neutrality'.[35] In the bourgeois utopia of a 'perfect' city, motion comes to subjugate obstruction. Yet there is no 'certainty' that the subjugation is 'predetermined', complete, and irreversible. There have been moments in history when obstruction has dictated the terms of motion (for instance, in Chapter 5). In the interplay of motion and obstruction, the city becomes a unity of opposites—a dialectical unity, a whirlwind. The urban historical materialist must grasp the on-ground and contingent relationship between unity and contradiction: when and how the conjuncture of difference is set in, when and how difference turns into conflicts, and when and how the conflict gets resolved 'either by creating new differences or by sliding slowly into indifference'.[36]

Marx targeted political economists as the messengers and legitimizers of accumulation, or capital's self-propelled expanded reproduction.[37] A student of urban dialectics must target the planners, engineers, valuers, and lawmakers

---

the more local processes of daily transportation, movement through public space and the travel of material things within everyday life.' According to Urry, the new century is marked by mobility (and not structures or positions) that comes to 'condition' social relations. John Urry, *Societies Beyond the Social: Mobilities for the Twenty First Century* (London: Routledge, 2000). On the contrary, I define motion as a structural force in a mode of production—one that 'conditions' human action and social intercourse. Under the capitalist mode of production, motion attains a hegemonic form—a norm to follow and a metaphor for progress and development. Likewise, obstruction is not a proxy for immobilities or moorings. It refers to the concrete human agency that conditions motion in the course of history. Nonetheless, I consider these two frameworks in complementary terms, inhabiting the same neighbourhood of ideas and politics. The new 'mobility turn' in social theory contains a distinctly twenty-first-century strain of economy and politics affected by hypermobility, containerization, 'just-in-time' delivery, instantaneous communication, and so on. My concerns about obstructed motion—on the other hand—is grounded in the twentieth century.

[35] Chakrabarty, 'Two Histories of Capital', 66.
[36] Henri Lefebvre, *Marxist Thought and the City*, trans. Robert Bononno (Minneapolis: University of Minnesota Press, 2016), 42.
[37] In Marx's more technical rendition, capital accumulation entails a rising organic composition of capital expressed as the ratio of constant (c) and variable capital (v), or c/v.

in the same vein as bards of motion. A critique of motion-centric urbanism can only advance through obstruction, and it begins with an immediate[38] urban phenomenon: 'the street'.[39]

Property, Territory, Accumulation

Property, territory, and the city have existed beyond the capitalist mode of production. However, under the capitalist mode of production, property and territory conjoin with capital accumulation to constitute cities differently and transform urban experience in distinctive ways. While property has attracted some attention in India's urban historiography, I see it as just one vertex of the triad—property, territory, accumulation—a framework necessary to understand the modern city. One of my central concerns is to follow this triadic encounter in the specific historical context of twentieth-century Calcutta.

Lefebvre explains the role that the real estate sector plays in the modern city of capital accumulation. According to him, real property plays the role of a 'safety valve' when capital shows the tendencies of the rate of profit to fall.[40] How does this happen? 'As a mix of production and speculation', says Lefebvre, the real estate sector 'oscillates between a subordinate function as a booster, flywheel or back-up—in short, as a regulator—and a leading role'. Private and public construction usually 'generates higher-than-average profits'. Investment in 'the production of space' involves 'a higher proportion of variable as compared with constant capital'. Part of the reason is because the construction sector has a mix of small and large corporate firms and the work of excavation, framing, and so on, calls for the employment of large armies of workers who are mostly paid low wages and are migrants. In this sector, living labour cannot be iteratively replaced by labour-saving automation (dead labour). Thus, the real estate sector can generate a 'mass of [absolute] surplus value'. A large chunk of this surplus value is pumped into other sectors that are witnessing a falling rate

---

[38] Immediate means 'the elementary appearance before mediations'. Recollect the first sentence of *Capital*, vol. 1: 'The wealth of those societies in which the capitalist mode of production prevails, presents itself as "an immense accumulation of commodities," its unit being a single commodity. Our investigation must therefore begin with the analysis of a commodity.' Marx, *Das Capital*, vol. 1, 27.

[39] In our first sight, the city appears as a massive collection of streets.

[40] Lefebvre, *The Production of Space*, 336. Marx defines rate of profit as the ratio of profit to investment. As relative investment increases, the rate of profit tends to fall, assuming a constant rate of surplus value/rate of exploitation.

of profit, while a significant portion remains with the real estate players. Real estate's imbrication in the overall economy thus comes to defer an extended 'interruption of the economy-wide circuit of capital'.

Lefebvre writes: 'The mobilization of space becomes frenetic and produces an impetus towards the self-destruction of spaces old and new.'[41] He cautions, 'Investment and speculation cannot be stopped, however, nor even slowed, and a vicious circle is thus set up.' As the real estate sector is summoned to save capital, the city enters a vicious cycle: 'A strategy based on space … must be considered a very dangerous one indeed, for it sacrifices the future to immediate interests while simultaneously destroying the present in the name of a future at once programmed and utterly uncertain.'[42]

The capitalist unfreezing of space has harsh consequences, warns Lefebvre. It happens through loot and plunder of the commons (Marx would call it 'primitive accumulation of capital') or giving concession to the landowners in terms of ground rent. Once land is released from the 'stability of patrimonial inheritance', it acquires the mobility of exchange value. Each 'exchangeable space' enters the market. Once in the market, the real property's connection of price with value is elastic. This relationship gets further disturbed by speculation. Speculations enable price to liberate itself from value. In other words, the law of value is compromised: 'Fraud itself now becomes a law, a rule of the game, an accepted tactic.'[43] Civic authorities of the capitalist world must come to terms with land speculation by including speculative prices in their compensation packages. Speculations become intense during or after a devastating war.

In South Asian cities such as Bombay, Calcutta, Karachi, and Rangoon, speculation became rampant during the First World War, as the war-induced boom money could not find long-term and sustainable productive outlets such as immediate investment in the industrial sector. In these cities, real estate emerged as a destination of investment and a veritable source of revenue for the city corporations and the Improvement Trusts in the interwar period. The operations of the Improvement Trusts led to the shrinking of the existing housing market. The Trusts acquired vast tracts of land—in the name of public interest—beyond what was necessary to execute their projects and sold them in the open market at higher prices.[44] Landed property, which was the root of private property, was

---

[41] Ibid., 336.
[42] Ibid., 336.
[43] Ibid., 337.
[44] Debjani Bhattacharyya, 'Speculation', *Comparative Studies of South Asia, Africa and the Middle East* 40, no. 1 (2020): 51–56.

thus mobilized into the orbit of private property as a commodity, disregarding all kinds of sentimental sides of land ownership.[45] In Chapter 2, I discuss how, in Calcutta, such a strategy produced social dislocations and inter-communal tensions. The situation became so difficult that the civic governments had to pass successive rent control acts in the interwar period.[46] An attempt was made to separate profiteering and gamble from legitimate market speculation, which was believed to pave the way for 'the correct value of land and price of the property to emerge as discrete economic information'.[47]

Several recent historical works on Bombay, Calcutta, and Delhi have described how the property market and its players—small and big—operated when the Improvement Trusts began to open up considerable lands for exchange. Trust schemes opened up land in the inner cities through renewal and recycling of spaces, and in the frontiers by planned suburban developments.[48] The early-

---

[45] Karl Marx, *Economic and Philosophical Manuscript of 1844* (Moscow: Progress Publishers, 1959).

[46] Needless to mention, the rise of house rent is also the rise of ground rent—the interest on the 'plot' on which the house is located.

[47] Bhattacharyya, 'Speculation', 53. For a discussion about the separation between gamble of the bazaar and market speculation, see Birla, *Stages of Capital*. Birla pioneered the now booming field of colonial governmentality's encounter with the pre-existing South Asian market practices, leading to legislations predicated upon the distinction between the market and the bazaar.

[48] For Calcutta, see Debjani Bhattacharyya, *Empire and Ecology in the Bengal Delta: The Making of Calcutta* (Cambridge: Cambridge University Press, 2018). This is a larger study of land reclamation in an active delta of the Bay of Bengal where Calcutta stands today. Towards the end of this remarkable book, Bhattacharyya analyses the operation of the Improvement Trust in the land market and how speculations played a constitutive role in the formation of property deals between the state and the subjects and subjects themselves. Also see Nabaparna Ghosh, *A Hygienic City-Nation: Space, Community, and Everyday Life in Colonial Calcutta* (Cambridge: Cambridge University Press, 2020). Ghosh draws our attention to the ways in which Calcutta's Hindu and Muslim property owners negotiated with the Improvement Trust's tribunal by foregrounding the cultural values of land and property in their everyday life. She writes: 'Property owners inscribed emotive and material meanings to land as part of their everyday strategies to resist the Trust. In the process, their own identities as members of a religious community were reflexively produced' (90). For Delhi, see Anish Vanaik, *Possessing the City: Property and Politics in Delhi, 1911–1947* (Oxford: Oxford University Press, 2020). For Bombay, we have a host of recent works on urban property. See Rao, *House, But No Garden*); Shabnum Tejani, 'Disputing "Market Value": The Bombay Improvement Trust and the Reshaping of a Speculative Land Market in Early Twentieth-century Bombay', *Urban History* 48, no. 3 (2021): 572–589; Nikhil Rao, 'Space in Motion:

twentieth-century urban improvement schemes further valorized urban land as it became a prime outlet of capital. This ultimately produced an indistinction between rent and interest, allowing rent to be a measure of price. Determining the rent of properties, then, became a site of negotiation between the land-hungry state and the property owners, buyers, and sellers, and between property owners and their tenants.[49]

One of the significant aspects of this new urban property historiography has been a shift of the focus from planning to private investment in property as the 'primary loci of urban development'. Patterns of investments in urban property were 'already tied up with the patterns and cycles of accumulation in other sectors of the economy'. Vanaik finds evidence in late colonial Delhi of the inter-sectoral mobility of capital 'between urban construction (or land purchases) and industry (in the 1940s), or between commerce and real estate (in the 1930s)'. This establishes that production of space had already become an unalloyed part of the circuits of accumulation.[50] Moreover, as Vanaik points out, 'production of urban space was an important means' for the buoyancy of the credit market itself.[51]

As Vanaik has shown for Delhi, similarly in Calcutta it was a common knowledge in the interwar era that Marwari jute speculators also took part in

---

An Uneven Narrative of Urban Private Property in Bombay', in *Rethinking Markets in Modern India: Embedded Exchange and Contested Jurisdiction*, ed. A. Gandhi, B. Harris-White, D. Haynes, and S. Schwecke (Cambridge: Cambridge University Press, 2020), 54–84. Together, these works have brought our attention to the urban land question, which remained in the margins of urban history for many decades. Economic histories of the cities were much more concerned with the colonial state's fiscal policies concerning urban planning and trade data. Urban social historians avoided the land question almost exclusively.

[49] For long, Marxist accounts of urbanization and cities have used 'urban rent' as a conceptual grid to understand state–society–capital relations. David Harvey, *Limits to Capital* (Oxford: Blackwell, 1982); Anne Haila, *Urban Land Rent: Singapore as a Property State* (Oxford: Wiley-Blackwell, 2015). In this context, speculation in real estate—understood as a set of techniques to materialize the future to the present—transpired as a key constituent of colonial governmentality. Debjani Bhattacharyya has demonstrated how the colonial civic institutions sought to tame urban rent and land market by separating land speculation that produced 'scientific rent' and the illicit indigenous tendency to 'rent profiteering' that pinched the tenants. Debjani Bhattacharyya, 'Provincializing the History of Speculation from Colonial South Asia', *History Compass* 17, no. 1 (2019): 1–11.

[50] Vanaik, *Possessing the City*, 56–57.

[51] Ibid., 74.

urban property speculation and circulated capital in these two sectors, especially in the couple of years after the First World War. They made quick money during the War years and found no immediately available investment destination other than 'fixing' it in urban land.[52] Between the 1930s and the 1950s, they used their urban landed possessions as mortgage security for long-term bank loans to invest in jute mills.[53] Speculation was the vehicle for capital's inter-sectoral mobility. A great deal of it occurred throughout the interwar era and during the Second World War. Moreover, these developments in the property market had enormous social implications. In central Calcutta—as the book reveals—speculation in real estate intensified ethnic, religious, and class animosity among its declining Bengali gentry, enterprising Marwari traders, the working-class Hindu, and Muslim populations.

Keeping this new historiographical trend in mind, I focus on two relatively understudied aspects in the theme of urbanism and urban property. First, historians have largely restricted themselves to the pursuit of private property, land acquisition (the conflict between private property and the 'public purpose') and compensation. Through these, they have woven city-specific narratives about colonial institutions, social practices, and the life of property in political mobilizations such as communal riots. As they follow private property archives, their research tends to get restricted to the world of the 'rate-paying' and almost exclusively male propertied class, who were also the enfranchised

---

[52] Alamohan Das, *Amar Jiban* (Dash Nagar: 1949). From a street hawker and subsequently an acid manufacturer, Das became a jute speculator during the First World War. After many twists and turns in personal and business life, Das became a premier jute miller and banker in the 1940s and the 1950s. He was a Bengali Mahishya by caste (an entrepreneurial middle caste in south Bengal). For a detailed analysis of Das' career and what it says about the frontiers of post-colonial capital accumulation, see Ritajyoti Bandyopadhyay and Ranabir Samaddar, 'Caste and the Frontiers of Postcolonial Accumulation', in *Accumulation in Post-colonial Capitalism*, ed. Iman. K. Mitra, Ranabir Samaddar, and Samita Sen (Singapore: Springer), 189–214.

[53] P. T. Nair drew my attention to this switch story in 2008. I found corroboration of this from the Kanoria Jute Mill activist Prafulla Chakrabarty in 2017. Rajat Kanta Ray mentioned that the interwar era witnessed the switch of indigenous bazaar capital towards industrial investment. In Calcutta, the Marwaris were the agents of this transfer of capital. Rajat Kanta Ray, 'The Bazaar: Changing Structural Characteristics of the Indigenous Sections of the Indian Economy before and after the Great Depression', *Indian Economic and Social History Review* 25, no. 3 (1988): 263–381, see 264–267 for the exact reference.

population of these cities.[54] Studying colonial cities through private property, rent, and enfranchisement[55] has its own core concerns, but also leaves out certain matters of significance.[56] These studies have not paid attention to the urban commons and consequently the relationship between private property, public space or property, and the urban commons. This book goes beyond the domain of formalized property, both private and public, to consider the dynamic *inter-conversion* between property and urban commons, which makes capital accumulation in and through space possible.

While the conversion of commons into private or public property is well documented, one has also witnessed the conversion of public and private spaces into commons in the phenomenon of the communal aggregation of neighbourhoods and gated communities, serving a particular community exclusively. The communal cleansing of ethnic or religious minorities from a majority-community-dominated neighbourhood and the concentration of certain minority populations into ghettos because of civil war are more examples of such

---

[54] A notable exception is Vanaik's treatment of property market and communal mobilization in the last chapter of *Possessing the City*.

[55] In the interwar era, a new economic and political order began to gain ground in Indian cities such as Calcutta. After the passage of the Government of India Act of 1919, the colonial bureaucracy pulled out significantly from urban governance. Local self-government and public works were 'transferred' to the charge of a minister selected by a provincial legislative council. In the meantime, the electoral base for the city corporations was enlarged beyond the payers of municipal property tax to include all who paid a rent of at least ten rupees a month. The electorate was further enlarged in 1935 to allow a vote for the persons paying at least five rupees a month as rent. Thus, during the interwar period a significant section of the urban lower-middle-class population entered the realm of electoral politics. Rao, *House, But No Garden*.

[56] In Delhi, Anish Vanaik calculates that 'women's control of property was rare'. However, the data suggest some interesting patterns when one intersects religion with gender. Vanaik finds that 'there were a stark differences between the abilities of Muslim and Hindu women to control property'. He found that Muslim women 'constructed almost two-and-a-half times as many structures as Hindu women'. In Delhi, the communal figures of construction were divided almost equally by Hindus (about 50 per cent) and Muslims (about 40 per cent). Vanaik, *Possessing the City*, 67–69. In central Calcutta, the construction activities were almost exclusively controlled by the Marwaris and the Hindu rentier class in the early twentieth century, with the former superseding the latter by 1910. Proceedings of the 33rd Meeting of the Works Standing Committee held at the Central Municipal Office, 22 March 1921, Corporation of Calcutta.

forms of conversion and commoning. In both instances, new spaces emerge that are open to the members of certain communities and vital for their life and labour.

There is, however, another way in which commons form in the cities. Urban commoners such as street hawkers, refugees, and pavement dwellers encroach upon public properties and turn them into collectively occupied spaces, as we see in Chapters 1, 4, and 5 in this book. As Gidwani (in the context of Indian cities) points out,[57] such commons presuppose 'being-in-common' or 'using resources in more or less shared and nonsubtractable ways, through practices'.[58] There are two crucial dimensions to the commons that the urban commoners create. First, the commons are the source of livelihood and/or dwelling for them and, second, they use the commons 'through variable local arrangements that are more or less equalitarian, incorporative, and fair' in order to dwell and meet livelihood necessities'.[59] These commoners direct a portion of labour's use value to the growth and upkeep of the common resource. The bourgeois law of property sees these commons as unlawful possession or privatization and encroachment of property by commoners and the dispossessed and criminalizes such practices. In Calcutta, for instance, it is widely believed by certain sections of the middle class that the hawkers encroached upon public spaces and unlawfully privatized them. I revisit this hegemonic common sense about the hawkers' privatization of public spaces in Chapter 5 and show how the hawkers developed an ethic of commoning while justifying their encroachment of sidewalks for livelihood.

Such commons, however, develop as pockets in the shadow of the property regime as subservient entities and often lose their separate identity. The state may reclaim them as property or some commoners may indeed privatize them as exclusively belonging to them. In Calcutta, the refugees did transform commonly and collectively encroached spaces into well-demarcated private properties by mobilizing the Lockean notion of self-improvement and individual labour. Nonetheless, it is important to maintain the conceptual separation between property or commodity (where labour's use value is harnessed for capital) and the commons in order to track how spaces metamorphose and are produced in cities under capitalism.

Private and public property's link with urban commons is a central and recurring theme of this book. Most studies on urban property ignore this connection as a significant component in the production of urban space and

---

[57] Vinay Gidwani, 'Six Theses on Waste, Value and Commons', *Social and Cultural Geography* 14, no. 7 (2013): 773–783.
[58] Ibid., 774.
[59] Ibid., 775.

thus succumb to a statist view—as opposed to the commoners' view—of urban property. In this book, I argue that the metamorphoses of property—from private to public and vice versa, and from property to commons and vice versa—are important in conceptualizing the triadic relation of property, territory, and accumulation in an urban context (Chapters 1, 2, and 4).

The second aspect of the city, apart from urban commons, that I foreground in my analysis is territory as the 'kernel' of both city and property. Urban historians of property in India have not yet delved into the territoriality of property. Scholars of territory often hold that territory is a province of state power and sovereignty—Foucault said, sovereignty expresses itself in territory.[60] Scholars of property, on the other hand, take territoriality of property for granted in the forms of margins, boundaries, and exclusions that define a property as a legally guarded relationship between people and a resource. Rarely do territory and property meet in an exposition of the city.[61]

When we walk through a city, we navigate a series of private and public properties demarcated by 'refusal and permission'.[62] The territorial aspects of property are expressed as enforcement, adjudication, registration, prohibition, and exclusion. As a specific form of spatial classification, territory structures and materializes property in the socio-spatial universe of the city, while property acts as the conceptual core of territory and 'frames its identities and organizes its habits'.[63] Territoriality of property comes clearly to the surface in moments of ethnic and communal violence,[64] civil wars, violent spatial and demographic restructuring of urban localities through road-building and sanitizing (Chapters 2 and 3), and land grab in the territorial frontiers of the city (Chapter 4).

---

[60] Michel Foucault, *Security, Territory, Population: Lectures at the Collège de France 1977–1978*, trans. Graham Burchell (London: Palgrave Macmillan, 2007).
[61] Nicholas Blomley, 'The Territory of Property', *Progress in Human Geography* 40, no. 5 (2016): 593–609; Stuart Elden, *The Birth of Territory* (Chicago: University of Chicago Press, 2013); A. M. Brighenti, 'On Territory as Relationship and Law as Territory', *Canadian Journal of Law and Society* 21, no. 2 (2006): 65–86.
[62] Blomley, 'The Territory of Property', 594.
[63] Ibid., 596.
[64] We may mention three works on urban communal riots that placed urban territory at the heart of analysis. Ghanshyam Shah, 'The 1969 Communal Riots in Ahmedabad: A Case Study', of a dozen studies included in the well-known volume by Asghar Ali Engineer (ed.), *Communal Riots in Post-independence India* (Hyderabad: Sangam Books, 1984), 175–208; J. Mukherjee, *Hungry Bengal*; and Ranabir Samaddar, 'Policing a Riot-Torn City: Kolkata, 16–18 August 1946', *Journal of Genocide Research* 19, no. 1 (2017): 39–60.

We have already noticed that Lefebvre connected urbanization with the logic of capital accumulation. To him, it is a structural connection. The second circuit of capital—as Lefebvre calls urbanization, to distinguish it from the conventional industrial circuit—is effective in the channelling of money in the production of space, financing, and speculation. For accumulation in and through real property, capital must destroy and rebuild the inner city (Chapters 2 and 3) and expand the territorial reach of the city in the fringe areas by annexing agricultural land, fisheries, commons, and low-lying marshy tracts (Chapter 4). In this process of urbanization, both the city and capital acquire a territorial dimension. Territory acts through enclosure and prohibition, or what Blomley calls the 'negative appropriation of space'.[65] At times prohibitions are visible with gates, railings, and ditches meant to obstruct 'trespass'. Yet, most of the times, prohibitions are subtle and spatially inscribed through the principle of zoning. Zoning is a territorial technology to divide space into designated areas and areas that are prohibited. These zones are further subdivided into public and private spaces. In this way, the city becomes a 'particular configuration of *territory*'.[66]

This triadic formation of property, territory, and accumulation acquired a different trajectory in the post-colonial context of mass democracy. Post-colonial Calcutta was shaped by powerful squatter and anti-eviction movements, strikes, and unregulated proliferation of fringe economies such as slum-based production and petty retail. These expanded territorially, but their proliferations did not lead to capital accumulation as per Lefebvre's analysis. Unlike capital's motion, the fringe economy—the so-called informal sector—sought proliferation, not so much profit and accumulation, and, therefore, unwittingly to a great extent, punctuated accumulation. Real property in the new frontiers and the old city came to be encroached upon for decades, obstructing the mobilization of space for capital accumulation. In post-colonial Calcutta, the second circuit of capital could not provide adequate relief to the first circuit (jute industry, for instance), which was already in a process of deceleration. By the 1960s, Calcutta reached a state when the city's connection with the processes of capital accumulation had snapped to a large extent. This phenomenon of urbanization *without* accumulation has remained under-studied in Calcutta's urban history. We shall discuss it at length in the next section and return to it more substantially in Chapters 4 and 5.

---

[65] Blomley, 'The Territory of Property', 602.
[66] Samaddar, 'Policing a Riot-torn City', 40 (emphasis original).

Space, Economy, and Polity

In 1911, Calcutta ceased to be the Empire's Indian capital. The most vociferous critique of the switch of capital to Delhi came from the city's non-official white circles who feared that their economic fortune and political influence over the colonial bureaucracy would decline once Calcutta lost its political clout within the imperial command. Over the preceding 100 years or so, the European business elite such as bankers, merchants, planters, and so on, and the members of the colonial bureaucracy such as the Indian Civil Service (ICS) officers and judges had consolidated close social ties via European clubs, sports in the Maidans, and matrimonial alliances.[67] In fact, they pointed out a key feature of colonialism in India, which thrived on a close liaison between law, trade, administration, and accumulation. When they failed, a large section of the white business class migrated to Delhi.[68] Their withdrawal from Calcutta initiated an irreversible process of capital's flight from Calcutta. In this connection, we may note that about 81 per cent of investment in Calcutta came from Europeans, while just 3 per cent of investment was contributed by Indian industrialists. In Bombay, the figures were 41 per cent (European) and 49 per cent (Indian).[69] This meant that Calcutta's economic prosperity was conditioned by and contingent upon British-owned farms and banks. Two of Calcutta's prime export commodities—tea and jute—were under exclusive British control. In other words, the departure of the administrative capital to Delhi in 1911 augmented the decline of Calcutta's economic fortune over the first half of the twentieth century.

Calcutta's economic dependence on European capital was exposed once the city was robbed of its political and bureaucratic dominance within the Empire. Since the First World War era, Calcutta's pre-eminence in the colonial economy had begun to erode. The global demand for jute declined during the interwar period and the British capitalists slowly passed on the mills to the

---

[67] Sumit Sarkar, 'The City Imagined: Calcutta of the Nineteenth and Early Twentieth Centuries', in Sumit Sarkar, *Writing Social History* (Delhi: Oxford University Press, 1997), 159–185. Also see Swati Chattopadhyay, 'Cities of Power and Protest: Spatial Legibility and the Colonial State in Early Twentieth-Century India', *International Journal of Urban Sciences* 19, no. 1 (2015): 40–52.
[68] Swati Chattopadhyay, 'Cities of Power and Protest'.
[69] Rajat Kanta Ray, *Social Conflict and Political Unrest in Bengal 1875–1927* (Delhi: Oxford University Press, 1984). These figures are also mentioned in S. Sarkar, 'The City Imagined', 164.

Marwaris.[70] Nonetheless, until the end of the colonial rule, Calcutta retained its comparative pre-eminence over Bombay by a shrinking margin.[71] By the time of the Second World War, the signs of decline became a trend and after 1947, Bombay surpassed Calcutta.[72]

The 'Partitioned Independence' accelerated Calcutta's economic decline. The city lost its jute-producing agricultural lands to East Pakistan, while retaining the mills and increasingly outdated fixed capital with itself. Over the next two decades, East Pakistan developed more advanced jute industrial complexes which contributed to industrial retardation in West Bengal's jute mill belt. Furthermore, Partition affected tea export as well. Most of this tea being produced in Assam and northern Bengal was transported on steamers via the Padma, the Brahmaputra, and their tributaries. Partition-related political developments obstructed the circulation of tea in the 1950s and the 1960s. The outcome was a steady decline in Calcutta's share in industrial employment vis-à-vis Bombay. Such retardations in Calcutta's export-oriented economy were

---

[70] Amiya K. Bagchi, *Private Investment in India, 1900–1940* (Cambridge: Cambridge University Press, 1973).

[71] Claude Markovits, 'Bombay as a Business Centre in the Colonial Period: A Comparison with Calcutta', in *Bombay: Metaphor for Modern India*, ed. Sujata Patel and Alice Thorner (Delhi: Oxford University Press, 1995), 26–46.

[72] For instance, if one studies per-capita bank deposits in the banks of Calcutta and Bombay, an estimate of 1943 shows that the Bank of Bombay collected four times more per-capita bank deposits than Calcutta, indicating the relative prosperity of Bombay. Furthermore, paid-up capital of companies based in Bombay was much higher than Calcutta between 1920 and 1935. Another indicator of Calcutta's decline was the clearing house data of banks based in Calcutta and Bombay. In 1913, total clearing house transactions in India were worth 65,035 lakh rupees. Calcutta had 51 per cent share of it, while Bombay's share was more than 17 per cent less (fixed at 33.7 per cent). Madras had less than 4 per cent share, while Delhi's share was reported as 'insignificant'. However, Bombay progressively narrowed its gap with Calcutta in each subsequent year. By Independence, the shares of the two prime cities were equal. In 1950, Bombay's share was 6 per cent higher than Calcutta's. Bimal C. Ghose, *A Study of Indian Money Market* (Calcutta: Baptist Mission Press, 1943). Also see Charles P. Kindleberger, 'The Formation of Financial Centers: A Study in Comparative Economic History', *Princeton Studies in International Finance*, no. 36 (1974). For an accurate summary of the comparative fortunes of Calcutta and Bombay, see Amol Agrawal, 'When Bombay Overtook Calcutta: A History of India's Financial Geography', *Mint*, 24 June 2017: https://www.livemint.com/Sundayapp/Z8DStEXICwm3MFvlE7PFXI/When-Bombay-overtook-Calcutta-A-history-of-Indias-financia.html, accessed 12 October 2021.

coupled with a sudden and remarkable demographic shock, as East Bengali refugees began to enter Bengal and Assam in large numbers.[73] In the context of economic decline and refugee influx, Calcutta's urban infrastructures were stretched to their limits. Every rail station, bus stop, sidewalk became part of petty retail trade.

On the political front too, 1911 was a crossroads. During the debate on the transfer of capital from Calcutta to Delhi, the Bengali *bhadralok* (gentlemanly) class—who participated so directly during the anti-Partition agitation—remained conspicuously silent. Painfully aware of the limitations of public opinion and the futility of public consultation in the colonial context, the only alternative before *bhadralok* nationalists was to develop 'a mighty and moral power among the people themselves, raised up by systematic propagandist work' that would make the 'ruling power uneasy'.[74] At the time of Gandhian agitation in the interwar period, a new culture of street agitation developed, which resulted in a 'new political vernacular that sought to capture power by controlling city space'.[75]

The last three decades of colonial rule witnessed the growth of comparatively more permanent infrastructure of mass mobilization. Historians who studied politics in the final decades of colonial rule have suggested that 'mass communalism' as a 'political force' arose in the subcontinent from the 'eruption of masses in politics' during the interwar period. Communal mobilization and territorial warfare in Calcutta between 1918 and 1926 bolstered the capability of 'mass action' (Chapter 2). The late 1930s saw the gradual development of political organizations outside the Congress fold with distinct political visions and agendas, which both widened and deepened the sphere of organized political activities among different sections of the masses (Chapter 1). By the time the city witnessed the Hindu–Muslim Riot of 1946 (Chapter 3), it already had an extensive framework for competitive political mobilization.

Moreover, the expansion of the electoral space and nationalization of the Municipal Corporation during the interwar years played a crucial role in generating a new configuration between the city, the empire, and the nation. Newly organized groups such as the industrial and transport working class,

---

[73] Amiya. K. Bagchi, 'Studies on the Economy of West Bengal since Independence', *Economic and Political Weekly* 33, no. 47–48 (1998): 2973–2978.

[74] *New India*, 29 July 1905, quoted in Swati Chattopadhyay, 'Cities of Power and Protest', 48.

[75] Ibid.; Tanika Sarkar, *Bengal 1928-1934: The Politics of Protest* (Delhi: Oxford University Press, 1987).

women, students, and municipal workers asserted their presence on the streets, facilitating the proliferation of the spaces of agitation in the newly paved thoroughfares, open spaces, and parks. During the Non-Cooperation–Khilafat agitation, women and school students came out for picketing on the public streets, blurring the boundary between the private and the public.[76] By 1946–1947, these agitations ultimately succeeded in decolonizing the white-exclusive urban spaces (Chapter 1). However, mass politics in the late colonial era converged with and manifested as mass communalism in the subcontinent, especially in the cities (Chapters 2 and 3). As the theatre of mass action, urban streets played a significant role in forging and facilitating this relationship among the mass, the nation, and the state.[77]

Despite the spread of Gandhian agitation, until the very last days of colonial rule, legislative politics continued to be a domain of elite engagement, even when it involved lower-caste groups and minorities. Within this limited domain, subject-citizens influenced the government by forming various 'pressure groups'. The scope of mass agitation in the streets was inherently limited. But the mid-century transition to popular sovereignty and mass democracy intensified the spirit of popular politics in cities (Chapters 4 and 5). Between 1947 and 1952, there was a fundamental transformation in the subject position of ordinary Indians, as the new republic entered a conditional settlement with its adult citizens. Each one of them was now a voter of equal value within a unified electorate and therefore each adult citizen could, in theory, become the ruler. It was under this precise condition that the ruled willed to be governed.[78]

This transition in polity empowered the refugees, hawkers, students, and the working populations to repeatedly stake claims to capital cities, as the centres of power and privilege. After 1947, occupying the hitherto restricted secretariat area, the streets around the Governor's House and the Maidans became a matter of political and agitational common sense in Calcutta. The people of the new post-colony appeared 'explicitly' in these hitherto racially segregated spaces of privilege of the alien ruling elite. These public spaces were repeatedly recreated in subsequent refugee agitation, the anti-tram-fare-hike protest, teachers'

---

[76] T. Sarkar, *Bengal 1928–1934*.

[77] Sumit Sarkar, *The Swadeshi Movement in Bengal, 1903–1908* (Delhi: People's Publishing House, 1973); Anindita Ghosh, *Claiming the City: Protest, Crime, and Scandals in Colonial Calcutta, c. 1860–1920* (Delhi: Oxford University Press, 2016); S. Das, *Communal Riots in Bengal*; Ray, *Social Conflict and Political Unrest in Bengal*; T. Sarkar, *Bengal 1928–1934*.

[78] Ornit Shani, *How India Became Democratic* (Cambridge: Cambridge University Press, 2018), 3.

movements, food movements, and trade union movements. However, since it is a creation of action, these spaces tended to be highly fragile and resurfaced only when accomplished via public action.[79]

In Calcutta, the late colonial period (the 1920s–1940s) was the prelude to that popular sovereignty. The crowd was already on the streets. With the eventual transition to popular sovereignty, political aspirations and energies of democracy exceeded the frame of institutional politics. In this context, poorer social classes learned to collectively encroach upon crucial physical infrastructures and make infrastructure itself the focus of their collective existence in the city. These people, who produced the street as a site of livelihood, secured legitimacy only within the discursive universe of popular sovereignty. By their sheer number, the urban poor—East Bengali refugees, slum and squatter colony dwellers, and street hawkers—became an essential player in the city's political sphere, forging new interfaces between space and polity.

The focus of urban planning also underwent a considerable transformation in the 1950s and the 1960s. The Improvement Trust, we have noticed, was an organization tasked to produce a sanitary city by removing *bustees* from the inner city (more discussion can be found in Chapters 2 and 4). Such an approach at the time of mass democracy proved impossible to execute. In fact, one of the early pieces of urban legislation that the new post-colonial state in Calcutta tabled was the Thika Tenancy Act of 1949 (West Bengal Act No. 2 of 1949), which stabilized the tenants' lease and occupancy rights in the *bustees* and took away the owners' right to sell the *bustee* lands in the open market.[80] In the early 1960s, the Ford Foundation–engineered Calcutta Metropolitan Planning Organization (CMPO) came up with the blueprint of a Bustee Improvement Programme (BIP) to improve the living condition of the city's two million *bustee* dwellers. This was the first major *in situ* slum redevelopment programme to tackle the growing influence of communists among Calcutta's poor. In the next couple

---

[79] To invoke Hanna Arendt, its singularity is that
    unlike the spaces which are the work of our hands, it does not survive the actuality of the movement which brought it into being but disappears not only with the dispersal of men—as in the case of great catastrophes when the body politic of a people is destroyed—but with the disappearance or arrest of the activities themselves. (Hannah Arendt, *The Human Condition* [Chicago: University of Chicago Press, 1958, 199)

[80] There were many subsequent amendments to this act in the following decades which ultimately led to the abolition of private ownership of *bustee* lands in 1981. All resumable *bustee* lands were vested under the state. The tenants were granted heritable occupancy right to the dwellings under a rental agreement with the state.

of decades, the BIP travelled far and wide in the post-colonial world with the Ford Foundation consultants and provided a template for urban development and 'stabilization' of the insurgent cities.[81]

The first three post-colonial decades (1947–1977) in Calcutta was also marked by a radical labour agitation. These decades earned a reputation for Calcutta in the capitalist world, that of a 'dying city'—a city of *gherao*, strike, and blockade. By the late 1960s, *gherao*, or encirclement of important seats of power in the city and in factories, became ubiquitous. It became a popular tactic of public agitation in Calcutta and in the industrial belts after the electoral Left came to state power for the first time in 1967. The early *gherao*s created a new legacy of protest in Calcutta.

The tide turned in the 1990s (Chapter 5 and Epilogue). From the mid-1990s, the electoral Left of Calcutta began to disown *gherao*. Already, India's economic liberalization (officially started in 1991) reoriented the major cities as competing with other cities to attract corporate investment in industry, infrastructure, and finance. The Left Front government in West Bengal became an aggressive proponent of this project of privatization and corporatization.[82] Calcutta's

---

[81] Andrew Rumbach, '"Between the Devil and the Bay of Bengal": The Ford Foundation and the Politics of Planning in Post-Independence Calcutta', *Planning Perspectives* 36, no. 5 (2021): 1025–1051.

[82] India's liberalization of the economy is widely considered to have opened up new frontiers of urban growth. The transformation of the Indian cities at the time of 'globalization' has been a widely discussed phenomenon. Several works in the first decade of the twenty-first century have talked about the gentrification of Indian cities and the neoliberal passage. See Partha Chatterjee, 'Are Indian Cities Becoming Bourgeois at Last?', in Partha Chatterjee, *The Politics of the Governed: Reflections on Popular Politics in Most of the World* (Ranikhet: Permanent Black, 2004), 131–147; Amita Baviskar, 'Between Violence and Desire: Space, Power, and Identity in the Making of Metropolitan Delhi', *International Social Science Journal* 55, no. 1 (2003): 89–98; Gautam Bhan, *In the Public's Interest: Evictions, Citizenship and Inequality in Contemporary Delhi* (Athens: University of Georgia Press, 2016); D. Asher Ghertner, *Rule by Aesthetics: World-class City Making in Delhi* (New York: Oxford University Press, 2015). There are also some remarkable new works exploring the rental regime and real estate developments unfolding in Indian cities in the post-liberalization context. See Llerena Guiu Searle, *Landscapes of Accumulation: Real Estate and the Neoliberal Imagination in Contemporary India* (Chicago: University of Chicago Press, 2016); Michael Goldman, 'Speculative Urbanism and the Making of the Next World City', *International Journal of Urban and Regional Research* 35, no. 3 (2011): 555–581; Shubhra Gururani, 'Cities in the World of Villages: Agrarian

slowness and 'crumbling infrastructures' became a matter of the regime's embarrassment before the global business community. Time and again, several self-corrected regime functionaries said in public that in hindsight they felt that their earlier support to *gherao* was wrong—'an immoral act'.[83]

We may recollect, this was also the time when the Left Front government evicted thousands of hawkers and squatters in the inner city in a bid to re-insert the city in the global network of capital accumulation.[84] This attempt failed. The hawkers returned to the sidewalks and continued to occupy new sites (Chapter 5). Even in the early 2000s, Calcutta remained a city of hawkers, pavement dwellers, trams (at an increasingly reduced scale), aged Ambassador cars, agitators, strikers, and dissenters—a city of obstructed motion. Being the products of primitive accumulation of capital themselves, the hawkers and squatters facilitated urbanization, which was always ambiguous. They upheld a culture that was critical of the city-associated culture of accumulation. They created a city where obstruction becomes the keyword instead of motion.

Urbanism and the Making of India's Urbanising Frontiers', *Urban Geography* 41, no. 7 (2020): 971–989; Sai Balakrishnan, *Stakeholder Cities: Land Transformations along Urban Corridors in India* (Philadelphia: University of Pennsylvania Press, 2019); Tom Cowan, 'The Urban Village, Agrarian Transformation, and Rentier Capitalism in Gurgaon, India', *Antipode* 50, no. 5 (2018): 1244–1266.

[83] 'Bandh Is Bad and Gherao Immoral, Says Buddhadeb', *Economic Times*, 27 August 2008.

[84] Operation Sunshine was the beginning of a series of cleansing processes in the next decade that sought to reclaim Calcutta from the 'decadence' of obstruction and popular politics. Before the campaigns for the 2006 Assembly elections started, the Election Commission banned 'political graffiti, banners, posters and the colourful plywood figures of party symbols' in Calcutta using a decades-old local municipal law that prohibits 'defacement' of public and private property. In an influential post-edit in *The Telegraph*, Partha Chatterjee argued that the ban on political graffiti, which had been part of the state's political culture for more than half a century, was part of a zeal among the high-up bureaucracy, the court, and the business elite to 'cleanse and sanitize the public political arena to rid the space of citizenship of all the noise, smell and gaudiness of a publicly mobilized plebeian culture that is now being seen as both an impediment to and an embarrassment for an India seeking to be become a world power'. Cited in R. Bandyopadhyay, *Negotiating Informality*.

Sources

To write this book, I used two hitherto unexplored urban archives at the record rooms of the Calcutta Improvement Trust (CIT) and the Calcutta Hawker Sangram Committee (HSC), besides the well-established repositories at the British Library, London; the National Archives of India, New Delhi; the West Bengal State Archives, Kolkata; and the Daily Notes of Calcutta Police (Special Branch), Office of Deputy Commissioner of Police (Special Branch), Kolkata.

During my PhD days, I got access to the HSC archives. This was a unique repository of conflict and negotiation between the union and the state being created and mobilized by the trade unionists and the hawkers themselves. In Chapter 5, I discuss the emergence of this archive. The remaining four chapters are primarily based on the Improvement Trust Records.

In 2011, I managed to secure access to this repository. A large portion of this collection was still out of academic circulation. Various scholars used the Trust's published reports and Annual Reports liberally,[85] but most of the unpublished primary materials were frozen in dust. In 2014, we—at the Centre for Studies in Social Sciences, Calcutta (CSSSC)—took the initiative to digitize a small portion of this repository containing the minutes of the Board of Trustees from 1912 to 1962. The repository became available for academic consultation at the CSSSC archives in early 2016.

This book took shape with the public appearance of these two archives and my involvement in making them accessible to historians. Combining these two disparate sources and building a narrative of the city through them was a considerable challenge for me which I accomplished in this book over the last ten years. I had to learn to import ethnographic sensibilities while handling the archives. An ethnographic take on records enabled me to treat the archives as socially and culturally constructed and maintained entities—that archive and archiving are outcomes of organizational contexts within which they are generated and preserved.[86]

---

[85] Most notably by Partho Datta in *Planning the City* and Nabaparna Ghosh in *The Hygienic City-Nation*.
[86] Ritajyoti Bandyopadhyay, 'A Historian among Anthropologists: Comments on "Politics of Archiving"', *Dialectical Anthropology* 35, no. 3 (2011): 331–339.

Conclusion

The twentieth century began with efforts at planned city-building and suburbanization. Motion was taken up by city planners as the keyword. The century ended with such planning being thwarted by obstructionism. The latter proclaimed itself as the hallmark of a democratic polity. Obstructionism built the late-twentieth- and early-twenty-first-century city of Calcutta, which expressed a logic of urbanization *without* accumulation and played out through ambivalent class and communal dynamics. In other words, I trace how the terms of the motion–obstruction dialectics transformed, leading to the emergence of a mass political culture in twentieth-century Calcutta.

I tell this story via Calcutta's streets. I imagine the streets as being in motion themselves, simultaneously settling and unsettling an urban social structure and unfolding in space with uneven temporalities. And yet that same street is also my epistemic field, offering a 'standpoint', a situated view of social processes and their histories.

1

The Making of the Modern Street
Engineers, Commoners, Agitators

The ground, in the words of one planner, is 'the traffic-flow-support-nexus for the vertical whole'. Translated, this means that the public space has become a derivative of movement. The idea of space as derivative from motion parallels exactly the relations of space to motion produced by the private automobile.... Today, we experience an ease of motion unknown to any prior urban civilization ... we take unrestricted motion of the individual to be an absolute right. The private motorcar is the logical instrument for exercising that right, and the effect on public space, especially the space of the urban street, is that the space becomes meaningless or even maddening unless it can be subordinated to free movement.... The city street acquires, then, a peculiar function—to permit motion....

—Richard Sennett[1]

We attain to dwelling, so it seems, only by means of building. The latter, building, has the former, dwelling, as its goal.

—Martin Heidegger[2]

Automobility began to emerge as a significant aspect of urban mobility in the west as well as in prime colonial cities such as Calcutta and Bombay in the last decade of the nineteenth century.[3] Automobiles became ubiquitous and

---

[1] Richard Sennett, *The Fall of Public Man* (London and Boston, MA: Faber and Faber, 1977), 14.

[2] Martin Heidegger, *Poetry, Language, Thought*, trans. Albert Hofstadter (New York: Harper & Row, 1971), 145.

[3] 'Automobility', writes John Urry, 'captures a double sense, both of the humanist self as in the notion of autobiography, and of objects or machines that possess a capacity for movement, as in automatic or automation.' Its introduction resulted in the notion of human freedom premised upon the individual's unrestricted mobility and his or her mastery over machine, space, and time. John Urry, 'The "System" of Automobility', *Theory, Culture and Society* 21, nos. 4–5 (2004): 25–39, quoted in 26. Paradoxically, automobility was also associated with the production of the

dominant in many of these cities by the 1940s. In South Asian cities such as Calcutta, automobiles had to share space and time with other, more primordial and slower, means of human locomotion throughout the twentieth century (and even the twenty-first), producing differential mobilities on city roads.[4] Their emergence necessitated and culminated in several significant urban spatial reforms, which began—as we have seen—as a counterinsurgency and public health measure in the mid-nineteenth century. Automobility gave these reforms a new orientation by which—as Richard Sennett mentions in the opening quote—public space turned out to be 'a derivative from motion'.

The streets that literally undergirded and made possible the modern automobile age came into existence in prime cities all over the world in the first half of the twentieth century. A set of new paving experiments facilitated and coincided with a host of other innovations, such as sidewalks, public squares, parks, and elevated tramways on green boulevards. These spaces materialized in the triadic encounters of engineers, commoners, and agitators. In giving shape to streets, both experts, who planned their construction, and users, who navigated their lives through them, ended up shaping each other in myriad ways.

I conceptualize the modern street as a synthesis of these two practices. First, street-building 'from above' by the architects of motion (as the opening quote by Sennett suggests) and, second, street-building 'from below' by its users, through obstruction, squatting, agitation, protest, and encroachment. If motion refers to the forces of circulation, obstruction—as a domain of human action—is a critique of a motion-oriented urban imaginary. The modern street emerges at the point where motion meets obstruction. These two forces develop what Marx calls a 'modus vivendi': 'a form in which they can exist side by side.'[5] This contradiction is immanent in the street, and it asserts itself 'in the antithetical phases' of the city's 'metamorphosis'.[6]

'commuting mass' in cities via public transport—started first by electric tramcars and suburban trains, and subsequently by buses. S. Chas Dunbar, *Buses, Trolleys and Trams* (London: Hamlyn, 1967). Also see C. Jefferson and J. Skinner, 'The Evolution of Urban Public Transport', *WIT Transactions on the Built Environment* 77 (2005): 75–84. Public transport in the cities also created public transport centres such as tram depots, bus terminuses, train stations, and so on, where the streets converged and masses gathered. These spaces also created possibilities for trade and commerce to concentrate around them.

[4] David Arnold, 'The Problem of Traffic: The Street-Life of Modernity in Late-Colonial India', *Modern Asian Studies* 46, no. 1 (2012): 119–141.

[5] Karl Marx, *Capital*, vol. 1 (Moscow: Progress Publishers, 1887), 71.

[6] Ibid., 77.

Engineer: The New Master of Space

The newly founded Calcutta Improvement Trust appointed the remarkable civil engineer E. P. Richards[7] as their Chief Engineer and asked him to submit a report on the Trust's course of action.[8] Richards and his team spent 15 months studying the city and extensively used a new technology of capture—the cameras—to document streets, vehicles, buildings, and neighbourhoods. The rather comprehensive report on the 'Condition, Improvement and Town Planning of the City of Calcutta and Contiguous Areas' in 1914[9] was ill-fated and was largely ignored by the Trust, but it received praise from many contemporary urban planners.

In this report, Richards pointed out certain 'striking defects' of Calcutta, particularly with regard to its streets. He found that 'the maximum density of building and population' was in pockets that had 'the least provision of roads and streets'. The city had a 'rectangular system of main roads, the meshes being many times larger than those of any other city'.[10] But what was more problematic to Richards was that the streets that formed the rectangular system had unequal

---

[7] In September 1912, the Calcutta Improvement Trust hired Richards as its Chief Engineer. In their meeting on 23 July 1912, the Trustees appointed Richards with a salary of 2,000 rupees per mensem rising to 2,500 rupees by annual increment of 100 rupees with a consolidated pay of 100 rupees for the upkeep of a car. Minutes of the 22th Meeting of the Calcutta Improvement Trust, 23 July 1912, *Proceedings of the CIT for the Year 1912–13* (Valuation Department), 1. Before joining the Trust, Richards worked as the Chief Engineer of Madras. He was born in 1873. After being trained as a civil engineer, he was appointed as a senior engineer with the Derwent Valley Water Board between 1901 and 1908. Here, he earned a good professional reputation. He was one of the founder-members of the Royal Town Planning Institute (1914). This Institute was one of the key players in canonizing the science of town planning through pedagogy and advocacy. Richard Harris and Robert Lewis, 'Introduction', in E. P. Richard's *The Condition, Improvement and Town Planning of the City of Calcutta and Contiguous Areas: The Richards Report*, ed. Richard Harris and Robert Lewis (London: Routledge, 2015), vii–xxii.

[8] When Richards conducted his survey, Calcutta was already an enormous metropolis with a 'population of one-and-a-quarter millions' concentrated in 30,000 acres of densely built-up land.

[9] E. P. Richards, *The Condition, Improvement and Town Planning of the City of Calcutta and Contiguous Areas: The Richards Report*, ed. Richard Harris and Robert Lewis (London: Routledge, 2015).

[10] Ibid., 19.

width varying in traffic capacity and no 'ordinary relation between width and position'.[11] He observed:

> Chitpore Road, perhaps the most important of the north and south traffic routes … is miserably narrow yet has to carry heavier traffic than the 60 to 70 ft. wide Cornwallis Street, and the 80 to 100 ft. wide Circular Road. Some of the best roads are so placed that they carry but a small traffic.

Richards also complained that the city lacked diagonals except for Harrison Road and Park Street. Moreover, it did not have a 'single true radial direct route out of or into the city's main focus'.[12] The chief obstacles to 'free main road extension' to the outlying roads connecting the hinterlands, according to Richards, were mainly the canals and railways to the north, northeast, and east. These, in his opinion, needed to be crossed by massive bridges.

Using a detailed description of jute traffic in the city, Richards criticized Calcutta's street system from a business standpoint as well. Raw jute was brought to Calcutta from Eastern Bengal and Assam by train, by the river, and by canal boats. On arrival and for months afterwards, hectic buying and selling of jute would occur in Calcutta markets, most notably in Hatkhola. Most of it would be prepared for shipping to European centres in jute mills that lined the 'west Hugli banks for miles above and below Howrah Bridge, and the east bank above Cossipore, and at Kidderpore'.[13] Another assemblage of jute presses and mills could be found in the northeastern industrial area. A few more could be traced in Aheeritolla, Neemtolla, Sovabazaar, and Hatkhola, situated between Chitpore Road and Strand Road (North). After preparation, an enormous volume of the jute would be re-carted to the railways and shipping areas. The remaining stock would be re-carted to the jute mart and moved from one warehouse to another in north Calcutta.[14] Richards describes this enormous logistical world thus:

> Every north and north-east country road on the outskirts of Calcutta is crowded with jute carts coming in and going out. The canal and its lock-basins are crammed and bunged up with barges of jute. The Hugli

[11] Ibid., 20.
[12] Ibid., 20.
[13] Ibid., 114.
[14] Ibid., 114.

riverside from Cossipore to below Neemtolla is in somewhat the same state; and nearly every railway yard and siding in the north, at Sealdah on the east, and Kidderpore in the south is filled with wagons of jute.[15]

The inland movement of jute between markets, warehouses, and transit centres happened via the proverbially slow bullock carts trudging their way through the lanes and by-lanes of the northern quarters of the city. The traffic pressure became much higher on reaching Chitpore. There were three primary jute-carting foci in Calcutta: (*a*) between Cossipore–Chitpore and Hatkhola market area, (*b*) between Hatkhola and the Canal Stores and northeast passes, and (*c*) between Sealdah and Hatkhola, and Sealdah and Cossipore–Chitpore.

To alleviate the situation, Richards proposed a north and south 'inner Strand Road culminating in Shyambazaar' along with a 'good riverside double-level road from at least Aheeritolla to Cossipore'. He then proposed an east–west road 'straight across from Hatkhola to Halisibagan [in Maniktola, east of Upper Circular Road] and over the Circular Canal.'[16] The new roads, Richards instructed, would have to 'cut through congested and insanitary neighbourhoods' of the northern quarters. Along the way it would valorize property prices, destroy *bustees*, and lead to an overall 'decongestion' of the city.

In planning new streets, Richards contemplated coordinating an indeterminate series of motile elements: how to simultaneously optimize the circulation of x number of bullock carts and y number of pedestrians, how to control miasmas and decongest neighbourhoods, how to defer the otherwise inevitable outbreak of an epidemic, how to minimize disorder, how to capitalize locked up urban property, how to prepare the city for automobility, all this while ensuring public order in the city. Thus, street planning under capitalism was the art of dealing with innumerable, intersecting, open-ended series of uncertain but probable elements and events, all of which had to be governed 'within a multivalent and transformable framework.'[17] In other words, the planner-engineer had to invent order out of what was identified as chaos. The goal was to attain maximum urban efficiency to ensure a smoother climate for capital accumulation. In this planning schema, the street was a subject of intervention in and of itself, in governing a city. In Calcutta, the Improvement

---

[15] Ibid., 113.

[16] Ibid., 115.

[17] Michel Foucault, *Security, Territory, Population: Lectures at the Collège de France 1977–1978*, trans. Graham Burchell (London: Palgrave Macmillan, 2007), 35.

Trust and the Municipal Corporation came under the command of this calculative rationality in the early twentieth century (Map 1.1).

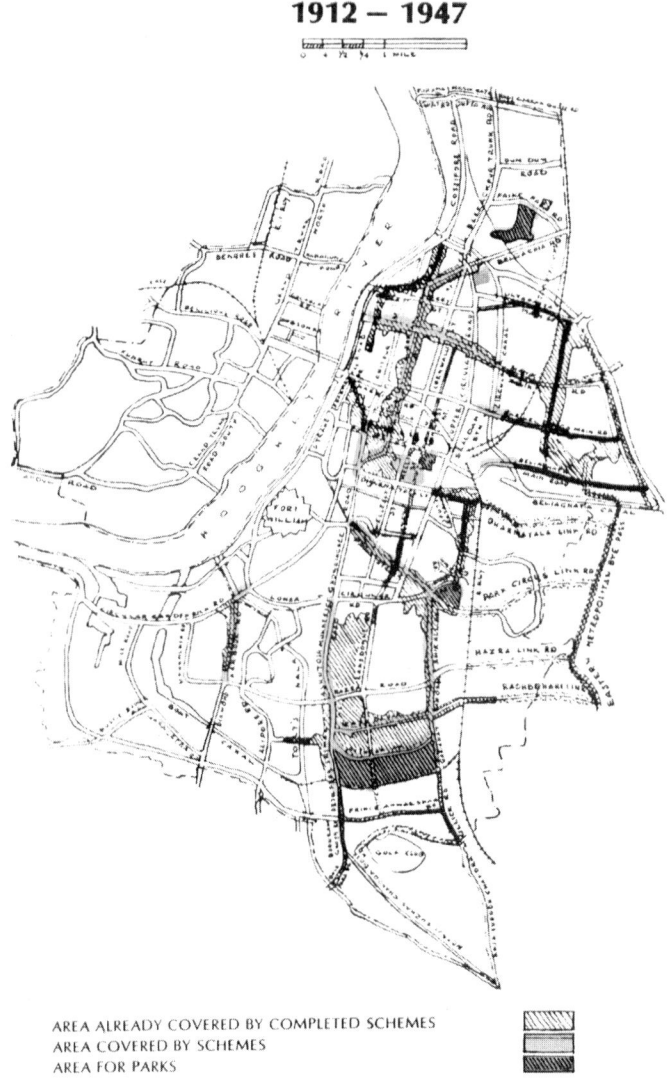

Map 1.1 The work of the Calcutta Improvement Trust between 1912 and 1947

Source: Partho Datta, 'Calcutta on the Threshold of 1940s', in *The Stormy Decades: Calcutta*, ed. Tanika Sarkar and Sekhar Bandyopadhyay (London: Routledge, 2015), 18–41, 19. The marked areas reflect the work of the Calcutta Improvement Trust between 1912 and 1947.

The Calcutta Improvement Act, 1911, provided for the laying down of new roads and street alignments, which were the basis of all the improvement schemes that the Trust undertook. There were four significant considerations before the Trust. First, the new streets would have to provide better communication throughout the municipal area. This would serve the dual purpose of facilitating traffic and commerce within the city and functioning as 'ventilating shafts' in densely packed neighbourhoods. Second, the Trust was required to connect the inner-city streets with the existing and proposed suburbs. This way, it was hoped, the inner-city population load could be reduced and the neighbourhoods of the sprawling city would integrate with the centre. The third function of the Trust's street schemes was to ensure surveillance, necessitated by both the integration of the city with its hinterlands and the growing migration of working-class people from all over the subcontinent. The fourth and last function of the new streets was to prepare the city for the impending automobile revolution that was expected to replace bullock carts and other animal-driven locomotion soon.

Together, these four functions constituted the civic government's policy realm. Thus, civic institutions of the twentieth century had to balance their hygiene function, business function, surveillance function, and traffic function. All these four functions presupposed a *motion-centric* understanding of the city, as a space for the smooth circulation and accumulation of capital. In this scheme of transformation, civil engineers such as Richards became the 'agents of liaison' between the 'three great variables of territory, communication and speed'.[18] In the twentieth-century city, the engineer was to become the new master of space.[19]

The Improvement Trust was entrusted with the unencumbered authority to institutionalize the engineers' view of the city, away from the fast-democratizing sphere of municipal politics. Richards' proposals might not have come to fruition

[18] Michel Foucault, *Power/Knowledge: Selected Interviews and Other Writings, 1972–77* (Brighton, England: Harvester, 1980).

[19] An exchange between the Bengal Chamber of Commerce and the Municipal Corporation dating back to 1910 had already emphasized the need for

> a special engineer with experience in road matters ... who would have under his care the whole question of road repairs and management, with of course an adequate staff of qualified officers to assist him: this official would be subordinate to the Chief Engineer and would have no other work to do than supervise the roads. (Minutes of the Proceedings of the 37th Meeting of the Roads, Buildings, Bustee and City Improvements Sub-Committee, held at the Municipal Office, on 24 January 1910, *Proceedings of the Calcutta Municipal Corporation for the Year 1910–1911*)

due to the fiscal conservatism of the colonial state, yet his views indicated the route the new authoritarian civic reforms would take at the time of high imperialism. For Richards, the new avenue-style streets represented an imperial civilizing mission—an intervention that would produce a city of motion, where the prime imperial commodity, jute, would circulate seamlessly from boats to warehouses to markets to factories and ultimately to the port. With the beginning of the automobile age, vital to the realization of this modern city of motion, a preoccupation with the street 'surface' became distinctly pressing.

Some Early Paving Experiments

The nineteenth-century Scottish engineer John Loudon McAdam gave his name to a type of road construction in which compressed layers of similarly sized crushed stones were used as paving material. Soon after, a coating of coal tar came to be used to stabilize macadam surfaces further—referred to as tarmacadam or tarmac.[20] This technology was adopted widely and, in the following years, various improvements were made to 'macadamized' roads, by adding different kinds of binding agents, to serve different purposes. For instance, in Calcutta in the 1870s, the engineering challenge that dominated discourses of street construction was the need for a more impervious surface foundation to prevent water from seeping into the subsoil. A common resolution was the use of water-bound macadam, in which the gaps between the stones were filled with a mixture of stone dust and water. But an increase in vehicular traffic at the turn of the century led to an alarming proliferation of dust and noise 'nuisance'. Moreover, the earlier stone surface was damaging to the pneumatic (inflated) tyre. Engineers worldwide began experimenting with a set of paving materials that could produce a non-porous but also dustless and smooth surface well suited to pneumatic tyres.

S. W. Goode, the early municipal historian of Calcutta, tells us that in 1904–1905, a new generation of municipal engineers devised 'an improved method of mixing the blindage[21] with the stone metal', a term used for crushed stones.[22] This

---

[20] While the use of tar on macadam surfaces started in the mid-nineteenth century, Edgar Purnell Hooley registered 'Tarmac' as a trademark in 1903.

[21] In conversation, present-day civil engineers described blinding in road construction as the filling of gaps on the ground to create a smooth, dry surface to work on. The 'blindage' generally used today is low-grade concrete or sand.

[22] S. W. Goode, *Municipal Calcutta: Its Institutions in Their Origin and Growth* (Calcutta: Corporation of Calcutta, 1916).

method was rejected after two unsuccessful attempts to implement it in 1907–1908 and 1909–1910 in Dalhousie Square East and College Street. The new surface was smooth, and it controlled dust and noise from vehicular traffic, but the edges of the road wore out quickly in the face of heavy traffic.[23] In 1910–1911, Messrs Bird and Co. spearheaded another experiment with an Indian patent stone[24] slag on the Gladwell system (a variation of the tarmacadam) and lithofalt (a kind of granite block). However, Goode found the experiment unsatisfactory.[25] Within a year of construction, these roads began to produce considerable dust. In the rainy season, mud began to loosen the stones, creating gaps between stones that affected wheels, hooves, and boots alike. The smaller stone plates began to break into pieces under heavy traffic, and the dust thus produced got amalgamated with sand in the gaps between stones. Further, mixed with animal excreta, especially horse manure, the small potholes (that resisted flushing) became the breeding ground of tetanus bacteria. The seepage of this substance downward made the sub-surface utilities, especially the water supply pipelines, vulnerable.

In the following year, the Corporation tried out wood-paving.[26] The forest department supplied 50 tons of *sal* wood-blocks from the Jungle Mahals free of cost to facilitate the experimentation.[27] Initially, the municipal engineers found that the wooden surface was considerably less dusty than other existing materials. However, in busy streets, wooden blocks proved less durable. They showed signs of undulation, and like macadamized roads, gathered animal excreta. The wooden blocks also reacted rapidly to temperature fluctuations and humidity, and in some places, they encroached upon the sidewalks.[28] The experiment was soon called off.[29]

---

[23] Ibid.

[24] The Indian patent stone, or IPS, formed by mixing metal oxides with cement, was a type of flooring used widely in India.

[25] Goode, *Municipal Calcutta*.

[26] Ibid.

[27] Ibid.

[28] It is important to note that in many metropolitan cities, especially in Victorian England, wood was widely used as a paving material in the 1860s and 1870s and subsequently rejected for very similar reasons. In addition, many contemporaries attributed the great fire of Chicago in 1871 to the inflammable creosote oil that wooden pavements had to be soaked in. Chris Otter, *The Victorian Eye: A Political History of Light and Vision in Britain, 1800–1910* (Chicago: University of Chicago Press, 2008), 94–95.

[29] 'Calcutta Roads: The Ideal Surface', *Times of India*, 23 April 1915.

The search for an impervious and durable surface continued. Besides coal tar, bitumen (often used interchangeably with pitch in road construction) also came to be used to layer street surfaces in Britain. Unlike tar, a hydrocarbon which was artificially derived through the destructive distillation of coal or petroleum, pitch or bitumen (a residue of the same process) could also be naturally occurring. The use of bitumen proved helpful in checking water contamination in the subsoil through seepage.[30] It was in this context that W. B. MacCabe, the Municipal Corporation's engineer, while on leave in Britain, collected some tarmacadam samples, which he brought back to Calcutta upon his return. The new mixture, however, proved unsuitable for Calcutta. Because of bitumen's low melting point, in the heat of summer, it became too soft for practical purposes. The difficulty, then, was to get a mixture that was reasonably hard in summer but at the same time would not become brittle at low temperatures.[31] Finally, MacCabe conducted a modification of Gladwell's tarmacadam in his laboratory. This led him to propose paving some of the city roads with a composition of tar and pitch to suit Calcutta's climate, as an experimental measure.[32] MacCabe held that earlier experimentations had failed partly because most of the roads had been paved with the residue of building materials (rubble) that contained lime in large quantities. This had impaired the adhesive quality of various dust-laying compounds being used.[33]

It was found that the initial cost of MacCabe's new system would be considerably higher than that of ordinary macadam. However, '... the waterproof quality of this surface was with the Calcutta climate a great asset, as the life of the road was thereby much increased'.[34] In 1913–1914 then, nearly 42,000 square yards of road were paved through this new version of tarmacadam at a cost of 99,000 rupees. The surface showed promising results for vehicles with pneumatic tyres. Nonetheless, it remained vulnerable to the hard-wheeled bullock-cart traffic.[35]

---

[30] Gjis Mom, 'Inter-artifactual Technology Transfer', *History and Technology* 20, no. 1 (2004): 75–96, quoted in 79.

[31] 'Calcutta Roads: The Ideal Surface', *Times of India*.

[32] Rai S. C. Mittra Bahadur, 'Modern Road Making and Maintenance—1', *Calcutta Municipal Gazette*, 28 November 1925.

[33] 'Calcutta Roads: The Ideal Surface', *Times of India*.

[34] Goode, *Municipal Calcutta*, 244.

[35] Ibid.

Thus, we find that at the start of the second decade of the twentieth century, some significant attempts were made to pave Calcutta with materials that could suit the topographic and climatic condition of the city. The change, however, was slow, fragmentary, irregular, and asymmetrical. In most of the early-twentieth-century cities, the coexistence of variously paved streets was a reality that requires a historian to investigate 'the black-box of competing technologies'[36] minutely. It is possible that one would find only minor differences between coexisting and competing paving technologies. What interests us, then, in resuming the story of street-building in Calcutta are the context-specific developments and discussions that settled the future in favour of a particular method over another.

The Age of Asphalt

In the history of automobile-friendly streets, asphalt occupies a key position. Asphalt, an aggregate bound by bitumen, is obtainable from natural reserves and produced by the fractional distillation of petroleum. Asphalt cannot be obtained from coal. It is an adhesive that has been in large-scale use as a paving material since the late nineteenth century. Scientific experimentations proved that both asphalt and cement concrete were water-resistant and damp-proof, thus enhancing the durability of built space. Their enormous capacity to, quite literally, hold a diverse range of things together made possible a kind of unity in the world of objects, which had considerable impact on human settlements and lived practices.

Before the 1910s, asphalt hardly appeared as a potentially important commodity to the colonial Government in India, as coal tar—abundantly available in Bengal Presidency—was commonly used in road construction.[37] When in 1902 the Assistant Political Resident stationed at the Persian Gulf reported the discovery of asphalt deposits in a hill called Jebbel Dukhan on an island, the response from the Government of India was 'cautious, restrained and overall unremarkable' to the extent that it even hesitated to depute a trained Geological Survey of India (GSI) staff to supervise the work of discovery at Bahrain.[38] Asphalt finally became a vital import for India during the years of

---

[36] Gjis Mom, 'Inter-artifactual Technology Transfer' (2004): 76.
[37] File B/2 Oils and Minerals, Bahrain, India Office Records and Private Papers, IOR/R/15/2/13, 11 Jan 1907–12 Nov 1917.
[38] In 1905, the asphalt market in India was still found to be considerably small 'not exceeding 1,500 tons per annum'. File 19/98 II, 128 (C 10) Naphta Spring Near Halul

the First World War. Several United States (US) oil companies (also producing asphalt) who invested in the European markets started feeling the shiver of the Great War by August 1914 when 'the pipelines suffered the worst month in history'.[39] Soon, Rockefeller's Standard Oil Company was compelled to divert much of its petroleum and petro-products to some British colonies, including India, mainly on account of its Romanian supply lines being cut off. The growing importance of asphalt in the construction industry, then, also coincides with a shift from coal-based binding agents to those derived from crude oil.

In the meantime—as we have seen before—MacCabe and his Indian interlocutor Rai S. C. Mittra Bahadur had already found that if tar in tarmacadam was replaced by bitumen and the stones were resized accordingly to fit in with this new adhesive, one could get asphaltic concrete (concrete bound by an asphaltic binder as opposed to cement concrete, which is bound by cement and water). MacCabe asked the city corporation to contact experts in the US' Standard Oil Company. Responding to this request, the Standard Oil Company sent one 'Mr Staber' to Calcutta in the early winter of 1916 with a consignment of liquid bituminous asphalt. Staber, MacCabe, and Mittra closely supervised the introduction of asphalt paving in the city with 2-inch asphaltic concrete initially 'from the portion of Chowringhee Road between Esplanade East and Kyd Street'.[40]

The European Association in Calcutta had in 1914 identified the problem of streets as essentially one of surface materials being laid on a weak and 'uncertain' base 'provided by the deltaic silt characteristic of the city'.[41] Soon after, a committee was set up with representatives from the Corporation, the Improvement Trust, and the Public Works Department (PWD) for the

---

Island + Miscellaneous Correspondence + Viceroy's Interview 1901; File 19/98 II Asphalt Deposit, India Office Records and Private Papers, IOR/R/15/1/317 28 Jan 1901–31 May 1911.

[39] *Wall Street Journal*, October 1914.

[40] Rai S. C. Mittra Bahadur, 'Modern Road Making and Maintenance—1' (1925). Also see File 5R/2 of 1919, PWD-MIS PUB. IMPVTS, 'Use of Oil, Tar and Pitch Compounds on Calcutta Roads' (Note by B. K. Finnimore, Chief Engineer, Bengal) (West Bengal State Archives [henceforth WBSA]).

[41] Calcutta, on the other hand, stood 'on the bank of a tidal river, with a considerable portion of its surface scarcely above the level of the highest spring tides; and a subsoil consisting for the most part of the fine silty sand, saturated with water'. William Clark, 'The Drainage of Calcutta', a paper read at the Bengal Social Science Congress, held at the Town Hall, Calcutta, on 2 February 1871.

standardization of road-construction methods in Calcutta. MacCabe was inducted into the committee as its expert. The committee recommended asphalt paving on a lime concrete foundation. It was found that this new surface worked very well to facilitate automobile traffic. At the same time though, several complaints of humans and horses breaking their pelvis were also registered. Thus, on 26 August 1918, a horse-drawn 'Phaeton carriage' crashed in Chowringhee as the horse allegedly 'slipped and crumbled'. The cart had two European women and a child inside. The passengers received 'major injuries' and were subsequently rushed to a hospital.[42]

The Age of Asphalt, then, was necessitated by and roughly coincided with the automobile age. In 1914, the colonial government had already passed the Motor Vehicles Act to streamline automobile traffic on roads. The fact that automobiles required separate legislation speaks of the fact that it had already emerged as a substantial problem in the realm of traffic governance.[43] By 1922, Calcutta had 9,438 private cars, 970 taxi cabs, 758 Lorries and 2,285 motorcycles plying on the streets.[44] The war released hundreds of wounded trucks and their (mostly) exhausted Sikh drivers on the streets of Calcutta. The European Association and the Bengal Chambers of Commerce (BCC) welcomed the arrival of trucks, anticipating the end of the 'bullock cart era'.[45] In 1921, the trucks gave birth to the first vernacular motorbuses when some of their owners started taking commuters from Kalighat and Kidderpur to Dalhousie in the course of a month-long tramways workers' strike. Wooden bodies were soon added, and the trucks were also given seats and proper entrances. These buses had temporary licences to transport passengers.[46] In 1922, 15 motor omnibuses

---

[42] 'Phaeton Crash on Asphalt', *The Statesman*, 27 August 1918.

[43] File 1-M-4 (11) of 1981, Nos. 319–326, MPI, dated Calcutta, 11 April 1918, from C. P. Walsh, Esq., Secretary to Government of Bengal, PWD, to All Members of the Committee, 'Summary of the Proceedings of the First Meeting of the Chowringhee Congestion Committee Held on the 10th April 1918' (WBSA). Also see File 1-M-4 (13) of 1918, 'Report of the Chowringhee Traffic Committee' (WBSA).

[44] *Annual Report on the Police Administration of the Town of Calcutta and Its Suburbs for the Year 1922* (Calcutta: The Bengal Secretariat Press, 1923).

[45] File 5R-1 of 1915, Proceedings 36 to 62, Government of Bengal PWD-MIS (Public Improvements), 'Standardization of Methods of Road Construction in Calcutta' (WBSA).

[46] Ahindra Choudhury, *Nijere Haraye Khunji*, vol. I (Kolkata: Saptarshi Prakashan, 2011).

were running on regular routes. Within five years or so, Calcutta had several bus routes. In 1921 alone, 12,884 motor car-related cases were reported to the Motor Vehicle Branch. The city Traffic Police dealt with an additional 9,078 cases and convicted 2,898 drivers for a traffic rule violation. The introduction of buses, taxicabs, and private cars overlapped for a long while with slow-moving animal-drawn and human-drawn vehicles. Together, they created a new image of the city and a new commuting public.

The existing, largely water-bound macadamized main roads of the city increasingly appeared ineffective in withstanding the suction of the new and expanding army of pneumatic tyres on Calcutta streets.[47] With the steady increase in automobile traffic since the 1900s, dust and noise seemed to have pervaded urban life in Calcutta. The increasing numbers of electric trams since 1902 added yet another set of vibrations to the usual hum on the streets. In 1907, the Mint Authority complained that traffic-induced vibrations were causing considerable problems in the operation of measurement units.[48] Even before this complaint was made, the Secretariat of the Foreign and Army Department at 5 and 6, Esplanade East, drew the PWD's attention to the 'great inconvenience caused to the officers and numerous visitors' due to 'the constant roar caused by vehicular traffic, coupled with the clanging of tram-car bells' making it impossible for 'ordinary speech to be heard in the Secretariat'.[49] The Municipal Commissioner's office was flooded with similar complaints about increasing dust and noise from government establishments and various 'ratepayers' associations'. The Star Theatre authority wrote a letter to the municipality describing how the vehicular roar made it impossible for Rabindranath Tagore to watch a particular show on the evening of 8 September 1915.[50] Property owners regularly claimed that due to the vibration on the street in the daytime and the reckless driving of loaded trucks at night, the buildings abutting major streets began showing early signs of cracks. Heavy vehicles, especially loaded trucks, created another problem. Several times heavier than automobiles, the trucks ran on hard rubber

---

[47] File 5R/2 of 1919, Serial 4, 10 & 11, PWD-MIS PUB. IMPVTS, 'Laying Tar Macadam and Constructing a Footpath on the South Side of Ochterlony Road on the Calcutta Maidan—Question of Specification', WBSA.

[48] 'Calcutta Roads: The Ideal Surface', *Times of India*.

[49] File 1M/5/1904, 1–9, April 1904, PWD-MPI, 'Proposed Alteration of Roads on the Portion of Calcutta Maidan Opposite the New Foreign Office and Military Secretariat' (WBSA).

[50] Chaudhuri, *Nijere Haraye Khunji*, vol. I.

wheels. Under their pressure, the existing roads of the city began to crumble.[51] Thus, asphalt paving in the winter of 1916 appeared to be timely and inevitable, especially to Calcutta's official circle, even though it was yet to become the uncontested paving material in London.

The Emergence of Avenues with Sidewalks

Asphalt paving was preceded by and coincided with the expansion of a subterranean drainage network. Covering up the existing open drains widened many existing streets in some instances and enabled new lanes to emerge in other cases, especially in neighbourhoods that had denser populations.[52] In some of the major streets, the newly acquired margins were given an elevation of sidewalks to segregate pedestrian traffic from other forms of locomotion. The paving experiments in cities, then, also coincided with other street reforms, such as the emergence of avenue-style streets with wide sidewalks, large intersections, and public parks and squares.

William Clark mentions how apart from providing a sanitary surface to the underground drainage infrastructure, the sidewalks also came to serve three other very crucial functions. First, the sidewalks were to protect the fancy gas-lighting facilities from aggressive traffic. Second, the sidewalks worked as an embankment to insulate abutting properties from seepage of stormwater from the increasingly convex streets. Third, the sidewalks were designed to give the commercial establishments a window-shopping public.[53] Goode calculates that in 1913–1914, more than six and a half lakh rupees (a lakh equals hundred thousand) were spent on the construction of sidewalks. The ever-increasing

---

[51] David Arnold writes, 'A sense of novelty particularly impressed itself on the consciousness of those who became first-time observers of, and participants in, the modern phenomenon of traffic.' Arnold, 'The Problem of Traffic', 121.

[52] Clark, 'Drainage in Calcutta'.

[53] Ibid. The commencement of the first footpath was rather unspectacular and was catalysed by the need to recycle the 'spare earth excavated in laying the sewers, ashes, building rubbish and broken bricks'. Thus, in 1858, the Municipal Commissioners wrote, 'The bricks have almost been wholly obtained from the house purchased and pulled down in opening the new street in Soorti Bagan, and the carting of the materials has been done by the conservancy establishment.' In 1858, it had been claimed by the Municipal Commissioners that 'nine tenth of the foot passengers make use of the sidewalk'. *General Report of the Commissioners for the Improvement of the Town of Calcutta for the Year 1857* (Calcutta: Military Orphan Press, 1858).

amount of corporation budget spent in elevating, maintaining, and constructing sidewalks suggests that in colonial Calcutta, sidewalks increasingly became a part of the routine public work done by the municipal authority.

As automobiles began to increase acceleration within a cluttered urban space, the structural and functional segregation between the carriageway (for automobile traffic) and the sidewalk (for pedestrian movement) emerged as a pervasive common sense among city planners, reformers, the police, and civic administrators. The macro-segregation of the street between the carriageway and the sidewalk was coupled with the creation of several small and interstitial spaces. Thus, within a street, one could identify travel lanes, parking lots, kerbside edges bordering the sewer channel and the outer sidewalk areas where one found lampposts, water taps, railings, newspaper boxes (in some cities), treelines, outdoor benches, and various kinds of doorway displays.

In other words, the street was gradually broken up into 'discrete zones', increasing the 'specialization of urban space'.[54] A new generation of urban professionals and reformers began to argue that spatial zoning in the principle of mono-functionality of spaces would ultimately ensure better circulation of bodies and things in the city. From the nineteenth century, parsing of spaces into 'discrete zones' began to be justified as serving 'public purpose'. The public purpose of the sidewalk, for instance, was to ensure a 'smooth system of movement'.[55] With the addition of raised sidewalks, the carriageway became larger but also 'more sharply differentiated from the other parts (increasing the amount of legal ambiguity about what the term "street" was meant to convey)'.[56] Pedestrians could still use the entire carriageway, but the centre became less and less convenient, and the footways dedicated to pedestrians more so. Soon, it was understood that the pedestrian was the only legitimate public on the sidewalk.

'The most suitable width of main roads' in 'the central portion of Calcutta' came up for discussion in an epistolary exchange between urban bureaucrat C. H. Bompas, who went on to become the Chairman of the Improvement Trust, and Patrick Geddes, the famous Scottish town planner, biologist, sociologist,

---

[54] Nicholas Blomley, *Rights of Passage: Sidewalks and the Regulation of Public Flow* (New York and London: Routledge, 2011), 61.

[55] Renia Ehrenfeucht and Anastasia Loukaitou-Sideris, 'Constructing the Sidewalks: Municipal Government and the Production of Public Space in Los Angeles, California, 1880–1920', *Journal of Historical Geography* 33, no. 1 (2007): 104–124, quoted from 110.

[56] James Winter, *London's Teeming Streets: 1830–1914* (London: Routledge, 1993), 100.

and humanist, who visited various Indian cities in 1914. At that time, the Trust was building a new avenue over the old Russa Road, connecting Tollygunge with Chowringhee. The Trust was also developing the old Halliday Street in central Calcutta into a grand north–south Central Avenue, which eventually connected the Esplanade with the northern quarters of Bagbazaar. Bompas starts by referring to three major functions of main roads:

> Firstly, they give access to the building sides which are laid out along them. In a large town the majority of the roads is of this nature and carries purely local traffic. Secondly, they may form the main arteries used by traffic proceeding from one part to another and more particularly between the suburbs and the centre. Thirdly, roads may constitute a very valuable form of open space; a tree planted strip 50 feet wide along a mile of road only occupies an area of about 5 acres or 15 bighas.[57]

Bompas then gives his measurement of width for an ideal avenue:

> If a width of 8 feet is taken as affording accommodation for a line of traffic and 2 feet allowed on each side of the road as occupied by gutter and sloping edge of the macadam 32+4=36 feet gives a roadway accommodating two streams of traffic in each direction and adding two 12 feet footpaths, we have a width of 60 feet. Adding 18 feet to the 36 feet roadway for a double line of trams we get a roadway of 54 feet. This will accommodate the same traffic as Old Court House Street, where the trams are in the centre of the roadway, is about 58 feet wide.... Adding 15 feet footpath in both the sides, we get a width of 84 feet and I recommend that this should be taken as the standard width for the roads which we have hitherto completed making 80 feet wide … I have explained in a previous note my reasons for thinking that for a third stream of traffic proceedings in a given direction 10 feet and not 8 feet should be added to the roadway. On a road of this character the footpaths should certainly not be less than 20 feet wide.[58]

In Bompas' plan, the sidewalk or footpath thus emerges as a minutely measured spatial category along with the other parts of the road. The road, the footpath, the macadam, and the roadside open space for plantation—all constitute

---

[57] Proceedings of the 124th meeting of the CIT, 7 December 1914, *Proceedings of the CIT for the Year 1914–15* (Valuation Department), 4.

[58] Ibid., 4.

a spatial complex in the colonial city. Geddes made certain alterations in the plan, considering the social and cultural specificities of the 'Indian crowds'. One of his proposals was to construct more sprawling sidewalks along the two sides of an avenue—wider than their European predecessors—because the prevailing caste tradition in India dissuaded pedestrians from using crowded sidewalks.

> If there is any point on which a newcomer to India may criticize with certainty, it is that engineers tend to imitate the narrow proportions of European pavements, and are then surprised at 'the perversity of the natives' in out upon the broad roadway they had planned for vehicles only! In this way the pedestrians hold up traffic, and I have been much struck in Bombay by the way the broad new roads of the Improvement Trust are thus rendered almost as slow going as the old narrow streets! The only course is to recognize the fact that the *caste tradition keeps the Indian crowd a divergent one*—and the close packed European pavement is here impossible. It must therefore be widened; and that substantially 17 feet as shown is not too much, and when possible, i.e., upon the great 150 feet avenue, twenty, including trees, is to be desired.[59]

Geddes also reminded the Trustees that for the sidewalks to attract more pedestrians, they had to be paved in such a way so that a 'bare feet' walker could also walk with relative ease:

> Another point, too much neglected, is to consider the quality of pavement or other road surface on bare feet, which are not so horny as we suppose but much more sensitive. In the hot season a pavement is too hot, in cold weather too cold … if Indians are to be kept out of the roadway, the pathways must be made less repellent than they often are (I have seen them left 'finished' in sharp red stone-chips, and of course unused, save by Europeans in boots!). Assuming then, express tramways and broad footpaths, one can still have a double avenue in the 15 feet portion though only single in that of 100 feet. The type is that of your figure too, but when expanded to 150 feet it will admit of a grass strip beside the footways.[60]

---

[59] Ibid., 8 (emphasis mine).
[60] Ibid., 8.

In their exchange, Bompas took the position of a technocrat who gave a universal template for the modern avenue. In this, he found that 'continental' planners were far ahead of British engineers: 'The cities on the continent of Europe have paid more attention than has been done in England to the construction of tree planted boulevards, keeping tramways on an elevated podium so as to avoid conflicts between automobiles and tramcars.'

On the other hand, Geddes developed his design of avenues by amalgamating town planning with sociological insights. While Bompas saw the new avenues from the standpoint of vehicular traffic, Geddes was more interested in observing them from the point of view of a barefoot Hindu Indian. Both, however, agreed that the new avenues should be wider than the usual streets to accommodate diverse users with minimal conflict.

Bompas and Geddes spoke of the city and its streets with an air of authority and ownership characteristic of expert opinion. Before them, technocrats like Richards, MacCabe, Mittra, and Staber were also confident that their informed interventions into the city's landscape would 'improve' the city, among other things, by easing the flow of traffic through its streets and 'decongesting' its neighbourhoods. Even if their actions were ultimately oriented towards enabling the circulation of capital in the city, in their personal trials and tribulations, planners and engineers were inspired by the idea of public good. But while the 'public' of the planner's imagination was an abstraction, the public that inhabited the city's streets—commoners—were real, agential actors. Like builders, technocrats, and engineers, commoners also functioned with a sense of ownership and authority over the street, but one that drew from lived experience rather than academic abstractions. And alongside planners, commoners played an equally decisive role, in both the planning and the shaping of the city.

Commoning the Streets

In 1909, street hawkers in Bombay were found to be 'engaged in a running battle with the police … at frequent intervals throughout the day the whole street is occupied by petty hawkers.… These men do not wish to go anywhere else and could not be induced to squat in special stands'.[61] In Calcutta, in 1913 alone, as

---

[61] Quoted in Prashant Kidambi, *The Making of an Indian Metropolis: Colonial Governance and Public Culture in Bombay, 1890–1920* (Aldershot: Ashgate, Historical Urban, 2007), 152. Also see Jonathan S. Anjaria, 'Unruly Streets: Everyday Practices and Promises of Globality in Mumbai' (PhD dissertation, Department of Anthropology, University of California, Santa Cruz, 2008).

many as 71,990 cases of sidewalk obstruction were prosecuted. In addition, 3,903 persons were 'summoned on police application for encroachment on footpaths'.[62] In 1914, Sir F. L. Halliday, the city's Police Commissioner, reports with much disgust that 'in a number of areas [of Calcutta], obstructions inflicted by hawkers prevail despite our sincere efforts to clear the pavements for pedestrian traffic'.[63]

Kidambi and Arnold quote similar expressions from Bombay and Madras, respectively, around the same time, which suggests that by the second decade of the twentieth century, the phenomenon of people occupying sidewalks began to be seen as encroachment and incited similar responses from the colonial government.[64] Arnold writes: 'In 1931 in Madras, more than four hundred families, mostly casual workers and unskilled labourers, were said to be squatting on the streets in the Harbour and Esplanade areas of the city or sleeping on warehouse verandas.'[65]

Additionally, the issue of how to deal with hawkers would continue to remain largely unresolved, for, even after the payment of fines, they would come back with baskets of goods, treating the fine as some kind of rent to occupy the footpaths. Commenting on the street culture in Bombay in the 1930s, Rajnarayan Chandavarkar says: 'Everything could be bought and sold on the streets of Bombay. Anything that might be bought was made. Any service which might be sought was offered. Most people were engaged in trades which were neither regular nor secure; some had to find their livelihood however they could.'[66]

Planners and engineers—the architects of motion—see the modern street as 'public space', as a property-bound relationship between public authority and members of the public. The latter can use the street as a right, balanced

---

[62] *Annual Report on the Police Administration of the Town of Calcutta and Its Suburbs for the Year 1913* (Calcutta: The Bengal Secretariat Press, 1914), 14.

[63] Judicial Department, Abstract of Proceedings, F. L. Halliday, Administrator, Calcutta Municipal Corporation, to Secretary, JD, Bengal, 15 September 1914, GOB, December 1914, A 49, p. 1432 (WBSA).

[64] Kidambi, *The Making of an Indian Metropolis*.

[65] David Arnold, 'Subaltern Streets: India, 1870–1947', in *Subaltern Geographies*, ed. David Arnold, Sharad Chari, David Featherstone, Vinay Gidwani, Mukul Kumar, and Sunil Kumar (Georgia: University of Georgia Press, 2019), 36–56, quoted from 42.

[66] Rajnarayan Chandavarkar, *The Origins of Industrial Capitalism in India: Business Strategies and the Working Classes in Bombay, 1900–1940* (Cambridge: Cambridge University Press, 1994), 81.

and constrained by a similar right of other members. As the trustee of public property, the state must protect all the rights of the public by imposing constraints on every user of the street. The idea of urban commons, on the other hand, transported from its rural milieu, implies shared claims to space in the city, based on 'use' rather than 'ownership'.[67] If public space concerns property, law, and 'exchange value', the commons are concerned with 'use value' and exist on the outside of the regime of modern property and law.[68]

Commoners, on the contrary, produce the street as they use it and inhabit it. They build the streets simultaneously with planners and engineers, but by dwelling in them—as the second chapter-opening quote by Heidegger suggests. Commoning the city streets collapses the act of building into the act of dwelling itself.[69] Commoners also govern the street, albeit differently from administrators, through locally shared sets of understandings and tacit ethical codes among

[67] In the nineteenth-century political economy and its critique, commons had a rural and frontier character whose enclosure led to the end of feudalism and the birth of the capitalist mode of production. Much later—in the early twenty-first century—the concept was urbanized when scholars began to see certain urban spaces and resources as commons that continuously evade the 'territorial grid of law'. Much like the rural commons, the urban commons, too, are governed by customs and 'variable local arrangements' between users who use them in 'shared and non-subtractable ways'. Vinay Gidwani, 'Six Theses on Waste Value and Commons', *Social and Cultural Geography* 14, no. 7 (2013): 773–783.

[68] Ibid.

[69] Labour historians have contributed more substantially than urban historians to shift our focus from the elite planners to the working-class city builders. They have drawn our attention to the connection between mass politics and the making of the cities in the high- and late-colonial era. Rajnarayan Chandavarkar, *The Origins of Industrial Capitalism in India: Business Strategies and the Working Classes in Bombay, 1900–1940* (Cambridge: Cambridge University Press, 1994); Nandini Gooptu, *The Politics of the Urban Poor in Early Twentieth Century India* (Cambridge: Cambridge University Press, 2001); Chitra Joshi, *Lost Worlds: Indian Labour and Its Forgotten Histories* (Ranikhet: Permanent Black, 2005); Aditya Sarkar, *Trouble at the Mill: Factory Law and the Emergence of the Labour Question in Late Nineteenth-Century Bombay* (New Delhi: Oxford University Press, 2018). This is just a small sample from a large body of literature. Another set of literature on communal riots developed the connection between mass politics and the city. Sandria. B. Freitag, *Collective Action and Community: Public Arenas and the Emergence of Communalism in North India* (Berkeley and Los Angeles: University of California Press, 1989). For a comprehensive historiographical review, see Surya. P. Upadhyay and Rowena Robinson, 'Revising Communalism and Fundamentalism in India', *Economic and Political Weekly* 47, no. 36 (2012): 35–57.

users. These are usually inclusive and fair. Capital, however, encounters this form of inhabiting the modern city street as an encroachment upon its spaces, as an obstruction to its motion and, consequently, as an enemy to be subjugated.

A joint product of building initiatives of both planners and commoners, the modern street, therefore, emerges in the friction between these contrary forces. The street embodies both these impulses. It is both public property and commons. If public space concerns the abstract and the universal, the common refers to the local, specific, qualitative, and contingent arrangements among its users.[70] The contradiction between the public and the commons plays out continuously in the life of the streets.

The ordinary city builders affected transformations of the new public spaces by repeatedly returning to the same site controlled by the authoritarian state, as we noticed in the aforementioned historical instances. They also generated new possibilities through which they could assert a presence in the city of capital. These actors were not organized yet; the repetitive, incremental, and collective actions of these 'non-collective actors' gave them an 'art of presence' in the face of persecution. It was made of fragmented yet similar activities by thousands, even if their actions were devoid of a clearly laid out ideology and leadership.[71]

The act of commoning through encroachments is, however, much older than the newly asphalted streets, public parks, and sidewalks of early-twentieth-century Calcutta.[72] This was a strategy that urban multitudes repeatedly undertook to live and dwell in the alien city whenever a new infrastructure was brought into being by the authorities. The issue of popular occupation of public drains, sewers, and sidewalks is periodically recorded as encroachments throughout the colonial period in official documents. As early as 1835, Lieutenant Abercrombie complained of numerous encroachments on public

---

[70] Gidwani, 'Six Theses'.

[71] Asef Bayat, *Life as Politics: How Ordinary People Change the Middle East* (Stanford: Stanford University Press, 2013, 2nd edn).

[72] We know that capital arose by transforming the commons into currency—a process that Marx calls the 'so-called Primitive Accumulation of Capital'. Commons is necessary to the function of capital, but they do not necessarily belong to capital's life-process by any natural connection. Commons had, for instance, preceded capital by centuries without giving rise to capital. In the cities of capital, commons both precede and succeed capital. See Dipesh Chakrabarty's illuminating discussion of money and commodity in the history of capital in 'Two Histories of Capital'.

drains and the blocking of traffic by 'shambles and booths erected on roadside'.[73] The legislation of 1876 empowered the municipal authorities to 'remove any wall, fence, rail, post, or other projection placed in, on, or over any public drain or sewer'.[74] In 1877, however, the *Annual Report of the Municipal Administration of Calcutta* emphasized having a 'suitable preventive legal provision' to prevent those they saw as 'unruly natives' from eroding the sidewalk space, indicating the futility of existing provisions to check encroachment.[75] Baldwin Lathan's 'Report on the Drainage and Conservancy of Calcutta', published in 1891, documented numerous examples of popular encroachment on sidewalks and the municipal administration's incapacity to maintain the 'order' of the public space. A new kind of crime—'public nuisance'—began to divert considerable attention of the police in prime cities such as Calcutta and Bombay, leading to state intervention in the 'social use of the physical environment'.[76]

Viewed from the street, one could argue that it was the multitudes on and of the streets—the commoners—who rescued the streets from an exclusive regime of property and exchange value. Their obstructionism opposed commodification. These 'discrete' and 'prolonged', 'surreptitious' and 'incremental' actions dismissed as encroachments, in fact, got consolidated and organized in the post-colonial era in the context of mass democracy and refugee influx. These so-called encroachments gave birth to normative forms of urban living, an aesthetic, and a political culture based on the interdependence of the commoners and the commons.

In my long experience of working with Calcutta's footpath hawkers, I have seen how the demolition of one stall in a particular area could lead to the destruction of a network of small economies that sustained not only the 'poor' but also the 'daily commuter' and the 'lower middle class'. It would also severely affect the way other hawkers carried out business. How does this happen? The large network of stalls, to which each individual stall belongs, becomes more than the sum of its parts. It provides the crucial condition for both the existence of the individual hawker and the latter's self-definition. Hawkers rarely exist in isolation; they cannot live devoid of this crucial connection to a network

---

[73] Quoted in Goode, *Municipal Calcutta*, 252.

[74] Ibid., 252.

[75] *Annual Report of the Municipal Administration of Calcutta* (Calcutta: The Corporation Press, 1877), 40.

[76] Anjaria, 'Unruly Streets', 25.

that exceeds both the capacity of its individual actors and the scope of their individual stalls. When, for instance, hawkers gather their stalls, new spaces between bodies and stalls are created whose internal cohesion and consistencies become vital for collective living. In many cities, hawkers collectively buy mini-generators and place them between two sets of continuous stalls. Electric wires move between stalls, not just occupying space but also producing quite a different play of light and sound on the street—a new atmospherics distinct to the street. The obstructions put up by the hawkers, then, enable myriad forms of urbanism to thrive.

Ironically, the street-as-commons is a favourite of the covetous accumulation economy as well, as the latter seeks to 'enclose' commons and turn them into property (read 'private' or 'guarded by law'). Urban capital, then, is frequently formed out of a public–private partnership that utilizes the logic and idiom of commons but gentrifies public space and secures it exclusively for its propertied citizens. A good example of this would be the gated communities where public streets are often turned into commons meant exclusively for the members of a residents' welfare association (RWA). Therefore, commoners—hawkers, vendors, and others who make the street their home—purpose a kind of urbanization, which is always ambiguous because they uphold a culture that is critical of the city-associated culture of accumulation.

The Beginning of Organized Street Agitation

Between 1913 and 1947, the Improvement Trust developed parks in densely built northern Calcutta, covering an area of more than 82 acres. It also added over 47-kilometre street extensions in the inner city and the suburbs. These new-found spaces provoked and enabled people to congregate, forge alliances, and lay claims on them by walking, protesting, vending, and dwelling in them. Agitational politics since the Swadeshi era flourished in the newly engineered streets and public spaces of Calcutta. In fact, one of the central aspects of agitational politics in the last four decades of colonial rule was to challenge the exclusivist nature of open spaces that the British had created in the colonial city. In the 'White Town' of Chowringhee and Dalhousie Square, many streets and parks were closed to native publics and were reserved for the exclusive use of the Europeans in Calcutta. It was mainly through public action on streets such as mass gatherings, rallies, and blockades that Calcutta finally witnessed the emergence of more inclusive public streets and public spaces in the post-colonial era.

A key feature of the anti-colonial mass mobilizations in Calcutta since 1905 had been to shift the venues of public rallies and meetings from neighbourhood recesses and community halls to open public spaces such as Beadon Square, College Square, and Wellington Square, and eventually to the highly restricted 'British' areas of the city, especially around the iconic Ochterlony Monument in the Maidans. Commenting on this new fever of mass awakening, historian Anindita Ghosh writes: 'Perhaps the most spectacular transformations took place on the city's streets, converting them from arteries of colonial authority and commerce to tributaries of mass protest, with performative posturing and ritual singing investing these everyday spaces with a rare moral authority.'[77]

During the Swadeshi era (1905–1911), protests were confined to the 'Indian areas', avoiding overt confrontation with authority. Apart from temples, meetings were regularly held on school and college premises (Eden Hindu Hostel, Ripon College, and City College premises in central Calcutta), in the residences of city notables such as the house of the Paikpara Rajas, the Marble Palace, and the Tagore Residence at Jorasanko, and important nationalist offices such as the press of the radical evening daily *Sandhya* at 193, Cornwallis Street. Numerous fundraising processions to aid striking press workers and clerks and to support Swadeshi enterprises connected disparate streets and neighbourhoods. Strikes by press workers, tramway men, carters, and railway workers disrupted traffic on several occasions. Municipal sweepers also joined the protests by converting certain portions of the city (wards 1 and 2) into a massive garbage vat. The white zone of the city was breached for the first time on 22 September 1905 when a breakaway section of students attending a meeting at the Town Hall entered the restricted zones of the Maidans, abused European strollers, and began pelting stones.

During the Swadeshi Movement, the very imagination of mass mobilization had a strong investment in physically and symbolically claiming the city's streets and other open spaces. In a couple of meetings in September 1905, Rabindranath Tagore suggested a plan for *rakhibandhan* on the day of Partition of Bengal (16 October 1905), 'transforming a traditional popular rite into a symbol of the brotherhood and unity of the people of Bengal'.[78] Sumit Sarkar writes:

> Bengal, and particularly Calcutta, witnessed truly memorable scenes of fraternization on that day, from which Muslim mullas, policemen

---

[77] A. Ghosh, *Claiming the City*, 283.
[78] S. Sarkar, *The Swadeshi Movement in Bengal, 1903–1908*, 287.

and even whites were not excluded. From early morning, huge crowds walked barefoot (the traditional sign of mourning) to the Ganga to bathe in its holy waters … year after year these rites were kept up, though may be on a diminishing scale—till the partition itself was abrogated.[79]

Protest marches during the Swadeshi era deliberately connected sites deemed 'holy' in Hindu sensibilities. At times, the protest rallies would touch upon the iconic river *ghat*s and temples. On some other occasions, marchers crossed the Empire's administrative district and went past the city's police headquarters at Lalbazaar. The protests sought to reclaim the city from the state authority by spilling out 'from the interiors of buildings and adjacent grounds to streets and the Maidans, a space that carried a long history of racial segregation'.[80] Such gestures were new in the Indian context, and they opened up a new conversation between urban space and nationalist politics.[81]

The tradition of street protest that the Swadeshi Movement initiated became more common and robust during the Non-cooperation and Khilafat agitation in 1921–1922. By this time, the participation of women and school students in street demonstration had become noticeable. The striking students discovered a 'novel method' of picketing at the entrance of the examination hall. On 17 January 1921, they blocked the passageway by lying flat on the College Street sidewalks. Alternately, the 'native quarters' of the city also made a statement by withdrawing from the streets totally on 28 January 1921 so that the visiting

---

[79] Ibid.

[80] Swati Chattopadhyay, 'Cities of Power and Protest', p. 50.

[81] In Calcutta, the tradition of street protest began in the last decade of the nineteenth century—precisely, during the promulgation of the Age of Consent Act in 1891 (Act X of 1891). Tanika Sarkar writes: 'Outside the official circles and the courtroom, an informal tribunal was in the making: street-level demonstrations, literally the first of its kind in India.' Surendranath Banerjee referred to the street protests while opposing the Bill. He said: 'It is impossible to talk about the bill without reference to the great and unusual agitation which it has given rise to in Bengal.' On 21 February, a huge Hindu crowd gathered in an 'unprecedented phenomenon of a mass demonstration at the Calcutta Race Course' and chanted: 'WE DO Not Want, We DO NOT Want, WE DO NOT WANT THE BILL.' This was the first time anti-colonial nationalist sentiments embraced the street and began communicating with the 'mass-in-the-making'. Tanika Sarkar, 'Intimate Violence in Colonial Bengal: A Death, a Trial and a Law, 1889–1891', *Law and History Review* 38, no. 1 (2020): 177–200, quoted from 195.

Duke of Connaught would be greeted with the sight of empty streets. On 16 September 1921, a 'monster meeting of 12,000 carters' took place under the presidency of Swami Biswanand, attended by Mahatma Gandhi and C. R. Das. Again, on 13 November 1921, the Calcutta Maidans hosted a 'mass meeting of Police constables' who were asked to quit their service and join the Non-cooperation agitation.[82]

The bazaars of the city emerged as key sites of protest, picketing, and *hartal* at this time.[83] In 1919, Gandhi drew on this phenomenon and nationalized *hartal* to oppose the Rowlatt Bill. A single date and time was fixed when the entire nation would observe a *hartal* simultaneously and put the circulation of commodities on hold as a mark of protest. By 1921, *hartal* had become an everyday street phenomenon in Calcutta, and thus it got integrated into the city's emerging political vernacular. By the time of the Non-cooperation–Khilafat agitation, the 'volunteer movement' became ubiquitous in Calcutta and it attracted the growing public participation of women and schoolchildren of the 'respectable class'.

In 1927, the Congress carried out a massive programme to boycott the all-white Simon Commission. The 'Simon go back' agitation awakened the Congress from a long slumber since the end of the Non-cooperation days, especially after the devastating communal riot of 1926. Around the same time, a new era of strikes began, involving the working class. Most of these strikes were organized by the Communists under the Workers' and Peasants' Party (WPP) and involved sustained and long-term organizational strategies. Long marches, *satyagrahas*,[84] and large-scale demonstrations became routine affairs.[85] In the agitations of the late 1920s, schoolboys and middle-class women were often seen taking a frontal position.[86] The involvement of women and children in street demonstrations meant that the police could not take

---

[82] *The Indian Annual Register: Chronicle of Events, 1921–22* (Sibpur: The Annual Register Office, 1923), 1–352.

[83] *Hartal*, or the closing of bazaars, had been a standard mode of protest in South Asia since the early nineteenth century. Time and again, local dissensions against the administration took recourse to localized hartals. Richard Heitler, 'The Varanasi House Tax Hartal of 1810–11', *Indian Economic and Social History Review* 9, no. 3 (1972): 239–257.

[84] *Satyagraha* refers to the Gandhian technique of passive political resistance.

[85] T. Sarkar, *Bengal 1928–1934*.

[86] Ibid.

recourse to its usual modes of repression in fear of enabling a sensational public discourse against the police administration. Needless to say, the coming together of people from different social groups to augment the 'crowd', which then took to the street in an act of protest, did not leave the carefully planned public infrastructure of the city untouched. Their collective movement through public thoroughfares adapted, manipulated and fashioned the city to cater to various popular purposes.

Breaching the 'White Town'

Throughout its colonial history, Calcutta's municipal jurisdiction was outside the organized industrial belt. In this, Calcutta was much like London and Barrackpore. The city was the centre of finance, trade, and commerce—a city of circulation. Industrial production happened in factories located in Howrah, Hooghly, and 24 Parganas. Unlike Bombay, Manchester, and Kanpur, Calcutta did not have a mill-going working class residing in the inner city. Therefore, Calcutta's working class was predominantly constituted by transit and transport workers, coolies, domestic and office servants, police constables, municipal workers, shopkeepers, and street hawkers. As a result, the relationship between the working class and urban space in Calcutta evolved differently from these cities.

Organizing these workers into unions required trade unionists to think beyond the shopfloor and working-class *bustees*. Most of these workers never lived in *bustees*. They resided instead on the streets in makeshift arrangements, as pavement dwellers. For these workers, then, the streets of Calcutta literally accommodated both their workspace and dwelling place, and consequently shaped the dominant narratives of workers' lives. Some of the earliest workers' unions in Calcutta developed among transport and logistics labourers, both of whom worked and lived ('squatted', according to municipal imaginations) in central Calcutta markets, *bustees*, sidewalks, rail stations, and near the port.[87] Unsurprisingly, streets were at the centre of their organization and mobilization. This becomes apparent in the early 1930s, around the Civil Disobedience Movement, when one such group—the up-country Hindu and Muslim carters—claimed the streets of northern and central Calcutta.

---

[87] There were some ethnic overlaps among these workers. For instance, many cart owners, or *chowdhuri*s, were also subaltern police officials and municipal supervisors, who hailed predominantly from the United Provinces.

On 9 February 1930, a group of Communist trade unionists formed a carters' union. Prominent among the leaders were Madan Mohan Burman, D. P. Golbole, Swami Viswananda, Abdul Halim, Abdul Momin, and Bankim Chandra Mukherjee. An 'up-country' sub-inspector of Calcutta Police was given the charge of 'labour officer' in the new union. Between 9 February and 30 March 1930, these leaders met with hundreds of carters at Halliday Park in Central Avenue, a new park that the Improvement Trust had developed in the 1920s. They decided to start a *satyagraha* against a set of new traffic rules that prohibited cart traffic in northern and central Calcutta streets for some hours in the day to avoid congestion. The next day, the carters and some rickshaw pullers observed a strike at the Howrah Bridge bottleneck. About 300 *satyagrahis* were prosecuted at the Jorabagan Police Court the following day, creating a public sensation. A large crowd gathered outside the court.[88] In response, the carters organized a large protest on the same day.[89] They untied bullocks from their carts at about noon, dismantled the wheels of the carts, and arranged them across the streets. They also unloaded carts carrying 'steel rails, corrugated iron and bales of merchandise, etc. across the road' to obstruct traffic. This form of protest affected traffic on Strand Road, Harrison Road, Central Avenue, Chitpore Road, and in many other adjacent streets.[90] A report in *The Bengalee* on 2 April 1930 described the scene as follows:

> The carters crowded the streets, footpaths and whole of Strand Road. The house tops and balconies being not exempted. The Police were busy removing the carts and cleaning the traffic but their attempt to do so proved abortive at times owing to the carter having re-piled up the carts on the roads.... Soon after, there was a fusillade of brickbats and three Police Sergeants were injured.[91]

In Cornwallis Street, the students and carters raised a barricade by 'placing carts, municipal dustbins and road materials'. In Harrison Road, the blockade was even stronger as the carts and municipal dustbins obstructed several

---

[88] 'Jorabagan Sensation: 300 Persons Sent up for Trial', *The Bengalee*, 1 April 1930.
[89] T. Sarkar, *Bengal 1928–1934*.
[90] 'Carters Defy Police: Serious Disturbance Near Howrah Bridge', *The Bengalee*, 2 April 1930.
[91] Ibid.

tramcars. Around this time, Police Commissioner Charles Tegart arrived at the Howrah Bridge bottleneck with enforcement and ordered firing.[92] The first day's firing left seven carters dead. A procession of as many as 500,000 people gathered to take the carters' bodies to perform the last rites.[93] According to an Intelligence Bureau report from 1935, the official Communist Press acclaimed the strike as the first barricade street fight with the police in India—which indeed it was.[94]

After this, in 1931, Oriya coolies of Burrabazaar conducted successful *hartal*s by refusing to carry bales of foreign cloth from warehouse to marketplace.[95] In April 1933, coolies joined carters and the city corporation's conservancy staff on a strike for a much-awaited pay structure review. As the police fired and arrested the protesting coolies, the crowd began to swell. News spread that 'three thousand carters and a thousand labourers of various descriptions … (had) paralyzed road traffic and showered bricks on the police'.[96]

The space for agitations and protests expanded much further in the mid-1940s.[97] An instance from 21 and 22 November 1945 will illustrate this expanding geography of protest in the city. On 21 November 1945, there was a nationwide call from the Congress and the Muslim League to observe the day as the 'INA Day'. Their objective was to bolster popular support for the unconditional release of the dismantled Indian National Army soldiers under trial. After a few lectures at a students' gathering in Wellington Square, the students decided to move towards the prohibited Dalhousie Square, the centre of the provincial government. The size of the procession kept increasing as it proceeded through Dharmatala Street. The city police intercepted the procession when it reached the 'New Cinema' landmark at 3 p.m. It barricaded the students 'from entering the prohibited area 'containing Bengal Govt. Secretariat, Legislative building, High

---

[92] T. Sarkar, *Bengal 1928–1934*.

[93] Ibid.

[94] Ibid.

[95] Ibid.

[96] Ibid., 164.

[97] Partha Chatterjee, 'The Political Culture of Calcutta', in *Calcutta: The Living City, Vol. II: The Present and Future*, ed. Sukanta Chaudhuri (New Delhi: Oxford University Press, 1990).

Court and Government House'.⁹⁸ At this time, another procession came along Central Avenue to join the one at Dharmatala Street. The two processions ended up facing each other on the two sides of the police barricade, in a tense 'race of patience' between the police and the students.⁹⁹ At about 6.45 p.m., the students attempted to break the barricade and proceed towards Dalhousie Square; the stalemate continued.¹⁰⁰ Eventually, to break the stalemate, the police fired on the assembled crowd of students, killing two and injuring many more. As per the Bengal government's version of events, the police were 'gently' persuading students to hold back from occupying the prohibited zone, but 'efforts by police to contain present crowds were strongly resisted, and police were subjected to stone-throwing which at times was very serious'.¹⁰¹

From the above description we find that in Dharmatala, crowd action was influenced and directed by its outside, or 'police action'. The police ran through the crowd and marked the boundaries that the crowd should not cross. The boundary was, however, fluid and mobile, subject to the trajectory of events. At one point, for instance, this police boundary split the crowd down the middle, thus establishing new barricades between two approaching groups. The crowds, meanwhile, continually improvised its movements in response to changes in police action, as both sides played on the fluidity of the boundary. Police action escalated gradually—tear gas, then *lathi* (baton), then bullet—thus maintaining the grammar of a 'civilized' and 'organized' force. This graded escalation, however, received a discrete and discontinuous response from the crowd. In the face of onslaught, the crowd would break apart into smaller groups only to reassemble and reengage the police simultaneously from different angles. In this manner, the 'outside' margin of the crowd, interfaced with the police, would become a prime mover for crowd action. The thresholds that would operate in the city centre, then, were produced through the dynamics of this crowd–police

---

[98] This area 'since 1937 had been one of the areas notified under Calcutta Police Act in which processions, demonstrations and meetings were not permitted'. In Telegram R, from Governor of Bengal to Viceroy, 413, dated 28th recd. 28 November 1945 (TOO-1940) (TOR-0830), Confidential. 2518-S, November 1945 Riots, NAI.

[99] 'A senior police officer described the stand-off in these words to a newspaper covering the incident'. In Telegram R, from Governor of Bengal to Viceroy, ibid.

[100] 'Police Open Fire on INA Day Procession in Calcutta: Two Persons Dead and over Fifty Injured', *Hindustan Times*, 22 November 1945.

[101] Bengal government's report to the Viceroy dated 28 November 1945, in Confidential. 2518-S, November 1945 Riots, NAI.

dialectic. The police restricted crowds from entering prohibited zones because they were entrusted with the enforcement of impregnable boundaries in the city. The crowds, on their part, pushed against these boundaries to obstruct the police's endeavour with the aim of decolonizing the prohibited zones of white privilege.[102] This protracted negotiation on the street between the police and people continued vigorously at this time.

Again, on the following evening, a large procession from Wellington Square began to move towards Dalhousie Square. It was obstructed precisely at the same place on Dharmatala Road, where a skirmish had broken out on the previous day. As the encounter began to spread to other parts of the city, the police once again opened fire, this time in several places—Dharmatala Street, Russa Road and Rashbehari Avenue intersection, and Shyambazaar Street and R. G. Kar Road intersection. Police firing left 11 dead and 44 injured.[103]

Yet again, on 11 February 1946, student activists of the Congress and the Muslim League conducted a 5,000-strong procession through various streets of Calcutta. That day, the police were prepared. They were seen parading the streets with teargas squads, machine guns, and *lathis*. The *People's Age* observed that the police were 'out to provoke a clash although the students maintained complete discipline and peace'. As the procession approached Dalhousie Square via Clive Street, the police obstructed its passage. However, the momentum of the procession was such that the barricade got pushed back. It was at this moment that a fresh regiment of armed Gorkha Police appeared. The *People's Age* reported:

> At first, the Police Officer approached Ananda Bhattacharyya, General Secretary of the Bengal Provincial Students' Federation, who told him that the processions demanded the right of passage peacefully.... The notorious Deputy Commissioner of Police, Samsud-Doha, shouted at the students, 'Either you go away, or I will smash you.' Ananda retorted amidst cheers, 'You can never smash us.' Thereupon 200 Policemen attacked the peaceful students for nearly one hour.... The brutality of the Police roused great indignation all over the city and enraged crowds collected at the street corners. Trams and buses were stopped in specific routes by passengers themselves and peacefully picketed

---

[102] For a perceptive analysis of crowd–police dialectic, see Deepak Mehta, 'Crowds, Mob and the Law: The Delhi Rape Case', *Contributions to Indian Sociology* 53, no. 1 (2019), 158–183.

[103] 'Police Again Open Fire in Calcutta: 11 Dead and 125 Injured on Thursday', *Hindustan Times*, 22 November 1945.

by the crowd.... In two places, police indiscriminately used tear gas and opened fire, which infuriated the people all the more. Cases of smashing up military trucks were also reported. By midnight, the whole city was burning with rage against the Police.[104]

Nearly three months after the firing at Dharmatala Street, on 12 February 1946, 'a mile-long procession'[105] comprising 100,000 people emerged from the same Wellington Square, followed the same route, and finally entered Dalhousie Square.[106] The occasion was to protest against the court-martial of the INA soldier Captain Abdul Rashid. Tracking these recurrent incidents makes evident that even under colonial subjection, people's agitations cumulatively pushed the boundary of the spaces of colonial power. At the same time, they expanded the geographic horizon of protests in the city. Thus, decolonization was already underway. The hitherto 'white spaces' of the city, located at the heart of colonial sovereignty, became a site where the acts of popular sovereignty were being exercised even before the colonial rule officially ended.

Sabotage of Public Infrastructures by Citizens

Finally, however, the Dalhousie barricades were decisively breached by the *citizen* crowd of Calcutta on the morning of 15 August 1947. On that day, Calcutta celebrated its first taste of freedom in a great festive disposition.

---

[104] 'Calcutta Students Demonstration Grows into Big Tide of Hindu–Muslim, Anti-imperialist Unity', *People's Age*, 24 February 1946.

[105] 'Military Called out in Calcutta', *The Statesman*, 13 February 1946.

[106] Ibid. Also see 'Governor Casy Issues a Stern Warning to Protestors. Extracts from a telegram by Governor of Bengal, to the Viceroy, dated 13 February 1946', File No. 5/22/46, Home (Political) Department, Government of India (NAI). The process of mass formation involved occasional crowd formation on the streets and squares, as we noticed in the preceding paragraphs. However, these crowds were not always 'disciplined' processions under the supreme command of a leader and under the observation of an organization. An instance from the Abdul Rashid Day in Calcutta on 12 November 1946 will testify to this fact. On 13 November 1946, the Governor of Bengal wrote to the Viceroy that a procession of 50,000 people crossed Dalhousie Square and entered the vicinity of the Lalbazaar Police Head Quarters; 'the crowd appears to have split up into gangs of hooligans spreading over centre of the town including European residential area'. It was further reported that these splinter mobs looted particular shops including the one that sold arms. Telegram R, From Governor of Bengal to Viceroy, 413, dated 28th recd. 28 November 1945 (TOO-1940) (TOR-0830), Confidential. 2518-S, November 1945 Riots, NAI.

At 1 a.m., following the famous 'Tryst with Destiny' speech by Jawaharlal Nehru 'at the stroke of midnight', the new Governor of West Bengal, C. Rajagopalachari, and Prime Minister, Dr Prafulla Ghosh, took the oath of office. The main flag-hoisting ceremony of the day was to take place in the Governor's House. Ordinary citizens of Calcutta gathered in thousands at the iconic main gate of the Governor's House in the morning. The city police tried to keep them at the gate, but as the Governor began his speech, the crowd overcame the police barricade and began to approach the Governor's podium. Sekhar Bandyopadhyay provides a vivid account of this public spectacle. As the Governor finished his speech and retired to his quarters, the crowd followed him inside the building. 'And then', writes Bandyopadhyay, 'for the next few hours, thousands of ordinary Calcuttans, many of them from a working-class background, roamed freely through the building.' At the time of return, many of them collected expensive furniture and other colonial-era 'memorabilia as souvenirs of a period of their history, which they thought now truly belonged to the past'.[107] They continued to break barricades of the erstwhile 'prohibited' buildings in the Dalhousie area throughout the day. They met the Governor in the adjacent Assembly House, and in the middle of his speech, they greeted him with the 'Jai Hind' slogan. Thus, they claimed their right to participate in the government of the post-colony. At least for a few weeks, they forgot the bloodshed between the Hindus and the Muslims. Nine days later, on 24 August 1947, Gandhi was greeted by more than 200,000 citizens in the previously prohibited Maidans. Gandhi described the situation 'as neither a miracle nor an accident, but an act of God'.[108]

The high and late colonial era legacy of public agitation left behind a 'rich repertoire of political actions and rituals'[109] for the post-colonial period. Central to this new political rationality was the idea that the 'people' were the final arbiter of what was right and legitimate and that for a political action to make an impact, one has to 'stage this "people" or a community in significant numbers'.[110] The moral force of a large gathering became proof of righteousness and truth. Thus, in the post-colonial decades it became a routine affair for political parties to

---

[107] Sekhar Bandyopadhyay, *Decolonization in South Asia: Meanings of Freedom in Post-independence West Bengal, 1947–52* (London: Routledge, 2009), 9.

[108] Ibid., 11.

[109] Thomas. B. Hansen, 'Democracy against the Law: Reflections on India's Illiberal Democracy', in *Majoritarian State: How Hindu Nationalism is Changing India*, ed. Angana. P. Chatterji, Thomas. B. Hansen, and Christophe Jaffrelot (Noida: HarperCollins, 2019), 19–40, quoted from 29.

[110] Ibid., 29.

mobilize masses from villages to occupy a central park in large cities such as Calcutta, Bombay, and Delhi. However symbolic it might be, occupying a big city gave a sense of empowerment to the 'village masses'. Occupying arterial city streets gave a sense of intervention in the stronghold of power. Thus, Calcutta's passage to popular sovereignty involved decolonizing the city's hitherto prohibited 'public' spaces. The bigger the gathering, the stronger the case. With the growth of opposition forces, 'this political vernacular of numbers, and the performance of public anger' began to emerge as a more complex force.

In the post-colonial decades, regional and linguistic movements, caste agitations, ethnic separatist movements, and trade union agitations routinely used the spectacle of public violence on government property (such as setting fire to the government buses, trams, train compartments, police vans, schools, hospitals, and so on) to express anger. At times, an entire neighbourhood would stand up against the police, destroy street furniture, and assert territorial claims over the street. A *Jugantar* report described such an incident during the anti-tram-fare-hike movement on 17 and 18 July 1953:

> We went to tour the area between Elgin Road and Purna Cinema a little after midnight. The residents of the locality discouraged us vehemently. We met a crowd at the Elgin Road and Ashutosh Mukherjee Road junction and they also asked us not to proceed. It was pitch-dark. We could see the tramlines burning a little ahead of us. We switched on the head light of our car, but immediately the crowd shouted and hurled stones on us. We turned off the light. We could feel the presence of a huge crowd. Some of them were making *mashals*. A group came to us with two young men at front. We shouted: 'we are from press' … then they allowed us to enter. Two young men with *mashals* in their hands showed us the way. The crowd cooperated now by removing tree trunks and junks from the road. We could see boys, young people and also elderly people among the crowd. We saw that some of them were busy uprooting the tram lines. Some middle-aged men were supervising them.… They were from middle-class educated families. We could see women standing at the terrace of the buildings by the roadside. We reached the Suburban School. In front of us, there was a wide empty main road. Across the road we could spot several police vans. Our guides told us that their area ended at that point and police's area began from the other side of the road. The in-between area was 'no man's land'.[111]

---

[111] Anwesha Sengupta, 'Anti-Tram Fare Rise and Teachers' Movement in Calcutta, 1953–54', in *From Popular Movements to Rebellion: The Naxalite Decade*, ed. Ranabir Samaddar (London Routledge, 2019), 48–84, quoted in 59.

For the law-implementing and peace-keeping forces, maintaining an appearance of public order was more important than actual prosecution for the 'offences against public tranquillity'. These offences were often intractable and were routinely termed as an expression of herd mentality. However, to maintain public order, the police would be empowered by the executive to take instant 'action', involving *lathi* charge, tear gas shelling, and even firing bullets.

There also developed the tradition of more mundane forms of public agitation over a range of issues concerning the operation of public infrastructures. Agitators would typically humiliate public officials and demand official apologies from them. A delay in the running of trains and buses, a power cut, waterlogging in the neighbourhood, broken streets and unrepaired sidewalks, potholes, open manholes, an overflowing garbage vat—any of these could incite agitation. The agitated public often demanded that a senior public official meet them and answer their questions. 'The ritual of humiliating officials', writes Dipesh Chakrabarty, 'speaks of a very particular form of power.' The agitations did not always yield much, but 'there is a certain pleasure and sense of authority in seeing the government losing face, to see its officers humiliated'.[112] This, according to Chakrabarty, was a specific post-colonial development. The colonial bureaucrats would hardly emerge before a subject crowd and tender a public apology.

Conclusion

This was how Calcutta's streets emerged in the early twentieth century through the actions of both generic and some individual actors who built them—its engineers, commoners, and agitators. The start of the story coincides with the beginning of the automobile age, when streets were imagined, envisioned, and constructed as enablers of motion—the quintessential quality of the modern city of capital accumulation. The fantasy of unencumbered motion, however, was soon obstructed as ordinary users of those same streets tailored them to suit their purposes. The agitators decolonized the streets, while the commoners transformed them into infrastructures of dwelling and livelihood. These streets were appropriated to provide the focus for collective living and popular action.

Thus, together, the engineer, the police, the commoner, and the agitator built the streets of twentieth-century Calcutta. Urban improvement schemes,

---

[112] Dipesh Chakrabarty, '"In the Name of Politics": Sovereignty, Democracy and the Multitude in India', *Economic and Political Weekly* 40, no. 30 (2005): 3293–3301, quoted from 3299.

helmed by the Municipal Corporation and the Improvement Trust, in the late nineteenth and early twentieth centuries, created new public spaces. Ironically, state initiatives to open up public spaces to facilitate movement also facilitated its obstruction. It gave birth to the 'mass'. Neither mass agitators nor street hawkers seemed inclined to settling in the narrow by-lanes. Those lanes were known for terrorist attacks on cops and incidents of stabbing at the time of riots. Agitators and commoners, instead, occupied the newly engineered public spaces and transformed them. Over the years, they developed an ethic of collective living in these spaces. This came to be the very essence of Calcutta's street culture. If engineers installed an infrastructure of speed through asphalt paving, agitators and the commoners punctuated it to achieve practicability. These punctuations, or obstructions, were just as central to the process of street-building as the visions of order floated by engineers and implemented by municipal and police officials.

I highlight the idea of obstruction here as providing a conceptual key to unlock the urban infrastructure. Conceptualizing the modern city in terms of motion (of bodies, things, and finances) has dominated academic common sense since the growth of research interest on urban settlements in the mid-nineteenth century. The motion narrative posits obstruction as its negation, which motion keeps on deferring until it can eventually be conquered. Obstruction's very final end, on the other hand, is the motionless, deathly city of de-accumulation. But we see in this chapter how obstructions, rather than ending motion, produce thriving urbanisms of many varieties. The streets can accommodate creative obstructions that actually enable motion, albeit of different kinds. Such obstructions, as those caused by hawkers and commoners, punctuate motion to produce a medium for exchange between bodies and things in space.

Moreover, at the other end of this imagined dystopia of motionlessness precipitated by obstructions, is the utopia of frictionless motion. One could argue that frictionless motion is really no motion at all, only slippage. I argue that obstruction is immanent to the city and must function as a positive category in urban studies.

2

The Regime of the Streets
Renewal and Riots, 1910–1926

Around the mid-nineteenth century, some of Calcutta's most densely populated *bustee*s were located in the area bound by Cotton Street in the north, Canning Street in the south, Halliday Street in the east, and Brabourne Road in the west. These *bustee*s were inhabited predominantly by poor Muslim tenants, but some rich Muslim Momin and Sarti merchants from Bombay also lived among them in more substantial dwelling houses. Although there had been a steady displacement of Muslims from the area because of slum clearance from the 1880s onwards, and affluent Muslim merchant families were also losing their presence in the area's trade profile, the construction of Harrison Road by the Municipal Corporation in the 1890s precipitated an extraordinary transformation of these neighbourhoods. This dense settlement of the city's poor turned into prime urban property almost overnight.

Buoyancy in the locality's real estate market brought on by the Harrison Road Scheme led to dramatic demographic upheavals in the heart of the city, thus creating conditions for social conflicts. Around this time, the city was also witnessing the emergence of mass nationalist and working-class politics, and the ways in which that impacted the nature and popular perceptions of urban space. In this chapter, I intend to show how the discourses and practices of property (shaped by colonial civic institutions) on the one hand and mobilizational politics on the other interfaced in the making of the urban milieu of early-twentieth-century Calcutta.

The Story of the Mosque near Harrison Road

In the late 1840s, Din Mahomed, a coachman of the wealthy Muslim city merchant Haji Zakaria,[1] had built a small mosque in the southern portion of

---

[1] Haji Zakaria was a wealthy Muslim merchant, who in 1857 built the iconic Nakhodka Mosque. Subsequently, the street was named after him and became

Armenian Street with his fellow *syces* and coachmen. A *bustee* of poor Muslim tenants, covering approximately 3 *bighas* of land, was located right opposite Din Mahomed's Mosque, on the north side on Amratola Street. In 1890, the Municipal Corporation initiated the construction of the new Harrison Road in the vicinity of the *bustee*. Drawn to the changing prospects of this area on account of its proximity to the projected new road, in 1902 or 1903, a Marwari firm, Gopi Ram Bhagat Ram, and a wealthy Muslim merchant, A. M. Ishabhai, bought over one half of the *bustee* each, for a total price of 110,000 rupees. Bhagat Ram built a four-storeyed mansion for his family on his share of the plot. In January 1910, he purchased Ishabhai's share as well, this time paying 110,000 rupees for only one half of the original *bustee* area. This 100 per cent increase in the plot's price within just seven years indicates the speculative boom underway in this area because of the Harrison Road Scheme.

In October 1910—when the communal 'trouble' began—Muslims were no more to be found in the northern segment of Armenian Street, as they were being steadily displaced by Marwari buyers like Gopi Ram Bhagat Ram. A 1910 report by Dundas, the officiating Commissioner of Police, tells us that 'with the inauguration of Harrison Road, wealthy merchants from the Burrabazaar and northern quarters bought land from lower class owners and tenants' who had hitherto occupied the areas along the fledging thoroughfare soon to become Harrison Road.[2] However, Muslims continued to live around Din Mohamed's Mosque and on both sides of the adjacent Amratola Lane (different from Amratola Street mentioned earlier). Several 'Mahomedan properties' still abutted Amratola Street and Gobinda Chandra Dhar Lane.

Meanwhile, on 29 October 1910, Dundas received a petition from the Marwari Association, asking him to stop a possible cow slaughter at Din Mohamed's Mosque on Armenian Street on the day of Bakr-Id festival.[3] After a 'thorough investigation' the police found that no cow slaughter had taken place in the mosque in the last four decades. They also found that a 'fifteen feet wall' insulated the inner spaces of the mosque from outside view and the designated

---

known as Zakaria Street. The mosque remained at the heart of many political and social activities of the Muslims in the city in the twentieth century.

[2] File No. 290. Serial Nos. 1–3, GoB, Police Department, 1910 (WBSA), 'Disturbances in Calcutta in Connection with the Bakr-Id festival, 1910', Letter No. 15992, dated the 17th December 1910, from the Commissioner of Police, Calcutta, submitting a report on the above subject, 1–7.

[3] Ibid., 1.

place for slaughter had adequate drainage to channel the sacrificial blood into the underground sewer outlet.[4] Having thus satisfied themselves about the discretion observed by Muslims on Bakr-Id, the police dismissed the apprehensions of the Marwari Association. The investigators reckoned that the real cause of Marwari agitation was not righteous religious indignation at ritual animal sacrifice in the neighbourhood. It was related, in fact, to Bhagat Ram's purchase of half of the erstwhile *bustee* land in front of the mosque in January 1910:

> The bustee has now been cleared, and the Marwari appears to intend to build, but so long as the sacrifices continue at the mosque opposite, he will be unable to let or sell the house to one of his own religion. Land anywhere near Harrison Road is naturally very valuable, and if there were nothing to offend the Marwaris Gopi Ram, Bhagat Ram & Co., would probably make a large profit. Accordingly, though nothing can be proved against him, it is the general opinion of everyone that Bhagat Ram started and did his best to keep up the present agitation.[5]

The displacement of Muslim *bustee* dwellers effected by the property boom, coupled with the brash assertions of power by the new wealthy Marwari residents, had begun to create collective resentment in the area. These resentments came to the surface as communal animosity. Neighbourhoods in this locality had already witnessed expropriation of poor residents in the past, most of whom were Muslims. After the Plague of 1898, the Municipal Corporation had demolished 325 huts in the nearby Baman *bustee* as a sanitary measure. Similar demolitions between 1901 and 1911 reduced the number of huts in Collinga *bustee* from 99 to 54. Therefore, the communal polarization in this neighbourhood of poor Muslims resulting from the entry of wealthy Marwaris, also drew from an older, more generalized experience of loss among its residents.[6]

In mid-1910, a Hindu extremist named Awadh Behari Lal *alias* Nitya Nandaji reached Calcutta from the United Provinces. Back home he had been known for his role in anti-cow-slaughter agitations. In Calcutta, Awadh Behari Lal found rooms in Suraj Mal's Dharamsala on Mullick Street. The street was at the centre of the Marwari quarters in Burrabazaar and very close to Din Mahomed's Mosque on Armenian Street. He began to attract several Marwari youths around him. On 7 December 1910, this gang was seen to parade the 'streets and lanes in the

---

[4] Ibid.
[5] Ibid., 2.
[6] *Census of India*, 1911, vol. VI, 'City of Calcutta', Part I, Report.

Burrabazaar quarter calling on everyone to close their shops until orders were passed stopping the cow-killing in the Armenian Street Mosque'. The 'Marwari boys went about boarding the tram cars and shouted "Mata Gai ki Jai".[7]

On 9 December, skirmishes took place on Harrison Road and the streets around it—lower Chitpore Road, Colootola Street, Halliday Street, Machooa (also written as 'Machua' and 'Mechua' in colonial documents) Bazaar Street, Cotton Street, Amratola Street, Amratola Lane, and Armenian Street. The Marwaris had armed 'up-country' *darwans*[8] on their behalf and local Hindu shopkeepers had joined hands with them. They clashed with Muslim shopkeepers, Muslim *bustee* dwellers, and itinerant Kabuli vendors. In the early evening, the Lieutenant Governor of Bengal himself visited the area and spoke with Bhagat Ram and his associates. He conveyed the 'Government's resolve to uphold non-interference in cow slaughter in the mosque premises'. Nevertheless, the battles between the two groups continued until 14 December 1910, leaving six individuals dead and several dozens injured.[9]

The animosity stoked by the Bakr-Id riot of December 1910 had long-term demographic implications for the neighbourhood. Marwari business owners began to replace existing Muslim coolies, coachmen, carters, and other workers in their firms and households with their ethnic and religious compatriots belonging to the working class. In the following years, they acquired more and more *bustees* from existing Hindu Bengali landlords, who were already in economic decline. The new Marwari lords of the *bustees* refused to rent out huts to Muslim workers. Muslims affected by these developments turned fiercely antagonistic towards Marwaris, a factor that fuelled persistent riots between these two groups, most prominently in 1918 and 1926.[10]

---

[7] File No. 290. Serial Nos. 1–3, GoB, Police Department, 1910 (WBSA), 'Disturbances in Calcutta in Connection with the Bakr-Id festival, 1910', Letter No. 15992, dated the 17th December 1910, from the Commissioner of Police, Calcutta, submitting a report on the above subject, 2.

[8] Ibid. It came to the notice of the city police that several hundreds of such men arrived at Calcutta from Bikaner a week before the incident.

[9] Ibid.

[10] S. Das, *Communal Riots in Bengal*. Here, it is essential to mention that in Bombay, the coexistence of factories and civic life gave birth to a specific urban material culture. The Bombay Improvement Trust could hardly ignore working-class housing issues for too long in its vision for a future city. On the other hand, Calcutta developed as an administrative centre and a transit hub, with numerous commercial establishments. In the first couple of decades of the twentieth century, only a minor part of the corporation area had modern industrial enclaves. The working class

As mentioned earlier, in early-twentieth-century Calcutta, religious polarization appears in a confounding conjunction with the Calcutta Improvement Trust's street-building initiatives. I have laid out the larger context of the Bakr-Id riot of December 1910 to break down the complex inner workings of this puzzling conjunction and also to illustrate it as part of the protracted process of urbanization. We find that the 'rational action' of street-building, the 'invisible hands' of the real estate market, and crowd action during communal outbreaks constituted each other in a complex fashion in producing the twentieth-century city.

Improvement by Recoupment

In 1884, the Municipal Commissioners appointed a 'Town Improvement Committee' to prepare 'a comprehensive report on structural and sanitary improvements' in the 'congested' central part of the city.[11] The Committee recommended a 'new and more direct route from Sealdah to the Hoogly bridge', which would 'open out' the densely built-up Burrabazaar. This would ease the circulation of goods and people between the two major railway transit hubs of the city—Howrah and Sealdah. The Committee planned to run the new street through 'the centre of the large Soortee Bagan and Kalabagan bustee'. It was hoped that this would enhance the value of properties in these thickly populated localities.[12] This proposed road was Harrison Road—a diagonal that cut across central Calcutta. It began at Strand Road in the west, along the river, and extended in the south-eastern direction, intersecting first Chitpore Road, then College Street, and finally ending at Sealdah.

---

was predominantly male and made up of transport coolies connected to transit centres and warehouses. In the absence of a unified shop floor, traditional trade unionism was significantly absent among transit workers. In this city, housing became a political question only in the second half of the twentieth century when the upper-caste Bengali refugee influx began.

[11] Municipal (Municipal), Proceeding No. 168–169, Acquisition of Land for Construction of a Road from Hoogly Bridge to Sealdah, No. 176, dated, Calcutta, the 27th January 1888, Letter from the Chairman of the Corporation of the Town of Calcutta to the Secretary to the GoB, Municipal Department (WBSA), reprinted in Atish Dasgupta (ed.), *Select Documents on Calcutta 1800–1900* (Kolkata: Directorate of State Archives, Higher Education Department, Government of West Bengal, 2011), 122.

[12] Ibid., 130.

The principle of 'recoupment' was a unique and controversial provision of the Harrison Road Scheme. The Chairman of the Corporation and some influential Commissioners were keen to acquire more land for the scheme than required for street-building. The idea was to use the extra land to simultaneously create a new line of frontage properties abutting the new street. They expected these properties to sell at a very high price owing to their new locational advantage. The premium could also be extracted from existing owners of these plots if they could afford it. This strategy had been successful in European cities since the 1870s.[13] It was hoped that 'recoupment' would recover some of the expenses of street-building undertaken by the Corporation, and later the Trust.

However, recoupment was met with severe opposition from many commissioners and legal experts, who questioned its legal tenability. This led

---

[13] Government of India (GOI), Home Munc., A, Nos. 33–36, October 1904, (NAI), 57. A Prussian street-alignment law enacted in 1875 appeared to have inspired the proponents of recoupment in Calcutta. A relevant section of the said law lays out the principle of recoupment as follows:

> It may be laid down by local enactment that when a new street is laid out or an existing street prolonged for the purpose of being built upon, and also when buildings come to be erected on existing streets, or parts of the streets not yet built upon, the promoter of the laying out operations, or the adjacent owners ... may be required to make a reasonable contribution towards or to meet the entire cost of the laying out and construction of the street.... (Ibid.)

It should be mentioned here that the very idea of recoupment had been in practice (if not in this name) for a long time. Thus, the Lottery Committee in Calcutta (1817) wrote:

> ... if it were proposed to make a road through ground which might on an average be produced at 100 Rupees per cottah and the value of the ground adjacent to the road should as soon as it was opened rose to 300 Rupees per cottah, one third of the quantity so purchased might be given up for the road and 100 Rupees clear profit be gained by the sale of the remaining two thirds ... the value of ground in Calcutta generally rise in proportion to its contiguity to a great thoroughfare and that upon this circumstance rested the possibility of effecting the improvement ... without expense, provided sufficient capital were advanced for the purpose in the first instance. (Lottery Committee, 3 February 1820, quoted in Kaustubh Mani Sengupta, 'Infrastructural Development and the Issue of Compensation in Colonial Calcutta', http://www.mcrg.ac.in/6thCSC/6thCSC_Full_Papers/Kaustubh.pdf, accessed 16 June 2021)

to the appointment of a municipal subcommittee, entrusted with identifying legal provisions within existing land acquisition and municipal laws that could make recoupment possible. The subcommittee proposed:

> That in taking up land for the new road, the Commissioners should follow the principle of acquiring a considerable strip of land outside the regular line of the proposed street, the precise width being settled by the Committee. This course should be followed not only with the object of reselling the frontage land at a profit, owing to the enhanced value due to the new road, but also to enable them to redistribute the frontage land in convenient building blocks.[14]

The issue at hand was finally decided by the Lieutenant Governor in 1888. He consented to acquiring a strip of land with a consistent width of 170 feet throughout the proposed street. A measurement of 50 feet of land on each side of the proposed street (total 100 feet) was kept for the new building line. However, recoupment continued to sit ambiguously among land acquisition laws. The Harrison Road Scheme was stalled for nearly four long years (between 1884 and 1888) because of its uncertain legality.[15] The proponents of recoupment creatively interpreted various sections of the Land Acquisition Act VI of 1870, Land Acquisition Act IV of 1876, and Calcutta Municipal Act VI of 1863.

However, this kind of land acquisition in densely populated stretches involved considerable expense on the part of the government as compensation to those who would lose their property to road construction. In fact, when contemplating the Harrison Road Scheme, an alternative project to expand the existing Cotton Street and Machooa Bazaar Street instead was also under consideration. But the cost of land acquisition in these densely settled streets was prohibitive, because of which the plan was abandoned. The difference in the estimated cost of land acquisitions between the two projects is represented in Tables 2.1 and 2.2, published in 1884. While the net cost incurred by the Corporation to build Harrison Road was estimated to be 1,020,000 rupees, for the expansion of Cotton Street and Machooa Bazaar Street it was 1,444,000 rupees.

---

[14] Municipal (Municipal), Proceeding No. 168–169, Acquisition of Land for Construction of a Road from Hoogly Bridge to Sealdah, No. 176, dated, Calcutta, the 27th January 1888, Letter from the Chairman of the Corporation of the Town of Calcutta to the Secretary to the GoB, Municipal Department (WBSA), reprinted in A. Dasgupta (ed.), *Select Documents on Calcutta 1800–1900* (2011), 123.

[15] Ibid., 123.

Table 2.1 'The cost of this scheme, based upon the "assessed" value of the houses and lands through which it passes increased 15 percent' (between 1884 and 1888)

Section of the roadway	The estimated cost of entire premises to be acquired	Deduct estimated price to be realized from surplus land resold	Net cost
From Strand Road to Chitpore Road (800 metres)	Rs. 19,00,000	Rs. 12,00,000	Rs. 7,00,000
From Chitpore Road to College Street (800 metres)	Rs. 9,00,000	Rs. 8,00,000	Rs. 1,00,000
From College Street to Sealdah (1.9 kilometres)	Rs. 6,50,000	Rs. 4,30,000	Rs. 2,20,000
Total	34,50,000	24,30,000	10,20,000

Source: Municipal (Municipal), Proceeding No. 168–169, Acquisition of Land for Construction of a Road from Hoogly Bridge to Sealdah, No. 176, dated, Calcutta, the 27th January 1888, Letter from the Chairman of the Corporation of the Town of Calcutta to the Secretary to the GoB, Municipal Department (WBSA), reprinted in A. Dasgupta (ed.), *Select Documents on Calcutta 1800–1900* (2011), 131.

Tables 2.1 and 2.2 give us an indication of the relation between road-building and land-pricing. First, Table 2.1 suggests that existing property prices were already quite high in the west (close to Strand Road by the river) but kept declining as one moved south-eastwards along the road. Thus, the initial stretch between Strand Road and Chitpore Road, which had a series of bazaars, was expensive to begin with. Consequently, there was a minor gap between the existing price and projected price, and the developing cost of this area would be high despite recoupment. Second, Table 2.2 clearly shows that existing property prices in the areas lying to the north of the Harrison Road diagonal, like Cotton Street and Machooa Bazaar Street, were higher than towards the south, in the vicinity of Harrison Road itself. These areas were part of Burrabazaar, inhabited mainly by the city's Marwari mercantile community. Third, anticipated returns from road building or widening would be the highest in the stretch in the middle of the road, between Chitpore Road and College Street. This section had residential neighbourhoods peppered with small shops,

Table 2.2 '[A]nd the corresponding cost of widening Cotton Street and Machooa Bazaar Street to 70 feet'

Section of the roadway	The estimated cost of entire premises to be acquired	Deduct estimated price to be realized from surplus land resold	Net cost
From Strand Road to Chitpore Road	23,70,000	13,90,000	9,80,000
From Chitpore Road to College Street	9,87,000	7,30,000	2,57,000
From College Street to Sealdah	6,07,000	4,00,000	2,07,000
Total	39,64,000	25,20,000	14,44,000

Source: Municipal (Municipal), Proceeding No. 168–169, Acquisition of Land for Construction of a Road from Hoogly Bridge to Sealdah, No. 176, dated, Calcutta, the 27th January 1888, Letter from the Chairman of the Corporation of the Town of Calcutta to the Secretary to the GoB, Municipal Department (WBSA), reprinted in A. Dasgupta (ed.), Select Documents on Calcutta 1800–1900 (2011), 131.

Note: This entire exercise was merely a rough assessment, both of 'existing' prices as well as 'projected' prices of the acquired land. They were based on speculative trends in the neighbourhood. The figures would have diverged from the 'actual' market prices at the time of acquisition. Nonetheless, the tables reveal an interesting gradation of property prices in the area.

with mostly Bengali Hindus and some Muslim proprietors. It also included the *bustee*s of poor Muslims, mentioned in the previous section. Because existing property prices were much lower here than in the first stretch, the projected jump in the prices after road construction was expected to be massive. Table 2.1 shows that the final stretch between College Street until Sealdah had low prices to begin with, but unlike the second segment, the projected prices here were also relatively humble. Generally speaking, since existing prices were high in the west and north but kept declining as one moved both south and eastwards, the cheaper localities that lay south (and eastwards) of the projected diagonal road would earn better recoupment returns. Thus, the south-eastern part of the proposed Harrison Road would have financed the expense of building its (north)western segment. Eventually, the new street was expected to carve out a lucrative property zone between Strand Road and College Street, the most dramatic transformation being wrought in the second segment, between Chitpore Road and College Street.

Particularly in this segment, when the recouped properties eventually came to the open market, the cultivated architectural baseline along Harrison Road ended up coinciding with a narrow ethnic (and class) line. As already mentioned earlier, Marwari business owners, who had, until then, lived in the Burrabazaar area in the north, started buying up the expensive but lucrative frontage properties along the new road from Hindu Bengali landlords. The street directory for the year 1910 suggests that the properties in the area north of the College Street and Harrison Road intersection came to be owned predominantly by Marwaris. In the directory, property owners bearing Hindu Bengali (upper caste) surnames, on the other hand, are concentrated in the area east of the said intersection, along with more Marwari owners. There was a very small number of Muslim property owners too on both sides. Most of these properties enlisted in the directory were commercial. In some cases, commercial establishments were owned jointly by Hindu Bengalis and Marwaris.[16] Overall, the 1910 directory suggests a clear trend of property distribution along ethno-religious lines, where Marwari property owners appear to have pushed erstwhile Hindu Bengali landlords eastwards along the road.

Thus, besides evicted poor Muslims mentioned in the previous section, Hindu Bengali landlords were also adversely affected by recoupment. In 1902, H. H. Risley called recoupment the 'most contentious aspect of an improvement plan', which profoundly affected the 'Hindu sentiment': 'One of the strongest sections of public opinion in Calcutta consists of the Hindus who own residential houses on sites where their families have lived for generations, and to which they are very strongly attached both on domestic and religious grounds.'[17]

We have already seen how communal animosity was stoked by property transformations on Armenian Street to the south of Harrison Road. Tensions further intensified as the Improvement Trust took over the execution of street schemes through recoupment from the Municipal Corporation. The Trust recouped hundreds of properties, especially for its Central Avenue Scheme (Scheme VII) and the Russa Road Widening Scheme (Scheme IV). It was

---

[16] *Thacker's India Directory for the Year 1910: Embracing the Whole of the Indian Empire* (Calcutta: Thacker, Spink & Co., 1911).
[17] GOI, Home Munc., A, Nos. 33–36, October 1904 (NAI), 11.

assumed that the Calcutta Improvement Act had legalized recoupment beyond any doubt. In fact, the proceedings of the Trust's board meetings and other published reports referred to the principle of recoupment as the prime mover of the improvement work. It was projected that 336 lakh (33.6 million) rupees could be added to the Trust's income through the sale of the recouped land.[18]

A careful look at the Calcutta Improvement Act, 1911, itself (with all its amendments until 1983), however, suggests that the term 'recoupment' never, in fact, appeared directly in it, allowing for multiple interpretations and contrary opinions to coexist. This legal ambiguity over recoupment would thrive in the Bar of the High Court for decades after, making it a site of intense contestation between the Trust and the city's Hindu rentier class who expressed dissent right at the time of debate around the Calcutta Improvement Bill, 1910.[19]

Even at the time, the judges in the High Court remained divided in their opinions regarding the Trust's right to recoup land beyond the active scheme areas. In August 1915, an Appellate Bench of Justices Asutosh Mookerjee and Cuming of the High Court pronounced a judgment favouring a property owner who had been adversely affected by recoupment.[20] Given this adverse ruling, on 16 October 1916 the Bengal government asked the Trustees of the

---

[18] Datta, *Planning the City*, 206.

[19] For instance, amendments to the Improvement Bill to allow for recoupment drew severe criticisms from Raja Reshee Case Law—representing the interest of the city's Hindu rentier class—who opined that the quantity of land to be acquired must not be too disproportionate to its intended purpose. 'Such a tendency', Law cautioned, might 'develop towards land speculation, or to interfere with the just rights of the people by taking much more land than what would be required for the recoupment of the cost of the main scheme'. Law mentioned that land acquisition under the Calcutta Municipal Act, 1899, had already deprived many rightful owners of their claim to their properties. There was, then, a palpable sense of loss suffered by Hindu Bengali landlords of central Calcutta at this time. See 'The Calcutta Improvement Bill, 1911, Preliminary Report of the Select Committee, Notes of Dissent, Clause 16 of the Schedule to the Bill—Proposed section 24A (1) for the Land Acquisition Act', Reshee Case Law, 27 February, 1911, Legislative Department, Government of Bengal, Papers Relative to the Bill to Provide for the Improvement and Expansion of Calcutta, The West Bengal Legislative Assembly Library.

[20] Appellate Civil, Before Sir Asutosh Mookerjee, Knight, Judge, and Mr. Justice Cuming, *Trustees for the Improvement of Calcutta v Chandra Kanta Ghosh*, Appeal from Original Decree No. 416 of 1915 against the decision of Babu Umesh Chandra Chakrabarti, Subordinate Judge, 24 Parganas, dated the 10th August 1915, *Calcutta Law Journal* 24 (1916): 246–271.

Improvement Trust to avoid undertaking fresh recoupments in 'scheme nos. VII, VIIA and XII'.[21] But in another case defending an appeal by Trustees, the Advocate General admitted that though recoupment was not directly mentioned in the Improvement Act, it was nonetheless 'assumed' as a 'means to acquire land'. He reasoned that the lawmakers had intentionally omitted the word to evade public criticism. The High Court Bench, however, found this claim 'ingenuous'.[22] Nonetheless, three subsequent High Court cases, between 1916 and 1920, reversed the judgment pronounced by Justices Mookerjee and Cuming.[23] Finally, the Privy Council in 1920 decisively reversed the judgment of Justices Mookerjee and Cuming and restored the Trustees' authority to recoup land.[24] Even after this, the colonial government failed to legislate recoupment owing to strong resistance from Hindu landlords.

Recoupment continued to be a powerful para-legal device to translate private property into a 'public good' and vice versa. This cycle enabled a constant flow of money into the Trust's exchequer, which in turn funded improvement works

---

[21] Proceedings of the 221th Meeting of the Calcutta Improvement Trust, 16 October, 1916, *Proceedings of the CIT for the Year 1916–17* (Valuation Department). It appears that different Benches of the High Court had different readings of the recoupment provision under the Calcutta Improvement Act. The lower court at Alipore too had varied judgments. *Annual Report of the Operation of the Calcutta Improvement Trust for the Year 1915–16* (Calcutta: Calcutta Improvement Trust, 1916), 35.

[22] Appellate Civil, Before Sir Asutosh Mookerjee, Knight, Judge, and Mr. Justice Cuming, *Trustees for the Improvement of Calcutta v Chandra Kanta Ghosh*, Appeal from Original Decree No. 416 of 1915 against the decision of Babu Umesh Chandra Chakrabarti, Subordinate Judge, 24 Parganas, dated the 10th August 1915.

[23] These cases and judgments were published in nationalist newspapers, causing much public uproar. For instance, Calcutta's leading nationalist daily, *Amrita Bazar Patrika*, published two reports on 18 and 22 May 1917 that suggested a tacit understanding between the Trust and the Chief Justice of the Calcutta High Court to rescue recoupment from the August 1916 judgment pronounced by Judges Mookerjee and Cuming. One of the reports mentioned that the complexity of residential properties in Calcutta and the emotional cost of recoupment on the affected property owners could only be appreciated by native judges. *Tarit Kanti Biswas, Printer... vs Unknown* on 27 June 1917, 45 Ind Cas 338 Author: L. Sanderson, Bench: L. S. Chitty, Fletcher, JUDGEMENT Lancelot Sanderson, C.J., 1–2.

[24] On 22 December, 1919, Bompas reported that the Privy Council had agreed to hear the Trust's appeal against the High Court judgment. Proceedings of the 367th Meeting of the Calcutta Improvement Trust, 22 December 1920, *Proceedings of the CIT for the Year 1919–20* (Valuation Department). Also see *R. C. Sen vs Trustees for the Improvement of Calcutta*, 21 January 1921, 64 Ind Cas 577.

elsewhere. Thus, recoupment became a means for the self-reproduction of 'improvement'. It embodied the necessary 'force' that ultimately set property in motion.

Just one instance of recoupment in the central city can give us a sense of its scale. In 1913, the Trust began its first recoupment experiment in Soorti Bagan. The delimited area for the scheme covered 14.4 acres of thickly built-up land with a population density of 333 persons per acre. Of the 5,000 individuals living in the scheme area, 1,100 were women. Two-thirds of the population comprised up-country working-class men. Of the 256 masonry buildings in the delimited area, 33 per cent was deemed unfit for human habitation, while only 12.5 per cent of buildings were satisfactory in the Trust's view. The Soorti Bagan Scheme projected 1,350 yards of road, 40 and 45 feet wide, and new masonry dwellings on 14 acres of land. Between September 1915 and March 1916 in Soorti Bagan 10 *bigha*s, 14 *cottah*s, and 9 *chatak*s of land was auctioned off to 36 buyers at an average price of 8,000 rupees per *cottah*.

Marwari business owners continued to benefit from these street schemes, even as the interventions added to the already seething resentments in the area. The Marwari Association (we met them briefly during the 1910 riot) welcomed the Trust's schemes, and even asked the Trust to widen and extend Armenian Street up to Halliday Street in the east to allow diversion of traffic from Strand Road towards the inner city. The Marwari Association also asked the Trust to widen Machooa Bazaar Street. Both proposals were subsequently accepted.[25] By 1916, Zakaria Street was widened and extended and 'building sites abutting on it were sold at a satisfactory price'.[26]

The improvement work and recoupment resulted in a land boom during and after the First World War (henceforth the War), which invited unregulated speculation in the land market. As a result, land prices became unstable. As a land dealer, the Improvement Trust itself fell prey to these fluctuations. It ended up buying land during the boom only to sell it off at slump time in several expensive schemes.[27] Eventually, in the face of growing public opinion against

---

[25] *Annual Report on the Operation of the Calcutta Improvement Trust for the Year 1912–13* (Calcutta: Calcutta Improvement Trust, 1913).

[26] *Annual Report on the Operation of the Calcutta Improvement Trust for the Year 1915–16* (Calcutta: Calcutta Improvement Trust, 1916).

[27] C. H. Bompas, 'Note on the Finances of the Trust, 14 January 1921', attached with the Proceedings of the 407th Meeting of the Calcutta Improvement Trust, 10 January 1921, *Proceedings of the CIT for the Year 1920–21* (Valuation Department).

recoupment, the Trust had to look for other means to finance its operation. As the War ended,[28] the Trust began to rely more on institutional borrowings. For instance, in 1920–1921, the Trust raised a loan of half a crore (a crore equals ten million). Chairman Bompas anticipated that in future the Trust would be operating 'mainly on borrowed capital', which might exceed a crore or more in the next year.[29] Eventually, borrowing became an enduring feature of the Trust's finance in the interwar decades. But by this time, recoupment had already changed the demographic pattern of central Calcutta. This was, however, in keeping with the Trust's other significant objective—the graded dispersal of population in the city.

Graded Population Dispersal

In the initial years of its operation, the Improvement Trust had devised a strategy for a layered population displacement to be achieved through its schemes. Iman Mitra has closely analysed the minutes of the Trust's board meetings to write about it in detail.[30] The idea was that improvement schemes would let loose an autonomous market process by which the upper-class population would displace lower-middle-class property owners and the working class occupying the *bustee*s. C. F. Payne, then a Board member, expected the population to 'move away in layers'. He added, 'The people from Burrabazaar would not go far, but they would displace others, who in their turn would go further afield till the class of people, who would be willing to live in Manicktolla, was reached.'[31] Thus, dispersal was expected to happen according

---

[28] In the later years of the War, the Trust had to cope with many unanticipated circumstances. The fall in the value of money seriously affected the Trust's operations since 1917. Furthermore, the Trust failed to raise funds on debentures. In this context, the Trust began selling surplus lands at its disposal to recover the already invested capital. The Trust suspended several of its ongoing and future building operations as actual expenditure exceeded the pre-war projections. Bompas, 'Note on the Finances of the Trust', ibid.

[29] *Annual Report on the Operation of the Calcutta Improvement Trust for the Year 1920–21* (Calcutta: Calcutta Improvement Trust, 1921), see Appendix C, 67.

[30] Iman Mitra, 'Towards a Rental Economy of the City: Calcutta Improvement Trust and Urbanisation in Calcutta in the Early Twentieth Century', paper presented at the 'Sixth Critical Studies Workshop' at the Mahanirban Calcutta Research Group, 2015, 6: http://www.mcrg.ac.in/6thCSC/6thCSC_Full_Papers/Iman.pdf, accessed 3 September 2020.

[31] Ibid.

to the class character of the affected populations. Working-class populations, it was hoped, would eventually get thrown out of the central city areas, under improvement. The Trust's Chief Engineer Maden and Chief Valuer Shrosbree claimed that it would achieve what they called 'a more natural gradation of values … throughout the town'.[32]

This form of zoning the city relied on an auto-corrective rental economy principle under speculative capitalism. We already know that the street schemes made significant interventions in the land market in the pursuit of improvement. 'This intervention', Mitra contends, 'was necessary to have a more cost-effective improvement mission….' In the context of the Trust's land acquisitions for this purpose, Maden and Shrosbree tell us:

> If the limits of the property to be acquired are determined so that, other considerations apart, all lands are acquired whose increase in value is in excess of the additional value conferred by the existence of buildings, the net cost of improvements will be reduced to the lowest possible extent.[33]

Mitra finds in this argument an intimate conversation with the theory of rent in classical political economy where 'rent as the surplus income from land is determined as excess over the price of the produce in the least productive plot of land. To make this model of differential rent work, one needed to know the sequence of different grades of land'.[34] In keeping with this model based on agricultural land, Maden and Shrosbree too proposed grading the acquired surplus land in the city. It would help reorganize the city thus:

> For example, the Trust might provide land available for the erection of bustee huts upon model lines in the suburbs and let it displace tenants from the city. The cheaper bustee land in the town thus vacated would be taken up in part by the displaced population of small pucca buildings in another improvement scheme, and the conditions would adjust themselves similarly throughout the whole area of the Trust's operations.[35]

---

[32] James Maden and Albert de Bois Shrosbree, *City and Suburban Main Road Projects, Joint Report, 1st July 1913* (Calcutta: Calcutta Improvement Trust, 1913), 66; I. Mitra, 'Towards a Rental Economy of the City'.

[33] Maden and Shrosbree, *Joint Report*, 66.

[34] Ibid., 66.

[35] Ibid., 66.

Hence, to facilitate layered population dispersal, the Trust had to simultaneously improve suburban areas so that the displaced population could find affordable housing solutions in those places. Moreover, connecting these suburbs with the central city through roads and public transport networks was an essential appendage of this vision of improvement. It was hoped that suburban developments—devoid of litigations—would precede the demolition work in the central city. This would enable rehabilitation of the expelled inner-city populations.[36]

Emphasizing the need to reconfigure the city's layout, Maden and Shrosbree wrote: 'The present planning of Calcutta has produced a concentration of land value in the vicinity of the existing main roads, whilst it has tended to retard the growth of value in the areas enclosed by main roads'. They proposed a set of new roads that would 'run for the greater part of their extent through back lands'.[37] As a result, they argued, when the proposed roads opened up, 'the frontages abutting upon them will be largely increased in value' and hence 'the general effect' would be that a 'more natural gradation of values will exist throughout the town'.[38] Maden and Shrosbree hoped that if their plan were followed, the Trust would lead to the most remarkable 'redistribution of property values that has ever taken place in India, if not in the world'.[39] At the core of this entire project of city-rebuilding lay a mechanism to transfer future forms of surplus to the present as the city's valuation.

However, Maden and Shrosbree cautioned that the redistribution of property prices throughout the city could lead to a 'sudden disturbance of the level of value' if the society at large failed to 'absorb surplus lands into development'. They contended that the Trust needed to execute improvement schemes in such a way as to keep the market 'occupied with enough, and no more than enough, land available for development'.[40] These two technocrats anticipated that the Trust would work as a land development corporation, willing to sacrifice its capital ultimately to finance improvements that would inevitably drive it towards loss and liabilities. Maden and Shrosbree were proved right about the future course that the Trust was to tread. Their apprehension that the Trust's operations might result in a massive and sudden disturbance of the level of property prices too proved to be true in the subsequent years.

[36] Ibid.
[37] Ibid., 66.
[38] Ibid., 66.
[39] Ibid., 66.
[40] Ibid., 66.

However, what they did not care to anticipate was that a class-based dispersal of the population in a city like Calcutta would result in the dispersal of its population along communal and ethnic lines as well. The 'invisible hands' of the market would enable mostly wealthy Marwari business owners to displace mostly poor Muslim tenants (often housed by Hindu Bengali landlords). Such a measure would also progressively convert dwelling spaces into commercial quarters and business districts. The complex class, ethnic, and religious tensions that this process fomented were often clubbed together in the archives simplistically as 'Hindu–Muslim riots', as we saw in the Armenian Street mosque incident in 1910. Thus, given the colonial state's policy of non-interference in communal affairs, a gradual Hinduization of the city proceeded via urban renewal, gentrification, and communal riots. All these forces operated through interdependent relationships in Calcutta in the first half of the twentieth century.

Central Avenue: Commercialization and Dislocations

Besides the east–west diagonal of Harrison Road, the need for a north–south thoroughfare between Chitpore Road and Cornwallis Street had been felt in the mid-nineteenth century itself. Alderman William Clark (we met him briefly in Chapter 1 as the person behind Calcutta's elaborate underground drainage scheme) projected such a street in his 1854 map linking up Bagbazaar in the north and Dharmatala to its south. This line resembled today's Central Avenue. Finally, in 1914, the Improvement Trust took up the 'Central Avenue Scheme' (Map 2.1). Bompas, the Trust's Chairman, was keen to ensure that the contrasting grandeur of the Tipoo Sultan Mosque and the Ochterlony Monument at the southern end of the proposed road gained unencumbered visibility within a single photo frame. Thus, work on the Central Avenue Scheme began with the destruction of a host of dwellings and shops to 'clear up' the Dharmatala and Bentinck Street corner. The Central Avenue Scheme was one of several urban renewal schemes that the Trust undertook during the War and the early interwar period (1914–1928). These schemes recycled more than 200 acres of prime land in the inner city and displaced at least 50,000 individuals from the densely populated neighbourhoods of Soorti Bagan, Jorabagan, Jorasanko, and Colootola—all in the vicinity of the Chitpore Road–College Street segment of the Harrison Road Scheme discussed earlier.[41] By 1931, Central Avenue touched Beadon Street in the north. When completed, it covered 201.1 acres of prime land, stretching over 3 miles with a consistent width of 100 feet.

---

[41] C. H. Bompas, 'The Work of the Calcutta Improvement Trust', *Journal of the Royal Society of Arts* 75, no. 3868 (1927): 199–219.

The affected localities were multi-ethnic and had a mix of classes. The upper-caste Hindu Bengali rentier class lived with an increasingly prosperous Marwari community, a lower-middle-class Bengali population, an Urdu-speaking Muslim trading community, mendicant Kabuli merchants, male students of various colleges under the University of Calcutta residing in messes and hostels, and thousands of (predominantly male) migrants from northern and western India. These migrants worked as *darwan*s and coolies. They also pulled rickshaws and drove bullock carts through the alleys of Burrabazaar. These migrant workers and Kabuli traders lived in the patrons' shops, servants' quarters, and footpaths. In the numerous *bustee*s that dotted the neighbourhoods, there was virtually no separation between life and work. Like in the case of the Harrison Road Scheme, the Central Avenue Scheme facilitated a speculative land market and reshuffled property ownership in these central Calcutta neighbourhoods along the axes of class and ethnicity.

The Scheme recouped lands and redeveloped buildings to host commercial establishments. It swallowed smaller by-lanes and neighbourhoods and disturbed a life-world that had developed in these places over centuries. Bimal Mitra's magnum opus *Saheb Bibi Golam* begins with an 'imaginative evocation'[42] of a disappearing central Calcutta lane:

> Between Bowbazaar Street and the fledging Central Avenue stood a spiral lane called Banamali Sarkar Lane, acting as a connector between two streets. Central Avenue has already eaten up half of this lane. The other half is still anticipating its imminent annexation. The Improvement Trust has been entrusted with the work of civic reform in this neglected neighbourhood. The lane begins where there was an *adda* of some *Hindustani Bhujiawalas* in a tin-roofed two-storeyed house. They sang 'Rama Ho' a month before the Holi, accompanied by a *khanjani*. From there, the lane moves eastward. Proceed a little and turn left and then right to reach Bowbazaar Street. When you enter Banamali Sarkar Lane, you are bound to think that it will hit the wall just a yard away. Gather courage and proceed, and you will get to see a thriving life along this moribund lane. The roadside rooms of all the dwarfed houses host shops of all kinds. Just at the edge of the first turn, you see the gold and silver shop of Beni Sarkar. The next one is 'India Tailoring Hall'. Proceed a little, and you see Prabhas Babu's 'Pabitra Khaddar Bhandar' (Sacred Khadi Shop). Next to this is Gurupada Dey's 'Swadeshi Bazaar'. When people queue up for *swadeshi* goods, it

[42] Datta, 'Calcutta on the Threshold of 1940s', 18.

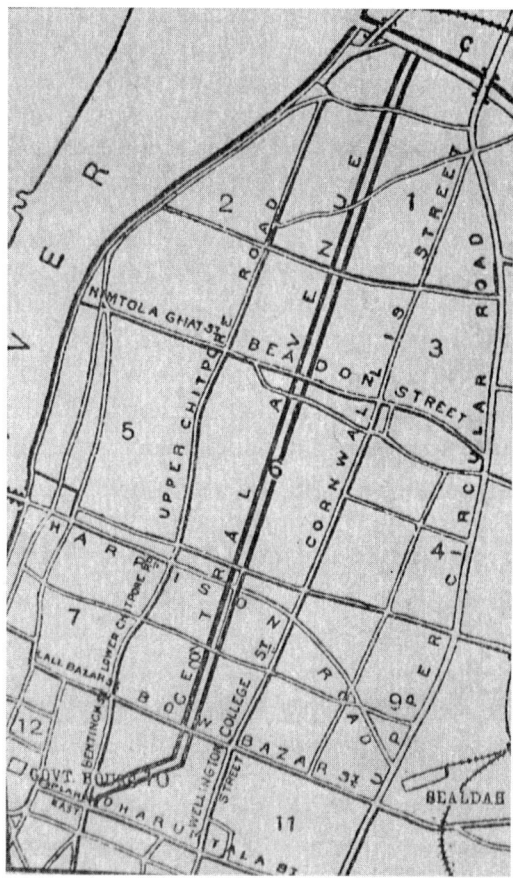

Map 2.1 The planned layout of Central Avenue in 1916

Source: Surendranath Sinha, 'The Central Avenue: Calcutta's New Thoroughfare', *Bengal Past and Present* 35 (1916), 72.

Note: The present names of some of the major streets have been indicated.

reaches the 'Sabuj Sangha' (a clubhouse). At times, the club organizes local events. That day, the whole *para* celebrates the victory of Sabuj Sangha and forgets about everything. The para cannot afford to fall asleep that day. Just after the club, one sees the proud signboard of the 'famous' astrologer Srimat Ananta Bhattacharyya's 'Sri Sri Mahakali Asram' where one can still find the proper medicine to bring back their lost fortune. The next shop is Bancharam's popular *telebhaja* (fried food) shop. Bancha is no more. Even his son Adhar is not seen these days. Akrur—Adhar's son—now keeps the tradition. This is about the eastern edge of the lane. Banamali Sarkar's dilapidated mansion occupies the whole of the western edge. Decades ago, this was one of the most luxurious houses in the whole of Central Calcutta. The Improvement Trust has served a legal notice in due course. The para has to find its way to other places as the lane has to give way to a sprawling avenue. There is a considerable discussion going on in Bancharam's shop regarding the Trust's notice.[43]

The Central Avenue Scheme converged with the long-term improvement operation in central Calcutta that had commenced in the earlier decade. In the nearby Colootola area, which was in the active catchment of the Scheme, population density declined by 32.5 per cent between 1911 and 1921, while Jorasanko witnessed a decline of population density by 3.2 per cent during the same census decade. In these two neighbourhoods alone, the Central Avenue Scheme acquired 33.3 and 22.6 acres of land, respectively.[44] The Census of 1911 noted that due to the demolition of 75 *bustees* in the Colootola, population density had come down from 282 per acre in 1901 to 255 in 1911[45] and 172 per acre

---

[43] Bimal Mitra, *Saheb Bibi Golam* (Calcutta: Mitra O Ghosh, 1953, translated by me). To understand the *para* phenomenon in colonial Calcutta, see Kaustubh Mani Sengupta, 'Community and Neighbourhood in a Colonial City: Calcutta's Para', *South Asia Research* 38, no. 1 (2018): 40–56. In this remarkable article, Sengupta shows how the 'rural foundations of the concept' assumed a new life in the colonial city, which profoundly impacted the city's evolving social structure. For a book-length treatment of the various aspects of *para*, see N. Ghosh, *The Hygienic City Nation*. This book tracks the *para* in the first half of the twentieth century, after establishing nationalist control over the city Corporation and showing how space evolved conceptually when the nationalist Corporation conceptualized it as a field of administrative intervention and civic pedagogy. This book also shows remarkable clarity on how the improvement work of the Trust resulted in intense proprietary negotiations in the *paras*. Studying the Trust's Tribunal records, Ghosh unravels how the *paras* reacted to and adapted themselves to a new authoritarian municipal regime. Swati Chattopadhyay's now-classic book opened a new way to bring the common, the intimate, and the domestic of the neighbourhood under a perceptive spatial analysis. Swati Chattopadhyay, *Representing Calcutta: Modernity, Nationalism and the Colonial Uncanny* (New York: Routledge, 2005). For a brilliant cultural analysis of the *para* in the late-twentieth- and early-twenty-first-century contexts of Durga Puja, see Tapati Guha-Thakurta, *In the Name of the Goddess: The Durga Pujas of Contemporary Kolkata* (New Delhi: Primus, 2017).

[44] *Census of India*, 1921, vol. VI, 'City of Calcutta', Part I, Report.

[45] *Census of India*, 1911, vol. VI, 'City of Calcutta', Part I, Report.

in 1921.⁴⁶ These figures indicate the magnitude of the impact of improvement operations in central Calcutta and the concealed violence of urban renewal.

A part of the Central Avenue was to run parallel to College Street. Between 1901 and 1911, land had been acquired to expand the campuses of the Presidency College, the Medical College Hospital, the University Law College, and some other public buildings.⁴⁷ This meant that a substantial amount of land was already out of the local land market.⁴⁸ In this context, any road-building schemes in this locality already meant a tremendous hike in land prices and house rents. The simultaneous clearing of land through the demolition of slums and lower-middle-class dwellings from the Central Avenue area once more enabled wealthy Marwari traders to gradually shift from the narrow alleys of Burrabazaar to the more lucrative frontal sites in the now transformed Colootola.⁴⁹ A redevelopment of Colootola also meant that a sizeable section of Muslim petty merchants, traders, shopkeepers, artisans, Kabulis, and workers were displaced from that area.

In 1915, in a particular segment of the Central Avenue Scheme, that is, the Central Avenue–Halliday Street Widening or Scheme VIIA, 335 objections were officially recorded from property owners and Ratepayers' Associations between Machooa Bazaar Street and Beadon Street. The Trust's 'Objection Committee' heard 62 objections from the area and, it seems, 'disposed of all the objections'.⁵⁰ Table 2.3 lists some of these objections raised by individuals who had interests in 'holdings' in a lane called Bhawani Charan Dutt (also written as 'Dutta' in colonial documents) Lane. At this time, Bhawani Charan Dutt Lane was predominantly a residential street,

---

⁴⁶ *Census of India*, 1921, vol. VI, 'City of Calcutta', Part I, Report.

⁴⁷ *Census of India*, 1911, vol. VI, 'City of Calcutta', Part I, Report.

⁴⁸ *Report of the Calcutta University Commission* (Calcutta: Superintendent of Government Printing, 1919). The presence of thousands of students from various districts of the subcontinent meant that there was a thriving house rent market in this area. The above Commission documents contain an important discussion about these hostels and messes from a disciplinary standpoint. For a social–historical approach towards this rental market and its relationship with the university and college campus life, see Bodhisattva Kar, 'Chatro Andaloner Itihaas Likhte Jaoyar Aage', Gautam Chattopadhyay Smarak Baktrita, Kolkata, 2017.

⁴⁹ Such a trend was registered in the Census of 1921. *Census of India*, 1921, vol. VI, 'City of Calcutta', Part I, Report.

⁵⁰ Progress Report for the Quarter ending on 31 March 1915, in *Proceedings of the Calcutta Improvement Trust for the Year 1915–16* (Valuation Department).

Table 2.3 Objections raised by property owners of Bhawani Charan Dutt Lane and their status in 1918

No. of Holding	Name of Objector	No. in File	Abstract of Objection	State of the Property in 1918
1, 1/1	Lalit Mohan Dey	16	Premises stands outside the limit of road line; willing to pay an exemption fee	Property not mentioned in the street directory; either abolished or annexed with the holding No. 2
3, 3/1, 3/2	Md. Ismail	11	Premises stands outside the road line; pleads exemption	Property not mentioned in the street directory
49, 50, 50/1	Musamat Chand Bibi	30	Will suffer loss and inconvenience; wishes a similar plot as compensation Halliday Street, Bhawani Charan Dutt's Street; alternatively Rs 6,000 per cottah as compensation	Property must have been abolished. Not mentioned in the street directory
51	Harish Ch. Ghosh	17	Sanitary house; pleaded hardship	Property must have been abolished. Not mentioned in the street directory
51/1	Smt. Bhuban Mohini Dassee and others	18	Same as above	Property must have been abolished. Not mentioned in the street directory

(Contd)

The Regime of the Streets

(Contd)

No. of Holding	Name of Objector	No. in File	Abstract of Objection	State of the Property in 1918
52	Iqbal Ahmed	Number not visible in the file	Sanitary house, built recently	The property got amalgamated with No. 54
54	Bulloram Dey	10	Asks for adequate compensation	Retains
55	Ganga Narayan Pyne	25	Family dwelling house; does not fall on the road line	Retains
55/1	Balai Chand Rana	26	Sanitary building: outside road alignment. Prays exemption without paying any fee	Retains
56	Sm. Sarat Kumary Dassee and others	24	Two-storeyed building: sanitary	Transferred to B.N., S.N., O.C. and SK Rana. 55/1 and 56 must have been amalgamated
57	Shama Chand Paul	27	Premises beyond the proposed street line: dwelling house; prays for exemption	Property must have been abolished. Not mentioned in the street directory
58	Dhirendranath Sen and Brothers	34	Premises outside the street alignment; acquisition for recoupment illegal; prays for the acquisition of only the required portion	Property transferred to Roti Kanta Pyne

(Contd)

(Contd)

No. of Holding	Name of Objector	No. in File	Abstract of Objection	State of the Property in 1918
59	Amrita Lall Sen and others	36	Locality highly developed and free from congestion; acquisition illegal: building sanitary: prays for exemption	Retains. *The owner was a pleader in High Court* and was well-known in the locality
59/1	Satish Ch. Roy and others	33	Premises outside the street alignment; acquisition for recoupment illegal; prays for the acquisition of the required portion	Property not mentioned in the street directory. It appears to have been amalgamated with 59 and 59/3.
59/2	Hemendra Nath Gupta and others	39	Same as above	Same as above
59/3	Kumud Behari Sen and others	43	Is the birthplace of Babu Keshab Chandra Sen: premises beyond the road alignment: sanitary building	Retains
59/4	Dhirendra Nath Sen and Brothers	35	Locality highly developed … acquisition of premises beyond road line is illegal; prays for exemption	Property not mentioned in the street directory.
59/5	Indra Kr Sen and others	42	Same as above	Same as above
60	Bolai Chand Mullick	40	Dwelling house; outside street line; proposed widening of the Halliday Street is enough	Same as above

(Contd)

(Contd)

No. of Holding	Name of Objector	No. in File	Abstract of Objection	State of the Property in 1918
61	Manmatha Nath Mukherjee	12	Asks for compensation	Same as above
62	Sm Khantomoyee Dassee	Do	Poor Hindu widow maintains herself and her family with the income from the premises; not required for the execution of the scheme; prays for exemption	Property transferred to M. C. Dutt

Sources: Precise of Objections at Scheme No. VIIA, *Proceedings of the Calcutta Improvement Trust for the Year 1915–16* (Valuation Department). For the right-most column, see *Thacker's India Directory for the Year 1918: Embracing the Whole of the Indian Empire* (Calcutta: Thacker, Spink & Co., 1919), 316.

marking the northern boundary of the Presidency College. The last column of the table records the status of the 'holding' three years later, gleaned from a 1918 street directory. It indicates the changes that took place in just one street in the area, within a couple of years.

From Table 2.3, it is clear that most residences that were recorded in 1915 as objecting to recoupments were subsequently 'abolished' or 'annexed' by adjacent properties, and had ultimately ceased to exist by 1918. A very small number of the inhabitants of the street 'retained' their houses. We know the Trust reconsidered its decision to acquire properties in the 59 series of the list. Nonetheless, the 1918 street directory suggests that all properties in the series were abolished except 59/3. This house was spared as the Brahmos wished to preserve the birthplace of their founder figure—Keshab Chandra Sen.[51]

---

[51] Report on Scheme VIIA, Halliday Street Widening, Precise of Objections at Scheme No. VIIA, *Proceedings of the Board of Trustees of the CIT for the Year 1915–16* (Valuation Department).

A later street directory,[52] for the year 1927, mentions only 23 properties in Bhawani Charan Dutta Lane. Between 1918 and 1926, the amalgamation of Halliday Street with Central Avenue had turned this street into a blind alleyway. By this time several residential properties were turned into commercial establishments, including a newly founded *mess-bari* at No. 33.[53] Nonetheless, Bhawani Dutta Lane continued to be a *para* for small property owners right until the 1950s. What changed, however, was that it became an upper-caste Hindu quarter exclusively. Before improvement work (until 1915), this lane had had quite a few Muslim property owners (see properties at 3, 3/1, 3/2, 49, 0, 50/1 and 52 in Table 2.3, for instance). The Muslim households disappeared by 1918. The case of Bhawani Charan Dutta Lane reinforces the conclusion that the Trust's work resulted in the simultaneous commercialization and Hinduization of properties in the localities in this area.

Moreover, a close look at a portion of Central Avenue where the erstwhile Halliday Street stood suggests a clear ethnic monopolization of properties by prosperous Marwaris. There is a stray file of 1921 that contains a reference to 13 new plots ranging between 2.5 *cottahs* and 4 *cottahs* that emerged in the annexation of Halliday Street. Between 1916 and 1919, the Improvement Trust sold 11 of these plots to eight 'Marwari businessmen' at prices ranging between 65,000 rupees a *cottah* to 92,000 rupees a *cottah*.[54] The Census of 1931 tells us that there was a 'Marwari exodus' from Jorabagan and Burrabazaar into large tenement houses on both sides of Central Avenue.[55]

---

[52] *Thacker's India Directory for the Year 1927: Embracing the Whole of the Indian Empire* (Calcutta, Thacker, Spink & Co., 1928), 241.

[53] *Mess-bari* refers to a rented house where individuals (mostly students and male clerks in the case of these quarters of the city) would get a dormitory arrangement for dwelling. An old acquaintance of ours in College Street (a book shop owner) recollected that some bookshop owners began to occupy the northern edge of the lane in the 1950s. In the 1970s, the state government acquired vacant land from the Trust at 6 Bhawani Charan Dutta Lane to house some government offices. Several food stalls occupied the southern edge of the lane (Presidency University side) after the government office at No. 6 became functional.

[54] Note by Rai Radha Charan Pal Bahadur and Raja Reshee Case Law, 22 January 1921. This is a typed five-page stand-alone loose file found by the author in the Improvement Trust Record Room. The file does not contain other address details.

[55] *Census of India, 1931*, vol. VI, 'City of Calcutta', Part I, Report, 8–9.

A comparison of properties between the street directories for 1918[56] and 1933[57] reveals some further readjustment of properties on Central Avenue, at the Balaram De Street intersection, which further attests to the commercialization of the area. A *bustee* land at 49 Balaram De Street inhabited in 1918 by 'lower class upcountry Mohamadans', for instance, was recycled into a solicitors' firm sometime between 1918 and 1933. No. 50 Balaram De Street, home to Naran Dassi and Naran Moti Devi (sex workers) in 1918, had disappeared in the 1933 street directory. By 1933, at least three new commercial properties were added to No. 52 Balaram De Street. In adjacent Central Avenue, all the property names recorded in the 1933 directory were non-residential-commercial. Thus, we have Kaviraj Promotho Nath Sen & Joshi and Co. at No. 14 Central Avenue, the Presidency Electric Co. at 28-B Central Avenue, and the Merzapore Building at P-18-B Central Avenue, which hosted several commercial addresses such as the New Bengal Motor Works and Store Enameling House.

In Zakaria Street—a 'predominantly Muslim area', according to Census of 1911—the work of the Improvement Trust changed the neighbourhoods 'beyond recognition'.[58] The 1918 street directory names only three properties, but in the 1933 street directory there are references to 54 properties along the same street. Of the 54 properties, the first 35 names between Lower Chitpore Road and Surtee Bagan (also written as 'Surtibagan' and 'Soortee Bagan' in colonial documents) Lane refer to commercial establishments owned or occupied by people bearing Muslim names. In the Soorti Bagan area, where the Improvement Trust had launched its first scheme, the remaining properties were both predominantly commercial and had owners or occupants with Hindu Bengali (upper caste) and Marwari surnames.

The above evidence shows that the work of the Improvement Trust in the central part of the city decisively converted dwelling spaces into commercial establishments. This happened through the erasure of *bustee*s to create space for the new and valorized 'frontage properties'.[59] The evidence also

---

[56] *Thacker's Indian Directory 1918*.

[57] *Thacker's Indian Directory 1933*.

[58] Note by Rai Radha Charan Pal Bahadur and Raja Reshee Case Law, 22 January 1921.

[59] Unfortunately, we do not have an exact estimate of the social composition of these *bustee*s as the colonial bureaucracy did not leave behind any 'socio-economic surveys' of these settlements. As a genre of research, socio-economic surveys became ubiquitous in the post-colonial period, in the twin effects of democracy and development. The colonial administration never bothered to meticulously record

attests to a growing predominance of Hindus in the area, specifically wealthy Marwari traders. While existing tenants were driven out from these parts unceremoniously, monetary compensations were handed out to erstwhile property owners as consolation. The process of arriving at and disbursing the compensation amounts became yet another site of contestations between the state and its subjects.

Compensation and Rehousing

The Calcutta Improvement Act, 1911, provided a valuer (we met valuer Shrosbree in a previous section) to handle property prices and disputes. He recommended terms of compensation to the Trustees. Usually, compensation was at the current 'market rate' established through the local rental records,[60] especially when sale records were not robust. A solatium of 15 per cent was added to the market rate. However, the *bustee* owners did not receive a solatium as the land was deemed to be 'run down' and devoid of value in its current use. This clause in the compensation package worked against the interests of the Hindu Bengali landed elite of Calcutta, who owned several central Calcutta *bustee*s. However, it favoured the investors who bought these properties as real estate sites such as the Marwaris.

The property owners had the right to challenge the valuer's decision in a special three-member Tribunal constituted by the President (usually a city notable), an assessor from the Bengal government and an assessor from the Municipal Corporation. The Tribunal, however, consistently adjudged disputes in favour of the Trust, betraying the fact that it was intended to function as a vehicle to bulldoze any opposition to the Trust's decisions. Table 2.4 showing disputes adjudicated by the Trust between 1922 and 1928 makes this clear.

The compensation package devised for petty house owners was different than that for owners of *bustee* land. At the Board of Trustees meeting on 27

---

the non-ratepaying populations of the city unless they posed a threat to the safety and the security of the propertied classes.

[60] The Improvement Trust's land acquisition Collector, J. C. K. Peterson, defined the 'net rent' as the return from the capital invested in the property. How to calculate net rent? Peterson tells us 'if we can find the rate of interest which this rent represents, it is then possible to ascertain the amount of the capital invested, i.e., the total value of the property'. J. C. K. Peterson, *Report on Valuation of Properties in Scheme No. 1* (Soorti Bagan Improvement Scheme) of the Calcutta Improvement Trust, 1913, 2.

Table 2.4 Suits and tribunal decisions between 1922 and 1928

Year	Number of Suits Filed Against the Trust	The Tribunal Decisions
1922	Five suits filed in small claims court, seven ejectment suits in small claims court	All decided in favour of the Trust, except one ejectment, which remained pending
1924	Twelve suits in small claims court	All decided in favour of the Trust
1926	Twenty-four suits in small claims court	All decided in favour of the Trust
1928	Fourteen rent suits	All decided in favour of the Trust

Source: N. Ghosh, *A Hygienic City-Nation*, 87.

November 1917, Chairman Bompas discussed the possibility of awarding petty house owners a mixed compensation basket. This basket included an alternative housing arrangement in the suburbs. In that case though, the rest of the compensation would be monetary, but not exceeding '50 percent of the value of the property acquired'. For tenants on rental agreements with property owners, the payment could include the cost of relocating to another property in the same scheme area, close by, also acquired by the Trust.[61] But what kind of land was being transferred to the displaced petty property owner? Bompas considered this to be a matter of policy principle and opined:

> Clearly, no one would require residential property in the occupation of its owner B, in order to re-house the displaced person A. Setting this case aside, it is advisable that the Corporation or the other authority should have the power to acquire a tenanted house in order to give it to A? or would it be right to acquire a bustee and evict the tenants in order to give the land to A? In the two latter cases, if it is decided to acquire, the owner will often raise the objection that he intended to use the property hereafter for the residence of himself or of his near relations. The same objection will be raised if we take possession of garden lands in the suburbs.[62]

---

[61] Proceedings of the 297th Meeting of the Calcutta Improvement Trust, 8 July 1918, *Proceedings of the CIT for the Year 1918–19* (Valuation Department), 4.

[62] Ibid., 4–5.

According to Bompas, the land-acquiring public authority must judge 'how far it is right for such an authority to compel the owner of a building site to part with it to A rather than to a purchaser or a tenant of his own choice.' From his long experience in this business, Bompas asserted that the evicted owner often demanded his reinstatement in the immediate surroundings of his former dwelling. This would inevitably result in the dispossession of some other residents of the neighbourhood, belonging to a more 'inferior class'. On the other hand, he opined, if the owner wanted to claim a better living, he would accept land compensation in another scheme area or in the suburbs. Here the compensation money would buy him a larger plot. However, only one evicted owner accepted such a condition out of the hundreds of owners of the 20 acres of prime land acquired for the Central Avenue Scheme by 1918. This exposed Bompas' vision of better living for the evictees as a disingenuous idea.

Deliberations over acquired residential properties aside, Bompas was ultimately of the opinion that the central city lands ideally be used for commercial purposes instead of residential purposes:

> ... for instance, Improvement Scheme No. 1 [Soorti Bagan] was definitely undertaken to allow of the expansion of Burra Bazar. As the business quarter grows, it must displace the population which previously occupied the ground, and this will, in the long run, be for the welfare of the city as a whole.

Eventually, a committee was set up to recommend what needed to be done with displaced petty residential property owners of the Central Avenue Scheme. The committee urged that the displaced owners be rehoused within the scheme area to avoid public discontent. However, finding a rehousing site within the Central Avenue Scheme area was not easy. Two vacant plots had been marked out at 22 Chora Bagan Lane and a *bustee* at 22 Ashutosh Dey Lane and Trust members Kumar Nagendra Nath Mullick and Radha Charan Pal urged the acquisition of these plots for rehousing. Most committee members, however, rejected the motion on certain legal grounds. Moreover, the owners of these plots marked out for rehousing, quite understandably, wanted to hold on to their properties until after the Central Avenue Scheme was complete, so as to reap higher profits.[63]

Eventually, Bompas dismissed the possibility of rehousing tenants of the acquired properties in the same area. He argued that the overall improvement of the land due to its proximity with the Central Avenue would make the price of land in this locality several times higher than the 'existing street-less,

---

[63] I. Mitra, 'Towards a Rental Economy of the City', 6.

partitioned mesh of properties'. 'It is desirable', he said, 'that building of some size and dignity should front on such a road. It would have been ridiculous for Haussmann when he made the Boulevards of Paris to have allowed them to be lined with small cottages.'[64] 'The only way of re-housing in these cases at a fair expenditure', Bompas added, was to 'compel the people, however reluctant, to move into the suburbs where land is cheaper' than in the inner city.[65] However, such a vision of dispersal could not materialize in Calcutta in the first couple of decades of the twentieth century. Later in this chapter we will see why.

Table 2.5 illustrates the pattern of rehousing of a small section of displaced *bhadralok* small owners in 1921. These men were proprietors of old residential buildings of central Calcutta that were mired in multiple claims to ownership and tenancy. Out of the 136 properties notified for acquisition along the emerging Central Avenue, the table gives us an idea of just 61 (45 per cent) owners who moved out. This points towards an official tendency to under-report the impact of improvement on the people displaced in the first decade of the Trust's operations.

Table 2.5 shows that out of a total of 109 cases of rehousing, 61 cases (56 per cent) came from the Central Avenue area. Of these 61, 15 house owners (24.56 per cent) could find an alternative offer within the Central Avenue Scheme area itself. An overwhelming number of displaced owners (38, that is, 62 per cent) moved to what was then the emerging suburb of Bhowanipore further south. To encourage the affected owners of the Central Avenue Scheme to move to Bhowanipore, the Trust—in September 1918—announced a concession scheme that offered 'either 33.3 percent of the value of the new site or 50 percent of the value of the old site'.[66]

Nabaparna Ghosh mentions that the Trust made some attempts to rehouse evictees by transferring the acquired plots in the Central Avenue Scheme to private real estate agents, who built apartment houses, initially intended for rehousing the displaced owners. Subsequently, however, they sold the apartments in the open market. Private agents such as Mr A. Stephen and J. C. Galstaun built 'modern' flats to replace the old structures. The first set of such buildings came

---

[64] Note by Chairman (C. H. Bompas) of the Calcutta Improvement Trust on Re-Instatement in Scheme, No. VII, attached with the Proceedings of the 307th Meeting of the Calcutta Improvement Trust, 4 September 1918, *Proceedings of the CIT for the Year 1918–19* (Valuation Department).

[65] Ibid.

[66] Proceedings of the 307th Meeting of the Calcutta Improvement Trust, 4 September 1918, *Proceedings of the CIT for the Year 1918–19* (Valuation Department), 3.

Table 2.5 Resettlement of the displaced *bhadralok* owners from various scheme areas in central Calcutta

Scheme from which displaced	Number of cases	Scheme in which rehoused
I: Soorti Bagan	1	I: Soorti Bagan
I: Do	5	V: Bhowanipore Area
I.B.: Link Road between Chitpore Road and Central Avenue, Soorti Bagan	1	I.B.: Link Road between Chitpore Road and Central Avenue, Surtee Bagan
IC: Surtee Bagan area	1	IV A: Russa Road Extension
IV: Russa Road Widening	2	V: Bhowanipore Area
IV: Do	1	IV A: Russa Road Extension
IV A: Russa Road Extension	12	IV A: Do
IV A: Do	2	V: Bhowanipore Area
V: Bhowanipore Area	9	IV A: Russa Road Extension
V: Do	12	V: Bhowanipore Area
VII: Central Avenue (between Machooa Bazaar Street and Beadon Street)	2	IV A: Russa Road Extension
VII: Do	24	V: Bhowanipore Area
VII: Central Avenue (between Machooa Bazaar Street and Beadon Street	3	VII: Central Avenue (between Machooa Bazaar Street and Beadon Street
VII: Do	1	VII B: Central Avenue (between Colootola Street and Bowbazaar Street)
VII A: Central Avenue (Halliday Street Widening)	2	V: Bhowanipore Area
VII A: Do	3	VII B: Central Avenue (between Colootola Street and Bowbazaar Street)
VII B: Central Avenue (between Colootola Street and Bowbazaar Street)	3	V: Bhowanipore Area
VII B: Do	2	VII B: Central Avenue (between Colootola Street and Bowbazaar Street)

(Contd)

(Contd)

Scheme from which displaced	Number of cases	Scheme in which rehoused
VII C: Maniktola Spur	5	IV A: Russa Road Extension
VII C: Do	6	V: Bhowanipore Area
VII C. S. (Chitpore Spur)	1	XIII: Park Street Widening (between Chowringhee and Wellesley Street)
VII C. S. Do	4	VII C. S. (Chitpore Spur)
VII C. S. Do	2	VII B: Central Avenue (between Colootola Street and Bowbazaar Street)
VII C. S. Do	1	IA: Surtee Bagan
VII D: Central Avenue (between Bowbazaar Street and Princep Street)	1	V: Bhowanipore Area
VII: Central Avenue (between Machooa Bazaar Street and Beadon Street)	1	V: Bhowanipore Area
R. K. D. S. Square	1	IV A: Russa Road Extension
R. K. D. S. Square	1	V: Bhowanipore Area
	Total: 109	

Source: Annual Report on the Operation of the Calcutta Improvement Trust for the Year 1920–1921 (Calcutta: Calcutta Improvement Trust, 1921), 22.

Note: Scheme names corresponding to the numbers are not given in the original table.

up in Park Street. Several other up-scale residential buildings, such as the Cohen Mansion in Ripon Street and Eliot Mansion in Eliot Street, came into being subsequently. Another private builder, Chowringhee Commercial Properties Limited, developed a new apartment complex with the ground floor being leased to modern commercial showrooms. These flats were clearly meant for a class wealthier than that which had just lost their dwellings in central Calcutta.

The plots in the suburb of Bhowanipore—earmarked for the Central Avenue evictees—were converted into what Ghosh calls 'a paradise for wealthy Bengalis: flats, villas, and the small palaces....'[67] The Trust opened up new areas for housing in other suburbs as well and designated neighbourhoods not only along lines of class, but also of religion. Thus, a new suburb near Kalighat and Chetla

[67] N. Ghosh, *A Hygienic City-Nation*, 82.

was reserved for Hindu commercial groups. The Trust also sold plots south of Alipore and west of Diamond Harbour Road to wealthy merchants and landed aristocrats from various rural districts of Bengal.[68]

Finally, the rehousing scheme of the Trust for the 'workmen' and 'dis-housed' *bustee* dwellers, in the period under review, was effectively confined to merely three blocks of three-storeyed tenement buildings. Each building had 248 rooms and four shops, capable of housing just '1,260 adults in Karbala Tank area and Ward Institution Lane'.[69] Only one of the three blocks of buildings was earmarked for the Muslims. For long, these *chawls* remained vacant. The dis-housed slum dwellers refused to move far away from their places of work, and those who moved refused to be rehoused 'against gravitation'.

After a while, the Trust opened the scheme to other social classes to recover costs. Let us consider one such instance. The Trust received an application from one Nirmal Chandra Mitter, who was 'ready to offer Rs. 750 a month for the three blocks for a twenty-year lease'. Mitter wished to take the two upper floors of the three blocks for the occupation of middle-class Bengalis but *only* if a gate were put on the staircases. Having thus secured his genteel clientele, Mitter agreed to leave the Trust free to lease the ground floors to 'whomever they liked'.[70] The Trust's deliberations over this application reveals its appetite for profit-making, barely concealed by its grudging attempts at rehabilitation.

In 1920, the Trust accepted that the occupants of these *chawls* were not 'persons of the poorest class' and noticed a 'growing tendency for the buildings to become occupied by clerks and poor students whom the Trust's operations have not displaced'[71]—a trend that continues with lower income group (LIG) constructions in Indian metropolises until today. Soon after, it decided to use parts of the three buildings (Blocks A, B, and C) for commercial purposes. Thus, the Annual Report for 1920–1921 shows the 'conversion of two ground floor dwelling rooms in Block "A" into shops and another two rooms on the top flat into restaurants and also a third top flat room in Block "C" into a restaurant'.[72]

To summarize then, the Trust's compensation schemes were unsatisfactory for its recipients and its rehousing schemes were severely compromised by its eagerness for profits. The limited space it developed for rehousing purposes was

---

[68] Ibid.

[69] *Annual Report on the Operation of the Calcutta Improvement Trust for the Year 1919–1920* (Calcutta: Calcutta Improvement Trust, 1920), 15–16.

[70] Ibid., 16.

[71] Ibid., 16.

[72] Ibid., 16.

permitted to be sold in the open market for profits. The structures themselves were built to attract better-off classes of city dwellers, and, consequently, all of this led to a steady gentrification of central Calcutta that had previously housed eclectic neighbourhoods. The Trust's schemes left in their wake a string of discontented property owners. But even more significantly, they failed the displaced working-class tenants of *bustees* worst affected by the Central Avenue Scheme. These lapses, coupled with the economic distress of the War years, would have dire consequences for the housing situation in the city in the near future.

Rent and Riot

The War caused a staggering 300 per cent hike in defence expenditure that significantly strained the entire financial structure of the Indian Empire.[73] War expenditure and a protracted embargo on the circulation of goods and services for non-war purposes led to a severe increase in the prices of essential commodities both in wholesale and retail markets. Still, wholesale prices hiked to a lesser extent in Calcutta (increased by 68 per cent at the end of December 1917 from the pre-War period) as against other premier port cities of the subcontinent such as Bombay (109 per cent), Karachi (466 per cent), and Madras (111 per cent). For the same period, retail price inflation at the end of December 1917 was recorded as follows: Calcutta (21 per cent), Bombay (29 per cent), and Karachi (35 per cent).[74]

The absolute increase in commodity prices was coupled with a differential increase of prices across sectors and commodities. For instance, in the premier urban areas of the Empire, such as Calcutta and Bombay, the price spike in essential commodities corresponded with a 'rent storm' in the housing market. In Table 2.6, I reproduce the 'variations in house rents' in the premier port cities 'as compared with the pre-war year, 1913'.

---

[73] Sumit Sarkar, *Modern India, 1885–1947* (New Delhi: Macmillan, 1983).

[74] In Calcutta, at the end of December 1917, the wholesale price of salt rose 498 per cent, metals registered an increase of 188 per cent, cotton manufactures 112 per cent, raw cotton 149 per cent, sugar 88 per cent, kerosene oil 53 per cent, and coal registered a hike of 160 per cent. The general level of wholesale price in Calcutta at the end of December 1917 was 68 per cent higher than the pre-War period; by contrast it was 13 per cent in August 1915, 26 per cent in August 1916, and 42 per cent in August 1917. India Department of Statistics, *War Prices and House Rents* (Calcutta: Superintendent Government Printing, India, 1918).

Table 2.6 'War prices and house rents: statistics showing (1) wholesale and retail prices, and (2) house rents, at the end of December, 1917, as compared with the pre-War level (July, 1914), August, 1915, 1916, and 1917'

-------	1913 (pre-war year)	1914	1915	1916	1917
Karachi	100	114	135	140	141
Madras	100	111	113	113	122
Bombay	100	103	107	117	118
Calcutta	100	104	105	106	109

Source: India Department of Statistics, *War Prices and House Rents* (Calcutta: Superintendent Government Printing, India, 1918), 8.

Table 2.6 shows that until 1917 the increase in house rent in Calcutta was much less spectacular when compared with the situation in Karachi and Madras. However, we know that there was nearly a 38 per cent hike in house rents in certain parts of the city immediately after, that is, in 1918.[75] In 1920, the Maharajadhiraja of Burdwan, Bijoy Chand Mahatab, a premier landlord and rentier in central Calcutta, told the provincial legislature that Calcutta was really on the brink of a 'second Bolshevik Revolution' with rental values more than doubling within a year in several cases.[76] On average, the government acknowledged a 50 per cent hike in house rents in Calcutta and its suburbs between 1917 and 1920.[77]

On 30 September 1919, the provincial government of Bengal appointed a committee to gather evidence on the 'abnormal' rise in house rent and property prices in Calcutta. After considering evidence from different parts of the city, the

---

[75] It was estimated that there was a 38 per cent hike in house rent in 1918. India Department of Statistics, *War Prices and House Rents*, 3. Also see Debjani Bhattacharyya, 'Hoarding Land': Interwar Housing Speculation and Rent Profiteering in Colonial Calcutta', *Comparative Studies of South Asia, Africa and the Middle East* 36, no. 3 (2016): 465–482.

[76] The Speech of the Hon'ble Maharajadhiraja Bahadur of Burdwan at the Legislative Council, List of Business—Item No. 5, Legislative Business, The Calcutta Rent Bill, 1920, Proceedings of the Bengal Legislative Council on Wednesday, March 31, 1920, Government of Bengal, Legislative Department, *The Calcutta Gazette*, Part IV-A, pp. 248–54. The Maharaja was a premier landlord of Bengal whose family enjoyed rent-collecting rights in Posta Bazaar and the whole of the Tiretta Bazaar on the western margin of the fledging Central Avenue.

[77] Ibid.

committee recommended an emergency Rent Control Act to monitor and cap the exorbitant rent profiteering by landlords. The Rent Committee submitted its report to the government on 23 February 1920.[78] One of the contributing factors of the 'rent storm',[79] according to the Committee, was the slump in building operations during the five years of War (1914–1918). This was due to the rising cost of engineering materials, lime, and brick. Further, during the War years, the Trust demolished 643 masonry houses to dispose of 468 *bigha*s of land at a much higher price than the acquisition cost. In this process, it dis-housed more than 50,000 individuals from the scheme areas.[80]

The housing crisis was doubly precipitated by the influx of even more workers to the city, attracted by the war-induced commercial and industrial boom in the city. For instance, the jute industry expanded from 69 to 85 factories between 1914 and 1923, with a 36.8 per cent increase in the workforce in Calcutta and the adjacent industrialized municipalities.[81] Meanwhile, a large quantity of prime land within the limits of the Corporation area stayed out of the housing market, locked up in the enormous Presidency secretariat and other government and business headquarters.[82]

Predictably, available evidence on the 'rent storm' suggests that it hit the central and southern parts of the city more severely—places directly affected by the Trust's street schemes—than other areas of the city.[83] In 1920, the Rent

---

[78] Ibid.

[79] I found this term in the speech of the Maharajadhiraja of Burdwan and in the subsequent Legislative Assembly discussions.

[80] *Report of the Committee Appointed to Enquire into Land Values and Rents in Calcutta,* Supplement to the *Calcutta Gazette*, 25 February 1920. The passage of the Rent Acts in various cities during and following the War caused intense anxiety among the liberal policymakers of the time. Everywhere—from the metropolitan to the colonial cities—they emphasized that any prolongation of such legislation beyond the exceptional years of the War would mean the state's interference in the 'natural process' of the market, which, when left to its own devices, would permit the formation of 'normal prices'.

[81] Bhattacharyya, 'Hoarding Land'.

[82] *Report of the Committee Appointed to Enquire into Land Values and Rents in Calcutta* (1920).

[83] The Speech of Hon'ble Rai Radha Charan Pal Bahadur, at the Legislative Council, List of Business—Item No. 6 and 6 A, Legislative Business, The Calcutta Rent Bill, 1920, Proceedings of the Bengal Legislative Council on Wednesday, March 31, 1920, Government of Bengal, Legislative Department, *The Calcutta Gazette*, Part IV-A, pp. 254–255. Regarding the connection between the rent hike and the Trust's street schemes, see Note by Rai Radha Charan Pal Bahadur and Raja Reshee Case Law, 1921.

Committee had circulated about 1,000 forms asking landlords and tenants about the current rental situation in the city. In 1919–1920, the number of masonry houses in the city was 36,000 (occupied by owners, tenants, commercial establishments, and warehouses), but the Committee got back only around 260 filled-in forms.[84] It is interesting that these eager respondents[85] came mostly from the neighbourhoods of Central Avenue, Bowbazaar, and Park Street,[86] all areas affected by the work of the Improvement Trust. Illustrating the rent situation in more such Trust-Scheme areas, the Maharaja of Burdwan, in his 1920 speech, further noted:

> In Lower Circular Road, the rent of three rooms has been raised from Rs. 100 to Rs. 175; in Elliot Road, the rent of a house with seven rooms has been increased from Rs. 220 to Rs. 400; in Zakaria Street, the rent of one room was Rs. 18, it is now Rs. 35; in Boloram De Street Rs. 80 was demanded a house let for Rs. 40 in 1916, and the rents of many flats south of Park Street have been raised from Rs. 200 or about to Rs. 400.[87]

The 'rent storm' did not leave European tenants unaffected either. Along central streets such as Theatre Road and Camac Street, where most European shops and dwellings were located, rents increased threefold. In the winter of 1920, *The Statesman* reported that many city dwellers checked into hotels, finding the rates cheaper than those for apartment houses.[88]

The War was followed by a short yet intense boom period (1919–1922). The 'rent storm' in the city assumed the severest form precisely during this boom. At this time, a large price gap developed between raw jute and jute products in

---

[84] The Speech of Hon'ble Rai Radha Charan Pal Bahadur.

[85] Ibid.

[86] The vicinity of Park Street up to Lower Circular Road used to host a sizeable section of British officials and British commercial establishments. Many of the buildings in this area were owned by native landlords. As a result, the British voice within the Rent Committee tended to side with the tenants. In his speech at the Bengal Legislative Assembly, Rai Radha Charan Pal Bahadur pointed out how the composition of the Rent Committee was tilted overwhelmingly in favour of tenants. Also see Note by Rai Radha Charan Pal Bahadur and Raja Reshee Case Law, 1921.

[87] The Speech of the Hon'ble the Maharajadhiraja Bahadur of Burdwan, 250.

[88] N. Ghosh, *A Hygienic City-Nation*.

eastern India, which opened up possibilities for wealth accumulation through speculation in the jute trade. Taking advantage of the opportunity, some prominent Marwari traders such as Swarupchand Hukumchand and G. D. Birla switched enormous commercial resources to industrial capital and began the first Indian-owned jute mills near Calcutta.[89] Its overlap with the 'rent storm' strongly indicates a possible link between returns from industrial jute production and speculation in the land market.

The Annual Reports of the Improvement Trust for 1919 and 1920 give us a sense of the magnitude of the increase in land prices.

The short-lived boom—coupled with the absence of a proper banking network, and the loss of credibility of government bonds during the War—created a kind of competitive anxiety among those who had made quick money during the War years.[90] In search of a reliable investment destination, they identified the rent gap in the inner city caused by the aggressive improvement work of the Trust.[91] Consequently, they began to hoard land for the indefinite future, not to build on it but to trade in it. Trading seemed more profitable because building activities would have a protracted turnover period. This kept the land out of the rental market, worsening the housing crisis. The Census of 1931, for instance, recorded 16 residents per household in the city. By 1941

---

[89] S. Sarkar, *Modern India*.

[90] Amiya Bagchi calculates that if the year 1914 is taken as the base year (that is, 100) for investment and profit of corporations (largely British-owned) that were in operation in Bengal, then the figure increased 7.5 times in 1916 and then came down drastically to 4.9 times in 1917. Amiya K. Bagchi, *Private Investment in India, 1900–1939* (Cambridge: Cambridge University Press, 1972).

[91] Shabnum Tejani reports similar real estate trends in Bombay during the War years and the early interwar period. For example, the Registration Department's Annual Report for 1917–18 recorded an 'extraordinary rise' in the value of property in Bombay. Land registration in 1919 showed a 64 per cent rise in the property prices. One P. B. Joshi attributed the hike to the merchant class of the city comprised of the 'Bhoras, Bhatias, Marwaadis, and Banias'. They bought plots from the Trust and resold them. Those who bought plots from them also sold properties back. As a result, land kept circulating in the market without any use value, causing a house famine in Bombay. See Shabnum Tejani, 'Disputing "market value": The Bombay Improvement Trust and the Reshaping of a Speculative Land Market in Early Twentieth-century Bombay', *Urban History* 48, no. 3 (2021): 572–589. It emerges from some stray evidence that the Trust's employees in Calcutta were also involved in land speculation, sold lands in *benami* and through private treaties. N. Ghosh, *The Hygienic City-Nation*, 80–81.

Table 2.7 Increase in land prices per *cottah* between May–June 1919 and January 1920

Town-Improvement Scheme Number	Rate per Cottah of Land (In Indian Rupees) in May and June 1919	Rate per Cottah of Land (in Indian Rupees) in January 1920
IV	3,620	9050
VII B	2,023	5,800
V	1,683	4,000

Source: N. Ghosh, *A Hygienic City-Nation*, 82.

that average rose to 27.5 persons per household. After this, the 'house famine'[92] became an ingrained feature of Calcutta.

As we have already discussed, the officials of the Trust had anticipated a layered dispersal of the population from the central city with the unfolding of various street schemes. But, according to the 1911 Census, in the decade before the Trust was established, population from the central city areas was already moving towards suburban wards and municipalities. The census shows that all the suburban wards outside Circular Road and Sealdah Station experienced an influx of population. In Beniapukur and Ballygunge, the population surged by 53.5 per cent and 28 per cent, respectively, between 1901 and 1911. In fact, Entally, Beniapukur, and Tollygunge registered a steady female population growth by 2,000, 5,300, and 2,700 respectively, indicating that it was permanent households that were growing, rather than footloose migrants. Therefore, when the Trust began to integrate these suburbs with the city proper through an extensive road network, these areas were already in the throes of a land crisis.

The crisis in the suburbs was exacerbated not just by the Trust's activities but also by land acquisitions undertaken by various railway and tramway companies in Talla, Belgachia, Paikpara, Ultodingi, and Ballygunge. A comparison made during the War revealed that the average price of Calcutta's suburban lands was 20 times higher than that of London's. However, during the same time, the average land price of Calcutta's inner-city areas was two to four times cheaper than that in central London.[93] This evidence reinforces the fact that when the

[92] Note by Rai Radha Charan Pal Bahadur and Raja Reshee Case Law, 1921.

[93] An exchange between Bompas and C. F. Payne gives us such a picture of the land market in Calcutta and its suburbs. Bompas informed Payne that during the War, the Trust had to acquire land in Calcutta's suburbs for 5,000 pounds per acre in some schemes. In reply, Payne wrote,

Trust took over renewal in the inner city, land prices in the suburbs were already extremely high. This meant that the price gap between the centre of the city and its suburbs was considerably less than imagined. As a result, there was minimal scope for the 'graded dispersal of population' and decongestion of the inner city by the movement of displaced people to the suburbs. No such movement took place even after the Trust had developed better communication networks between the city and its suburbs. If anything, in these suburbs, the presence of the railway yard obstructed any seamless amalgamation. The Trust's vision of graded population dispersal had failed.

Furthermore, the Trust's operations caused enormous hardship for small property owners, small tenants, and the working-class population in the inner city, especially during the War and the interwar period. The exceptional rental situation became a pretext for municipal officials to throw out some of the thriving trading activities of this area to the margins of the city, further adding to people's hardships. The Colootola–Tiretta Bazaar area had been an important transit centre for India's thriving hide trade. Several hide warehouses were located along and between Phears Lane, Harinbari lane, and Canning Street (west). In 1914, when the Central Avenue project was kicked off, the Corporation mandated the 'removal from residential areas of tanneries, knacker's yards, and blood, offal and gut factories' into the 'outlying areas' east of the railway tracks of Sealdah.[94] In addition, the Corporation transferred a substantial 'Mohamedan slaughterhouse' on Halliday Street to the Tangra area in the same year. Such ejectments heavily impacted the working-class population associated with such trades, who belonged predominantly to Muslim, Anglo-Indian, and Chinese communities.[95]

> Suburban land round London, with a good road frontage, main drainage, and all modern conveniences, cost roughly from 5 to 7 Pounds per foot frontage, and in especially convenient areas like Wimbledon it cost 10 Pounds per foot frontage, and sometimes more. That was roughly equivalent to from 1000 to 1500 Pounds an acre, rising, perhaps, in certain cases, to 2000 Pounds.
>
> Payne was the Chairman of the Calcutta Corporation in the 1910s. Upon return to London, he became a surveyor in London. See Bompas, 'The Work of the Calcutta Improvement Trust'.

[94] *Report on the Municipal Administration of Calcutta for the Year 1914–15* (Calcutta: Corporation Press, 1915), 23.

[95] Ibid., 26.

According to the Census of 1921, between 1911 and 1921, at least 90,000 individuals were removed from various inner-city *bustees*. Most of the evictees from the *bustees* were Muslims.[96] As *Satyagrahi* remarked in 1926, '… by all virtue of the Improvement Trust Act the condition of Calcutta is, indeed being improved day by day, but the town is at the same time, being gradually destitute of Musalmans'.[97] In 1927, another report observed 'a growing tendency among the Mohamadan workmen to migrate from the central parts to the eastern and south-eastern wards such as 14, 15, 16 and 48, 49.'[98] This pattern of the violence of urban renewal deepened existing fault lines in the Hindu-Muslim relationship in a Hindu-majority capital (Calcutta) of a Muslim-majority province (Bengal). It translated into an intense communal polarization. The migrant workforce—already segmented along religious lines—competed amongst themselves, in the midst of an economic crisis, to secure access to the city. This rivalry reinforced their mutual bitterness.

Two significant riots broke out in Calcutta in 1918 and 1926. These two riots had the most devastating impact in central Calcutta localities bound by Beadon Street in the north, Bowbazaar street in the south, Strand Road in the west, and College Street in the east. This was the same area that was being renewed by the Improvement Trust. The spatial and temporal overlap between the operations of the Trust and the riots is no mere coincidence.

In his study of these riots, Suranjan Das mentions that working-class Muslims ('butchers, dressers, craters, coolies and millhands') specifically targeted Marwari properties in central Calcutta. They ransacked food and garment stores belonging to Marwari owners. They also fought bitterly with the up-country Hindu cobblers, newspaper vendors, *goala*s (milk suppliers), coachmen, and *darwan*s stationed at Marwari firms, who worked as the riot's foot soldiers. Very rarely did Muslim mobs attack Hindu Bengali *bhadralok* properties in the area during these early twentieth-century riots. In fact, occasionally, Hindu workers and *bustee* dwellers joined hands with Muslims in the loot of garment stores and crop warehouses, suggesting definite class animosity at the heart of the riot. A contemporary Intelligence Bureau report also suggested passive complicity between the Hindu Bengali rentier class and Muslims of central Calcutta in this riot, as both imagined themselves as losing the city to the Marwaris.[99] In the 1926

---

[96] *Census of India*, 1921, vol. VI (Parts I, II), para 8. Also see Suranjan Das, *Communalism in Bengal* (1993), 75.

[97] Cited in Das, *Communalism in Bengal*, 75.

[98] Ibid.

[99] Ibid.

riot, which involved more intense violence compared to the 1918 riot, several Muslim Peshawari traders controlling the fruit trade from central Calcutta (mainly from Machua Bazaar) suffered heavy casualties. This establishes, yet again, a Trust-Scheme affected area as the nerve centre of the conflict.

The immediate context for both the riots in central Calcutta was set by the progressive commodification of the inner-city land by the Improvement Trust. While commenting on the 1918 riot, a Home Department official wrote:

> The savagery shown towards Marwaris by Muhammadans in Calcutta gives reasons for thinking that to some extent the cause of disturbances was local. Mr. Banerjee told me yesterday that the quarter in which the worst disturbances occurred used to be occupied by Muhammadans; that the Calcutta Improvement Trust had in the course of its operation acquired a good deal of land in that quarter and had resold it to Marwaris for the purpose of building substantial houses and shops; that the Muhammadans resented their eviction very keenly and vented their wrath on the Marwaris.[100]

During the riot of 1926, the Marwaris were seen to be much more prepared to take on the Muslims. On 11 April 1926 in the middle of a devastating communal riot,[101] the Marwari residents of Burrabazaar installed several barricades at all the entry points to the market. In those days, Burrabazaar—a densely built-up market-cum-dwelling locality—was spread over about 2 square kilometres crisscrossed by smaller lanes.[102] The musclemen in the employ of the Marwaris released bales of piece goods and carts at the narrow entry points and placed men armed with brickbats on the roofs of two- and three-storeyed buildings. A group of Kabuli traders were trapped inside this virtually impenetrable neighbourhood. They were kept as 'hostages'.

Three days later, the riots receded temporarily. We do not know when the Burrabazaar impasse was resolved and whether the Kabulis returned home safely. But what we do know—from personal correspondence between Rai Ramdev Chokhani Bahadur, a notable member of the city's Marwari community, and Sir R. N. Mookerjee, a pioneering Bengali industrialist—is that soon after the riot, the Marwaris began to demarcate areas, plots, *bustees*, and houses scattered

---

[100] Home Department, Political Branch, November 1918, Nos. 164–201, Note by J. Hullah, 19.9.18, (NAI), 5.

[101] 'Riots, Calcutta', House of Commons Debate, 3 May 1926, vol. 195 cc2-3. See for instance the Report on the Calcutta Riots of April 1926, First Phase—2nd to 15th April, Home (Poll.) File No. 11/VIII (NAI).

[102] Birla, *Stages of Capital*.

across central Calcutta as 'their areas'. They developed a militia of about 500 armed men (comprised of *darwans* and *jamadars* of the Marwari firms) and a group of volunteers who would patrol the streets and lanes in Burrabazaar and the entire area falling between Vivekananda Road in the north and Colootola in the south every night between 9 p.m. and 8 a.m.[103] Each Marwari trader and resident was asked to pay for the upkeep of the militia, according to their capacity. They divided the area into 15 zones for effective monitoring.[104] The groups were empowered with bamboo sticks and battery-powered flashlights. They thus classified and assigned spaces and properties (both public and private) as 'their' areas, which was an *in rem* right over space—not for the contract-bound specified audience, but 'for the world at large'.[105] In the mediation of territory, private and public (such as the streets) properties came to be *collectivized* as 'our property' as opposed to 'their' property—a form of commons that breeds majoritarian tendencies.

Muslims paid more dearly than the Hindus for the events of 1918 and 1926. For instance, during the 1926 riot, there was a mass exodus, as hundreds of people from all classes began to desert their homes in the affected areas. The Hindus and Marwaris left temporarily to take refuge in their suburban garden houses. The Commissioner of Police reported, however, that 'many

[103] *Darwans* and *jamadars* were two unionized groups. They were under the influence of the Hindu Mahasabha leaders such as Madan Mohan Malaviya and B. S. Moonje. Home (Poll.) File No. 187/26, (NAI).

[104] I found the entire description in Ramdev Chokhani's personal letter to R. N. Mookerjee on 11 March 1927. The letter can be found in the Calcutta Improvement Trust's Record Room at Sir R. N. Mookerjee's File. Both Chokhani and Mookerjee were notable Trustees of the Improvement Trust. Mookerjee's file contains several private and official correspondences and unpublished notes and lectures of Mookerjee (between 1918 and 1929). The file contained no further details when I consulted it in 2014. It should be noted that I could not trace an alternative source to corroborate this description. The government files (mentioned in Chapters 2 and 3) contain no reference of the Burrabazaar barricade and the informal policing of central Calcutta by the Marwari Association. It is, however, clear from government files that the Marwari Association had been continually active in neighbourhood control in the early twentieth century. Such a reference can be found in Chapter 2. It is also clear from police reports that the up-country *goonda* elements played a significant role in skirmishes and loots during the riots. See, for instance, the Report on the Calcutta Riots of April 1926, First Phase—2nd to 15th April, Home (Poll.) File No. 11/VIII, NAI. Also see S. Das, *Communal Riots in Bengal*, 92–93.

[105] Blomley, 'The Territory of Property'.

Mahomedans ... have left the city with the intention of remaining absent for some considerable time and have returned to their original homes'.[106] He believed that the number of Muslims who had deserted the city could run into several thousands. They likely never returned, and those who returned found it challenging to get their jobs back.

The riot of 1926 was followed by a period of a mutual social boycott by the two communities. Once again, the Muslims were at a significant disadvantage as Hindus and Marwaris, with their enormous financial power, joined hands to replace Muslim labourers with up-country Hindus. In early April, 'the Marwaris convened a meeting, in the course of which it was decided that Muhammadan labour should henceforward be employed as little as possible'. However, this restriction could never assume a general form as the wage for a 'Mahomedan worker in Burra Bazaar', when sourced locally, 'was considerably less than that of an up-country man'.[107] Thus, even though the internal borders of the city were redrawn in the riot, they remained unstable and volatile even after the city returned to its regular rhythm. The Trust's improvement activities had very clearly introduced new strains of tension within the already fragile social fabric of the city, and it gave way, in places, with increasing frequency and tragic consequences, especially for the city's poor.

Conclusion

Motion and obstruction are the opposing forces that produce the city. The impetus towards motion usually comes from above, and the need for obstruction, from below (their reversal is also possible, when, for instance, the police places barricades to obstruct a crowd in motion). By executing an ambitious inner-city renewal mission, the colonial administration attempted to achieve the fantasy of motion in the city. Two street schemes—Harrison Road and Central Avenue—were executed between the 1880s and the 1920s to ease movement through the so-called congested life-world of its colonized subjects. This official fantasy of seamless mobility visualized multiple flows that would set each other off. The expectation was that the building of a road would set off the commodification of land, commodification would enable the circulation of property in the market, a regime of property would create a vibrant rental economy, a competitive rental economy would gentrify the city's centre and push away the city's working classes to its margins.

---

[106] 'The Calcutta Riots', Extracts from the 'Report of the Commissioner of Police on the Calcutta Riots from the 2 to 15 April 1926', in *India in Home Polity, January–June 1926*, vol. I (Calcutta: The Annual Register Office, 1926), 81.

[107] Ibid.

But, as we have seen, it was ultimately a fantasy whose realization was stubbornly obstructed by ground realities. Recoupment was obstructed by public opinion and the 'graded dispersal of population' was obstructed by unexpectedly high property prices in the suburbs. Nonetheless, fantasies create their own realities. The city witnessed the devastating consequences that the Trust's initiatives had for thousands of ordinary city dwellers, mostly poor Muslims, as they were displaced from their homes, neighbourhoods, and places of work by wealthier residents of the city—in this case, Marwari business owners. Finally, its inequalities reinforced by the process of urban renewal worsened communal fault lines and created both the conditions and the occasion for violent communal conflict.

The forces of urban renewal and communal polarization have often constituted each other. Just as this chapter dealt with the ways in which street-building intensified communal animosity, the next chapter will elaborate on the ways in which the streets were, in turn, redrawn by communal violence. However, it should be pointed out that the co-constitution of these two forces does not mean that they shared a relationship of causality, that is, communal mobilization as the outcome of urban planning and vice versa. Nor do they have a continuous history of co-evolution. The experience of communal violence was diverse across neighbourhoods, and not every area touched by communal violence was rebuilt and re-planned by the Improvement Trust. But, in demonstrating the deep links between city planning and violent crowd action, I try to draw attention to the structural relationship that exists between the violent and the rational in the production of the urban. Moments of extraordinary violence illuminate this underlying unity.

3

City as Territory

Institutionalizing Majoritarianism

Throughout its colonial history, Calcutta had been a Hindu-majority city in the heart of a Muslim-majority province. Until the mid-twentieth century, despite bitter rivalry, the city's Hindu and Muslim populations inhabited shared spaces, even in areas populated chiefly by members of one community. In such localities, there were scattered pockets where people of the other community resided, creating a complex inter-communal sharing of neighbourhoods, infrastructures, and resources. Ghettos did not manifest to the extent they do today. However, the city's character began to transform slowly in the interwar decades due to the twin effects of urban renewal and communal mobilization, culminating in an utter territorial defeat of Muslims in the mid-twentieth century. One of the outcomes of this was ghetto formation in the city's margins. While ghettoization is a violent process, ghettos are also kept in place through violence.

This chapter looks at how the police as an apparatus of public order 'read' the city as a communally divided territory in moments of civil unrest. It also demonstrates how the cop–mob dialectic redrew, reinforced, and refunctioned the internal boundaries of the city. In this negotiation between the police and the mob, the street emerged both as a territory and as a zoning device. At the same time, the street (and the spatial order of the city) also shaped the tactics and the outcome of this urban warfare. In this light, I examine the police evidence of a series of communal occurrences spanning the first half of the twentieth century—including a communal civil war in 1946. In doing so, I track social infrastructures that developed around these riots and various forms of mass politics that further enforced the territorial reordering of Calcutta in the first half of the century. Finally, the chapter analyses the implications of these zoning exercises for the emergence of an internally segregated city in the post-colonial period. The discussion that follows examines the street and the ghetto as two distinct configurations of territory that frame the spatial reconfigurations of this period.

The Mob–Cop Dialectic

As discussed in Chapter 2, one of the areas affected by the Harrison Road Scheme, roughly bound by Cotton Street in the north, Canning Street in the south, Halliday Street in the east, and Brabourne Road in the west, became the nerve centre of the 1910 Bakr-Id riot. Hostilities began on 9 December 1910, around 5 p.m. Anticipating trouble, most shop owners and showrooms on Harrison Road shut business rather early. Only a few 'Mahomedan fruit and pipe shops' were open around Cross Street and Cotton Street. The Kabulis had already lost the workday as Marwari wholesalers had refused to open their shops at all on 9 December. They were idly squatting on the 'ledges of the closed shops', even as a large group of Marwaris gathered with their *darwans* 'on the pavements and about the corners of the roads, especially at Mullick Street corner'. The police patrol was unsuccessfully trying to persuade this potential 'mob' to disperse. As business in the Burrabazaar was shut, 'they had nowhere to go and nothing to do'.[1]

The Sub-inspector in charge of the police patrol was in Cotton Street when he heard about a fight in Harrison Road. He rushed to the spot and found that the Kabulis had been pelted with 'bricks and half-bricks from roofs and verandas of the Marwari houses' abutting Harrison Road. The news reached the Police Commissioner at Lalbazaar Head Quarters at 7 p.m. F. L. Halliday, the Commissioner, immediately rushed to the spot.

> When I arrived, I found an excited crowd of Mahomedans, and proceeding to Mullick Street saw that the Mahomedan shops which were left open had been looted and bricks were being thrown from the houses along Harrison Road, the Verandahs and roofs of which were crowded with Marwaris and their Hindu followers. The Mahomedans were picking up the bricks and throwing them back….[2]

Due to the protection offered by masonry buildings and elevation, the Marwaris had an advantage in this skirmish. Halliday found that the *darwans* and some 'Hindu *goondas*', on the instruction of their Marwari masters, had started the battle. Further investigations revealed that the rooftops of all the Marwari houses

---

[1] File No. 290. Serial Nos. 1–3, GoB, Police Department, 1910, Disturbances in Calcutta in Connection with the Bakr-Id festival, 1910, Letter No. 15992, dated the 17th December 1910, from the Commissioner of Police, Calcutta, submitting a report on the above subject (WBSA).

[2] Ibid.

had been well stocked with brickbats, stones, and sticks for days in advance. By the time Halliday started his investigation, he had some 200 armed constables with him. As the skirmish receded, he secured the area by disaggregating it into zones. Halliday, for instance, divided the stretch of Harrison Road, between College Street and the approach of Howrah Bridge, into six zones. Each zone had to be policed and brought under control. To do this, he 'established a patrol system under European sergeants—two sergeants and twelve men to each section remained on duty till midnight'. Halliday relied heavily on European officers and sergeants, whose presence in the conflict zone, it was believed, 'made a difference'.[3] Safe zones and secured corridors were needed so that trade and commerce could commence once again.[4]

On the morning of 10 December, by 7 a.m., Halliday had already received news of fresh disturbance in the area. Early in the morning, a handful of Muslim traders had gone to check their shops. A 'roving band of up-country darwans' had attacked them and some other stray Muslim pedestrians by stabbing them from behind. Some other Kabulis, who had barely woken up, had rushed to the spot, only to be welcomed by more brickbats from the 'Marwari houses'. Within a few moments, a severe riot was in progress.

Halliday commanded 28 European sergeants and 50 armed constables and mounted police 'to turn out at once'. He also sent an urgent message to the Duff College building, where a force was kept on reserve. As he reached the crossing of Chitpore and Harrison Roads, Halliday found about 120 policemen

---

[3] Ibid.

[4] In subsequent decades, this scheme earned a name: 'Harrison Road Protection Scheme'. *Proceedings of the Calcutta Disturbances Commission*, Monday, 20 January 1947 (Calcutta, Superintendent, Government Printing, Bengal). As we know, one of the central functions of the police as an 'institution of market' was to regulate and facilitate 'exchange, circulation, manufacture and marketing of goods and services'. Foucault, *Security, Territory, Population*, 437–438. In his *Lectures on Justice, Police, Revenue, and Arms*, Adam Smith assigns three functions to the police: cleanliness, security, and cheapness and plenty (that is, price control). In this remarkable lecture, Smith traced the word's origin to the Greek *polis*, which meant 'the policy of civic government'. He thus retains 'police' in the same lexical field with *polis* and policy. For an illuminating discussion on Smith's understanding of the police, see Peter Linebaugh, 'Police and the Wealth of Nations: Déjà Vu or Unfinished Business?', *Counter Punch*, 3 July 2020: https://www.counterpunch.org/2020/07/03/police-the-wealth-of-nations-deja-vu-or-unfinished-business/, accessed 21 September 2020.

from various local *thana*s caught between huge 'crowds of Hindus to the west and Mahomedans to the east of the road'. Showers of bricks were flying in all directions. Amidst the confusion, a Muslim pedestrian—'evidently a passenger from Howrah who came along by chance'—was stabbed before Halliday's own eyes 'by Hindu goondas'. They emerged 'from a side street' and escaped into it again before anything could be done. The mounted men, who had proved to be excellent in quarantining a crowd in the main street just the other day, could do nothing due to the width of lanes and spaces between buildings, 'where those goondas vanished'.[5]

Within half an hour, Superintendent Cregan brought reinforcements from the northern division. Halliday finally formed a further force of 100 armed policemen and about 400 constables 'beside the mounted sowars and European sergeants'. More contingents kept coming from all over Calcutta 'till five hundred constables with their officers were in the affected quarter'. Halliday then formed a cordon across 'Harrison Road and placed groups of police along Chitpore Road to the south and at the head of Mechua Bazaar, while superintendent Cregan was holding Upper Chitpore Road, Burtolla Street and all the streets to the north'. Halliday anticipated that the Hindus to the north of Harrison Road and the Muslims from their stronghold in Machua Bazaar to the south could 'invade each other's quarters'. In fact, many such attempts were made. However, Cregan held the police's north–south 'demarcation by chasing the most determined rioters and effecting some arrests'.

Harrison Road itself was also found to be a site of territorial warfare between Hindus and Muslims armed with 'sticks, pieces of iron and any other weapon they could seize'. Halliday expected that a 'big racial riot' would occur, 'which was likely to spread through the quarter and even the rest of Calcutta'. Failing to 'disperse the rival factions or even continue to hold them apart', Halliday rushed to Fort William to solicit military assistance, leaving Deputy Commissioner Tegart in charge. By 10:30 a.m., 'two hundred men of the Rifle Brigade under the command of Major Harman arrived'. Within an hour or so, 56 soldiers joined them under the command of Captain Purvis. This military deployment

---

[5] File No. 290. Serial Nos. 1–3, GoB, Police Department, 1910, Disturbances in Calcutta in Connection with the Bakr-Id festival, 1910, Letter No. 15992, dated the 17th December 1910, from the Commissioner of Police, Calcutta, submitting a report on the above subject (WBSA).

finally made the 'rescue' of Harrison Road possible. The mobs dispersed to the side streets.[6]

Soon after, the Kabulis attacked Panna Lal's mansion in Machua Bazaar. Panna Lal was a prominent Marwari wholesaler of piece goods. His was an 'isolated Marwari house' in that quarter, otherwise dominated by Muslims. Despite brickbats showering from the rooftop, the Kabulis managed to break open the gates and loot the house. Halliday rushed to the spot with a squadron of Sikh Cavalry. However, before they 'could surround the place, all the Kabulis, who had been gradually making off since the Police arrived, made good their escape over some partly finished buildings at the back'. Only two looters were caught inside the house. The brawl subsided by late afternoon, after a trip by the Lieutenant Governor to the affected quarters.[7]

The early twentieth century was marked by numerous such incidents of isolated and sporadic mob action, described as riots. It is evident from police reports that the spatial and architectural order of the city shaped the course of the action during such riots. Thus, in a report on the 1926 riot, Officiating Police Commissioner J. E. Armstrong wrote: 'These actions subsided as suddenly as they arose. The particular feature of this warfare which was most difficult to control was the stabbing of individuals by small roving bands … who pounced on their victims without the slightest warning and vanished in a moment.' These groups would be provided 'excellent cover by the labyrinths of small lanes and gulleys'.[8] The assailants would immediately find shelter 'amongst their coreligionists', which made it impossible for 'a patrol arriving even within a few moments of the occurrence to ascertain whether they had gone or to obtain the slightest clue to their identity'.[9] In most of the cases, the Commissioner reasoned that firing would have caused enormous civilian casualties. He also wrote that deploying large, armoured vehicles did not work beyond the sprawling main streets. 'Chasing the goondas with any vehicles is difficult', wrote Armstrong, 'because of the unexpected obstruction of walls and buildings.' 'Moreover,' he wrote, 'chasing in horseback, cycle or motorcycle means that one hand is engaged.' Armstrong felt that *goondas* could easily confuse the constable by

[6] Ibid.

[7] Ibid.

[8] J. E. Armstrong, ESQ. OBE, Commissioner of Police (offg.), Report on the Communal Riots of July 1926: 14 to 25 July 1926 (Calcutta: Bengal Government Press, 1926), L/PJ/6/1921, The British Library, London.

[9] Ibid.

twisting his movement at the turn of an alley or a lane: 'His superior knowledge of the locality makes him invincible.' In such a context, wrote Armstrong, 'the most that could possibly be done was to keep flying patrols continuously operating in the affected area and to search for bad characters and lethal weapons in the gulleys down which the assailants had disappeared'. While the police patrols were busy suppressing more spectacular battles on the major streets, these 'breakaway elements' held sway over the lanes and by-lanes of the city. Armstrong observed that 'the "goonda" element of the population participated freely in the rioting, and the fact that all the available Police were fully occupied in the suppression of open rioting and other acts of violence made it difficult to deal with them effectively'.[10] The easy dispersal of mobs was a repetitive feature of riot-policing in early-twentieth-century Calcutta. Ironically, it betrayed an underlying, more organized warfare involving localized, targeted, and precise attacks on the communal rival.

The colonial state—in the long run—addressed these riots in two ways. Its first intervention was legal. To control the up-country workers who acted as the foot soldiers in the early-twentieth-century riots, the colonial government passed two crucial laws between 1923 and 1926. The 'Bengal Act I of 1923', popularly known as the 'Goonda Act', empowered the Calcutta Police to book criminal elements in apprehension of a disturbance. In 1926, another new Bill titled 'The Presidency Area (Emergency) Security Bill, 1926' became the Bengal Act III of 1926.[11] It supplemented the usual criminal laws by vesting exceptional powers in the police and the local government on the pretext of protecting life and property in the 'Presidency Area' in times of 'emergency'.[12] The Detective Department was empowered to directly collect information on attempts to subvert the 'tranquillity' of the city, over and above the local *thanas*. The Act also empowered the Police Commissioner of Calcutta and District Magistrate of the 24 Parganas to expel suspects from the 'Presidency Area' for three months, even if the said persons did not have a past criminal record with the police.[13] The Government Member of the Bengal Council mentioned that often the *goonda* gang leaders were 'persons of standing' in the city, coming

---

[10] Ibid.

[11] Ibid.

[12] Henry Moncrieff-Smith, 'British Empire: British India', *Journal of Comparative Legislation and International Law* 10, no. 3 (1928): 141–149.

[13] Ibid.

from respectable families. The Act would enable the police to round up such people based on intelligence inputs about them.[14]

These colonial-era Acts were premised upon a racialized understanding of 'bad characters' who allegedly indulged in crime and public disorder. Urban riots, however, repeatedly transgressed racial stereotypes. Consider the instance of a riot that engulfed northern Calcutta in October 1907. The cops on duty reported that *dhangars*, up-country carters, and other 'menial municipal workers' participated in rioting and looting.[15] However, as darkness advanced, the class distinction between the 'bhadralok type' and the 'lower-class type' broke down. The Officiating Chief Secretary of Bengal, Edward Gait, found it very disturbing that some Bengali *bhadralok*, too, participated in shop-looting with the *goondas* of the affected areas.[16] What is more, the up-country *goondas* appeared to have merged with up-country constables, and together they looted shops.[17]

The second intervention was to undertake an authoritative change in the city's built form. This was necessary because in these early-twentieth-century riots, the spatial layout of the city enabled particular kinds of evasive crowd action. We find that during a riot, shop-looting would start around dusk. The rioters would in fact put out street lamps to enforce darkness. Moreover, they had better knowledge of the buildings, spaces between them, neighbourhoods, and alleyways than the police. Using this knowhow, the crowd assembled in main streets would disperse 'at every point on the arrival of the police and flee into lanes and gullies, and owing to the darkness of the night, no arrests could be

---

[14] Ibid.

[15] The British officials all over India had a certain entrenched idea about the civic working class. During the plague crisis in Bombay in 1897, Municipal Commissioner P. C. H. Snow wrote: 'Scattered as they are through every portion of the city in large numbers, any unrest or tendency to strike among them immediately affects other numerous low-caste natives, and any development of panic or alarm straightaway spreads to their immediate surroundings.' Snow, however, did not forget to mention the critical role that these municipal workers played in the operation of the city: 'On their presence or absence ... depends the safety or ruin of this vast and important city', and that without them, 'Bombay would be converted into a vast dunghill of putrescent ordure'. Arnold, 'The Subaltern Streets', 46.

[16] Report of the Chief Secretary, Bengal to the Secretary, Government of India, Home Department, File (Poll), D/19/8 of 1907 (WBSA).

[17] Ibid.

made ... those throwing stones from the house also escaping from back exits'.[18] Such frustrations were frequently expressed by officers being interrogated after a riot. Evidently, during riots, the city appeared spatially illegible, sometimes even to the native policemen who had worked for years in nearby police stations.

Thus, the early-twentieth-century riots exposed the beleaguered state of colonial authority enforcing order in the urban landscape. For instance, in the riot of October 1907, the crowd that formed on the streets dissolved the line between the criminal and non-criminal populations. Suddenly, in the darkness of those October nights, the whole subject population appeared delinquent to the official gaze. The city virtually passed into the hands of the mob. To the senior bureaucrats of the British Empire, it was an unmistakable sign of the collapse of normal government and a breakdown of the police as a disciplined and disciplinary force. Moreover, the communication hierarchy of the police force would often crumble as the riots progressed.

Historian Swati Chattopadhyay compares New Delhi and Calcutta in terms of spatial legibility to give us a significant contrast.[19] 'If New Delhi produced a clear description of the imperial state in the 20th century, making it visually explicit, Calcutta defied this form of legibility.'[20] This is why, she argues, the shift of capital in 1911 should be read as a 'significant spatio-political gesture'

---

[18] Suranjan Das, 'The Calcutta Riots of 1907: An Investigation into Crowd Behaviour', *Proceedings of the Indian History Congress* 40 (1979): 587–603, see 592.

[19] Swati Chattopadhyay, 'Cities of Power and Protest: Spatial Legibility and the Colonial State in Early Twentieth-Century India', *International Journal of Urban Sciences* 19, no.1 (2015): 40–52. In May 1907, the *Sandhya* carried a series of recommendations for every nationalist householder of the city. Some of them were as follows: 'rooftops of each shop and house be stocked with bricks, bombs and other instruments of offence, and houses and shops be converted into small fortresses', 'let no one stir out of home without *lathis* or small weapons'. Another piece in the same periodical declared the arrival of a new light bomb, 'that must be kept in every house' (Chattopadhyay, 'Cities of Power and Protest', 50). Coupled with Hindu religious sentiment, the *paras* were increasingly becoming sites of nationalist territorial assertion around *chandimandaps*, *kalibaris*, clubs, libraries, and playgrounds. In Muslim-dominated neighbourhoods, mosques became the principal sites of communal and political mobilization. No wonder that several of the Improvement Trust schemes in the next decade were run through these neighbourhoods to render them legible and governable.

[20] Chattopadhyay, 'Cities of Power and Protest', 40.

on the part of the colonial state in imagining a 'new relationship between state, city and politics'.[21]

As we have previously noticed, the Improvement Trust's spatial mobilization in the interwar years was directed to produce a more legible urbanscape in central and northern Calcutta. The new public spaces that came into existence as a result were the sites of a new articulation of communal territorial warfare just before India won independence.

An Urban Civil War

Nearly two decades after the intermittent rioting of the early twentieth century, recounted in the previous section, the city witnessed its next major escalation of communal tension in August 1946, exactly a year before India and Pakistan attained freedom. The riot of 1946 exceeded its predecessors in all aspects. In the third week of August 1946, the violence left about 15,000 dead, 100,000 injured, and 2,000,000 individuals homeless. The official estimate was, of course, much more conservative.[22]

A Calcutta Disturbances Commission of Enquiry was set up to look into the riots of 1946. One of the first things that the Commission did was to prepare a clear map demarcating 'predominantly Hindu localities, predominantly Moslem localities ... the border of the No-Man's land ... mixed localities ... aristocratic Moslem localities such as Park Circus ... four prominent bustees' in Kalabagan,

---

[21] Chattopadhyaya also points out for Calcutta that the nationalist movement in the Swadeshi era, on the other hand, 'inaugurated a new way of thinking the city as a political space'. Ibid., 42.

[22] The Riot of 1946 has been a well-researched topic. For a general understanding of the sequence of events before, during, and after the riot, see S. Das, *Communal Riots in Bengal*; Joya Chatterji, *Bengal Divided: Hindu Communalism and Partition, 1932-1947* (Cambridge: Cambridge University Press, 1995); Claude Markovits, 'The Calcutta Riots of 1946', *Online Encyclopaedia of Mass Violence*, 5 November 2007: http://www.sciencespo.fr/ceri/en/ouvrage/oemv, accessed 15 June 2021; J. Mukherjee, *Hungry Bengal*; Nariaki Nakazato, 'The Role of Colonial Administration, "Riot Systems" and Local Networks during the Calcutta Disturbances of August 1946', in *Calcutta: The Stormy Decades*, ed. Tanika Sarkar and Sekhar Bandyopadhyay (London: Routledge, 2015), 267-319; Samaddar, 'Policing a Riot-Torn City'. For testimonies and oral history accounts, see Debjani Sengupta, 'A City Feeding on Itself: Testimonies and Histories of "Direct Action" Day', in *Sarai Reader 06: Turbulence*, ed. Monica Naurala (New Delhi: CSDS, 2006), 288-295.

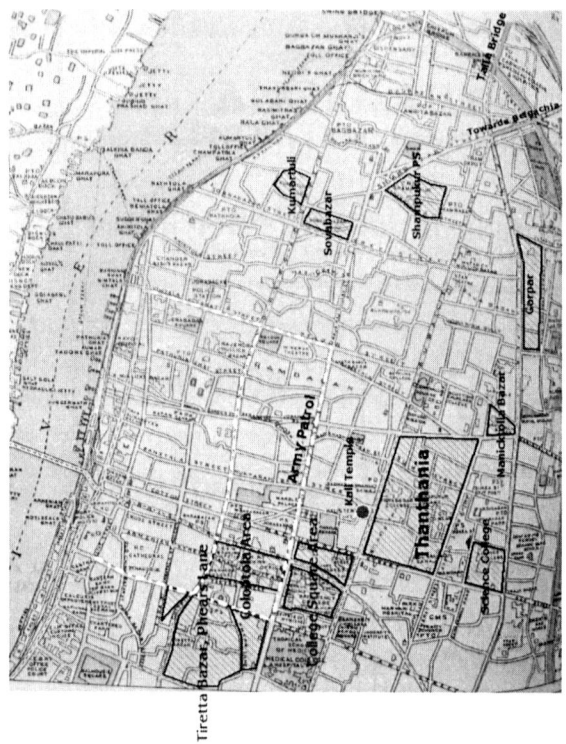

Map 3.1 1946 Riot Map-1: 'North Calcutta'

Source: Extracted from *Thacker's Indian Directory 1945: Embracing the Whole of the Indian Empire* (Calcutta: Thacker, Spink & Co., 1946).

Mehdibagan, Rajabajar, and Watganj' (Maps 3.1–3.3).[23] The Advocate General of Bengal was entrusted with the responsibility to come up with such a map, to make the Commission's task of fact-finding easier. Witnesses appearing before the Commission were asked to describe and mark their activities during the days of the riot on the map.

N. H. Khundkar was the Officer-in-Charge of the Burtolla Police Station (the outlined box in Map 3.1).[24] Khundkar gave a 5.5-page affidavit detailing his activities on the first two days of the riot—16th and 17th. He answered as

---

[23] Ranabir Samaddar, *Ideas and Frameworks of Governing India* (New York and London: Routledge, 2016), 16.

[24] Calcutta Disturbances Commission of Enquiry, Proceedings from Friday, the 14 February 1947, P. W. 13, Interrogation of Mr N. H. Khundkar, Officer-in-Charge, Burtolla Police Station, 5–46, 17 February 1947, 47–84, 18 February 1947, 85–104.

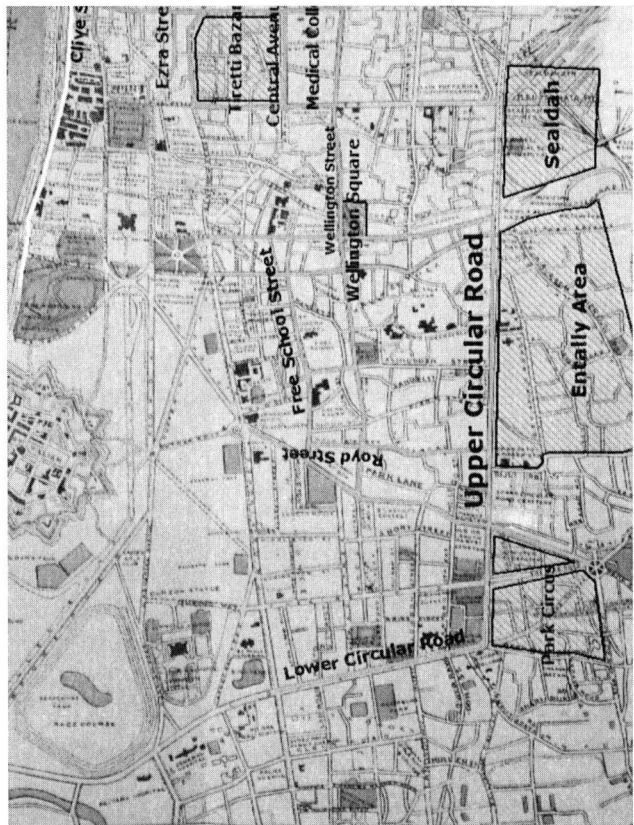

Map 3.2 1946 Riot Map-2: 'Central Calcutta'

Source: Extracted from *Thacker's Indian Directory 1945*.

many as 1,706 queries on the first day of his interrogation, making it one of the most extended interrogation sessions. What emerges from his deposition is a complex sociology of the civil war that calls into question existing paradigms of comprehending crowd action. It appears that Khundkar was operating from an epistemic space that was mutually incommensurable with that of the counsels. They 'cut the world differently' to comprehend the civil war. Khundkar's 'thick description', illustrated in the following paragraphs, frustrated the Commissioners. In the end there was a *crisis of comprehensibility*—as the Commission's failure to uphold the 'regime of truth' became apparent.

According to Khundkar's written statement, the Assistant Commissioner (his boss) of the 'North Town' jurisdiction telephoned Khundkar, at 7:30 a.m. on

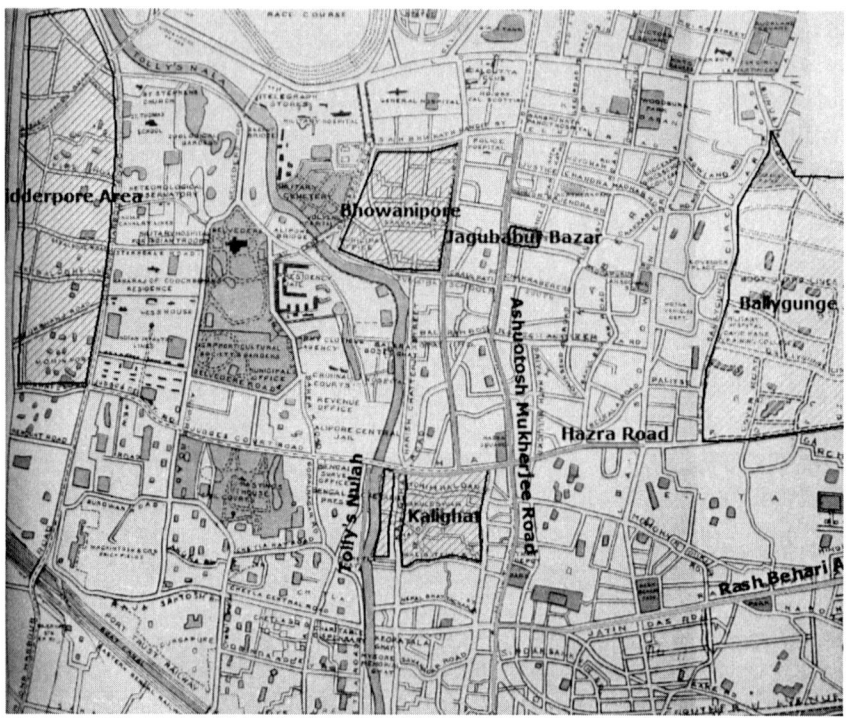

Map 3.3 1946 Riot Map-3: 'South Calcutta'

Source: Extracted from *Thacker's Indian Directory 1945*.

16 August 1946. He asked Khundkar to proceed to the junction of Beadon Street and Upper Circular Road without delay. A riot between Hindus and Muslims had been going on there for a while. Khundkar rushed to the spot with two lorries and six armed men. He found a 'very big crowd' of Hindus on Beadon Street in the west and another crowd of Muslims 'of similar dimension' (note the measurement Khundkar was giving: 'very big'/'similar dimension') at the 'east end of Beadon Street'. The police managed to persuade both parties to return.

Then, at 8:45 a.m. Khundkar met the Assistant Commissioner and the Deputy Commissioner (North) on 'Vivekananda Road, east of its crossing with Upper Circular Road', where a fight appeared to be imminent. On the Deputy Commissioner's orders, he dispersed the crowd formation once. But when he returned to report, yet again 'a crowd of Muslims from the east advanced up to the crossing' and a 'Hindu mob' from the opposite direction 'marched forward'. Before they could interface, the police 'drove them away'. Soon after, the Muslim crowd gathered further east along Vivekananda Road, only to be confronted by a crowd of Hindus that suddenly emerged from a street. This time both the parties began to 'swell to such a dimension' that Khundkar found it difficult to disperse them with the small force at his disposal. So the Assistant Commissioner formed two groups and with Khundkar approached the crowds from the northern and the southern ends. Around 9:30 a.m., when Khundkar returned to the same Beadon Street and Upper Circular Road junction where he had started from, he found that more trouble had broken out at the junction of Kerbala Tank Lane and Upper Chitpore Road.[25]

His description of events became thicker as the day proceeded. At 3:20 p.m., Khundkar had to rush to a 'Muslim bustee at 76/1 Cornwallis Street, south of Rambagan Theatre'. Once there, Khundkar, Sub-inspector Zaman, and a few armed men found that the *bustee* had been surrounded by a Hindu crowd advancing from Cornwallis Street and Sahitya Parishad Street. The crowd had already begun to set fire to some eating places and was approaching the *bustee* aggressively to set fire to it next. With much difficulty, Khundkar pacified the mob. Then he posted two pickets at Sahitya Parishad Street and Cornwallis Street and hurriedly returned to the *thana*.

As he reached there, he heard that a mob had attempted to break open a house at 32/2 Beadon Street. He had also noticed a crowd forming near the *bustee* at 76/1 Cornwallis Street on his way back to the *thana*. As evening approached, Khundkar rescued the Muslims trapped in the *bustee*. At about 4:30 p.m., Khundkar rescued another 500 Muslims from the adjacent Ram Chand Ghosh Lane, where a locality was being raided by a 'big Hindu mob'. The mosque was irreparably damaged, and 'about 12 or 13 dead bodies were found lying inside it, and four dead bodies were found lying on the lane and two very severely injured persons too were lying on the lane'. All these bodies were 'Muslim looking'. Hundreds of Muslims continued to remain trapped in the lane. Khundkar's team rescued another 100 Muslims from the lane and drove them back to the *thana*. On hearing the lorry engine, 1,000 'low-class Hindus armed with daggers, knives and lathis' chased the rescue party. Khundkar ordered several rounds of firing. He then proceeded with the rescued on foot (with the injured ones in the lorry) along Beadon Street 'from a distance up to Chattoo Babu Bazar'. On the way, they rescued many more Kabulis and Bengali

---

[25] Calcutta Disturbances Commission of Enquiry, Proceedings from Friday, the 14 February 1947, P. W. 13, Interrogation of Mr N. H. Khundkar, Officer-in-Charge, Burtolla Police Station, 5–46, Exhibit P.

Muslims. When Khundkar reached the *thana*, he found about 5,000 Muslim evacuees squatting in the premises. A small gang of 12 Hindu evacuees from Nandan Bagan *bustee* also joined them.[26]

Let us get a sense of the population in the jurisdiction of Burtolla Thana. Question numbers 106 to 118 dealt with this subject:

> Q. 106 (B. A. Siddiky): 'If you can, will you give us the population within your jurisdiction?'
> Witness: 'According to the Census of 1937, the population was 67 thousand and odd.'
> Q. 107 (Siddiky): 'You mean 1941 census?'
> Witness: 'No, 1937.'
> Q. 108: 'That is the Police census you say of?'
> Witness: 'That was a census we obtained the results from the Commercial Museum of the Calcutta Corporation. Then after that, another Census was held in 1942 and the population at present, and we can safely say, has increased by 33 per cent.'
> Q. 110: 'Can you give us the proportion of the Hindus and Muslims living in your jurisdiction?'
> Witness: 'Muslims were not more than 9 per cent., or a little bit more.'
> Q. 111: 'Are they spread over the whole area in your jurisdiction, or are they in pockets?
> Witness: 'They have got bustee areas, Muslim pockets here and there.'[27]

Visibly dissatisfied with this answer, Siddiky asks:

> Q. 112: 'Will you kindly name these pockets in your area?'
> Witness: 'One was in Ram Chand Ghosh Lane. Then in Musjidbari Street. It has got no particular name. This pocket is in Musjidbari Street. Then to the south of it is Ram Chand Ghosh Lane. Then there is one Muslim pocket there in Central Avenue. There is a mosque that bears a number of Musjidbari Street. At the crossing of Musjidbari Street and Central Avenue, there is a mosque, and near it, there are two or three houses. Three Muslim families used to live in the rooms attached to the mosque.'[28]

[26] Ibid., Exhibit P.
[27] Ibid., 16.
[28] Ibid., 16.

City as Territory

Q. 113 (B. Somayya): 'There are no houses apart from the mosque?'
Witness: 'No.' Khundkar continues, as if he was taking 'Their Lordships' through the lanes of his jurisdiction: 'Then Gulu Ostagar Lane. Here is also a Muslim pocket. There were big buildings and huts here, about eight houses. Then we come to near about Beadon Row. Hereabout was a mosque and attached to the side of the mosque; three or four Muslim families used to live in some rooms attached to the mosque. There were also two or three huts close by. Then we come to what is called Chidam Mudi Lane. Near about is a mosque. Nobody used to live here, but the Mutawalli and three or four families used to live at this place. This is called Blacquire Square. This is in Hari Ghose Street. It falls on Grey Street, and it comes out from Beadon Street. About this place, there was a mosque about halfway off. This is opposite Bhim Ghosh Lane. Here, there were no Muslim residents, but there were 2, 3 or 4 shopkeepers, Biri and cigarette sellers—Muslim shopkeepers. Then here is the police station and we are on Cornwallis Street. About this place, there is a mosque.'[29]

Q. 114 (President): 'Just north of the police station?'
Witness: 'Not exactly north; it is North West. Here we have got a big mansion, thereafter the residence of a Hindu gentleman. Then the mosque. By the side of that mosque, in the rooms attached to the mosque, some Kabulis used to reside. Then this is Raja Raj Kissen Street, and this is Sahitya Parishad Street. These are two populous streets. Between these is Goabagan Cattle Market.'[30]

Q. 115 (Mr Somayya): 'Do any Muslims live there?'
Witness: 'There are Muslim cattle dealers, and some Hindu cattle dealers live mostly this side on the Sahitya Parishad Street, and the north side lives Muslims. On the north side of Raja Raj Kissen Street, there are some cattle huts, cattle khatals they are called, almost close to Upper Circular Road. We have Muslims here.'[31]

Q. 116 (Somayya): 'Scattered?'
Witness: 'Almost compact, around the cattle market except on the south where the Hindu cattle dealers live. This we come to the crossing of Upper Circular Road and Vivekananda Road. This is not exactly opposite the crossing. Here we have a market called Maniktolla Market. There is a mosque, and there are few residential

[29] Ibid., 16.
[30] Ibid., 17.
[31] Ibid., 7.

huts as well as shops—Muslim shops. Here there was a Hindu shop also. This is called Nandan Bagan bustee, between Circular Road and Raja Dinendra Street.'[32]

Q. 117 (do): 'Is that all Muslim area?'

Witness: 'No mixed area. Muslims were very few, scattered all over. Here is a bustee at No. 76/1 Cornwallis Street, just west of the police station. This is a mixed area...'

Q. 118 (do): 'Was there any Muslim bustee behind Ram Chand Ghosh Lane?'

Witness (understanding that the President has no sense of the place): 'This is not near Ram Chand Ghosh Lane. It is south of that Lane and north of Sahitya Parishad Street.'[33]

What is important in this long conversation is how Khundkar handled a set of seemingly objective demographic questions regarding how many of which communities lived where by providing more of a visual or pictorial, that is, qualitative, description. In other words, instead of treating them as a series of census questions that could then be tabulated and analysed, Khundkar took the Commission members through a visual or pictorial and primarily qualitative description of his jurisdiction. Although he began with some census figures, the description increasingly moved to intimate details of neighbourhoods— houses, buildings, shops, residential quarters, streets, lanes, and mosques. It resonated with the way a long-time resident of the place would relate to their neighbourhood, rather than a disinterested enumerator. Clearly perplexed by the unexpected quality of this description, the President of the Commission quipped redundantly, '... and you have gathered a fair knowledge of your jurisdiction by this time?'

The whole deliberation of the Commission was replete with a desperation to zone-mark the city along religious lines. The results were frustrating. A counsel asked another police officer: 'Was Hatibagan belonging to "Section A" a Hindu area?' He replied: 'Hatibagan, predominantly Hindu area except some pockets of Muslims in little of Bagbazar, a little of Mohanbagan—just pockets.' What about 'Section B'—Beniatola? 'A little upper Chitpore Road, Muslim area, I mean Muslim shops, mainly a Hindu area.' Consider 'Section C': 'Duliapara Lane and Ram Chandra Ghosh Lane—a Muslim pocket, Muslim traders in cows, some milkmen—otherwise a predominantly Hindu area.' Yet further information was called for. For instance, 'is Phulbagan Bustee a Muslim area?' 'There are

[32] Ibid., 17.
[33] Ibid., 18.

Mohammedan houses as well as Hindu houses there.' A counsel clarified: '… also that part between Mitra Lane and Marcus Square is entirely Mohammedan.' The deponent replied: 'No, there is a lot of Hindu houses also.'[34]

Did Khundkar answer the questions posed? Yes and no. Khundkar did not merely outline the Hindu–Muslim demography in his jurisdiction. He gave a complex description of the lived reality of communal distribution in the area that defied the frame through which the Commission members were prepared to understand the conflict. The Commission members were trying to 'fix' the populations in time, space, and ratio. Khundkar, on the other hand, described mobile geographies and entangled realities of inter-communal, inter-ethnic and inter-class sharing of space. This understanding enabled him to contend with a set of mobile crowds that were attacking various portions of his jurisdiction while continuously switching locations.

Consider, for instance, this rather funny exchange:

> Q. 219 (Siddiky): 'Tell us about Dhulipara. You have got a fairly good idea of that locality?' [Note, he asked this question after Khundkar described to Their Lordships the features of his jurisdiction.]
> Witness: 'I think so'. [A no-nonsense answer.]
> Q. 220: (Siddiky): 'I will help you with this map. (Hands in a sketch.) You will show how many Muslim houses are there, just to refresh your memory. A little west of Minerva Theatre. You see the sketch I have given you.'

At this point, Somayya, another counsel, asked: 'What is it that you have given him?' Siddiky replied: 'A sketch just to refresh his memory about Dhulipara. I have sketched it myself and have given it to him just to refresh his memory as to what roads are leading into this Dhulipara Bustee.' Then, Khundkar took out the map, displayed it and explained it to 'Their Lordships'.

> Q. 221 (Siddiky): 'What would have been the Muslim population of this Dhulipara, the number of Muslims living in that bustee and the houses … 100, 150, 200?'
> Witness: 'It would be no less than 700, perhaps 750.'[35]

The discussion continued for the whole day on the 14th in this circular manner. It was evident that Calcutta's spatio-demographic reality was difficult to zone-mark. On several occasions, the counsels wanted Khundkar to specify the

---

[34] Samaddar, 'Policing a Riot-torn City', 49.
[35] Ibid., 23.

'composition of the crowds'. How many Hindus and how many Muslims? Did they belong to the working class or the *bhadralok* class? For instance, at one point, Siddiky asked him to specify the 'composition of the two mobs': 'I mean of what class they were composed?' Khundkar replied: 'Of the Muslim mob, some were wearing Pyjamas, some lungis … and of the Hindus, I saw young men, Bengali young men. Kalwars and low-class people on both sides.'[36]

Siddiky, a representative from the Muslim League in the Commission, was inclined to project the comparative innocence and victimhood of the Muslim community of the city. But Khundkar's replies captured the complexity of the violence such that it frustrated any easy conclusion. At one point, Siddiky asked: '… by this could you judge that the mood of this Hindu mob was very bad?' But Khundkar replied: '… the mood was bad on both sides. Equally bad.' Then, Siddiky anxiously asked Khundkar to give a 'pocket-by-pocket' breakup of the plight of the Muslims where Hindu mobs attacked them.[37] He took up the instance of Musjidbari Street *bustee*: 'This one is not a bustee proper, but there are a few Muslims living here and there within a radius of a few yards. Is it not?'[38] To this, Khundkar reiterated his earlier position: '… all the Muslims are living side by side.'[39] 'How many Muslims are living there?' Khundkar replied: '… there are about six pucca buildings and huts also.'[40] Siddiky stopped Khundkar and asked to provide precise numbers: '… did I not ask for a number?' 'May be 100,' replied Khundkar. 'And would you tell us now what happened to these 100 Muslims of Musjidbari Street?' Khundkar replied: '… nothing happened to them….' 'Not a single Muslim was killed?' 'Not a single Muslim was killed *because Hindus protected them.*'[41] Siddiky pointed out that, after all, the entire Muslim population was evacuated from the place for safety. Therefore, they lost 'hearth and home. They might not have been killed to the last man.'[42] Khundkar chose to remain silent.

As already discussed, the disturbance of 1946 took on the dimensions of an undeclared civil war. The crowd movement sharpened religious boundaries in

---

[36] Ibid., 18.
[37] Ibid., 22.
[38] Ibid., 20.
[39] Ibid., 20.
[40] Ibid., 20.
[41] Ibid., 20–21, emphasis mine.
[42] Ibid., 21.

space. Its strategic formations through mobile territories claimed the streets while traversing them. In so doing, the crowds dissolved social distinctions to function as a transitory whole. Thus, the Commission found a liaison between *bhadralok* elements, the terrorists, and the *goonda*s in the crowds. The police chased the crowds to disperse them into more easily recognizable mobs. The crowds retaliated by chasing the police patrol or escaping from it. The sporadic and discrete mobility of the mob–police dyad produced a shifting spatiality in the city. On being pursued by the police, the crowds would disappear and re-form a few yards further or elsewhere. This continually kept the police patrol on the move in different directions throughout the city, blurring the boundaries of legal jurisdictions of different *thanas*.

Thus, Khundkar would frequently be seen crossing his jurisdictional boundaries to chase the crowds. This added another layer of difficulty for 'Their Lordships' of the Commission, in their retroactive efforts to track his movements comprehensively. 'In the second paragraph, you say at the junction of the Upper Circular Road and the Vivekananda Road you met the Deputy Commissioner North.... Is this within your jurisdiction?' Khundkar confirmed that it was outside his jurisdiction. 'Is his (Mr Manik Mullick's) residence within your jurisdiction?' Khundkar replied: 'No, that is not in my jurisdiction, but is on the border.'[43] Again, consider interrogation number 59: 'The next paragraph starts with, at 9 am, you saw dead bodies strewn on Grey Street, B. K. Paul Avenue. Is this area that you mention within your jurisdiction?' Khundkar replied: 'I found in Grey Street and Central Avenue some dead bodies. Central Avenue, North of Grey Street, is within the jurisdiction of Shampukur P. S., not within my jurisdiction, and the portion of Grey Street that I mentioned is within my jurisdiction, close to B. K. Paul Avenue.'[44] Consider one last instance in interrogation number 123: 'In normal times, which are the spots, I should call black spots, from where you can anticipate some troubles?' Khundkar replied: 'Troubles in normal times we apprehend from the brothel area in Sonagachi and from Rambagan area which is on the border of my jurisdiction.'[45]

Throughout the Commission's proceedings on 14 February 1946, Khundkar continued to define his jurisdiction in terms of its *borders*—the interfaces it had with other *thanas*. The Commissioners struggled to pin down the nature of this

---

[43] Ibid., 13.
[44] Ibid., 13.
[45] Ibid., 17.

borderland. They seemed preoccupied by its repeated transgression during the riots. How to tackle a situation when it bordered with another territory? When such a question was asked, Khundkar gave a reply that did not precisely answer the question: 'From your evidence, I have gathered, Mr Khundkar, that incidents which took place on the border line, should be dealt with by both the thanas. Is not that so?' Here is Khundkar's blunt reply: 'Those that occurred in my jurisdiction, it was my first duty to deal with them instead of asking the other police station to deal with it.' The interrogator felt satisfied and clarified: '... that is to say that irrespective of the line, if anything happened within your views, I take it, it would be your duty to deal with it.'

However, the boundaries emerging from the civil war did not neatly overlap with the formal boundaries of the police stations. In the dialectic of boundary-breaking and boundary-preserving exercises, lines continuously moved with the mobile bodies that took the form of a crowd only by breaking and refunctioning these boundaries. Police chasing the crowds to maintain the boundary between two rival communities and the crowd chasing the police to disrupt that boundary was, in fact, a recurring theme in Khundkar's deposition. Those were the moments in which power and violence intercepted each other on the street, simultaneously instigating and electrifying those who took part in this game.

Thus, the Commission's session with Khundkar remained inconclusive for want of a common measure. In other words, they failed to engage satisfactorily with each other's ways of seeing the world.[46] Hence they often talked at cross-purposes—when the Commission sought census data on population, Khundkar could only find names, mosques, some houses, and a few huts. Their conversation exposed conceptual incompatibilities that highlighted the limits of their communication. Khundkar's voice was recorded, but it was hardly heard. By the time Khundkar's affidavit was read, its 'context' had already ebbed away

---

[46] A member expressed his expectation that being a 'Muslim man' and an 'ordinary citizen', Khundkar should have his own anticipations of the meaning of the Muslim League's call for 'Direct Action'. Khundkar clarified that his Muslim identity did not make him a member of the Muslim League. He further said that 'direct action' did not carry any particular message to him beyond the fact that there would be a general *hartal* in the city. At places, traffic might be obstructed, as it happened on numerous occasions during his career as a police officer. Khundkar also anticipated that some Hindus might join in the protest with the Muslims. Thus, Khundkar saw the significance of the Direct Action Day in continuation with a host of street protests that had become part of the city's normal rhythm in the previous decades. Ibid.

into 'archival compost'. The more the witness clarified his affidavit, the more it appeared incomprehensible to 'Their Lordships'.

Ultimately, the Commission decided to end its deliberations without producing a report on its findings. It was argued that the time had changed, as Independence with territorial Partition of the subcontinent approached. Any further deliberation of the Commission would hardly serve a purpose in the changed context. As Samaddar puts it, the Commission was an exercise in an armistice—'a mode of declaring truce until the final positions were announced'.[47]

Khundkar's sessions with the Commission also pointed to the fact that the Hindu–Muslim communal segregation of the city remained an unfinished endeavour until the 1946 riot, despite a repeated convergence between the violence of city rebuilding and that of communal polarization, throughout the twentieth century. Janam Mukherjee points out that the majority and minority community had localized characters— 'the prevailing territorial dynamic of local dominance'—as he calls it.[48] There were Hindu *paras* with Muslim households and vice versa. The civil war of 1946 disturbed this equation fundamentally by 'de-housing' around 10 per cent of the city population over a few months. Still, until Independence—as we have seen over this section—Muslims retained their territorial claim over some portions of the city.

The Social Infrastructure of Violence

We find that communal mobilization since the 1920s developed a durable social infrastructure of violence in the city. Its internal boundaries remained unstable as long as communal riots remained limited to episodic mob violence and momentary crowd action. Since the 1926 riot, however, both Hindu and Muslim groups showed a much more organized investment in territorializing neighbourhoods. The Hindus were undoubtedly more advanced in this regard. Besides the revivalist Arya Samaj, workers became members of various neighbourhood clubs and *akharas*. The Commissioner of Police reported significant involvement of these social and cultural organizations in conducting planned assaults on the enemy community. In addition, he mentioned the involvement of certain clubs and volunteer groups that came up in various neighbourhoods with the intention to protect Hindu temples.

---

[47] Samaddar, *Ideas and Frameworks of Governing India*, 204.
[48] J. Mukherjee, *Hungry Bengal*, 218.

Immediately after the outbreak of Attacks on religious institutions on the 3rd April, proposals were made to organize defence parties for the protection of Hindu temples, Some defence parties were actually formed, notably the 'Bray Club' in the jurisdiction of the Bartola police-station, the South Calcutta Defence Force under the presidency of Mr. S. N. Haldar, and another band of Bengali youths, who, under the leadership of Pulin Das, Nanda Ghosh and Nera Ghosh, defended the Kali temple in Kalitala.[49]

Several Muslim associations such as the Jamiat-i-Ulema and Tanzeem-ul-Mussalman, too, were seen to have played a very active role in popular mobilization during the riot. A few names (along with their geographies) of local clubs, *akharas*, and associations playing an active role in communal mobilization and in organizing 'defence parties' to protect property from the enemy community are given here.

The growth in quasi-political and social activities of clubs began during the Swadeshi era. It gained new momentum, however, in the 1920s, with the nationalist capture of the city corporation, following the Montague–Chelmsford Reforms, the Non-Cooperation–Khilafat Movement, and the brief Swarajist moment in Bengal politics. The mushrooming of relatively more permanent and formal associations and organizations for large-scale political mobilizations in the 1920s has been pointed out by Partha Chatterjee as well.[50] These organizations played an essential role in the *paras*' social, political, and cultural life, and were known to have controlled the local real estate and rental market.[51]

[49] 'The Calcutta Riots', Extracts from the 'Report of the Commissioner of Police on the Calcutta Riots from the 2 to 15 April 1926', *India in Home Polity, January-June 1926*, Vol. I (Calcutta: The Annual Register Office, 1926), 81.

[50] P. Chatterjee, 'The Political Culture of Calcutta', 27–33. For a detailed discussion of the mushrooming of clubs, their activities and typology, see Soumita Mazumder, 'The Clique of the Club: A Small History of Nationalism in Calcutta, 1920–1946' (M.Phil. dissertation, CSSSC, 2016). For an understanding of the nationalist politics in Calcutta in 1920s, see Rajat. K. Ray, *Urban Roots of Indian Nationalism* (New Delhi: Vikas Publishing House, 1979).

[51] Let me mention just an example of the clubs' involvement in local real estate affairs. A club in Shinghee Lane, registered in the name of Shimla Byayam Samiti, mediated a property dispute between the family members of Ashutosh Chandra Mittar, residents of 13 Beadon Street, over a 2-*cottah* plot located close to the intersection of Beadon Street and Central Avenue. The Improvement Trust had recently acquired the plot under the Central Avenue Scheme. The plot fetched compensation for the

One of the most prominent trends in the Non-Cooperation-Khilafat Movement was recruiting volunteers by forming the 'volunteer corps'.[52] In addition, there were other associations, not formally affiliated to the Congress, but offering a cadre base in response to the call of Congress leaders. For example, Chittaranjan Das used the Bengal Young Men's Association podium to create a solid cadre base at the neighbourhood level.[53] The Bengal Provincial Khilafat Committee was also active in building neighbourhood-based volunteer corps. By 1921, 400 volunteers worked on behalf of the Khilafat Committee and the Calcutta Muhammadan Committee.[54]

These civic associations were key players in reorganizing the neighbourhoods and their internal boundaries during and after each riot. The famous Simla Byam Samiti (see Table 3.1) was in fact founded during the 1926 riot. It offered free-of-cost *lathi* training to about 500 Hindu boys on Vivekananda Road.

Mittar family (94,000 rupees), which one of its members, Brajendra, claimed as belonging to his family segment. On 27 December 1926, the patron and founder of Shimla Byayam Samiti called a *salishi sabha* (arbitration meeting) in the presence of all the claimants of the property and the local notables. What we get to know from the record is that the *sabha* was successful in resolving the dispute. Correspondence between Ashutosh Mittar and Dr. S. C. Banerjee (President of the Improvement Trust's Tribunal) between 18 February and 3 March 1927. This correspondence has four letters, between Mittar and Banerjee, regarding the aforementioned dispute. This is a loose file kept along with the Trust's Proceedings for the Year 1927–1928.

[52] An Intelligence Bureau report in 1921 found 10 'seva samitis' operating in Calcutta with 897 members who were given rigorous physical and military training under a well knit command structure. The Bengal Provincial Congress Committees organized and sponsored at least nine volunteer corps in various city neighbourhoods with 1,072 members. Often, the volunteers were paid workers of the Congress. In November 1921, a circular from the Bengal Congress announced two posts—captain and vice-captain—for its volunteer association with a salary of 75 rupees and 50 rupees respectively. The circular also announced two members in each police station area of the city with a monthly wage of 15 rupees. Individual volunteers used to get a daily wage to organize pickets. See Mazumder, 'The Clique of the Club'. For a discussion on the role of these associations in the 1946 riot, see Nakazato, 'The Role of Colonial Administration'.

[53] Mazumder, 'The Clique of the Club'. A report published in 1925 in Swarajya Party's organ, *Forward*, stated that the association deployed its volunteer service at different bathing *ghats* of the city, especially in Bhowanipore and Kalighat, for the lunar eclipse on the midnight of 8 February 1925.

[54] Mazumder, 'The Clique of the Club'.

Table 3.1 Names of local clubs, *akhara*s, associations, and their addresses in 1927

Name	Location
Akhara of Maheswari Bhavan	4, Sovaran Bysach
Arya Kumar Sabha	19, Cornwallis Street
Arya Samaj	19, Cornwallis Street
Bajrang Parishad	201, Harrison Road
Barrabazar Hindu Sabha	160, Harrison Road
Bengal National Militia	71, Mirzapore Street
Bengal Ex-service Association	209, Cornwallis Street
Calcutta Hindu Sabha	50, Bagbazar Street
Central Calcutta Youth Association	18/4 Akrur Dutta Lane
Cow Protection League	19, Cornwallis Street
Digambar Yuvak Jain Samity, Mahabir Reading Club	82/1 Lower Chitpore Road
Hindu Mahasabha	160, Harrison Road
Hindu Relief Committee	160, Harrison Road
Mahabir Dal	25, Grey Street
Navin Sangha	15, Gopi Bose Lane
Probuddha Samity	2, SriKrishna Lane, Shyampukur
Rajput Nava Yuvak Dal	402, Upper Chitpur Road
Rashtriya Sangha	College Street Market
Shobuj Sangha	38, Kali Mitra Ghat, Bagbajar
Saraswati Samity	4, NimuGosai Lane
Simla Byam Samity	9B, Singhee Lane
Tarun Samity	6, Nivedita Lane
Bengal Provincial Tanzim Committee	13/1 Wellesley Square
Calcutta Young Muslim Association	1, Kaiser Street

(Contd)

(Contd)

Name	Location
Kidderpore Muslim Volunteers	7, Ekbalpore Lane
Kidderpore Young Muslim Association	39, Mominpore Road
Bengal Provincial Tanzim Committee	13/1 Wellesley Square

Source: List of *sabha*s, *samiti*s, *akhara*s, and gymnasiums found active during the 1926 disturbances, GB-IB Records, Serial no. 162/27, F. 303/27, 1927 (WBSA).

After enrolment, these volunteers were commanded to protect the Thanthania temple and Sikh Gurudwara at Burrabazaar during the riot and were sent to Pabna to protect the riot-affected Hindus of the district.[55] Soumita Mazumder's archival research on the subject tells us that there was a merger of activities of the Congress Seva Dals and Hindu volunteer organizations. Mazumder found official intelligence documents suggesting that numerous *akhara*s and physical education clubs joined the Hindu Mahasabha to avowedly regenerate and protect their religion. Mazumder wrote: 'Following the riot [of 1926], the growing popularity of Hindu Mahasabha further indicates how religion has come to be regarded as a "natural" binding element of nation.'[56] Nakazato pointed out that by the 1930s, a segment of these associations 'had developed into paramilitary forces'.[57] Such associations played an even more important role during the riot of 1946.[58] In this context, an introspective observation of the Government of India in 1947 may be consulted:

> By 1938 it was becoming apparent that the volunteer movement in India was gaining both in point of members and in intensity, even though organization and control were lacking in full efficiency. With the outbreak of war in September 1939, the pace began to further quicken and in the first half of 1940 there was hitherto unpatrolled activity throughout the country.... At the same time, increasing communal mistrust, combined with a general apprehension of internal disorder or external aggression, gave a strong impetus to volunteer activity in several provinces.[59]

[55] Ibid.
[56] Ibid., 80
[57] Nakazato, 'The Role of Colonial Administration'.
[58] The clubs remained an important socio-political institution in neighbourhoods in the post-Independence era. They played an essential role in the social reorganization of refugee populations in various areas of the city.
[59] Nakazato, 'The Role of Colonial Administration', 284–85.

During the civil war of 1946, such volunteer groups played a significant role in planning and executing attacks. All the major political parties had their volunteer groups ready to engage in warfare. The Muslim League had its powerful 'Muslim League National Guards', while the Congress kept a group of disciplined volunteers ready 'in each locality of Calcutta when the rioting broke out'. The Congress divided the city into 36 or 37 blocks and kept local volunteers ready for 'action'. The volunteers knew their locality well and were well-trained in using knife, sword, and bomb. The Hindu Mahasabha, too, had the Hindustan National Guard posted in various corners of the city.[60]

As the war intensified from the evening of 16 August, these groups submitted to the more amorphous mobs comprising—as one police report put it—'the lower classes' of the two communities.[61] With the disappearance of the *bhadralok* and the voluntary associations from the streets, the *goonda*s took over. Volunteer organizations reappeared after 22 August again, when the violence receded, to conduct relief and rehabilitation for their coreligionists, and to reconstruct affected *paras*.[62] For instance, one of the old residents of Beadon Street talked about the involvement of the Simla Byayam Samiti in expelling an entire Muslim *bustee* and an adjacent red-light quarter in nearby Hartaki Bagan Lane after the riots. The vacant huts were offered to seven or eight Hindu families who had lost their homes in Muslim-dominated Beliaghata and Beck Bagan during the riot.[63]

---

[60] Oral History Transcript No. 301: Shree Surendra Mohan Ghose, NMML. Also see Nakazato, 'The Role of Colonial Administration'.

[61] Nakazato, 'The Role of Colonial Administration'.

[62] My interview with Achintya Kumar Ghosh (18 March 2006), who lived in Jorabagan during the civil war. He was 15 when the civil war took place. His father—Prafulla Chandra—was a prominent member of the Hindu Mahasabha. About 167 refugee camps were set up by various clubs and socio-religious organizations such as the Ramakrishna Mission and the Bharat Sevasram Sangh. Around 66,000 refugees were taken care of by these organizations. Mazumder, 'The Clique of the Club'. Also see the following two important IB files in this regard: Relief Organizations Functioning in Bengal, G.B, I.B records, Serial No. 715, File No. 199/47, 1947 (WBSA); and Relief Organizations Functioning in Bengal, File No. 199/47, Serial No. 715, 1947 (WBSA).

[63] Interview with Achintya Kumar Ghosh.

A Decisive Defeat

Earlier, we have seen that even during the 1946 riots, it was difficult for the police officers working on the ground to zone-mark the pockets of the city as exclusively Hindu or Muslim. The neighbourhoods were mixed even in places where Muslims were in a clear minority in census terms. But the creation of Pakistan and Calcutta's settlement with India, coupled with the disbandment of the Bengal Provincial Muslim League and a spectacular influx of Hindu refugees in the city, produced objective material conditions for the ultimate territorial marginalization of the Muslims in Calcutta. Hindu upper-caste refugees found leaders in all the established political parties of the day—a leadership capable of keeping the district-level mass leaders out of the core power structure of the ruling Congress Party and the Left opposition. The Muslim leadership within the Congress, on the other hand, lost ground in territorial reorganization and the factional squabbles within the party structure. The Partition produced two new minority communities—the Hindus in East Pakistan and the Muslims in West Bengal.

Nearly five years after the August 1946 riot, the Census of 1951 published a 50-year trend of the Hindu–Muslim population ratio in Calcutta (Table 3.2). The census figures registered a decline of the Muslim population in Calcutta between

Table 3.2 Fifty-year trend of Hindu–Muslim population ratio in Calcutta

Year	Hindu Population	Muslim Population	Muslim Population as a percentage of the Hindu Population
1901	603,310	270,797	44.9
1911	672,206	275,280	41.0
1921	725,561	248,912	34.3
1931	796,628	281,520	35.3
1941	1,531,512	497,535	32.5
1951	2,125,907	305,932	14.4

Source: *Census of India*, 1951, vol. VI, Part III, 'Calcutta City', XV. Also cited in Joya Chatterji, 'Of Graveyards and Ghettos: Muslims in Partitioned West Bengal, 1947–67', in *Living Together Separately: Cultural India in History and Politics*, ed. M. Hasan and A. Roy (New Delhi: Oxford University Press, 2005), 222–249.

1941 and 1951 by 191,603 individuals. The West Bengal government recorded a flight of 130,000 Muslims by 1951 because of the 'fear of disturbances'.[64] The 1961 Census found a near elimination of Muslims from certain wards of the city and a consequent rise of Muslim concentration in some others like Park Circus, Ekbalpore, Bowbazaar, Karaya, Narkeldanga, and Beniapukur. By 1961, Muslims were almost totally expunged from the northern, eastern, southcentral, and southeastern wards of the city. Many of these wards also witnessed refugee resettlement throughout the 1950s.[65]

Scholars such as Joya Chatterji[66] and Anwesha Sengupta[67] have recently drawn our attention to the various ways in which the near elimination and ghettoization of Muslims happened in the post-Partition years. For example, Chatterji shows how the Hindu refugees slowly but systematically occupied mosques, graveyards, and other properties under the Waqf board. At times, such encroachments were coupled with communal violence.

These scholars refer to such an outbreak of communal violence in February 1950. Wards 15 and 16, along with areas adjacent to Beadon Street, Amherst Street, and the working-class areas of the eastern frontier of the city[68] were severely affected by the February violence. A section of the Congress workers, the RSS, and the Hindu Mahasabha activists were actively involved in this violence. Golwalkar's presence in the Burrabazaar area of the city on 15 and 16 February was not a mere coincidence.[69] Certain neighbourhood clubs in the affected areas were actively engaged in evicting Muslims and settling Hindu refugees in the vacant houses and hutments. Such a case was reported in the Lalbagan area

---

[64] J. Chatterji, 'Of Graveyards', 229.

[65] M. K. A. Siddiqui, *Muslims of Calcutta: A Study of Their Social Organization* (Calcutta: Anthropological Survey of India, 1974), 16.

[66] J. Chatterji, 'Of Graveyards'.

[67] Anwesha Sengupta, 'Becoming a Minority Community: Calcutta's Muslims after Partition', in *The Stormy Decades: Calcutta*, ed. Tanika Sarkar and Sekhar Bandyopadhyay (London: Routledge, 2015), 434–458.

[68] This area is also known for the city's China Town and for tanneries, oil mills, hide warehouses, slaughterhouses, and petty waste recycling units inhabited predominantly by Dalits and Muslims. This was also an area where several slums were established by local landlords to house refugees and lower-middle-class families. See Jyotirindra Nandy's novel *Baro Ghar Ek Uthan* (Kolkata: Dey's Publishing, 1955).

[69] J. Chatterji, 'Of Graveyards'.

in north Calcutta. In this *bustee*, one 'Lallbagan Seva Samiti' claimed to have resettled 650 refugee families in 229 vacant houses earlier occupied by Muslim tenants. The Samiti received active encouragement from the northern district committee of the Congress Party.[70]

A remarkable feature of violence during the trouble of 1950 was the proliferation of the cases of mob lynching of Muslims inside Muslim *mohallas*, often situated in the city's margins.[71] What is important to note here is its continuous, mundane, and unofficial nature. During her investigation, Mridula Sarabhai encountered such a case at Ismail Street in Entally:

> The incident in Ismail Street coincided with the Prime Minister's visit to Calcutta on 6 March 1950 ... on or about 8 March; I visited the place, saw the injured and heard the complaints of Hindus and Muslims. Hindus claimed that they were in the minority. It was the Muslims who were the aggressors. But the Muslims had another story to tell. From the type of devastation, one could not understand the Hindu claim...It was quite apparent the persons who were sleeping were attacked. From the way the doors and windows, even the lavatory doors, were broken, one could see the place had been the victim of a consorted attack and all this in a Muslim Mohalla only.[72]

During the riot of 1950, some allegations were made regarding the role of the police. An eyewitness, for instance, complained that a mob was led by people in khaki, 'giving the appearance of belonging to either the police or the military'.[73] It was also alleged that the patrolling police parties intentionally delayed

---

[70] A. Sengupta, 'Becoming a Minority'.

[71] It is important to note that communal outbreaks since the 1950 event tended to concentrate only in the known Muslim areas, leaving the rest of the city unaffected. Thus, the carnage in 1964 took place in pockets such as Taltala, Jotasanko, Kareya, Beniapukur, Amherst Street, Beleghata, Entally, Watrgunj, and Garden Reach. A. Sengupta, 'Becoming a Minority'. Another point to be reckoned with is the fact that the geography of these disturbances clearly shifted to the margins of the city even though certain old epicentres appeared in the list of areas.

[72] 'Mridula Sarabhai's Report on the Communal Situation and Riots in Calcutta in 1950', in *The Trauma and Triumph: Gender and Partition in Eastern India*, vol. 2, ed. Jasodhara Bagchi and Subharanjan Dasgupta (Kolkata: Stree, 2009), 206–267, quoted from 263. This seven-page fact-finding report is the only surviving record of the carnage of 1950 in the public domain.

[73] S. Bandyopadhyay, *Decolonization in South Asia*, 51.

action and helped the Hindu mobs do their job. The remarks of some of the prominent Muslim legislators in the assembly before and during the carnage also revealed a sense of insecurity among Muslims in the city. Already on 6 February 1950—a couple of days before the carnage—S. K. Rafiq mentioned the following, which talked about the silent complicity of the administration in these various instances of violence:

> These troubles do not start in the daytime; they always take place at night. And as usual, it takes time for the Police to arrive. The Police arrive not only one or two but sometimes three or four hours after the occurrence. Those who live near College Street and Mechuabazaar junction know how certain people, members of a certain community, tried to interfere with the *Kotwali* in the market, resulting in loss of properties and injuries to members of the minority community.[74]

The next day, another member of the House, Husan Ara Begum, reported how Muslims in Maniktala, Narkeldanga, and Paikpara were intimidated and forced to quit their neighbourhoods.[75] She claimed to be unable to trust the state machinery. Muslims in thousands fled to locations they perceived as safer like Park Circus, Beniapukur, Narkeldanga, Zakaria Street, and Kidderpore.[76] The jute mills and other factories in the industrial townships around Calcutta had to close production due to the flight of Muslim workers. Sekhar Bandyopadhyay says that about 25,000 Muslim refugees were squatting in and around the Park Circus Maidan during the riot days.[77]

By the third week of March 1950, these refugees were all gone. The British Consulate speculated that they had 'mostly migrated to Pakistan'.[78] According to the East Pakistani Press, about 1,100,000 Muslims crossed the international borders by 22 May 1950. While this may be an exaggeration, the official West Bengal figure of 4,37,612 was a rather conservative estimate. Joya Chatterji believes that about a million Muslims left for Pakistan after Partition and 70 per cent were from West Bengal.[79]

---

[74] A. Sengupta, 'Becoming a Minority', 441–442.

[75] Ibid., 443.

[76] *The Statesman*, 1 July 1950. Also see S. Bandyopadhyay, *Decolonization in South Asia*, ch. 2.

[77] S. Bandyopadhyay, *Decolonization in South Asia*.

[78] Ibid., 55.

[79] Ibid.

There is no precise date available for when the violence of 1950 began, and indeed, it did not end with Jawaharlal Nehru's subsequent visit to the refugee city. In the next one and a half decades, February 1950 became a norm rather than an exception. The cleansing of the Muslim community continued and remained largely unreported (in media) in the refugee-dominated localities. In 1964, Nirmal Kumar Bose found nine wards—3, 14, 16, 33, 34, 77, 78, 79, 80—in northern, north-eastern, eastern, and southern Calcutta where refugee Hindus had displaced Muslim labourers and artisans.[80]

A proud (late) Chitta Dey told me how he headed several raiding gangs to the Muslim quarters in Bijoygarh and Azadgarh in 1951–1952 and compelled them to leave those places. According to Dey, raiding Muslim areas was a part of their 'fight for freedom'. During the riot of 1964, the Muslim residents of the Asutosh Colony migrated to the Muslim-dominated Tiljala. They never returned. An elderly resident of the colony remembered: 'Though there were no killings or violence, the Muslims were intimidated by the local refugees.'[81] Similarly, Sajal Sengupta, a resident of Shahidnagar Colony, commented: 'Muslims had some properties in this area. They started leaving as refugees started to settle down.'[82] The riot in 1964 ravaged Muslim-dominated neighbourhoods in Amherst Street, Sealdah, Taltola, Entally, Beniapukur, and Beliaghata in the central-eastern parts of the city, Garia in the south, and squatter colonies along the Sealdah–Ballygunge rail track.[83]

One direct impact of the sustained communal tension in the 1950s and 1960s was a growing crowding of Muslims of all classes in some of the pockets of the city, especially in southeastern fringes such as Tangra, Tiljala, and Topsia. Take the instance of the Dhobiatala Camp near the Dhapa garbage dumping station. Here, 48 riot-torn Muslim families were stationed in 1964. An estimate of 1992 shows that this particular camp had a population of 5,000 individuals, of which 4,543 were Muslims.[84]

---

[80] Nirmal Kumar Bose, *Calcutta 1964: A Social Survey* (Bombay: Lalvani Publishing House, 1968).

[81] Anwesha Sengupta, 'Political History of Calcutta: 1947–1977': https://www.sahapedia.org/refugee-colonies-kolkata-history-politics-and-memory, accessed 14 September 2020.

[82] Ibid.

[83] Suranjan Das, 'The 1992 Calcutta Riot in Historical Continuum: A Relapse into "Communal Fury"?', *Modern Asian Studies* 34, no. 2 (2000), 281–306.

[84] Ibid.

As is shown in parts of this chapter, Calcutta lost its complex character of inter-communal sharing of space in the post-1946 years, as Muslims were pushed to certain exclusive pockets in the southeastern and southwestern pockets of the city, where their overall invisibility was compensated by the locally concentrated hyper-visibility. The wealthy Hindu-minority population in Garden Reach, Metiaburuj, and Park Circus began to desert their ancestral places and moved to exclusively Hindu neighbourhoods between the 1970s and 2000s. A complex intertwining of the cultural othering of ghettos, real estate, and communal tension came to constitute the structural relationship between the city and its minority ghettos.

Latent Violence

Calcutta remained relatively free from significant incidents of explicit communal fury during the long Left Front regime in West Bengal (1977–2011). There were, however, numerous incidents of group violence as government initiatives led by the Municipal Corporation, the Improvement Trust, and later the Calcutta Metropolitan Development Authority (CMDA)[85] began the planned expansion of Calcutta eastwards. This expansion engulfed slums and squatter colonies along the rail track between the areas of Park Circus in the north and Bagha Jatin in the south—areas that had hosted a substantial section of Muslim and Dalit populations. Eventually, Bijon Setu (bridge/flyover) over the Ballygunge rail station, along with Sukanta Setu over Jadavpur rail station, became prime vehicles for the eastward expansion of Calcutta, culminating in the massive Eastern Metropolitan Bypass project (started in 1973). In subsequent decades, it led to a substantial real estate boom and peri-urban growth in these neighbourhoods and the East Calcutta Wetlands area. Urbanization in this area remained a matter of intense conflict, while it continued to keep the significant political regimes well-funded to run their everyday machinery.[86]

---

[85] The Calcutta Metropolitan Development Authority (CMDA) came into being in 1970 through a Presidential Ordinance. It took up many of the operations of the Trust in the subsequent years. The Trust came under the CMDA's administrative control in 1973 and became a department of the CMDA in 2017. Between the 1950s and the 1980s, the Trust constructed three overbridges to facilitate the southward and eastward migration of Calcutta. The next chapter talks about two such overbridges in some detail. The expansion of the jurisdiction of the Corporation in these areas happened in phases over three decades since 1973.

[86] Ananya Roy, *City Requiem, Calcutta: Gender and the Politics of Poverty* (Minneapolis: University of Minnesota Press, 2002).

The expansion of the real estate market in the city's eastern fringe further marginalized the working-class Muslim and Dalit populations of the city. The real estate operators lobbied aggressively with the government to shift the tanneries that employed thousands of Muslims and Dalits to areas further south and east in newly formed industrial hubs, citing pollution as a reason, and then proceeded to recycle these lands into new middle-class residential quarters. As a result, the slums that still existed in these areas lost their immediate livelihood contexts, forcing their residents to find employment elsewhere or in other sectors within the informal economy. Moreover, the loss of proximity between life and labour made life more expensive and unsustainable in these slums, which enabled a faster real estate transition in these fringe areas.

The Left Front government successfully checked the outbreak of communal riots for over three decades. However, it did very little to address the structural imbalance between the majority and minority communities regarding their access to social infrastructures such as health, education, and employment. The Sachar Committee Report (2006) explicitly stated that the state of West Bengal had failed to provide primary resources for the uplift of its Muslim citizens. It was pointed out that the literacy rate of Muslims in Calcutta was much lower in 2006 than it had been in 1947. The Left Front government also failed to eliminate the latent communalism that continued to inform the city's *bhadralok*. It may be argued that the period of Left rule enabled latent majoritarianism by subsuming communal and caste contradictions into class issues. Nor could the government make the Muslims of the city feel secure about their futures. The spectre of riots continued to loom large among the city's Muslims. Thus, for the Muslims of Calcutta—as this section showed—the experience of Independence coincided with a durable territorial and social marginalization.

During her ethnographic study of Park Circus—a Muslim-majority neighbourhood of Calcutta—several Muslim 'gentlemen' explained to Anusuya Chatterjee why they could never move out of the Park Circus locality despite being economically solvent. They gave two reasons. First, they informed that the housing market in Hindu-dominated *para*s and apartment complexes was not open to Muslims. Second, they told her that the Muslim middle-class citizens feel safe when they live close to Muslim-dominated working-class quarters. Thus, a respondent told her:

> ... Muslims must live together ... I remember what happened in 1992–93. Hindus from Darapara (a nearby Hindu slum) came and attacked us with swords and lathis; they tried to burn down our houses. The police never come when you need them. Because our people were

> prepared, they could stand up to it. Even women knew that they should heat up oil and keep it ready to throw at the enemy. Together we could prevent them from entering our slum.... When Muslims live together people are forced to think twice before attacking them.[87]

Chatterjee's vignettes suggest that the memory of riots and the market economy of rent enforce each other to make ghettos durable. They further allude to the fact that social relationships between the majority and the minority communities are established in the course of significant incidents of violence that took place at specific historical moments. Well after these events are over, even for people who have not directly experienced them, they serve as mnemonic warnings of the 'permanent warfare' between communities that can erupt at any time and must be kept at bay. For Muslims in the ghetto, peace is when war is fought elsewhere. Thus, one of Chatterjee's Muslim respondents says:

> Muslims to a large extent slowly overcame the fear of 1992 before Gujarat happened. The latter has really shaken the Muslims; look at what happened in Gulbarg Society [in Ahmedabad] ....it was said to be in a cosmopolitan area and home to affluent Muslims. It makes us think many times before purchasing a house/flat outside a Muslim area.[88]

However, this remains an uneasy and differently violent peace. The segregated ghetto does not so much mean the end of communal violence as its displacement and transformation into other forms and modalities. Existing as an outcome of efforts to ward off and escape from large-scale, major violence, the Muslim ghetto marks and underwrites the *latent violence* of a majoritarian city. Let us take a closer look at this through a few ethnographic vignettes of how latent violence affects the lives of Muslims in present-day Calcutta.

Instance 1

In 2013, I interviewed several Muslim students studying in various colleges in the College Street area and Jadavpur University. Most of the students I met were from a number of districts of West Bengal, living in private boarding houses and as paying guests (known in Calcutta as 'PG'). All of them had a story to share with me regarding their difficulties with house hunting. Usually, Hindu

---

[87] Anasuya Chatterjee, *Margins of Citizenship: Muslims in Urban India* (New York and London: Routledge, 2017), 151.
[88] Ibid., 152.

owners refuse to rent out their PG arrangements to Muslim students, I was told. Most of my respondents could only find accommodation in Muslim localities from Muslim landlords. One such student said that he found a PG arrangement in Park Circus though his college was in Jadavpur—nearly 5 kilometres away. Another person named Labani added a rather interesting twist to this narrative. She was in search of a PG arrangement in a refugee-dominated neighbourhood in South Calcutta. Upon hearing her name, the owner was convinced that she must be a Hindu girl and was glad to offer her a shared room. On the day of her move, Labani had to deposit a photocopy of her voter ID. The owner discovered that Labani's surname was 'Jangi'. This surname was unheard of among the Hindus, and it was extremely rare for even the Muslims. In addition, the word means 'militant' in English. The landlady asked Labani to pack up and move out immediately.

I then followed the trail and met some PG owners in the Jadavpur University area, where I too have lived as a PG in the early 2000s. First, I met Mr and Mrs Chatterjee, who lived in Jadavpur Central Road. The couple was well known for their close friendship with a noted Revolutionary Socialist Party (RSP) leader in the neighbourhood. Mr Chatterjee's father was a prominent refugee activist of the 1950s who played an active role in settling Hindu refugees in Jadavpur's catchment areas. In many ways, the Chatterjees could be identified with the progressive, educated, and liberal *bhadralok* milieu of our times (that is, disavowal of caste and religious conservatism in *public* and its performance in *private*). After the marriage of their only daughter, they decided to start a PG for boys. When asked if they had any Muslim students then living in the PG or whether they would like to accept a Muslim boy sometime in the future, Chatterjee replied:

> You know, we do not believe in casteism or communalism. We will be thrilled to have a cosmopolitan culture in our PG. But, the parents ... you know.... They are from smaller towns. They lack urbanity. They don't understand that intercommunal living is a part of good education.... Therefore, we have not so far accepted any Muslim boys. After all, everybody should consent to live together.

I went to many housing societies with the same question. I received two types of answers: (*a*) 'we do not wish to live with the Muslims because they are culturally different' and (*b*) 'we have no issues, but we fear that our neighbours won't accept a Muslim family'. This is how the contemporary rental economy creates and reproduces the communal segregation of the city patterned by the earlier and more explicit violence of slum clearance and riots.

Instance 2

In the aftermath of the 1992 riots that broke out in different parts of the country following the Babri Mosque demolitions, the Calcutta Police rounded up several innocent Muslim young men from various slums in Topsia, Tangra, and Park Circus. When they were released after interrogation, they complained that the police had made them chant 'Jai Shree Ram'. My respondents from these slums repeatedly told me that they were constantly under special surveillance and were regularly summoned for interrogation whenever there was a crime in the city. Seabrook and Siddiqui draw our attention to the case of Ajijur Rahaman Sardar.[89] He was caught for his alleged involvement in an armed robbery in Tiljala, Calcutta, on 22 June 2007. Subsequently, he was acquitted for want of evidence but remained in jail on unsubstantiated charges.

In another similar case in late 2007, a 27-year-old man named Aftab Alam Ansari was arrested by the Calcutta Police on 27 December 2007. He was then handed over to the Uttar Pradesh Police, for purportedly transporting explosives for the 'court blasts' in Uttar Pradesh.[90] After prolonged agony suffered by Aftab and his family, the Uttar Pradesh Police admitted that their counterparts in Bengal had committed a mistake. It may be noted here that Aftab's father was a pensioned state government employee. Unlike Ajijur Rahaman Sardar, Aftab and his family were not slum dwellers, and they came from a historically Hindu-dominated mixed-class neighbourhood of Baranagar.

Reporting similar stories from Mumbai, Thomas Blom Hansen quotes a former corporator from a Muslim-majority area:

> The police call this a 'notorious area'. Whenever anything happens, they come rushing in and arrest people, mostly charge-sheeters and notorious characters but also innocent boys.... Crying mothers would come to my office. I had to go to the police station at least three times a week to plea with them, to ask them to let these boys go.[91]

---

[89] Jeremy Seabrook and Imran Ahmed Siddiqui, *People without History: India's Muslim Ghettos* (London: Pluto Press, 2011).

[90] 'Cop Goof-up on Calcuttan', *The Telegraph*, 15 January 2008: https://www.telegraphindia.com/india/cop-goof-up-on-calcuttan/cid/627463 (last accessed on 9 August 2020).

[91] Thomas B. Hansen, 'Democracy Against the Law: Reflections on India's Illiberal Democracy', in *Majoritarian State: How Hindu Nationalism Is Changing India*, ed. Angana. P. Chatterji, Thomas. B. Hansen, and Christophe Jaffrelot (Noida: HarperCollins, 2019), 19–40.

Hansen calls this a 'regime of low intensity terror'. In a majoritarian city, ghettos enter the majority common sense as permanent exceptions, 'notorious areas'. These neighbourhoods become the self-evidence of criminality. When Hansen asked a police official why such anticipatory measures were necessary, the latter's reply confirmed this public common sense: 'Well, it is a security precaution. We are trying to find people who know something. These people have so many secrets, we know that.... When you let them sit like that for some hours, people crack, you see.... We get a lot of information this way.'[92]

A retired Muslim police Inspector in Calcutta named Aziz (name changed) informed me that the police had installed extra *chowki*s (police posts) in Muslim slums in the aftermath of the 1992 riots. Initially, he thought that those were temporary installations. However, not only did they remain, but the number of such installations also continued to grow, especially in the early 2000s, in the context of a series of bomb blasts in Indian cities. 'The Muslim neighbourhoods', he continued, 'were the ones where they first installed CCTV cameras.... This happened just before I retired.' He informed me that the British had a conscious policy to keep communal check-balance in the 'forces'. This, according to Aziz, was reversed slowly in the post-colonial decades: 'Now, you will hardly see Muslims in good numbers in any of the levels, in any of the branches.' He said the Intelligence Bureau and the Special Branch (both intelligence wings) saw a systematic exclusion of Muslim officials after 1992.

Instance 3

On 13 January 2020, I visited an Aadhaar registration centre in Muslim-dominated Beniapukur in connection with another ethnographic research project. As I entered the premises, I saw a long queue of all age groups, from old ladies to children. I was puzzled since I knew that the area's local residents had all completed their Aadhaar formalities already. Fearful of losing out in the 'identity race' set up by Aadhaar, they had enrolled themselves at the very inception of the scheme. Initially, I thought that the queue must have something to do with the passage of the Citizenship Amendment Act, 2019 (CAA). Upon investigation, I realized that this was a usual sight in that Aadhaar Centre, unconnected to the CAA. Numerous Muslim citizens came every day to the Centre to get the spelling of their names corrected. Why? One Zeeshan told me that in four of his crucial identity documents—birth certificate, school certificate, voter ID, and Aadhaar—there were at least three versions of his name

---

[92] Hansen, 'Democracy Against the Law', 26.

(Jishan, Zishan, Zeeshan). This ambiguity had caused him many difficulties in all kinds of situations and he was anxious to put an end to it. A perceptive old lady told me that *sarkari* (government) officials (predominantly Hindu) regularly found these Muslim names culturally alien to their regular vocabulary. So, they imposed what they thought would be the correct spelling of a given name. The second clerk would find it difficult to accept the judgement of his predecessor and would 'correct' the spelling once again in the next document. The cycle goes on. The Aadhaar registration centres in these neighbourhoods never cease to exhaust their utility.

My ethnographic vignettes refer to a situation where violence towards the minority is routinized as a self-reproducing system. This chapter traces the twentieth-century history of violent minority oppression in Calcutta, where gradually sporadic acts of lynching replace the large-scale riot as the dominant form of physical violence, demographically heterogeneous neighbourhoods turn into pure and sanitized zones through the expulsion of minority elements, and clear territorial demarcations of space, access, and resources mark out the everyday experience of minority citizenship. However, the erasure of minority traces in the city makes certain practices associated with minority communities hyper-visible. After Independence, violence towards the minority community in Calcutta has increasingly taken an everyday form. These micro-aggressions have contaminated their experience (and documents) of formal citizenship, as seen in the Aadhaar name correction efforts we have just discussed. As a result, every Muslim in Calcutta grows up afraid that they are losing out and lagging behind. It is a strange kind of blackmail where the minority citizens must conform to an imposed norm of 'good' citizen behaviour. The burden of proof always lies on them.

Conclusion

This chapter is a history of the city traced through incidents of both overt and covert communal violence, spread across the twentieth century. It begins with examining the re-territorialization of certain parts of Calcutta during and after some of the major communal outbreaks. In my analyses, both cops and the rioting mobs emerge as foot soldiers of a demarcating force that enforces this re-territorialization. The discussion on the communal cleansing in 1946 and 1950 shows how a particular kind of ghettoization of Muslims took place after the 'partitioned independence' that erased the colonial era intermixing of populations to produce census-legible and communally segregated neighbourhoods in Calcutta. After Independence, Muslims in

India were reduced to a much smaller minority. Unable to take on the Hindus in territorial conflicts like before, minority ghettos attained a durable shape after Independence. Simultaneously, majoritarian violence assumed a latent form—always present in the urban common sense—in which the minority ghetto stood out as simultaneously an obstruction to the capitalist mobilization of space and as a 'threat' to 'security'.

For the Hindu majority and the majoritarian state, the Muslim ghetto represents a site where preparations are always underway for an imaginary battle that will eventually reduce Hindus into a minority. The ghetto is seen as the haven for radical ideas, Kashmiri terrorists, and Pakistani secret service interlopers. In this majoritarian view, the majority appropriates the tribulations of the minority, so that none can escape the spectre of the threat of minoritization in the city.

Thus, moving across the moment of post-colonial founding, the chapter tracks specific pathways of majoritarianism that unfolded in Calcutta both under colonial rule as well as under the post-Independence Left Front regime committed to a secularist ethos. I have argued that the normalization of communal zoning through a segregated real estate market, and the sustained criminalization of the Muslims through the twentieth century (leading into the twenty-first), produced a majoritarian urbanscape in spatial, social, and cultural terms. This history has shaped Calcutta's majoritarian common sense, which grew consistently along with—perhaps even enabled by—various 'progressive' ideas of democracy and development under successive secular regimes. This majoritarian common sense operates as a form of tacit violence that affects everyday life practices and the chances of Muslim populations of the city. The chapter shows that Calcutta's post-colonial passage to democracy and development is integral with the production of a marginalized minority population and its territorial manefestation as ghettos.

4

Frontier Urbanization

The mobilization of space ... begins ... with the land.... The mobilization is next extended to space, including space beneath the ground and volumes above it. The entirety of space must be endowed with exchange value. And exchange implies interchangeability: the exchangeability of a good makes that good into a commodity, just like a quantity of sugar or coal; to be exchangeable, it must be comparable with other goods, and indeed with all goods of the same type. The 'commodity world' and its characteristics, which formerly encompassed only goods and things produced in space, their circulation and flow, now govern space as a whole, which thus attains the autonomous (or seemingly autonomous) reality of things, of money.

—Henri Lefebvre[1]

In the historical struggle over property rights, the antagonists on either side of the barricades have used the weapons that most suited them. Elites, controlling the lawmaking machinery of the state, have deployed bills of enclosure, paper titles, and freehold tenure, not to mention the police, gamekeepers, forest guards, the courts, and the gibbet to establish and defend their property rights. Peasants and subaltern groups, having no access to such heavy weaponry, have instead relied on techniques such as poaching, pilfering, and squatting to contest those claims and assert their own.

—James. C. Scott[2]

If ghettos were the sites of surveillance and control—as we have seen in Chapter 3—frontiers represented lawlessness and chaos that needed to be counteracted to transform them into suburbs. Suburbanization in the context of early-twentieth-century Calcutta was a conscious planning response to the problems of inner-city 'congestion', public health breakdown, and industrialization. Some of the suburbs—such as Alipore and Cossipore—were already developed in the

[1] Lefebvre, *The Production of Space*, 336–337.
[2] James. C. Scott, *Two Cheers for Anarchism: Six Easy Pieces on Autonomy, Dignity, and Meaningful Work and Play* (Princeton and Oxford: Princeton University Press, 2012), 12.

nineteenth century as highly gentrified spaces dotted with upper-class garden houses. But most of the frontiers of the city to the south and east that were developed through the twentieth century were still forested, low lying, and marshy, and punctuated by natural bodies or water at the turn of the century. These spaces could not be brought to planned urbanization without remaking them as worthy of building activities. Forests needed to be cleared, ponds were to be drained out, dried, and filled, and lowlands needed to be raised with additional soil. Taming the frontiers thus required a considerable logistical mobilization. These frontiers were mobile zones where urban planning could be more radical than the central areas. These spaces were at the margins of authority and order, where the 'wild' and the 'tamed' played a game without cancelling out each other.[3] If the idealized modern city represents motion, the taming of the urban frontier produces a historicized topology of obstructed motion.

We may remember that James Maden and Albert de Bois Shrosbree had emphasized on a rigorous synchronization between the inner-city renewal schemes and suburbanization in the frontiers. They insisted that the suburbs must be kept ready to absorb the shock of population dispersal activated by the Calcutta Improvement Trust's inner-city schemes. However, the Trust encountered a practical obstacle in the form of unexpectedly high land prices in certain suburbs (in the north and west) while developing this coordinated approach of renewal and suburbanization during the First World War and its aftermath.[4] We briefly talked about this in Chapter 2. To the south and east, land prices were still cheaper, but these frontiers were not instantly ready for suburbanization. In this chapter, we go further and investigate an actual instance of suburbanization in the southern frontiers of Calcutta to explain the challenges that the Trust faced there. The chapter probes into the institutional and social experience of street-building and suburb construction in the southern frontiers which involved violent enclosure, commodification of land, accumulation, and discontent. Private contractors of labour, soil, and filling and building materials are ubiquitous in this story of frontier urbanization.

The chapter then takes us through the early post-colonial era of urbanization. Space-making in the southern frontiers in the 1950s was spearheaded by a mass encroachment movement—popularly known as *jabardakhal*—by Partition refugees and migrants from other districts of West Bengal, especially from the

---

[3] Wendy Pullan, 'Frontier Urbanism: The Periphery at the Centre of the Contested Cities', *Journal of Architecture* 16, no. 1 (2011): 15–35.

[4] For Colonial Bombay, see Rao, *House, but No Garden*.

adjacent 24 Parganas. When compared with the enclosure and commodification of land undertaken by the Improvement Trust in urbanization schemes of the late colonial era, 'space-making through encroachment' after independence presents a contrasting picture. In the latter case, urbanization happened through the decommodification of encroached-upon properties and the conversion of 'wastelands' into habitable properties through popular acts of reclamation. These two modes of frontier urbanization and spatial mobilization in the south involved an intense inter-conversion between private property, public property, and the commons. In this sense, frontier urbanization was very much constitutive of the city.

Urbanization in the frontiers re-centred Calcutta. By the second half of the twentieth century, it had added places, between Lower Circular Road in the north and Prince Anwar Shah Road in the south, to the 'inner city'. Two avenue-style streets—Russa Road and Rashbehari Avenue—were prominent players of change in places to the south of Lower Circular Road. The process began in and around Russa Road in the mid-nineteenth century. It was accelerated further in the 1910s, when the Trust initiated suburbanization schemes in Bhowanipore and began the construction of Rashbehari Avenue in the 1920s. Rashbehari Avenue and places south and east of it underwent dramatic transformations in the early post-colonial decades in the hands of squatter groups and footpath hawkers. The frontiers were tamed to breed genteel urbanity into the planned suburbs. Subsequently, they underwent a sustained process of plebianization in the post-colonial era of democratization. This is the story that this chapter chronicles.

Marshland to City: The Changing World of Russa Road

In Chapter 1, I referred to an exchange of notes between C. H. Bompas and Patrick Geddes on the widening of Russa Road that connected the southern suburbs of Bhowanipore, Kalighat, Chetla, and Tollygunge with the White Town in Chowringhee. In 1912, the Improvement Trust undertook to widen one part of Russa Road (the stretch between Lower Circular Road in the north and Tolley's Nullah in the south) to facilitate traffic between the southern suburbs and the city. In 1837, James Ranald Martin, in his 'Medical Topography of Calcutta' introduced the neighbourhoods of Russa Road as follows:

> I conceive then, that putting out of question the Sundarbans and the Salt-water Lake, that the thickest of trees and jangal, weeds, pools, small stagnant tanks, and jheels, which abound on each side of the

road from Chowringhee, Brijeetullah [near today's Rabindrasadan-Exide junction], to the end of Russapaglah [today's Tollygunge], on each side of the Kalighat Road, on the Tolly's Bridge, on each side of Tolly's nullah, and the road on the right of the nullah as far as the Insane Hospital, where the eye can hardly find any equality of surface except on the jheels and tanks, and where the wild indigo, and noxious weeds are growing in all directions—all this being situated south of the presidency, must be constant source of disease and disorders, many of which would vanish, if this pestilence could be removed. And if I am not mistaken, I can trace illness from this very source (these weeds) to certain houses in Chowringhee where in occasionally uninhabited houses, in the compound, and round the tanks is to be found, jangal indeed, which much add greatly to the malaria which is blown from the Russapaglah jangals over the Chowringhee part of the presidency.[5]

Martin declared that this unruly frontier needed to be tamed for the sake of Chowringhee—the centre of the European quarters in Calcutta. Else, the frontier would, one day, invade the centre and turn it into a frontier. Thus, the frontier appeared to be a wilderness that had to be distrusted, concurred, civilized, and capitalized. For nearly a hundred years, since the publication of the aforementioned report, certain areas between Lower Circular Road and E. B. Railway lines continued to be described as *terra nullius* of a sort in colonial documents—uninhabited, untenanted, and unencumbered by legacies and social norms. The Improvement Trust saw it as a frontier open to be transformed into a modern suburb. The Trustees hoped that a new urban society would emerge in this suburb, away from the stubbornly 'unmodern' native quarters of the northern city.

Russa Road occasioned several transformations in the area—especially in the village called Bhowanipore—since the third decade of the nineteenth century. Let us take the northern stretch of this road between Lower Circular Road and Hazra Road (this stretch is now Asutosh Mookerjee Road). Table 4.1 illustrates the increase of holdings in this stretch of Russa Road between 1796 and 1939. The holdings include residential, commercial, institutional, and bazaar holdings.

Until 1910, this stretch was predominantly residential, as the holding descriptions in the street directory suggest.[6] However, if we compare the street directories between 1910 and 1933, we see a growing commercialization of the

---

[5] Cited in Keya Dasgupta, 'Genesis of a Neighbourhood: The Mapping of Bhavanipur' (Occasional Paper 175: Centre for Studies in Social Sciences, Calcutta, March 2003), 21.

[6] *Thacker's India Directory for the Year 1910.*

Table 4.1 Holdings along Russa Road between 1796 and 1939

Year	Number of Holdings
1796	3
1825	13
1856	23
1863	34
1886	50+
1906	100+
1939–40	130+

Source: Keya Dasgupta, 'Genesis of a Neighbourhood: The Mapping of Bhavanipur' (Occasional Paper 175, Centre for Studies in Social Sciences, Calcutta, March 2003), 21.

holdings in this stretch. By 1933, this stretch was predominantly a commercial area—a trend we noticed in many other central Calcutta streets during the same period.

The area between Lower Circular Road and Hazra Road—on both sides of Russa Road—developed rapidly after three streets were opened in the first few years of the twentieth century. These include Harish Mukherjee Road (earlier known as Bediapara Road), Lansdowne Road, and Hazra Road's extension to Kalighat. Caste-Hindu, middle-class Bengalis appear to have occupied the newly released properties along these streets.[7] A sizeable section of them were urban professionals such as lawyers and doctors. There was also a craze among the educated rural middle-class *zamindars* of Bengal to buy plots in these areas and build sprawling houses as their urban dwellings. By the 1920s and the 1930s, their power in rural society had declined irreversibly. Several of them left village life and began to live in Calcutta. They would only visit their estates occasionally to collect dues. Thus, a section of the Bhawal family (the brother of Rani Bibhabati)[8] and the Uttar Para family built residences in Lansdowne

---

[7] *Thacker's India Directory for the Year 1933: Embracing the Whole of the Indian Empire* (Calcutta: Thacker, Spink & Co, 1934).

[8] Partha Chatterjee, *A Princely Impostor? The Kumar of Bhawal and the Secret History of Indian Nationalism* (Ranikhet: Permanent Black, 2002).

Road, while the *zamindar*s of Gobardanga bought a house in Elgin Road. There were quite a few such instances scattered in Bhowanipore.[9]

On Harish Mukherjee Road—one of the key thoroughfares of Bhowanipore—the street directory of 1910 shows a stark differentiation between the eastern and the western edges. The western side (toward the Tolly's Nullah) retained its old demographic and habitational form with a mixed population. There were substantial Muslim households in Benimadhab Nandan Lane and Bechu Doctor Lane, and various caste-based Hindu artisanal communities who were the earlier inhabitants of Bhowanipore.[10] The eastern edge of Harish Mukherjee Road, on the other hand, showed remarkable property- and land-use transformations in the first decade of the twentieth century. Members of the Bengali Hindu upper-caste professional class (mainly lawyers and doctors) bought properties along the eastern side. New two- and three-storeyed residential houses with imposing balconies and French windows adorned the place by the second decade of the twentieth century.

In nearby Elgin Road, there were 60 holdings in 1886.[11] Most of these holdings had belonged to Europeans, along with some Bengali professional class and *zamindar* owners such as R. C. Banerjee (*zamindar* of Gobardanga) at 5A, Subhas Chandra Bose's family at 38/2, and so on. There had been a concentration of Christian families in Elgin Road around the Congregational Church at No. 43.[12] From the mid-1940s, the Europeans began to sell their holdings to the members of the prosperous Marwari community. Thus, by the mid-1950s, Elgin Road became a Marwari-dominated neighbourhood.[13]

---

[9] The rich *zamindar*s had invested in Calcutta's bazaars and real estate since the eighteenth century (for example, the Burdwan Raj family). The Tagores, for instance, had their urban seat in Jorasanko, while their estates were in eastern Bengal. It was a new trend for the middle and smaller *zamindar*s to shift to Calcutta in the 1920s and 1930s. Those who had even smaller estates invested and shifted to nearby district headquarters. By the 1960s, the migration of the rural rentier middle class to towns and cities was almost complete.

[10] Most of the Muslims in the western flank of Harish Mukherjee Road deserted the neighbourhood during and after the civil war of 1946. They moved to Park Circus.

[11] K. Dasgupta, 'Genesis of a Neighbourhood'.

[12] *Thacker's India Directory for the Year 1933.*

[13] If in the early decades of the twentieth century, the Marwaris moved from Burrabazaar to Harrison Road and Central Avenue, by the 1940s, they moved further south, down the Lower Circular Road.

In his autobiography, noted actor Ahindra Choudhury has left behind a graphic description of the transformation of Russa Road and surrounding areas in Bhowanipore, Kalighat, and Chetla after the Trust started operations in 1912.[14] Notable among his subjects of description were the large Porabazaarer *bustee* and Porabazaarer *math* (playground), which were significant landmarks in the intersection of Russa Road and Sambhunath Pandit Street. This *bustee* stood on 10–11 *bigha*s of land. The Trust started its demolition work in late 1912 from this *bustee* towards the south, up to Chaulpati Road. Within a few years, new buildings came to adorn Russa Road. Choudhury remembers a water pavilion (*jaltungi*) close to the crossing of Russa Road and Sambhunath Pandit Street, on the western side of Russa Road, which disappeared during the Trust's operations.[15] Choudhury also talks about a Tram Company facility with horses' stables at Lower Circular Road and Russa Road (North). All these properties were taken over and redeveloped by the Trust during the first decade of its operation in this area. The Tram Company's facility became an exhibition ground and was later handed over to the Calcutta Club. Choudhury recollects how the roar of land-filling became routine every night for more than a decade. Cartloads of earth and rubbish were poured into low-lying areas and ponds in his Bhowanipore neighbourhood (see Appendix 4A.2).

To enforce the widening of the main roads—especially Russa Road—a new law (Act III of 1915) came into force from 14 April 1915.[16] It gave the Improvement Trust the power to 'lay down the line of projected public streets and prohibit the erection of new buildings within such lines'.[17] This new Act led to the further displacement of populations in the southern scheme areas. Thus, in 1918, Reverend Canon Banerjee—in charge of St Mary's Church in Elgin Road—complained that a 'large number of his congregation had been driven to leave the neighbourhood' on account of the excavation area of the Trust. He also complained that apart from the *bustee* dwellers, several of his co-religionists belonging to a 'better class' were also 'driven out due to the recent

[14] Choudhury, *Nijere Haraye Khunji*, vol. I.

[15] It was a 'circular summerhouse built in the centre of a tank'. The *New Calcutta Directory* of 1863 mentions that the property belonged to Heeralall Seal—a notable merchant prince of central Calcutta.

[16] *Annual Report on the Operations of the Calcutta Improvement Trust for the Year 1915–16* (Calcutta: Calcutta Improvement Trust, 1916).

[17] Ibid., 11.

increase in house rent'. Banerjee reported that the situation was graver in the stretch between 'Peepulputty Lane and Ram Mohun Dutt Road'.[18]

Rashbehari Avenue: The Making of a New 'Inner City'

Ahindra Choudhury referred to an east–west roadway, popularly known as 'Dhakurer Rasta' (Road to Dhakuria), which started a little south of the Kalighat Tram Depot and ended in the Ballygunge Rail Station. That road traversed through a vast rural landscape and remained busy on weekdays, as it was a link between Alipore Court and Ballygunge Station. There were shops and stables to serve the passengers and villages along the road.[19] This road was the precursor to today's Rashbehari Avenue.

Like many streets and lanes, the history of Calcutta's famous Rashbehari Avenue is also entangled with the city's underground drainage system. The Municipal Corporation's objective was to set up a drainage system for the city's southern suburbs, as Bhowanipore and Ballygunge were becoming lucrative upper-middle-class and middle-class destinations. By the first decade of the twentieth century, it became amply clear to civic authorities that siltation in the Bidyadhari River would put the entire drainage network into trouble.[20] Therefore, a short-term solution at the authority's disposal was to keep on expanding the spill area. As a part of this endeavour, the Corporation acquired a tract of 'marshy land' lying between the Ballygunge Rail Station to the east and Chetla to the west to set up a sewerage line.[21]

This area between Russa Road to the west and Gariahat Road to the east was full of 'low-lying marshes' with a 'malarious reputation'.[22] In 1920, the

---

[18] Proceedings of the 303rd meeting of the Calcutta Improvement Trust, 5 August 1918, *Proceedings of the CIT for the Year 1918–19* (Valuation Department), 2–3.

[19] Choudhury, *Nijere Haraye Khunji*, vol. I.

[20] C. C. Chatterjee, *Calcutta Drainage Works: A Brief History* (Calcutta: The Corporation Press, 1921).

[21] Sumanta Banerjee, *Memoirs of Roads: Calcutta from Colonial Urbanization to Global Modernization* (New Delhi: Oxford University Press, 2016).

[22] The quoted term was in frequent circulation among the British Trustees of the Improvement Trust. Proceedings of the 124th meeting of the Calcutta Improvement Trust, 7 December 1914, *Proceedings of the CIT for the Year 1914–15* (Valuation Department).

Improvement Trust acquired this entire tract.[23] The Trust was entrusted with sewering the area to the south of Hazra Road and building a road between Chetla and Ballygunge Rail Station. As it came to be known, the 'Main Sewer' ended in the Hooghly River after crossing Kalighat.[24] This sewer enabled the city authority to reclaim acres of 'swampy and low-lying tracts of land' in the area bounded by Russa Road to the west, Ballygunge Rail Station to the east, Hazra Road to the north, and the Eastern Bengal Railway Lines to the south. This newly reclaimed land became a real estate destination in the interwar decades.

The scheme was known as 'Scheme XV: The Main Sewer Road'.[25] The Main Sewer Road divided the reclaimed land into two halves. Over the years, the Trust subsidized a tram route over the road. It also enabled filtered water, electricity, and gas connections for the newly built houses and apartments, especially in the area bounded by the Gariahat Road to the west and Russa Road to the east (Scheme XV-B). Eventually—in the mid-1930s—this wide avenue became a lucrative middle-class residential and commercial quarter with apartment houses above and showrooms on the ground floor.

Within a couple of years of the initiation of Scheme XV, the Trust's valuer presented a plan for the aforementioned area, which was devised keeping in mind the trends in the real estate market as observed before. The plan read as follows:

> In the present Scheme I find it difficult to lay-out suitable plots without adding a number of new roads; and cul-de-sacs. It has been found out from experience that plots of a larger area than 9 to 10 kottahs, cannot find a ready market now-a-days and the alterations are designed in such a manner that the majority of the plots will not exceed ten kottahs. I have suggested the omission of the four small open spaces situated at the junction of Lansdowne Road Extension and the Main Sewer Road and in order to compensate for the total area of open space I have increased the size of the open space at Nos. 92 and 93, Monoharpukur Road.[26]

---

[23] *Annual Report on the Operations of the Calcutta Improvement Trust for the Year 1920–21* (Calcutta: Calcutta Improvement Trust, 1921).

[24] Banerjee, *Memoirs of Roads*.

[25] *Annual Report on the Operations of the Calcutta Improvement Trust for the Year 1920–21*.

[26] Proceedings of the 498th meeting of the Calcutta Improvement Trust, 6 November 1922, *Proceedings of the CIT for the Year 1922–23* (Valuation Department), 349.

By 1928–1929, a sprawling park came up in the intersection of the Main Sewer Road and the Lansdowne Road on a 20-*bigha* plot. The Trust's Annual Report of 1928–1929 describes the park as follows:[27]

> It includes a full-size football ground, eight tennis courts, and a children's playground. A shelter is provided in a central position for general use. The footpaths are paved with asphalt and lighted by electricity, and the park is surrounded by a border of crotons, hibiscus and other shrubs.

Besides these civic facilities, the entire area was given an elevation by accumulating and levelling earth excavated from what has now become the Dhakuria Lake (then designated as an 'excavation area'). This was done to keep the Scheme area free of waterlogging in the rainy season.

In addition, the Trust executed a special sub-scheme for the stretch of the Main Sewer Road between Russa Road and Gariahat Road (Scheme XV-B) 'to provide building sites, create new and improving existing means of communication and facilities for traffic, and affording better facilities for conservancy ... [and] to lay out new streets and alter existing streets in the area'.[28] It publicized the prime plots along the new avenue and the adjacent areas through frequent advertisements in magazines and newspapers. One such advertisement that appeared in the *Calcutta Municipal Gazette* on 12 December 1931 declared that the 'sites' were 'eminently suitable' for shops, flats, and 'dwelling houses'.[29] By 1935, Gariahat—the centre of this newly planned neighbourhood—marked the southern physical boundary of Calcutta. The imagination that Gariahat was the 'end' of the city persisted for long among the *bhadralok*. Living in the north and west of Gariahat, for the *bhadralok*, was coterminous to claiming a certain rootedness with the city.

When completed, the Main Sewer Road became a 100-foot-wide avenue divided neatly by a green and elevated boulevard that hosted a tramline from Russa Road to Ballygunge Station. The avenue covered a 9-foot wide sewer. In early 1929, the Trust named it 'Ballygunge Avenue'. During the same year, the Trust handed over the avenue to the Corporation, then under the nationalist leadership. On 20 May 1931, the Corporation officially renamed the Ballygunge

---

[27] *Annual Report on the Operations of the Calcutta Improvement Trust for the Year 1928–29* (Calcutta: Calcutta Improvement Trust, 1928).

[28] Banerjee, *Memoirs of Roads*, 142.

[29] Ibid.

Avenue Rashbehari Avenue, after noted barrister, politician, and philanthropist Rashbehari Ghosh, who in the Swadeshi era had established an indigenous match factory in a nearby locality.[30]

Several members of the city's *nouveau riche*, who made a quick fortune during the two World Wars, invested a portion of their wealth in the land around the Main Sewer Road. By 1933, Rashbehari Avenue hosted more than 606 substantial residential and commercial properties that carried its address.[31] Unlike properties on the Central Avenue, which were bought up by Marwari proprietors, properties on Rashbehari Avenue came to be owned predominantly by Hindu Bengali upper-caste owners. Barrister J. C. Mukherjea (one of the early residents of Rashbehari Avenue), who went on to become a member of the Trust and the Chief Executive Officer of the Calcutta Corporation in the early 1930s, wrote to Surendranath Tagore that both the Trust and the Corporation had an 'unofficial agreement' for settling the Bengali *bhadralok* class in this new neighbourhood.[32]

Gradually, several Bengali luminaries among the intelligentsia started moving to this area, often residing in rented apartments. Noted fiction writer Pratibha Basu settled in one such apartment house at 202 Rashbehari Avenue in 1936 along with her husband, Buddhadeva Bose. The latter was one of the central figures of Bangla literature in the post-Tagore era. The Basus left behind numerous recollections of Rashbehari Avenue, the neighbourhoods surrounding it, and their apartment-living at 202 spanning three decades. They called their apartment 'Kabita Bhavan' or the 'House of Poetry'. In one of his autobiographical

---

[30] Ibid. Also see Choudhury *Nijere Hariye Khunji*, vol. I.

[31] *Thacker's Street Directory, 1933.*

[32] Surendranath Tagore was a nephew of Rabindranath. After retiring from the Indian Civil Service, Satyendranath (Surendranath's father) lived in Ballygunge. His children and in-laws settled in the new neighbourhoods around Rashbehari Avenue. I found a reference and summary of this letter dated 17 April 1930 in a correspondence between Saibal Gupta and Jadunath Sarkar. Saibal Gupta was the Chairman of the Trust and Jadunath Sarkar was a famous historian. They lived in two neighbourhoods adjacent to Rashbehari Avenue. The historian asked the bureaucrat if it was really true that the Trust sold plots to Bengalis even when it could have sold the plots to Marwaris at better prices. In reply, the bureaucrat quoted from the letter referred to here. Ashoka Gupta showed me a copy of Sarkar's letter and referred to a page in Saibal Gupta's diary for the details of his reply. The date of entry was 24 March 1956. Ashoka Gupta was a freedom fighter, a close political associate of Gandhi, and Saibal Gupta's wife. She died in 2008. My exchange with her took place in March 2005.

accounts, *Amar Jouban*, Buddhadeva wrote how from the window of their living room at Kabita Bhavan, he could see the modern apartment houses in 'New Ballygunge'.[33] The living room of Kabita Bhavan became well known for many *addas*. Numerous autobiographies of noted intellectuals of the city carry the memory of Kabita Bhavan and Rashbehari Avenue.

In her autobiography *Jiboner Jalchhabi*, Pratibha Basu recollected how, while house-hunting, they found a 'to let' advertisement in front of house 202. It was a modest two-bedroom apartment with all modern amenities, comprising two ceiling fans (that Pratibha and Buddhadeva had failed to acquire so far), a big toilet with a massive south-facing window, and a bathtub, basin, and shower. The kitchen had an electric furnace fitted with a chimney. Both Prathibha and Buddhadeva portrayed the new house and the street as a setup that represented modern and progressive middle-class living, away from the madding crowd of the city's traditional neighbourhoods. Buddhadeva recollected how the shadow of the *sonajhuri* trees on the asphalt in the daytime ignited his literary imagination.[34]

The upper-caste and middle-class residents of this neighbourhood were very vocal about the sanitary conditions of the locality. Thus, one M. N. Basu, who lived in P-92 Lake Road, objected to the continued existence of a pail depot in the vicinity of a *bhadralok* quarter. He wrote to the Corporation's mayor that he had purchased the property, assuming that the depot would be removed as soon as the new residents occupied their houses. He further wrote: 'Apart from a thousand and one other inconveniences, the number of flies ... has increased to such an extent that even at night, we are disturbed by these in hundreds, if not in thousands.'[35]

The pail depot in question had many predecessors in slums, stables, and artisanal workshops that occupied the area along with the adjacent villages of Dhakuria and Mudiali in the early twentieth century. These establishments had supported the aristocratic living of the Europeans and the erstwhile princely family of Mysore in Tollygunge. However, these villages had to make way for the ever-expanding city from 1913 onwards when the Trust widened the Russa Road. Gradually, some new slums sprang up behind Rashbehari Avenue—in Kankulia Street and Panditiya Road—to similarly serve the requirements of its new *bhadralok* settlers.[36]

---

[33] Buddhadeva Bose, *Amar Jouban* (Calcutta: M. C. Sarkar & Sons, 1967).

[34] Pratibha Basu, *Jiboner Jalchabi* (Kolkata: Ananda, Falgun 1418).

[35] Banerjee, *Memoirs of Roads*, 141.

[36] Ibid.

In Central Calcutta—as we have seen—the Trust was constrained by the city's existing social and architectural orders. Dislocations led to various kinds of social tensions—as we have witnessed in previous chapters. The social dislocations in the south may have been far more significant and its transformations far more radical. However, the official archives yield only a handful of legal disputes. In the south, the Trust faced a very different kind of resistance. For instance, in 1922, Babu Amulya Dhan Addi, a local notable and a member of the Bengal Legislative Council, complained about repeated theft and armed robbery of excavated soil, building materials, and rubbish in areas close to the Main Sewer Road. He also complained about the theft of dismantled wooden materials and bricks from the demolition sites in Russa Road.

Addi suspected that local *bustee* dwellers and villagers were involved in these acts. He complained that these gangs would raid the sites at nights, but due to the enormity of the demolition and building works in the area, proper surveillance was impossible. Moreover, these gangs were protected by 'goonda elements' and rice dealers of Chetla and Tollygunge, 'who started a thriving black market in building materials'. There were several dozen rice mills in Sahapur, Chetla, Alipore, and Tollygunge (see Appendix 4A.1). 'The rice dealers,' reported Addi, had access to large vessels. Some of these mills and their warehouses were reported to be used for stockpiling the raided materials.[37] Eventually, they smuggled the stolen materials to several parts of Calcutta and 'faraway places in eastern Bengal, Bihar and the United Provinces via Tolley's Nullah'.[38]

Thus, the frontier of Calcutta—like any other frontier—revealed itself as a horizon of peril and possibility.[39] It was simultaneously inside and outside of capital accumulation. Its taming also ignited accumulation. As Anna Tsing points out, a frontier is a liminal space where boundaries of 'law and theft, governance and violence, use and destruction' are blurred. She further says: '… these confusions change the rules and thus, enable extravagant new economies of profit—as well as loss.' If inner-city renewal led to the consolidation of capital over a limited space, frontier urbanization meant a proliferation by which 'the

---

[37] Proceedings of a Meeting of the Committee Appointed to Hear Objections to Improvement Scheme No. XV-B, held on Wednesday, the 22 March 1922 at 1.30 p.m. (Calcutta Improvement Trust Record Room).

[38] Ibid.

[39] Subhra Gururani and Rajarshi Dasgupta, 'Frontier Urbanism: Urbanization beyond Cities in South Asia', *Economic and Political Weekly* 53, no. 12 (2018), 41–45.

expansive nature of extraction comes [came] into its own'.[40] In the southern frontier of Calcutta, (frontier) urbanization took place through two different modes, each mode characterized by complex and variegated processes, which nonetheless played out differently. These two modes are outlined below.

Frontier Urbanization Mode 1: (Sub)urbanization, Accumulation, Dispossession

As the Trust moved southwards, Chief Engineer James Maden cautioned that construction work in the south would be very different due to the nature of land (low-lying, forested, watery, and marshy) in the newly acquired sites. In an explanatory note (dated 24 June 1914) to the Trust's Chairman C. H. Bompas, Maden cautioned that an ad hoc arrangement of landfilling—in practice in the inner city in the hands of 'petty contractors'—would make the task in the southern suburbs more chaotic. He reasoned that 'such contractors would simply excavate other tanks as near as possible to the ones to be filled' to curtail the cost of transportation, which would lead to 'an indefinite multiplication of the original cost of filling the first tank' and consequently, 'the same, or a greater, tank area would remain'. Maden calculated that the ongoing southern schemes (IV, IV-A, V) would require approximately 9,000,000 cubic feet of earth, which could be obtained by excavating a 5,000 x 650 feet plot of land to a depth of 20 feet. The 'excavation area' would eventually take the shape of a massive lake for which at least a 400-*bigha* land plot was needed.[41]

Maden knew that excessively low-lying and forested areas east of Ballygunge Station or the Saltwater Lakes would not serve the purpose. Transporting such a massive quantity of earth would require thousands of bullock carts and a road that could withstand the load of heavy cart traffic. Finally, Maden zoomed into a 'low-lying' and 'practically uninhabited area at the extreme south end of Ballygunge'.[42] He insisted that this particular area lacked the prospect of being used for 'building purposes' due to 'its proximity to the railway and its bottled-up position'. Moreover, the land price appeared affordable, at just 20 rupees per *cottah*. This was important since the area acquired for excavation would eventually have to be 'paid for by the various schemes' in the southern

---

[40] Tsing, *Friction*, 26–27.

[41] Proceedings of a Meeting of the Works Committee, 29 June 1914, Letter no. 897, from James Maden to the Chairman Bompas, 24 June 1914, Note, pp. 2–5, *Proceedings of the CIT for the Year, 1914–15* (Valuation Department).

[42] Ibid.

suburbs. Moreover, the selected spot was within a mile of active scheme areas in Russa Road, which meant that the transport cost would also be minimal. Maden opined that a lake embraced by a massive park could be built in this area, which would eventually become a 'veritable civic asset': 'A park scheme embracing a lake of this magnitude, which would allow of sailing and rowing, etc., would undoubtedly become one of the chief attractions of the city.'[43]

On 13 July 1914, the Trust's Board passed a resolution favouring the acquisition of a 412-*bigha* land plot 'to the south of the Dhakuria Road in Ward No. XXI at an estimated cost of rupees 1,60,000 to be used as an area from which earth could be obtained for filling lands in the southern section of the town'.[44] The whole excavation area was bounded to the north by a line drawn east and west from Keyatala Lane and Gariahat Road to Shanagar Lane, and bound on the south by the E. B. Railway, east by Gariahat Road, and west by Russa Road (south).[45]

The Trust's records tell us that this land had belonged to 'petty property owners' residing in nearby villages. There was already a large pond belonging to the Contai Raj estate—a premier *zamindari* estate of Midnapore. Apart from that, there were 'lowlands' where Bagdis—an 'untouchable' caste—'squatted for generations'. They earned a livelihood by picking various kinds of *saak* and herbs and selling them in nearby urban neighbourhoods as itinerant vendors. They also worked in various garden houses owned by the rich that dotted Russa Road and Tollygunge in those days. Some of them were hired for manual work in nearby rice mills. There were some *bedes*—snake charmers—who 'squatted' there, as 'snakes were to be found in abundance' in this area.[46] It is clear then that much of this area, rather than being privately owned, functioned as shared commons, which sustained lower-caste marginal populations, servicing nearby urban areas. The acquisition of 412 *bigha*s of land in this area, then, meant enclosure of these commons.

---

[43] Ibid.

[44] Proceedings of the 104th Meeting of the Calcutta Improvement Trust, *Proceedings of the CIT for the Year 1914–15* (Valuation Department).

[45] Proceedings of the 206th Meeting of the Calcutta Improvement Trust, 12 June 1916, *Proceedings of the CIT for the Year 1916–17* (Valuation Department).

[46] Proceedings of a Meeting of the Committee Appointed to Hear Objections to Improvement Scheme No. XV-B, held on Wednesday, the 22 March 1922 at 1.30 p.m. (Record Room of the Calcutta Improvement Trust).

Frontier Urbanization

The Bengal government approved the Trust's proposal for land acquisition for excavation on 14 December 1915.[47] The Trust's land acquisition collector reported an increase in land price by more than 3.1 per cent within the year. In his explanation to the government for this price hike, Bompas reasoned:[48]

> The increase in the estimate is ... chiefly because since the Trust Scheme was first mooted along the Russa Road (South), transactions in the land have taken place within and near the area proposed for acquisition. The sales indicate a level of values much higher than was anticipated, and there is a ground for suspicion that they have taken place in anticipation of acquisition proceedings.

Bompas admitted that there was little concrete evidence to prove the element of speculation involved in the quick rise of land prices in the area. 'However,' added Bompas, the 'collector would be unable to ignore the evidence these transactions afforded'. In his autobiography, Ahindra Chaudhury, too, remembered how some of his forward-looking neighbours and 'people from the city' began to buy all available plots to the east of Russa Road.[49] It needs to be remembered that the First World War had already broken out when the Trust surveyed land acquisition in the area. Thus, the *Annual Report of the Trust for 1915–16* mentioned the increase in land speculation as 'Government Paper was no longer

---

[47] From Under Secretary to the Government of Bengal to the Chairman, Calcutta Improvement Trust, Letter No. 2688M, Municipal Department, Municipal Branch, 27 November 1915, Appendix D (Excavation Area), *Annual Report on the Operations of the Calcutta Improvement Trust for the Year 1915–16* (Calcutta: Calcutta Improvement Trust, 1916), 67. The government's declaration reads as follows:

> Whereas it appears to the Governor in Council that land is required to be taken by Government at the expense of the Calcutta Improvement Trust for a public purpose, viz., for the purpose of obtaining a sufficient supply of earth for the operations of the Trust and for the construction of a Park and Lake in villeges Mudiali, etc. ... it is declared that for the above purpose a piece of land measuring more or less 412 bighas ... is required within the aforesaid villages of Mudiali, etc.

The name Mudiali has survived until date, but nothing of its rural world.

[48] From C. H. Bompas to the Secretary, Government of Bengal, General Department, Municipal Branch, No. XXVII-1/4, 25 October 1915, Appendix D (Excavation Area), Annual Report for the Year 1915–16, 66–67.

[49] Choudhury, *Nijere Haraye Khunji*, vol. I.

looked on as a safe investment'. Already, there was a severe rise in the price of building materials, including brick. The prospect of cheap brickmaking from the earth in the excavation area made the Trust keener on acquiring this land despite the price hike.[50]

Ahindra Choudhury remembered the massive mobilization of workers and bullock carts in the excavation site, the stockpiling of earth by the side of the Russa Road, and the sale of rubbish as well as the materials acquired from the demolished buildings (see Appendix 4A.2). 'Everything appeared to have a market,' he wrote.[51] Similarly, Premendra Mitra, who studied in the nearby South-Suburban School and frequented 202 Rashbehari Avenue in the subsequent decades, wrote eloquently about losing the 'simple way of life' in the suburb. In his novel *Agamikal* (Tomorrow), published in 1934, Mitra said:[52]

> The day brings in engineer's measuring tapes, the road-rollers, account-books of the contractor and the crowbar of the coolies, while the full-moon night moans. Perhaps both are real. The city is coming of age. Someone loses his garden and others—their farmland. Huts with round leaves give way—the ponds fill up; date, palm, and coconut trees bow down—the city is moving forward.

Within a decade of the start of the excavation work, Rashbehari Avenue and the Lake (created out of the large excavation pit) became a lucrative Bengali middle-class residential destination. The plots sandwiched between Rashbehari Avenue and the Lake were sold between 800 rupees and 1,800 rupees a *cottah* from the mid-1920s onwards.[53] In the 1940s, the sale value increased considerably and moved between 2,800 and 3,000 rupees.[54]

The Trust's southern advance facilitated the growth of private contractors and builders who accumulated capital through the Trust's tenders.[55] One of the major

---

[50] *Annual Report on the Operations of the Calcutta Improvement Trust for the Year 1915–16*.

[51] Choudhury, *Nijere Haraye Khunji*, vol. I.

[52] Premendra Mitra, *Agamikal* (Kolkata: Indian Associated Publishing Co. Ltd., 1953), 225. The passage has been translated by Kaustubh Mani Sengupta.

[53] Choudhury, *Nijere Haraye Khunji*, vol. I.

[54] Civil Appellate Jurisdiction, The Province of Bengal (Appellant) vs. The Board of Trustees for the Improvement of Calcutta (Respondent), 20 February 1946, *Calcutta Weekly Notes*, 825–837.

[55] Appendix 4A.2 showcases some such enterprises, the type of works they performed between 1916 and 1920, and the quantum of money being pumped in the production

works that these contractors performed was excavating soil from the 'excavation area', producing brick, and mobilizing rubbish to fill ponds and raise low-lying areas in schemes IV, V, and XV. The Trust guidelines specified that the contractor 'must allow in his tender for tank filling, for the cutting down and removal of all such trees and other growths, including the grubbing out and removal of all roots'.[56] When the real work of excavation began, it was gradually realized that during the dry season, the contractors could excavate more earth than they could carry away. The surplus earth was stacked by the side of Dhakuria Road. In the rainy season, the surplus earth would have to be used because fresh excavation was found to be impossible as 'the remaining untouched portion' of the excavation area 'would be under water ... and consequently, unworkable'.[57]

From the list of eligible contractors in Appendix 4A.2, it seems that Hindu Bengali entrepreneurs dominated the sector. There were some joint stock initiatives in the form of engineers' collectives (such as the Calcutta Engineering Society), but there was a discernible tendency towards the formation of family firms in the construction business. There were a few Marwari entrepreneurs in this business such as Natiram Sagarmal & Co. and M. L. Dalmiya & Co. The latter became a prominent player in the southern schemes. Dalmiya specialized in land filling and developing parks in south Calcutta. He was credited with at least two iconic parks of the south—Deshapriya Park and Park Circus Maidan. By the mid-twentieth century, M. L. Dalmia & Co. became an influential developer and circulated capital between construction, tea, and logistics sectors.[58] Some of these

---

of space. It also reveals the extent to which labour, logistical, and financial mobilization in the south diverged from the Trust's central city renewal operations.

[56] 'Note on Excavation Area', Proceedings of the 280th Meeting of the Calcutta Improvement Trust, 2 April 1918, *Proceedings of the CIT for the Year 1918–1919* (Valuation Department).

[57] Chief Engineer's Note regarding Excavation Area, Proceedings of the 319th Meeting of the Calcutta Improvement Trust, 13 January 1919, *Proceedings of the CIT for the Year 1918–1919* (Valuation Department).

[58] M. L. Dalmiya was the founder of the MLD Group of enterprises which now employs more than 5,000 employees and is considered one of the key players in tea and packaging industries. Dalmiya's career trajectory is illustrative of the circuit of accumulation in which Calcutta's southern expansion became a chapter. In a conversation with me in 2010, M. L. Dalmiya's grandson and famous cricket administrator Jagmohan Dalmiya told me the following about MLD's business trajectory: M. L. Dalmiya began his career in the early twentieth century as a wholesaler in tea and a petty jute speculator. He routed some of his savings in the

contractors were granted lease in the excavation area and set up temporary brick fields. One such entrepreneur, S. Bagchee (Appendix 4A.2), took the contract of brick-making in 1920–1921 and again in 1921–1922.[59] Calcutta Engineering Society (CES) earned quite a name in brick-making at the excavation area and selling excess brick beyond their Improvement Trust contracts to the Trust for its other operations.[60]

Extensive building work in the emerging suburbs also facilitated small- and medium-scale enterprises producing house building and engineering materials in the 1930s and the 1940s. Historian Sumanta Banerjee traced some such enterprises from advertisements. Dutta & Company offered 'galvanised baths, buckets, stoves, lanterns, enamels' while P. C. Coomar & Co. (Appendix 4A.2), Architects, Builders and Contractors, claimed to be 'specialists in drainage and waterworks'.[61] Bengal Belting Works Limited (still in operation) manufactured 'belting and hose pipe as good as the best of the imported kind made under

---

construction industry in the second decade of the century, when the demand for contractors became particularly high in the frontiers of the city. By the 1950s, M. L. Dalmiya & Co. became one of the most well-known construction tycoons in the city. The company bought acres of land falling between Chetla in the east and Diamond Harbour Road in the west—a place now known as New Alipore. It got most of the contracts in developing a planned neighbourhood in New Alipore in the mid-1950s. The company managed to secure contracts during the development of Salt Lake in the 1950s and 1960s. Jagmohan's father, A. P. Dalmiya, was interested in going back to the family's initial investment in the tea trade. The second and third generations of the family saw a shift in the company's involvement from tea wholesale to tea plantation. It reinvested some of the profits from the Calcutta construction business in buying tea estates in north Bengal in the 1940s and the 1950s when the European planters transferred their tea estates to Indian entrepreneurs. Jagmohan Dalmiya took over the family's construction business in 1959–1960. One of his first construction works was the building of Birla Planetarium in Chowringhee (1963).

[59] Calcutta's expansion in Salt Lake in the 1960s and the 1970s, in eastern wetlands in the late twentieth century, and beyond Salt Lake in Rajarhaat in the early twenty-first century is dominated by the figures of the private 'promoter' and 'contractor' who connived with the local regime functionaries to grab land from small holders, fishermen, and farmers. The story of Dalmiya, Bagchee, and the CES gives us an (incidental) early genealogy of such figures in the real estate market.

[60] Note by the Hon'ble Rai Radha Charan Pal Bahadur, Proceedings of the 380th Meeting of the Calcutta Improvement Trust, 26 April 1920, *Proceedings of the CIT for the Year 1920–1921* (Valuation Department). For the specification of the contract between the CES and the Trust, see Proceedings of the 384th Meeting, 25 May 1920. *Proceedings of the CIT for the Year 1920–21* (Valuation Department).

[61] Banerjee, *Memoirs of Roads*.

expert Indian management by Indian capital and labour and at a much cheaper rate'.[62] Under S. K. Roy & Sons, Bengal Belting Works Limited became a prime supplier of engineering materials to large-scale housing, government, and railway projects.[63] These firms had backward linkages with engineering workshops clustered in Howrah.[64]

By the late 1930s, Rashbehari Avenue had become the new inner city in the expanding south. In 1936, the famous Jay Engineering Works Ltd was registered in Calcutta, and it was given a 120-*bigha* plot to the south of the Lakes, crossing the E. B. Railway lines.[65] This firm was given large-scale contracts to make various kinds of munitions during the war years, especially sewing machines to meet the requirements of the Supply Department of the Central Government. The factory produced hurricane lanterns, enamels, paints, cooking ranges, and electrical appliances such as ceiling fans. Ceiling fans became a ubiquitous item of middle-class living in Calcutta in the 1930s and 1940s.[66] The founding of such a factory in the southern frontier of the city set in motion urbanization and land-use transformations in the south. A whole industrial belt emerged near this factory in the late colonial and early post-colonial decades, where Bengal Lamp, National Instruments Limited, Sulekha Ink factory, and Krishna Glass were located in close proximity to each other.

The presence of these factories led to the creation of a fringe economy around them. Some entrepreneurs started small ancillary manufacturing units in the vicinity of these factories, while several others opened roadside eateries for

---

[62] Ibid., 153.

[63] See the advertisement of 'The Bengal Belting Works LTD' in *Prabuddha Bharata*, January 1942, 7.

[64] Despite a boom in indigenous entrepreneurial activities in Calcutta's construction sector during the interwar era, British monopoly over certain commodities such as the cast iron pipes required in drainage and water works remained unchallenged. Thus, the Trust's Chairman reported the government's sanction 'to the acceptance of the tender amounting to Rs. 2,95,548-11-0 of the Associated British Engineers Limited, Calcutta, for the supply and delivery of cast iron pipes for stores'. Proceedings of the 397th Meeting of the Calcutta Improvement Trust, 4 October 1920, *Proceedings of the CIT for the Year 1920–1921* (Valuation Department).

[65] Out of this 120-*bigha* plot, 35 *bighas* were acquired in 1928 by the Improvement Trust to build a model dwelling settlement for the evicted populations from the Trust's various schemes in the south. The settlement never came into existence. See Sir R. N. Mukherjee Private File at the Record Room of the Improvement Trust.

[66] *Report of the Indian Tariff Board on the Sewing Machine Industry* (Bombay: Government Central Press, 1947).

workers, visitors, and customers. New working-class neighbourhoods came up around the factory premises on Prince Anwar Shah Road, Poddar Nagar, Bikramgarh, Katjunagar, and Jadavpur.

The Trust's expedition in the southern frontiers of Calcutta facilitated and coincided with large-scale enclosures, dispossession, logistical scaling-up, infrastructure-building, accumulation, and working-class formation. Those dispossessed in this enclosure and urbanization process also hit back through multiple raids in the newly developing sites. Amulya Dhan Addi, who complained about the raids and disorder, also wrote that the local 'lower class' people were seriously antagonistic to the 'labourers brought from outside by the contract agencies' who squatted for years, 'making temporary villages near the excavation area'. There were incidents of conflict between these two groups in the 1910s and 1920s. Eventually, the Trust ordered the private contractors working in the excavation area to source labourers from the affected locality. This was indeed a compromise that the Trust had to arrive at.[67]

Frontier Urbanization Mode 2: *Jabardakhal* as (Sub)urbanization *without* Accumulation

Let us now present another mode of frontier urbanization that took place in Calcutta and its adjacent areas in the aftermath of India's Partition and Independence. This mode contrasted with the previous mode in many fundamental ways—the most fundamental contrast was urbanization's relation with accumulation. The prime mover of spatial mobilization in this mode was *jabardakhal*.

Jabardakhal refers to how poorer social classes claimed crucial physical and social infrastructures collectively and made those infrastructures the focus of collective existence in the city. Despite its doubtful legality, *jabardakhal* became a recognizable form of claiming space during the middle of the twentieth century, amidst massive colonization of land, locality formation, growth of fringe economies, and mass democracy. It forged new interfaces between space and polity and became a critical colonizing and urbanizing agent in the frontiers of Calcutta.

After Partition, the city moved further south because of unprecedented demographic pressure. By 1951, Calcutta had an official population of 433,000

---

[67] Chief Engineer's Note regarding Excavation Area, Proceedings of the 319th Meeting of the Calcutta Improvement Trust, *Proceedings of the CIT for the Year 1918–19* (Record Room Copy).

refugees. This was a very conservative official estimate. For instance, it excluded about 50,000 displaced families in various illegal refugee settlements that came up almost overnight between 1949 and 1950.[68] In 1952, the number of squatters' colonies in Calcutta, 24 Parganas, and Nadia reached 242. That apart, there were several stray colonies in the city proper like the one that grew in the parks around Dhakuria Lakes. Several refugee settlements sprang up in areas between Gariahat–Rashbehari Avenue and Garia–Tollygunge. Table 4.2 summarizes only a few prominent instances of squatter colonies that emerged in the southern and southwestern frontiers of Rashbehari Avenue and Gariahat. There were several other colonies between Tollygunge and Behala and between Garia and Tollygunge, along N.S.C. Bose Road.

Before the refugee influx began, areas such as Regent Colony (Ajadgarh), Naktala, and Ranikuthi (bordering Netaji Nagar) had acres of prime land walled up in garden houses of the city's gentry. Most of these properties were encroached upon by the refugees, causing a virtual suspension of private property in these emerging frontier suburbs. In 1954, there were at least 131,008 families settled on privately owned lands. According to Prafulla Chakrabarti's estimate, approximately 2,390,049 acres of land came under refugee colonization in the 1950s which included privately owned properties, state properties, and properties in the hands of state corporations. Negotiations between the private and public owners, the refugee associations, and the state continued for several years. They involved violence,[69] agitation, and displacements of refugees as well as of the existing populations by refugees.[70]

---

[68] Uditi Sen, *Citizen Refugee: Forging the Indian Nation after Partition* (New Delhi, Cambridge University Press, 2018).

[69] An instance will suffice. Sometime in April 1951 a pregnant woman was killed during a battle between the landlords and refugees in Poddarnagar. There was also a case of police firing in Dhakuria, killing a woman—Binapani Mitra. Prafulla Chakrabarti writes: 'The eviction operations of the private land owners were more in the nature of raids in the colonies by hoodlums and the police. They threw themselves upon the newly erected shanties and razed them into the ground ... occasionally they met with organised resistance and they killed.' Prafulla Kumar Chakrabarti, *The Marginal Men: The Refugees and the Left Political Syndrome in West Bengal* (Calcutta: Naya Udyog, 1999), 80–81.

[70] Acquisition of Land for Bikramgarh Squatters Colony P.S. Tollygunge, File No. 15 (2) 63-BI, 1963, Ministry of Home Affairs, Rehabilitation Department, 1963, NAI. This file mentions 78 houses and properties deserted by the Muslim owners during the setting up of a squatters' colony in Bikramgarh.

Table 4.2 Refugee encroachment of properties in south Calcutta

Name of the Colonies	Properties Encroached	Number of Families in 1954
Bijoygarh (the biggest colony) near Jadavpur	Varying types of land including the American Army barracks, 'good habitable properties', patches of agricultural land	3,000
Baghajatin near Jadavpur	Habitable high land and low-lying land close to the rail tracks	1,000
Jadavgarh in Garfa	'Low and jungle land': 70 *bigha*s approximately	340
Sahid Nagar in Dhakuria	'Jungle land, low and marshy land': 50 *bigha*s approximately	200
Netaji Nagar (Tollygunge)	High and habitable land: 150 *bigha*s approximately	600
Ramgarh (between Jadavpur and Tollygunge)	'Mixed land': 30 *bigha*s approximately	250
Arabinda Palli (Behala)	'Low and marshy land': 30 *bigha*s	250
Ajadgarh	'High lands': 60 *bigha*s approximately	600
Bikramgarh (backyard of Jay Engineering Factory)	'High lands' and some 'green fields': 15 *bigha*s approximately	206

Source: Based on 'Squatters' Colonies', *The Economic Weekly*, 5 June 1954: 631–634.

Very soon, the 'refugee question' entered the domain of electoral politics. In the by-election in mid-1949, Sarat Chandra Bose cobbled together the nucleus of a Left united front and won by 13,550 votes against the Congress candidate in the South Calcutta constituency. Congress's own report attributed this embarrassing defeat to the government's 'mishandling of the refugee problem'.[71] Gradually,

---

[71] Report to Dr. Pattabhi Sitaramayya, President AICC, on the cause for Congress Failure in the South Calcitta by-election, by A. K. Ghose, President NCDCC, in 'By-election in the South Calcutta Constituency—Sarat Chandra Bose vs. Suresh Chandra Das, File No. 3-11-B, 1949, Digitized Private Papers of Sardar Patel, NAI. Bose's victory brought to surface the crisis and factionalism within the ruling Congress government. In a press conference, Nehru proclaimed Congress's defeat as the people's verdict against the state government. The anti–Chief Minister factions within the state Congress unit led by Ambika Ghosh and Surendra Mohan Ghosh mounted pressure on the Chief Minister. This crisis continued from June 1949 to

the Left and other smaller political parties emerged as important political constituencies that offered the new post-colonial electorate the possibility of advancing pressing issues such as the housing crisis and unemployment to the forefront of political debate. In this political climate, *jabardakhal*, or forcible colonization by refugees, became a powerful agent of urbanization in the frontiers of Calcutta—from Kanchrapara to Sonarpur and from Bongaon to Budge Budge.

It is evident that the refugee crisis and the politicization of encroachment led to a complex transformation of property in mid-twentieth-century Calcutta. On the one hand, *jabardakhal* led to large-scale de-commodification of private and public properties on which refugee settlements developed. On the other hand, refugees and migrants transformed erstwhile 'wastelands' into usable, and hence, exchangeable properties by encroaching on them. Thus, in the 'waste lands', encroachments gave birth to private property, turning encroachment into an act of value formation and valuation—a positive human energy and a force that produced space.[72] These two circuits of property coexisted for decades in the new frontiers of the city. Consequently, most of the squatter colonies had a mix of dwelling land, agricultural land, marshy and low-lying land, and inhabited and uninhabited land. This is evident in the descriptions of the newly colonized lands in Table 4.2.

In early 1951, the Government of West Bengal devised a strategy to draw 'a line between high-price and low-price lands'.[73] The government would persuade the owners of low-price lands to sell them to refugees through amicable settlements, but refugees occupying the high-price lands would have to be evicted. It was only after many protests, roadblocks, and street agitations by refugee associations in 1951 that the government agreed to find rehabilitation for the refugees before evicting them from the high-price lands. It was decided that the refugees would be resettled in nearby low-price lands to avoid further devastation of their livelihood. But as a space of negotiation opened up, refugee associations began to bargain over the prices of both high-price and low-price lands. These negotiations revealed how properties in places such as Tollygunje, Jadavpur, and Dhakuria had been kept inflated by the *zamindar*s and real estate

---

January 1950—until Bose withdrew from active politics. He died in February 1950. See Prafulla Chakrabarti, *The Marginal Men*.

[72] Himadri Chatterjee, 'Partitioned Urbanity: A Refugee Village Bordering Kolkata', *Economic and Political Weekly* 53, no. 12 (2018): 93–100.

[73] Prafulla Chakrabarti, *The Marginal Men*, 83.

speculators during the Second World War and after Independence. The refugees demanded a fair pricing mechanism of property, considering its valuation before the war in 1939 or just after the war in 1946.

The government, moreover, found it difficult to trace new rehabilitation sites in the already populated fringes of the city. As Prafulla Chakrabarti notes, 'it simply had not the power to dismantle 149 colonies and evict 1,49,280 people (29,856 families)....'[74] Ultimately, the government decided to acquire the land occupied by 148 refugee colonies spread across Calcutta, 24 Parganas, and Nadia without evicting the residents. This acquisition was to happen in the name of a 'public purpose'.[75] Each refugee household in these colonies would be entitled to a one-time government credit of 1,875 rupees (maximum) to regularize their holding.[76] The refugee households were required to return this money to the government in 20 years. Until then, the property would remain under a mortgage with the government. This strategy, which received legal sanction through the Rehabilitation of Displaced Persons and Eviction of Persons in Unauthorised Occupation of Land Act, 1951, resulted in the freezing of landed property in the colonies for many years. In these resettled areas, there was thus a virtual disappearance of the real estate market. Refugees developed vast stretches of uninhabited areas by dwelling on them. Yet they could not afford to push those into the market as the properties were essential for their livelihood and social reproduction.

Thus, one of the effects of *jabardakhal* was a virtual withdrawal of urban property from the real estate market for at least four decades. The near disappearance of the land market in this vast stretch of land for such a long time created a kind of incremental urbanization *without* accumulation. *Jabardakhal* enforced the dismemberment of capital congealed in land in the urbanizing frontiers. In summary, while frontier urbanization mode 1 represents motion, urbanization through *jabardakhal* or urbanization without accumulation (mode 2) refers to the creative force of obstruction.

Eventually, the refugees got land titles in the colony areas only in the 1990s, which led to a property boom in neighbourhoods between Jadavpur and Garia, and Garia and Tollygunge. Many refugee families capitalized their holdings,

[74] Ibid., 80.
[75] Ibid. Metaphorically, this was an undoing of recoupment in Chapter 2.
[76] Acquisition of Land for Bikramgarh Squatters Colony P.S. Tollygunge, File No. 15 (2) 63-BI, 1963, Ministry of Home Affairs, Rehabilitation Department, 1963, NAI. Acquisition of Land for Regularization of Harakali Squatters' Colony, P.S. Dum Dum, Ministry of Home Affairs, Rehabilitation Department, 1965, NAI.

sold surplus land, developed apartment houses, or rented out their houses to college students. The post-colonial city grew along with the proliferation of the people's economy in the city as well as the frontiers.

The property negotiations in the fringes affected the new inner city regularly. Two Left-wing refugee associations by the names of United Central Refugee Council (UCRC) and Refugee Central Rehabilitation Council (RCRC) conducted regular protest rallies, demonstrations, and gatherings throughout the city, keeping the Maidan, parks, the Legislative Assembly, and the Government House (Rajbhavan) areas echoing with anti-landlord sloganeering. By 1951, writes Prafulla Chakrabarti, 'Calcutta became the city of processions, the nightmare city'. He further says:

> Processions, demonstrations and meetings, traffic jams, brickbats and teargas shells and lathis coming down in showers, burning tramcars and buses, and occasional firings—these became the hallmark of the city. Calcutta had experienced demonstrations and mammoth meetings, lathi-charges, teargas shells and bullets during the intoxicating days of the trial of the INA heroes. But at no time in its history these were part of its daily life.[77]

Thus, during the anti-eviction agitations or the *jabardakhal* movement of the 1950s, the city learned to live with agitations, demonstrations, and processions. Deshapriya Park and Park Circus Maidan became two popular sites of demonstration, along with the Maidan in Chowringhee. The agitators—men, women, adults as well as children—came from faraway places in the suburbs. Prafulla Chakrabarti writes: 'They came in trains, buses and trucks which disgorged their load at different terminal points in Calcutta where processions were formed.'[78] These continuing processions put Calcutta in a state of constant siege in the first two post-colonial decades.

Rashbehari Avenue—the new inner city—witnessed a transformation in the context of the *jabardakhal* movement. From the mid-1950s, footpath hawkers began to encroach upon the sprawling sidewalks and by the late 1960s, the entire stretch of the street had become a marketplace.

---

[77] Chakrabarti, *The Marginal Men*, 90.
[78] Ibid.

Claiming Rashbehari Avenue: Proliferation of the People's Economy

Urbanization in the older, central parts of the city took place through the proliferation of wholesale markets (such as Burrabazaar, Posta Bazaar, Hatkhola Bazaar) and numerous organized retail bazaars in the eighteenth and nineteenth centuries. However, in the twentieth century, urbanization in the southern parts occurred via *jabardakhal* that took the form of proliferation of unorganized retail. The refugee city thus came to be dotted with unorganized marketplaces. These marketplaces and shops blurred the boundaries between public space and commons, and the public and the private. Let us consider one of the early cases of encroachment by the hawkers.

According to police records, on 17 June 1955, some refugee men encroached upon the frontage premises of 195 Rashbehari Avenue, which was then a plot of vacant land having an interface (shared boundary) of about 226 feet with the sidewalk. The men—calling themselves 'refugee hawkers'—placed several *taktaposh* (wooden platforms with four legs), blocking the Rashbehari Avenue frontage of the plot. These hawkers were associated with the West Bengal Hawkers Association of 12 Ballygunge Garden in Calcutta. The association published a circular in Bangla stating that the hawkers had been permitted by the government to set up a refugee hawkers' corner (more discussion on the refugee hawkers' corners can be found in Chapter 5) at the said junction. Further, the circular said that the hawkers' corner would be inaugurated by Shri Arabinda Bose on Tuesday, 21 June 1955 at 5 p.m. The circular was disseminated widely[79] and a modest gathering assembled at the refugee corner's inaugural function. The speakers—most of them were from the Left-wing Workers Party of India (WPI)—talked about the refugee problem, unemployment, and the need for many such hawkers' corners in the city to aid the livelihood of thousands of unemployed youths.[80] Within a year or so, the frontage of 195 Rashbehari Avenue became a thriving marketplace.

The hawkers informed the Municipal Corporation—the proprietor of the encroached-upon sidewalk—that the police had permitted them to occupy the sidewalks. Three days before the inaugural function, on 18 June 1955, the

---

[79] *Sudhir Kumar Banerjee v. The Commissioner, Corporation of Calcutta* (High Court of Judicature at Calcutta), Matter No. 183 of 1959, 17-11-1960, In the Bench of Justice D. N. Sinha.

[80] SW 636/55, 82, ORS 4328, 25 June 1955, 12. 47, Office of the Deputy Commissioner of Police, Special Branch, Calcutta, Government of West Bengal, Daily Notes of Special Branch of Calcutta Police.

Officiating District Engineer (IV) of the Municipal Corporation had intimated the Ballygunge Police Station about this encroachment and requested the Officer in-Charge (OC) to 'remove obstructions' from the sidewalk. When the OC asked the hawkers to show the 'permission' for the hawkers' corner, they cited a verbal communication between the Deputy Commissioner of Police and the union leaders. They also showed trade licenses under Sections 218–219 of the Calcutta Municipal Act, 1951, which acknowledged and authorized them as traders. The Officiating District Engineer of the Corporation (IV) wrote a letter to the Deputy Commissioner of Police, requesting him to clear encroachments, but even after repeated reminders, and assurances from the police, the Corporation received no formal reply on the matter.[81]

In October that year, the hawkers approached the Commissioner of Police for permission to encroach upon the said sidewalk. The Commissioner of Police permitted the hawkers to set up a purely non-permanent hawkers' corner during the Puja season which would end on 25 October 1955. The Commissioner warned, however, that the hawkers must vacate the site at once if there were any complaints from the public or the property owners.[82] The Puja season of 1955 passed peacefully. The hawkers' corner remained and began to attract more hawkers.

Sudhir Kumar Banerjee—one of the owners of the plot on 195 Rashbehari Avenue—came to know about the encroachments only in March 1959. He came to visit the plot with the intention of developing it into a set of residential buildings, and realized that with hawkers blocking the entrance to his property, the price of the plot would be far less than its market price. Therefore, Banerjee requested the Commissioner of Police to clear obstructions from the frontage of his property, but he did not receive any reply.

On 30 September 1959, Banerjee and other owners of the plot moved the High Court. The Court's ruling was predictable. It severely reprimanded the Corporation and the police for failing to protect the rights of the public to an unencumbered sidewalk. The judge (Deep Narayan Sinha) mobilized various legal provisions that criminalized obstructions and held these two government organizations responsible for 'chaos in the city'. He particularly reprimanded the Commissioner of Police for issuing a 'formal permission without any reference to the Corporation of Calcutta'—the owner of the sidewalk. In his defence, the

---

[81] *Sudhir Kumar Banerjee v. The Commissioner, Corporation of Calcutta.*
[82] Ibid.

Commissioner of Police talked about unemployment and the livelihood of the refugees and asked the Court to investigate the matter from a humanitarian angle but failed to persuade the judge who ordered an immediate removal of the obstructions along the frontage of 195 Rashbehari Avenue.[83]

The hawkers' corner in front of 195 Rashbehari Avenue was dismantled after this judgment. By encroaching on a sidewalk and obstructing a building plot, it threatened both public and private property simultaneously. But the deliberations of the court case indicate that hawkers enjoyed the sympathies of government officials, who oversaw the implementation of order and enforced law. Elaborate scenes were witnessed on the day of eviction. The hawkers protested and blocked Gariahat Crossing for two hours and attempted to burn a tramcar. Nonetheless, the eviction happened.[84] Within a few months, however, the hawkers returned and restarted the hawkers' corner. This time, there were many more hawkers involved. Their establishments extended beyond the Gariahat Crossing and extended towards Basanti Devi College on Rashbehari Avenue.

Throughout the 1960s, hawkers clustered on the sidewalks of Gariahat Road and Rashbehari Avenue. Refugees who had migrated from East Pakistan were already part of the existing textile and garment trading networks in Bengal and beyond. Hence, they started sidewalk stalls at Gariahat, selling textile products, specializing mainly in traditional handloom *saris*.[85] Through the proliferation of sidewalk hawking, Gariahat emerged as a veritable destination for many inter-

---

[83] Ibid.

[84] SW 636/59, 102, ORS 4987, 12 January 1960, 17, 32, Office of the Deputy Commissioner of Police, Special Branch, Calcutta, Government of West Bengal, Daily Notes of Special Branch of Calcutta Police.

[85] The refugee hawkers were also familiar with textile products and artisanal communities in West Bengal bordering East Pakistan. This was due to the existence of several inter-district trading channels. These networks were reshuffled and reinvented as 'illegal' with the emergence of two nation-states in the subcontinent. Further, the Partition led to a violent geographic dislocation of peasant and artisanal communities. Many skilled artisanal communities found a settlement in different refugee camps in West Bengal and bordering districts. One often finds that refugee traders in Calcutta had village, kinship, and other social ties with these artisanal groups. Besides, the context of rehabilitation and struggle for citizenship created a new sense of bonding between various groups, manifested through diverse economic activities. Such networks allowed for a more enduring relationship between street vendors and refugee weavers.

district retail networks through artisanal connections forged across dispersed refugee settlements.

By the mid-1960s, the sidewalk hawkers successfully erected semi-permanent structures on sidewalks and the Gariahat Boulevard. Political theorist Sudipta Kaviraj, who spent his childhood and youth in the Deshapriya Park area, recollected this transformation as follows:

> By the mid-1960s, the pressure on the city in simple demographic terms was so immense that enterprising shopkeepers who could not afford rents in properly built-up shops constructed 'temporary' shacks along the pavements of main streets to vend their slightly cheaper wares.... The small shops gradually established themselves and were regarded, by a combination of economic pressures, as part of the neighbourhood. Roads around Deshapriya Park used to have wide pavements, too wide for the park's good. Because of their width, it was possible to build relatively small shacks right next to and backing against, the beautiful ironwork railings. In a few years, the park railings entirely disappeared from view, and the entire outside perimeter became an unbroken row of shops backing onto the park, hiding it completely from view from the tramway and from pedestrians walking on the main road.[86]

Thus, for Gariahat and Rashbehari Avenue, the first couple of post-colonial decades stood for momentous transformations. On the one hand, it was an era of spatial democratization if we think from the perspective of footpath hawkers and refugee activists. But, on the other hand, it was a time of decadence and loss when we look at it from the standpoint of Rashbehari Avenue's middle-class residents. The Basu family of 202 Rashbehari Avenue—Pratibha and Buddhadeva—left for the United States in late 1960 and came back sometime in 1963. When they returned, a new world welcomed them to Rashbehari Avenue.

> I have described Rashbehari Avenue more than once in this autobiography. Upon our return from the United States, we found it very hard to recognize our beloved street. We had already witnessed the growth of a hawkers' corner in Gariahat when we left for the United States. We noticed that the hawkers' corner was slowly engulfing the sidewalks towards our side, deep inside Rashbehari Avenue. When we returned, the sidewalks of Rashbehari Avenue had already been invaded. We felt very bad. The hawkers were not provided with basic

---

[86] Sudipta Kaviraj, 'Filth and the Public Sphere: Concepts and Practices about Space in Calcutta', *Public Culture* 10, no. 1 (1997): 83–113, quoted in 105.

civic facilities. In the absence of a public toilet, the entire street became a massive latrine. The odour and noise destroyed the tranquillity of Kabita Bhavan. Gone are those days when we could see Singhi Park from our window and notice well-dressed men and women strolling around the neighbourhood. We found it hard to accept the plight of that beautiful street.[87]

Buddhadeva and Pratibha had to endure their Rashbehari Avenue address for another three years. In July 1966, they finally moved further south in Naktala.

Refugees were not the only population to build this new city. Others, too, joined hands. Demographically, the most numerous among the new migrants to the city were the ex-peasants from the South 24 Parganas district (Sundarbans).[88] These fringe economies—soon to be labelled the 'informal sector'—were concerned with the basic needs of an urban living, both for the sellers and buyers. This people's economy functioned at the subsistence level for the social reproduction of the post-colonial metropolis. Sidewalk hawking in Gariahat was the symptom and the outcome of the flourishing of this people's economy. It engulfed a vast stretch from Ranaghat in the north to Sonarpur in the south, converting each rail station into a marketplace, and the land along the rail tracks into a continuous world of squatter colonies.[89] Encroachment of Gariahat's sidewalk was a part of this larger story of encroachment.

---

[87] P. Basu, *Jiboner Jalchabi*, 265. In the 1960s, the stretch between Garia and Tollygunge became a new residential destination for the city's intelligentsia and the middle class. This area was dotted with gardens and garden houses, where Calcutta's well-to-do families came to spend weekends. However, as *jabardakhal* became aggressive in the surrounding areas in Garia, Jadavpur, and Tollygunge, the owners began to sell their lands and houses to middle-class buyers.

[88] Consider the case of Ratan Mandal, who had a tea stall in Gariahat when I began my field research in the mid-2000s. He had had a small house and a few *bighas* of agricultural land in Canning, in South 24 Parganas, the southern hinterland of the city close to the Sundarbans. He had to sell his meagre property to pay the debt he had incurred during a rainless summer in 1965. Like many of his countrymen, Ratan came to Calcutta to test his luck. He found a place in Gariahat to start a humble tea stall.

[89] Anwesha Sengupta, 'The Railway Refugees: Sealdah, 1950s–1960s' (IDSK Working Paper, id: 11759, 2017): https://ideas.repec.org/p/ess/wpaper/id11759.html, accessed 11 November 2021.

Frontiers of Gariahat: Bridges and Their Underlying *Bustee*s

The presence of the inner city presupposes an outlying area that would delineate the former's territorial limits. For Chowringhee in the nineteenth century, for instance, places beyond Lower Circular Road constituted a frontier. Similarly, in the mid-twentieth century, Rashbehari Avenue and Gariahat, places further south and east—separated by railway tracks running between Sealdah and the industrial town of Budge Budge—constituted a frontier. In the nineteenth century, frontiers were characterized by natural wilderness that needed to be tamed. In the second half of the twentieth century, frontiers were marked by the fringe economy—footloose workers, refugees, and urban slums—that needed to be brought under control. What becomes evident is that the dialectic of the inner city–frontier must continue for the city to proliferate.

Let us first consider the instance of Gariahat's southern frontiers. In the late 1950s, the Government of West Bengal began integrating the new frontiers to the south of Gariahat, separated from Gariahat by an east–west railway track running between Ballygunge Rail Station and the industrial town of Budge Budge. It included places such as Selimpur, Jadavpur, Bagha Jatin, and Garia, which came to be thickly populated by the refugees and internal migrants from South 24 Parganas. The government was keen on bringing these areas into the purview of centralized surveillance and policing. They appeared too dangerous to remain 'outlying areas' and 'loosely connected to the city', as Saibal Gupta, the Chairman of the Improvement Trust, reasoned in 1958.[90] The concentration of refugees and migrants from 24 Parganas in these areas posited new administrative concerns for security. Thus, a bridge over the rail tracks was deemed necessary for the territorial consolidation of Calcutta in the 1950s. The Improvement Trust was asked to construct such an overbridge. The overbridge—soon to be known as 'Dhakuria Bridge'—was to extend Gariahat Road southwards up to Bagha Jatin and Garia. This overbridge was responsible for the emergence of Gariahat as an important transit and retail centre.

The land acquisition documents associated with the Dhakuria Bridge Scheme paint an accurate picture of the area in 1959:

> The lands to the west of the existing Gariahat Road should not present any difficulty. In view of a pre-existing Corporation alignment, all the buildings on that side had been set back, and the strips we propose to acquire are almost wholly vacant.... To the east of Gariahat Road,

---

[90] 'Dhakuriar Prastabita Overbridge', *Anandabazaar Patrika*, 22 October 1958.

there are one or two pucca structures, but the bulk of the land within our acquisition limit consists of a big timber yard standing on premises No. 31. The front belt of that land is essential for the construction of our high level and low-level roads.... South of the railway line the lands are almost vacant and should not present any difficulty.[91]

As the Trust proceeded with building work for Dhakuria Bridge, numerous complaints were raised by individuals who occupied the timber yard: 'They were displaced people from East Pakistan [now Bangladesh] and had taken a lease of marshy lands, filling up and reclaimed it, and established a large timber yard.'[92] Of the 58 objectors, 33 earned their livelihood as timber workers and carpenters. At the same time, the rest were involved in 'grocery, stationery, smithy, clay modelling, tailoring, transport, tea houses, and even coaching classes for school students'.[93] In 1961, the Trust's Chief Valuer noticed 'the presence of twelve huts within the fencing around the railway track' that interfered with the construction of the overbridge.[94] Four out of those 12 huts belonged to people of refugee origin, but the rest were constructed by people migrating from 24 Parganas. By the early 1970s, thousands of squatter-dwellers occupied the two sides of the rail track.[95]

These squatter-dwellers maintained contacts with the Communist Party of India (Marxist) (CPI[M], then in the opposition. There were several occasions when government departments tried to free encroachments along the railway track. In 1965, for instance, the Railway Department attempted to build a wall to encircle the settlement. The residents responded by forming a human chain. Again, during the Emergency (1975–1977), the authorities destroyed several huts. The residents acted through the Communist Party of India (CPI), which was then in alliance with Indira Gandhi's Congress. The CPI leaders were able to negotiate with the government, and 'the threat passed'.[96]

A second transformation of Gariahat and its adjacent areas accelerated in the late 1970s and early 1980s, when the Improvement Trust built a second

---

[91] Asok Sen, 'Life and Labour in a Squatters' Colony' (Occasional Paper 138: Centre for Studies in Social Sciences, Calcutta, October 1992), 6.
[92] Ibid., 6.
[93] Ibid., 7.
[94] Ibid., 7.
[95] Ibid.
[96] P. Chatterjee, *Politics of the Governed*.

overbridge above Ballygunge Rail Station, connecting Rashbehari Avenue with Kashba, a slum-dominated neighbourhood (in the 1970s and 1980s) to the east of Ballygunge Rail Station. The idea was to connect the inner city—now to be understood as Gariahat and Rashbehari Avenue—with the newly constructed road called the Eastern Metropolitan Bypass. Kashba fell between Ballygunge Rail Station and the Bypass. This overbridge was one of the last major infrastructural works undertaken by the Trust. Bijon Setu,[97] as it came to be known, was also used to tame the insurgent spaces on the eastern edge of the railway tracks (connecting Sealdah with Ballygunge) that threatened civic life in the 1960s and the 1970s. In these decades, the other side of the rail tracks was considered the natural end of Rashbehari Avenue's urban modernity—where wagon breakers, Naxalite insurgents, and impoverished migrants from 24 Parganas and lower-caste Bangladeshi refugees crowded the neighbourhoods.

Kashba remained a centre of various kinds of conflicts and mob action long after Bijon Setu became functional. On 30 April 1982, Bijon Setu witnessed a massacre when a local mob burnt alive 17 monks of the Ananda Margi sect on the charge of child-lifting. A little over a year earlier, on 29 January 1981, *The Statesman* surveyed the localities along the eastern and the western flank of the Sealdah–Canning and Sealdah–Budge Budge railway lines.[98] The staff reporter visited the slums of Kashba, and the 'sprawling clusters of huts and shanties of Panchanantala, Gobardanga, Jagannath Ghosh Road [which emerged from the Kankulia Road, we discussed in this chapter], A. T. Chatterjee Road, Dhakuria, Kalupara and Benibag' on both sides of the railway lines. The reporter found that most of the slum dwellers either were from South 24 Parganas or were 'low caste refugees from Bangladesh'. The lanes were narrow, the street light inadequate. The men in these slums worked mostly as vendors, street hawkers, and daily labourers, while women worked as domestic help in 'middle class households of Gariahat–Rashbehari Avenue, Southern Avenue and Jodhpur Park areas'. The report says:

[97] In August 1974, Bijon Basu, the Executive Engineer of the Improvement Trust and the person behind this overbridge, was murdered in full public view. Basu was on a train from Santoshpur to Sealdah when between Dhakuria and Ballygunge a gang of robbers attacked a group of women in his compartment, who were returning from a marriage ceremony. Basu tried to intervene on their behalf. An argument ensued. In the end, the goons pushed him from the running train. Basu died on the spot. The overbridge was subsequently named after him.

[98] 'Where Political Patronage Sustains Gang Warfare', *The Statesman*, 29 January 1981.

Though there are railway tracks in the area, wagon breaking is not a problem at the moment, though it was so more than five years ago, when the residents and slum dwellers had organized resistance parties to control the menace. A resident of the Panchanantala Bustee said that they had formed such parties because the railway police used to make indiscriminate arrests in search of criminals. The construction of an overbridge over the Ballygunge Station, too, had aided the movement of the Police in the area.

The survey found that most of the criminals residing in these slums were snatchers, highway robbers, and dacoits who operated elsewhere. These gangs were also known for smuggling rice and extorting money in the Dhakuria bazaar area. Gang wars over the spoils were commonplace. Another Panchanantala resident recounted a recent intra-gang clash over the spoils of a robbery near the 17A bus stand. Subsequently, the gang split: one went to the opposition Congress (I) camp for protection and the other sought refuge in the ruling CPI(M). One group had a better hold over the Panchanantala Bustee, while the other had control of the slums of Jagannath Ghosh Road and Gobardanga. During the elections, political parties frequently submitted themselves to these gangs: 'Leaders of a gang wield considerable authority over residents of their stronghold and can intimidate to vote for one political party. It is easy to enlist names of false voters in the voters' list in slum areas. Authority over criminals facilitates such enlistment.'

Eventually, Bijon Setu, along with Sukanta Setu in Jadavpur (over Jadavpur Rail Station), became a prime vehicle of expansion of Calcutta to the east, culminating in the massive Eastern Metropolitan Bypass project (started in 1973). In subsequent decades, the 'Bypass'—as it is popularly called—fuelled extensive real estate developments in Kashba, Dhakuria, and the East Calcutta Wetlands. When I entered Jadavpur University in 2000, the university area was already popularly considered a part of the inner city (Jadavpur became a part of the Calcutta Municipal Corporation in 1984). By that time, the southern frontiers shifted beyond Garia. Thus, Calcutta remained dynamic in the twenty-first century by mobilizing its frontiers.

Conclusion

Over the last four chapters, we identified planned urban renewal, communal cleansing, planned suburbanization, and *jabardakhal*—as entangled forces in the metamorphoses of Calcutta. If the Improvement Trust was the engine of urbanization through motion, then soil raids, working-class militancy, and *jabardakhal* emerged as the forces of urbanization by popular action. Or we may choose to call it urbanization through obstruction, which transformed Gariahat and Rashbehari Avenue from a frontier gateway to a new inner city. In other words, the force of frontier urbanization set the inner city or the centre in motion.

Ironically, the institution in Calcutta that bore the brunt of *jabardakhal* the most was the Improvement Trust. All the vacant houses and acres of inner-city land acquired or built over decades became disputed refugee settlements. Just to cite an example, in 1959, the Trust raised a severe complaint of encroachment in the Lake, which had just been renamed Rabindra Sarovar after the poet. The Trust raised concern over the state government's delay and inability to pay rent for the Lake Medical College and Hospital lands now 'under the occupation of refugees'.[99] The Trust also noted a reduction in rent collection as 'a considerable number of tenants' (specifically those in the Industrial Housing Scheme at Chaulpati Road) had 'surreptitiously' allowed their flats to pass into the unauthorized occupation of outsiders. Some disputes are still alive in the court, and the Trust spends a substantial portion of its revenue in these litigations.

In the course of time, the Trust was absorbed into the Calcutta Metropolitan Development Authority (CMDA) as merely a department. Subsequently, the Trust was expelled from its imposing office building at 5 Clive Street (now Netaji Subhas Chandra Bose Road) and was shifted to a more modest building in the formerly Tiretta Bazaar (adjacent to Central Avenue, now named after Netaji's political mentor C. R. Das), close to a massive garbage vat. Today, the Trust maintains a bare office floor whose approach and staircases shelter numerous pavement dwellers, and it struggles to clear the dues of perhaps the last batch of its permanent staff members.

As we have noticed in previous chapters, the Trust was brought into being to secure the colonial bureaucracy's claim over Calcutta from the arena of democratizing municipal politics in the early twentieth century. It constituted an apparatus of the colonial mode of governing the city. The precondition for its efficiency was an authoritarian right over space under colonial sovereignty. The Trust's notion of urban improvement was incompatible with mass democracy, which enabled a different relationship between space and polity under popular

---

[99] Chairman's 'Note on Slum Improvement and Rehousing of Slum Dwellers', Proceedings of the 1907th Meeting of the Calcutta Improvement Trust, 20 August 1955, *Proceedings of the CIT for the Year 1955–1956* (Chairman's Copy).

sovereignty. Hence, the decline of the Improvement Trust in Calcutta was bound to set in during the post-colonial era. In the 1910s and 1920s, the Trust thrived by recycling the inner-city slums and acquiring land in the frontiers without facing direct popular resistance from the erstwhile users. The Trust was able to create wealth in Calcutta by means of the development and trading of property. It did so via strategic devaluation and revaluation of asset values at certain junctures in the interwar period. The operations of the Trust enabled certain investors in real estate to capitalize on upward revaluation of asset values. This strategy met with occasional challenges during the interwar period when land prices went out of the Trust's anticipated levels but it collapsed completely when refugees, slums, and squatter-dwellers entered the city's electoral arithmetic and politicized displacement. Calcutta's *jabardakhal* movement was symptomatic of this new era.[100]

---

[100] The post-colonial regime of 'development' had to come to terms with the 'people' along with various population groups who developed their own constituencies in the legislature. P. Chatterjee, *Politics of the Governed*; Stephen Legg, 'Postcolonial Developmentalities: From the Delhi Improvement Trust to the Delhi Development Authority', in *Colonial and Postcolonial Indian Geographies*, ed. Stuart Corbridge, Satish Kumar, and Saraswati Raju (London: SAGE Publishing, 2006), 182–204.

Appendix 4A.1 Rice mills in the vicinity of Scheme IV

Area	Name of the Rice Mill	Name and Surname of the Owner(s)
Chetla	1. Rice Mill of N. C. Kawaji	Unknown
	2. Progress Rice Mill	Unknown
	3. Kali Rice Mill	Unknown
	4. Rice Mill of Kalinath Chakrabarty	Kalinath Chakrabarty
	5. Choga Rice Mill	Unknown
	6. Annapurna Rice Mill	Unknown
	7. Mill of Sitanath and Pannalal Das	Sitanath and Pannalal Das
	8. Mill of Bhagabatchandra Sadhukhan	Bhagabatcharan Sadhukhan
	9. Rice Mill of Devi Shaw	Devi Shaw
	10. Cchagmal-Haranaran Rice Mill	Unknown
Alipore (mainly Alipore Road)	11. Lakxmijanardan Rice Mill	Unknown
	12. Diamond Rice Mill	Unknown
	13. Kamala Rice Mill	Unknown
	14. Gauranga Rice Mill	Unknown
	15. Durga Rice Mill	Nagendranath Sarkar
Tollygunj	16. Rupnaran Rice Mill	Unknown
	17. Ganji-Saji & Co. Rice Mill	Unknown
	18. Bibhakar Rice Mill	(Unknown)
	19. Nanci-Kuvarji Rice Mill	Unknown
	20. Tribhuvan Rice Mill	Unknown
	21. Rice Mill of Rajnarayan Roy	Rajnarayan Roy
	22. Gaur-Bishnupriya Rice Mill	Jogen Mondal

(Contd)

(Contd)

Area	Name of the Rice Mill	Name and Surname of the Owner(s)
Sahapur	23. Satyanarayan Mill	Unknown
	24. Annapurna Rice Mill	Gopal Chandra Das
	25. Rice Mill of Krishnakali Shib-Krishna Roy	Shibkrishna Roy
	26. Rice Mill of Mahendranath Gayen	Mahendranath Gayen
	27. Daktarbabu & Co. Mill	Unknown
	28. Rice Mill of Taraprasanna Karmakar	Taraprasanna Karmakar
	29. Rice Mill of Basanta Saha	Basanta Saha
	30. Khekuria & Co. Rice Mill	Unknown
	31. Gobinda Das Rice Mill	Gobinda Das
	32. Rice Mill of Nanda Jana	Nanda Jana
	33. Rice Mill	Jogin Das
	34. Rice Mill	Pannalal Das
	35. Rice Mill	Gopal Das
	36. Rice Mill	Ramsundar Das
	37. Rice Mill	Upendra Sarkar
	38. Rice Mill	Upen Dutta
	39. Rice Mill	Binoykrishna Das
	40. Rice Mill	Kunja Ghosh
	41. Rice Mill	Sudhamadhab Mondal
	42. Emerald Rice Mill	Unknown
	43. Union Rice Mill	Unknown
	44. Rice Mill	Srikrishna Saha
	45. Gazi Miyazan Rice Mill	Unknown
	46. Rice Mill	Nagen Das

(Contd)

(Contd)

Area	Name of the Rice Mill	Name and Surname of the Owner(s)
	47. Rice Mill	Anadh Basu
	48. Ramdeo-Rameshwar Rice Mill	Unknown
	49. Rice Mill	Nibaran Paul
	50. Rice Mill	Sukomol Marwari
	51. Rice Mill	Aswhini Hajra
	52. Rice Mill	Rashik Dula
	53. Rice Mill	Purna Chandra Dutta
	54. Rice Mill	Ghosh & Co.
	55. Rice Mill	Upendranath Ghosh
	56. Rice Mill	Rajababu & Co.
	57. Rice Mill	Mahendra Guin
	58. Rice Mill	Rishi Hajra
	59. Rice Mill	Md. Yashin
	60. Rice Mill	Bhutnath Hajra
	61. Shib Durga Rice Mill	Unknown
	62. Rice Mill	Basanta Kumar Roy
	63. Jagatlakshmi Rice Mill	Unknown

Source: Computed from Santoshnath Seth, *Bange Chaltattva* (Kolkata: Tara Press, 1332 B.S.) and Department of Commercial Intelligence and Statistics, 1925 (Calcutta: Government of India Central Publication Branch, 1925).

Appendix 4A.2 Contractors and the Trust's operations, 1916–1928

Name	Winning Tender (in rupees)	Year 1916, 1918, 1919, 1920	Scheme
B. B. Sarkar	1. 21593	1. 1916	1. VA (Bhowanipore, Beltola Road section): Road construction and sewerage work
	2. 26879	2. 1916	2. VB (Bhowanipore, Beltola Road section): Road construction and sewerage work
	13616	1918	V (Bhowanipore): Road construction sewerage work
Biswas & Co	18342	1916	IIA (Cornwallis Street): Road construction
	41851	1916	II (Shyambazaar Bridge Road): Road construction
	25915	1918	V (Bhowanipore): Road building, sewerage work
	78930	1919	VII (Central Avenue>from Mechuabazaar Street to Muktaram Babu Street): Road construction, drainage work
	2576	1919	V (Bhowanipore): Road construction, sewerage work
	72825	1919	VII (Central Avenue): Road construction and drainage work
	256862	1920	VIII (Park Street Extension): Road construction and drainage work
	2576	1920	V (Bhowanipore): Road construction and drainage work
	3704	1920	V (Bhowanipore): Construction of 24-inch diameter brick drain from Bakulbagan Road to Road no. 14
P.C. Coomar & Co	3238	1916	Chitpore Road (Sewerage work)
	24262	1918	V (Bhowanipore): Road construction and sewerage work
	15462	1919	V (Bhowanipore): Road construction and sewerage work in Puddopukur area

(Contd)

(Contd)

Name	Winning Tender (in rupees)	Year 1916, 1918, 1919, 1920	Scheme
	14656	1919	IA (Surtibagan>Tara Chand Dutta Street): Road building and drainage work
	7839	1919	V (Bhowanipore): Road construction and sewerage work
	33508	1919	IC (between Zacaria Street and Colootola Street): Road construction and drainage work
	76550	1920	XIV (Shyambazaar Park): Concerning the embellishment of the park, urinals, Mali house and adjacent roads
Natiram Sagarmal & Co.	8841	1.1916	1.III (Wards Institution Lane): Road construction
	8380	2.1916	2.I (Surtibagan): Road construction and drainage work
	36460	1918	V (Bhowanipore): Road construction, sewerage work
	90692	1918	IVA (Russa Road Extn.): Road construction, sewerage work
I.N. Ghose	55498, 56915	1918	IVA (Russa Road Extn.): Two Tank filling, 10 feet deep, 15 feet deep and per 1,000 cubic feet.
	34857	1918	IV (Russa Road Widening): Tank filling
	27513	1918	V (Bhowanipore): Road construction and drainage work
	5100	1918	Excavating earth from plot B of the Excavation Area to a depth of 15 feet
	3169	1919	I (Surtibagan): Taking up and relaying paving slabs and]aying plastically laid pavement of patent stone in the footpaths of cross streets
	48335	1919	V (Bhowanipore: Northern Park): Road construction and Drainage work

(Contd)

(Contd)

Name	Winning Tender (in rupees)	Year 1916, 1918, 1919, 1920	Scheme
	78548	1919	VII (Central Avenue): Road Building, Drainage work
	13580	1919	Tank filling and Land raising in the Excavation Area
	9800	1919	V (Bhowanipore): Tank filling and land rising
B.B. Chatterjee	88889	1916	1. V (Bhowanipore): Drainage and sewerage work at Road no. 13
	39554	1916	2. V (Bhowanipore): Drainage and sewerage work at Road no. 13
	39554	1916	3. V (Bhowanipore): Surface water drains at Road no. 13
	23896	1918	V (Bhowanipore): Road construction and drainage work
	18037	1919	V (Bhowanipore): Road construction and drainage work
	21098	1919	V (Bhowanipore): Road construction and drainage work
	32620	1919	V (Bhowanipore): Road construction and drainage work
	12857	1919	V (Bhowanipore): Road construction and drainage work
	80225	1920	XII (Park Street Widening): Road construction and drainage work
	16830	1920	V: (Bhowanipore): Road construction and associated work
S. Bagchee	159600	1920	Excavation Area: Brick making during 1920–21 and 1921–22 winter season
M.L. Dalmiya (Babu Moni Lall Marwari)	15980	1918	V (Bhowanipore): Tank filling
	21457	1918	IV (Russa Road Widening): Tank filling, land raising
	15963	1918	V (Bhowanipore): Road construction, drainage work
	2506	1918	IV (Russa Road Widening): Construction of a masonry building and a public urinal at Dwarka Nath Mitter Square

(Contd)

Frontier Urbanization

(Contd)

Name	Winning Tender (in rupees)	Year 1916, 1918, 1919, 1920	Scheme
	15017	1919	V (Bhowanipore): Construction of the Southern Park
	23148	1919	V (Bhowanipore): Road construction and drainage work
	9341	1919	X (Ripon Street Triangle): Drainage work
	24605	1919	IV (Russa Road Widening>Hazra Square): Construction of Park roads, compound wall, Mali's house. Urinal
	9326	1919	V (Bhowanipore): Construction of the combined latrine and urinal, a Mali house, fixing wrought iron railings and gates in Southern Park
	5650	1919	IV (Russa Road Widening): Developments of Dwarka Nath Mitter Square
	32250	1920	IV (Russa Road Widening)
Cooperative Engg Society/ Calcutta Engg. Society	54924	1919	IV (Russa Road Widening): Tank filling and raising land
	19734	1919	VIII (Park Street Extension): Land raising and tank filling
	20690	1919	IVA (Russa Road Extension): Tank filling and land raising
	250271	1919	IVA (Russa Road Extension): Road construction and drainage work
	19700	1920	IVA (Russa Road Extension): Tank filling and land raising
	252891	1920	IVA (Russa Road Extension): Road construction and drainage work
Capital Engg. Company	206356	1919	IVA (Russa Road Extn.): Construction of Main Road west side only up to Road No. 8 including subsidiary Roads Nos. 3, 4, 5, 6, 7 and 8 and Halderpara Road
	11479	1920	XII (Ballygunge Circular Road to Swinhoe Street): Drainage work

(Contd)

(Contd)

Name	Winning Tender (in rupees)	Year 1916, 1918, 1919, 1920	Scheme
R.K. Chatterjee	17893	1919	V (Bhowanipore): Road building and drainage work around southern Park
	29040	1919	V (Bhowanipore): Road building and drainage work
B. Lahiri & B.C. De	8050	1916	I (Surtibagan): Carting away surplus earth from Tarachand Dutta Street
	33800 Contract being awarded with S.S. Mookerjee	1918	IV (Russa Road Extension): Tank filling and land raising
	14337 Contract being awarded with S.S. Mookerjee	1918	V (Bhowanipore): Tank filling and land raising
J. Ovani & Co.	69360	1919	VII (Central Avenue): Road construction and drainage work
	33648	1920	Model dwelling at Bow Street: Road construction and drainage work

Source: Prepare by author from Proceedings of the Calcutta Improvement Trust (1916–1928).

I have chosen one enterprise from the above list—M. L. Dalmiya—for further investigation during the interwar period between 1921 and 1928 in the southern schemes of the Calcutta Improvement Trust comprising Schemes IV (Russa Road), V (Bhowanipore), and XV (Rashbehari Avenue).

M. L. Dalmiya:

Scheme	Year	Amount (in rupees)
IV (Russa Road widening): Filling of a tank at no. 49 Kansaripara Road	1921	5530
IVA (Russa Road Extension): Laying ground for tramlines	1921	19821
V (Bhowanipore): Road construction and drainage work	1922	2628
V (Bhowanipore): Construction of a shelter in Southern Park	1922	1887
XVC (Rashbehari Avenue): Filling and raising low lying area in the intersection of Gariahat Road and Ekdalia Road	1924	14316
IVA (Russa Road extension): Filling of a dhobi tank	1924	9370
XVD (Lansdowne Road Extension): Filling and raising ground	1924	13200
XVB (Rashbehari Avenue): Laying out a park at Manoharpukur Road	1927	12306
XVB (Rashbehari Avenue): Laying out a public park at the junction of Lansdowne Road and Main Sewer Road [Deshapriya Park]	1927	38956
XVB (Rashbehari Avenue): Constructing a pathway round the football ground at public park at the junction of Lansdowne Road and Main Sewer Road [Deshapriya Park]	1928	4300

Source: Prepared by author from the Proceedings of the Calcutta Improvement Trust (1921–1928).

5

Durable Obstructions, Spatializing Motion

The History of Footpath Hawking in Calcutta

The frontiers of Calcutta witnessed a demographic revolution in every direction in the 1950s and 1960s. The city's economic deceleration, which had set in after the First World War, became more acute after 1947. Amidst an irreversible economic decay—through the 1950s and 1960s—refugees from East Pakistan and economic migrants from West Bengal's rural districts came to populate not only inner-city *bustees* and squatter colonies in the city, but also places beyond the city's civic limits. A report published in the *Economic Weekly* in 1954, for instance, noted how vacant stretches of land outside the city, between Dum Dum and Barasat, came to be populated by refugee squatter groups in the early 1950s:

> Beyond the proper city limits of Calcutta, there are vast lands which are mostly marshy and are full of jungle and mosquitoes, without roads or good water for drinking, and unhealthy. Even the garden houses of Dum Dum, Barangore, Barrackpore, and Kamarhati have such surroundings. …between the industrial belt and Calcutta, away from the Ganges, there were neither villages nor factories before the squatters came. The squatters brought life to this forlorn area. They cleared the jungles, built roads, raised the level of the land by piling up earth on it, sank tube wells, and then built their huts.[1]

Besides claiming land by invoking the Lockean logic of individual labour and self-improvement, these squatters and *bustee* dwellers—refugees and rural–urban migrants alike—contributed to the creation of an enormous and diverse fringe economy in Calcutta, which, by the 1970s, had come to be known as the 'informal sector' at the instance of the International Labour Organization (ILO).[2] Every morning, people commuted to the city from these new suburbs and *jabardakhal* settlements to eke out a living and returned home in the evening,

---

[1] 'Squatters' Colonies', by A Correspondent, *Economic Weekly* (5 June 1954): 631–634, quoted from 631.

[2] Harold Lubell, *Urban Development and Employment: The Prospects for Calcutta* (Geneva: International Labour Office, 1971).

in suburban trains and buses. Commuting became a mass phenomenon. Along with it came informally settled marketplaces in train compartments, rail stations, tram depots, and bus terminuses.

A section of the urban poor, especially those who migrated from West Bengal's rural districts, made the sidewalks their 'home' and stayed there for years and decades. Squatting on Calcutta's sidewalks and parks on a large scale began during the Famine of 1943, when thousands of people from Bengal's rural districts—especially from Midnapore and 24 Parganas—temporarily entered Calcutta in search of food. This tide receded after the Second World War. However, people from these districts began to settle on the sidewalks incrementally on a more permanent basis after Independence. Decades later, in 1987, a census survey of Calcutta's 'pavement dwellers' found that 15.2 per cent of a total population of 55,000 dwellers came from the southern subdivisions of the 24 Parganas alone.³ A previous survey on pavement dwellers in 1975 had mentioned that the largest chunk of them came from Canning, Sundarbans, and Jaynagar areas of the 24 Parganas district, who reported flood and agrarian distress as the two most prevalent causes of migration.⁴ These pavement dwellers were engaged in as many as 30 kinds of professions, including domestic work, transport work, daily wage earning without any specific regular jobs, construction work, rag-picking, ad hoc sanitary work in hotels and restaurants, and other commercial establishments, sex work, begging, and so on.⁵ Themselves products of the primitive accumulation of capital, pavement dwellers, *bustee* dwellers and squatters produced an urbanization that was always ambiguous.

---

³ N. Vijay Jagannathan and Animesh Halder, 'Pavement Dwellers of Calcutta 1987: A Socio-Economic Study, April 1988', Economic Planning Cell, Calcutta Metropolitan Development Authority, collated in *Metropolitan Kolkata: An Anthology of Socio-Economic Studies and Survey Reports of KMDA, 1970–2004* (Vol. IV: *1986–1992*) (Kolkata: Socio-Economic Planning Unit, Directorate of Planning and Development, Kolkata Metropolitan Development Authority, 1988), 109–171.

⁴ Sudhendu Mukherjee, 'A Report on the Survey of 10,000 Pavement-Dwellers in Calcutta, February 1975, Under the Shadow of the Metropolis: They Are Citizens Too', Calcutta Metropolitan Development Authority, Calcutta, 1975. The survey was conducted between September 1973 and March 1974. The report is collated in *Metropolitan Kolkata: An Anthology of Socio-Economic Studies and Survey Reports of KMDA, 1970–2004* (Vol. 1: *1970–1979*) (Kolkata: Socio-Economic Planning Unit, Directorate of Planning and Development, Kolkata Metropolitan Development Authority, 1988), 183–330.

⁵ Jagannathan and Halder, 'Pavement Dwellers of Calcutta 1987'.

They upheld an urban culture that was a critique of the culture of capital accumulation, normally linked to cities. They created a city where obstruction became the keyword instead of motion.

In this context, 'footpath hawking' became one of the most significant sources of livelihood for the urban poor. The hawkers sustained an enormous low-income urban population with supplies of food and other essential commodities at low cost. They also sourced and sold commodities made by squatters and *bustee* dwellers. The hawkers, in turn, were sustained by these low-income urban consumers and producers. This cycle of economic interdependence, or people's economy, kept Calcutta viable amidst crises. Lower establishment cost, self-exploitation and unpaid family labour, and smaller profit margins enabled the hawkers to sell commodities and services at a lower price when compared with established shops in the same commodity market. This enabled them to survive competition. In operationalizing this people's economy along footpaths, hawkers and other urban commoners actively 'produced' space in the city. One might ask: What kind of space did they produce? What kind of alliance, knowledge, and politics did they forge, and what kind of exclusion did their actions generate?

By the 1970s, footpath hawkers had emerged as an organized political force in the city, turning the sidewalk into a veritable livelihood resource for ordinary city dwellers struggling for survival. The city administration began to see them as causing obstruction to public mobility—one that needed to be quarantined and, if needed, bulldozed. In this chapter, I unpack this specific form of obstruction to reveal how the hawkers both caused and navigated urban transformations in Calcutta in the post-colonial decades. In doing this, I also illustrate how their history is intertwined with that of the state and capital. Organized encroachment of sidewalks by hawkers, I argue, was a form of 'durable obstruction' that 'spatialized motion' or distributed motion across spaces.

There were many political and ideological manoeuvres that made obstruction durable. The creation of trade unions to resist eviction and to reclaim sidewalks was one such manoeuvre. Trade unionism in its advanced form was informed by an emergent 'worldview' around obstruction. As operatives in the field of action, hawkers developed an intricate understanding of the world around them, which they accessed and transformed through mass action. In doing so, they operated with a 'coherent' and conveyable worldview—a 'theoretical understanding'—of their everyday street-level activities, particularly in relation to the operations of the state and the market.

Mass action and trade unionism by footpath hawkers instituted a culture of obstructionism in the city. Earlier, I defined obstruction as the realm of ordinary people—engaged in 'practical activities'—that punctuates the objective forces of motion and makes urban sociality possible. Obstruction is dialectically opposite to motion. But like every dialectical relationship, it engages with motion by creating its condition of being. Obstructionism, then, is a 'conception' of the world (worldview) from obstruction's standpoint.

The culture of obstructionism emerges at the point when this worldview resolves the contradiction between a tacit consciousness that unites them in anti-eviction mobilizations and a consciousness that has been 'internalized' via traditions, value systems, prevailing ideas, and institutions—a borrowed conception of the world. The latter form of consciousness manifests in normal times when the hawkers assist the state with their archives of database or submit to accumulation by acting on the fringes of society as a safety valve by helping the exploited classes to survive on low wages. Obstructionism holds together this dyadic relation with motion—on the one hand, motion is subverted; on the other, it is accommodated by being punctuated. In one, it unites the hawkers with other oppressed classes during anti-eviction mobilizations, and in another, it submits to the state–capital complex and forms a continuum of subordination, giving motion a grip on the soil and a local material and cultural form.

At the time of intense political mobilization in the city, obstructionism challenges motion's claims to be universal. This is a moment charged with the possibility of a breach, of difference. It is followed by a bid to hegemonic power by espousing an alternative universal. The assertions emerge from counter-publics. Then comes the ambition for a counter-hegemony—from pleb to people. However, this is never a straightforward, linear, progressive passage. As the history of hawkers' struggles in Calcutta shows us, there are twists and turns at every moment, and it generally ends up compelling motion to accommodate obstruction, thereby producing a punctuated motion before it moves on.

Durable Obstruction: The Proliferation of Footpath Hawking

The hawkers were remarkably successful in colonizing Calcutta's sidewalks between the 1950s and 1990s. According to Tushar Talukdar—a former Commissioner of Police of Calcutta—the number of hawkers crossed a hundred thousand within the limits of his jurisdiction by the mid-1990s. In these decades, the hawkers transformed the city into a vast and continuous retailscape. Spatial expansion of footpath hawking between the 1950s and 1980s added a new aesthetic dimension to the sprawling avenues of Calcutta. The hawkers set up their stalls in front of buildings and shops, occupying the 'frontage'. Another group set up stalls at the kerbside edge of the sidewalk, forming a corridor in the middle for pedestrian traffic. They added tarpaulin sheets above the stalls for protection from the sun and rain. These roofs merged with one another and thus produced a continuous shed over the sidewalk, making it convenient for the pedestrians to walk in summer and monsoon days. They bought generators collectively and placed them between two sets of continuous stalls. Electric wires moved between stalls, producing a play of light and noise on the street. Evidently, the post-colonial metropolis took a new aesthetic form.

There appears to be four significant moments of proliferation of hawking units on sidewalks: in 1951–1956, 1964–1969, 1971–1972, and 2011–2013. The first two moments were connected to the continuous refugee influx from East Pakistan.[6] The third moment was marked by the Indo-Bangladesh War that released a fresh set of refugees from Bangladesh. The fourth and the latest moment was associated with the electoral victory of the populist Trinamool Congress in the state Assembly, which explicitly encouraged footpath hawking.

Over these decades of spatial expansion, the demographic profile of the hawkers underwent some noticeable change. A large section of hawkers before 1947 were up-country Muslims, Bengali Muslims, and up-country Hindus. According to Ashok Ghosh—a veteran Left-wing trade unionist (belonging to the All India Forward Bloc), who was also one of the first organizers of footpath-hawking—the hawkers of his childhood (1920s–1930s), squatting in the main streets of north and central Calcutta, were mostly Hindi- and Urdu-speaking men.[7] On the other hand, hawkers of the early post-colonial era had a mix of educated upper-caste refugees as well as landless (mostly) Dalit economic migrants from various districts of West Bengal.[8] When I interviewed the hawkers of Gariahat (between 2006 and 2011), once a refugee stronghold, my respondents

---

[6] Nandini Dasgupta, who wrote the first authoritative account of Calcutta's 'petty traders', mentions that until the mid-1960s, a significant concentration of hawkers could only be found in areas around Sealdah and College Street, Kalighat and Bhowanipore, and Park Circus. She shows with precision how over the 1970s and 1980s petty trading engulfed the rest of the city. Nandini Dasgupta, *Petty Trading in the Third World: The Case of Calcutta* (Aldershot: Avebury, 1992).

[7] Interview recorded by the author on 13 March 2009 (transcript available at the Hawker Sangram Committee [HSC] archive).

[8] Ibid.

frequently remembered the presence of college-educated refugee hawkers who conducted their trade in the boulevard until the mid-1970s. I could track several of them who had gradually moved up in the economic order and become school teachers, corporation clerks, and shopkeepers in nearby markets.

After Partition, Ashok Ghosh recollected, there was a progressive Bengali-Hinduization of footpath hawking—a trend consistent with the *jabardakhal* movement and ghettoization of Muslims discussed previously. Ghosh also mentioned that hawking was common in the 1930s, but those hawkers encroached sidewalks as individuals or as small groups. They used easily collapsible and light-weight materials for their stalls. Encroachment took the form of an avalanche only in the 1950s, in the context of a mass democracy and sudden refugee influx. This was also the time when hawkers began using more permanent materials (bamboo, wood, and corrugated tin sheds) to build their stalls. Thus, collective encroachment accompanied a more durable claim to space.

In inhabiting the streets for their livelihood, both for survival and with intent, hawkers proactively remade them into sites of social reproduction. I tracked several hawkers who gradually moved up in the economic order and became school teachers, corporation clerks, and shopkeepers in nearby markets. For instance, Biren Bose and his younger brother Atin came as refugees from Dhaka in 1948. They got a plot in Bikramgarh refugee colony. In 1951, the Bose brothers (Biren was 18 and Atin was 16) floated a garment stall in Gariahat Boulevard. While Biren continued education until the matriculation level, he persuaded Atin to go to college and earn a higher degree in physics. Atin used to help Biren in the evening at the shop. After graduating from Asutosh College, Atin got an offer for higher studies in the newly founded Jadavpur University. Jadavpur had opened a night college for working people at this time. After graduating from Jadavpur's night section, Atin returned to their boulevard shop more permanently. After three years of struggle in the job market, Atin became an assistant teacher in a newly established, government-aided Bengali-medium high school. He managed to earn extra money by offering private tuitions to school students and eventually gathered enough capital for his elder brother to start a garment shop in Jadavpur by 1972. Biren rented the Gariahat stall out to two hawkers from Bongaon—Bimal Mandal and Tapan Roy. Bimal and Tapan migrated to Bongaon from Jessore during the Bangladesh War of Independence. They were just two of numerous *namasudra* (Dalit) refugees who migrated to West Bengal. In 1987, the Bose brothers agreed to pass on the stall to Bimal and Tapan in lieu of a one-time payment of 6,000 rupees. None of these transactions happened on paper. The stall changed hands with the mediation of several local hawkers and two trade union leaders.

The story of the Bose Brothers is a common one among the upper-caste refugee hawkers in Gariahat, Rashbehari Avenue, Shyambazaar, Hatibagan, and Sealdah areas. It illustrates a larger process of caste-based demographic reorganization of the city's 'informal economy' that took place in the 1970s and the 1980s. The upper-caste refugees started several informal enterprises to eke out a living just after they migrated to Calcutta. Eventually, some of their family members were able to use extended family and social networks to get better employment in subsequent decades. Atin Bose, for instance, remembered how a local school master gave him free tuition and how some *para* elders passed down textbooks to him even while in college. As upper-caste hawkers found avenues of upward mobility and exited hawking, Dalit refugees and migrant workers took their place. However, unlike their predecessors, they did not have access to a *bhadralok* network of *jabardakhal* colonies to chart a way out.

In later years, there has been a noticeable disappearance of refugee identity among hawkers working between Shyambazaar–Hatibagan in the north and Gariahat in the south. When I conducted a survey in 2013 of a randomly chosen group of 480 hawkers in Calcutta's 21 major intersections,[9] I noticed that only 81 out of 480 (16.87 per cent) hawkers being interviewed identified themselves as refugees. Thirty-eight of the 81 confirmed that they inherited the business from a senior family member. The rest—43 hawkers—confirmed that they had started the business themselves. Of the 43 refugee hawkers who started business on their own, 31 were *namasudras*. The highest concentration of refugee hawkers was found in three areas: Gariahat–Rashbehari Avenue (22), Sealdah (17), and Hatibagan–Shyambazaar (14). However, over 80 per cent of the hawkers interviewed (399 out of 480) did not report a refugee connection in 2013. A total of 188 hawkers (39.17 per cent) reported that they were from North and South 24 Parganas. Of the 188, 65 commuted daily on suburban trains to reach their hawking area. Many of them, in refugee hotspots such as

---

[9] The survey was done on behalf of a hawkers' union and with the aid of the union's members. Arguably, this is a very small sample. By 2013, there were more than 20,000 stalls in the vicinity of 21 intersections (if one takes a 100-foot radius of each crossing-point). For the most part, my research with the hawkers was qualitative, ethnographic, and historical. Nonetheless, it does provide some quantitative understanding of the social and economic processes involved in footpath hawking. I am thankful to Rimpa Ghosh for assistance during the survey and data entry.

Gariahat and Sealdah, confirmed taking over hawking establishments from upper-caste refugees of the 1970s.

I also found that 105 (21.9 per cent) hawkers had migrated from Bihar and Uttar Pradesh, decades back. They reported that they lived in nearby slums or spent nights on the sidewalk. Of these 105 long-term interstate migrants, 52 hawkers had their immediate family members residing with them. By contrast, 53 all-male hawkers reported that they remitted about 25 to 30 per cent of their income to their families back home. Thus, interstate migrants were only about one-fifth of the total population being interviewed, and out of them, nearly a half had ceased intense familial connections with their relatives in other states.

Thus, looking backwards from 2013, we get a sense of increasing social dynamism among the hawkers. Hawking, as a means of survival on Calcutta streets, developed as a response to large-scale dispossession induced by economic distress and Partition-linked migration. Different social groups came in and were replaced by other groups while a social infrastructure of obstruction remained available to those who were in need of it. In old industrial neighbourhoods such as Prince Anwar Shah Road, some former factory workers became footpath hawkers when the Jay Engineering Works factory (see Chapter 4) closed down and gave way to a giant shopping mall and an upper-middle-class enclave. Obstructions become durable when they make space for mobility among human actors—when motion gets folded into obstruction. However, routine eviction drives and a certain level of itinerancy produced a continued illusion of impermanence. This impermanence masked, in fact, an agility that helped these street establishments survive over decades, despite the efforts of unsympathetic governments that saw hawking as obstructions in the city.

One of the sources of this 'agility' is the relatively low setting-up as well as running costs. Some of my ethnographic findings from the 2013 survey (mentioned previously) can be considered in this context. On the source of initial funds, 394 out of 480 (82.09 per cent) hawkers confirmed that they depended on their family sources to start a business, while only 43 hawkers (less than 9 per cent) reported debt from close family friends and parents' employers. Another 43 (less than 9 per cent) hawkers took loans from moneylenders at high interest rates. All the hawkers confirmed that they became financially self-sufficient within three to five years of business. Those who failed had to exit the profession. The data here indicates that footpath hawking was not a credit-driven enterprise. I also found that more than 20 per cent of hawkers could marginally expand their enterprise within a decade (2003–2013), although in most cases, the size remained the same for many years. Taking 2013 as a standard year of entry to hawking, I calculated that their initial non-recurrent expenditure ranged between 6,800 rupees and 13,500 rupees. That apart, they needed 1,580 rupees to 2,020 rupees a month to keep the business at the same level. Depending on the monthly profits (assuming that hawkers reported a somewhat conservative figure), I estimated that proceeds from their daily sales would range between 6,750 rupees and 18,000 rupees. Thus, even the most conservative estimate of profits would have been higher than the government-mandated minimum wage. Over 87 per cent of the hawkers I interviewed sold commodities at 5 to 10 per cent less than the regular retail shops and bazaars and yet reported making sufficient profits to sustain themselves and the size of their businesses. Moreover, each enterprise directly served units of more than seven individuals (including workers and dependent family members), besides the owner-investor. Thus, my enquiries and estimates show that hawking was a viable economic activity for a large section of city dwellers and that footpath hawking remained a stable enterprise even in 2013, despite economic fluctuations.

It is thus evident that the proliferation of footpath hawking follows a different logic from that of organized capital.[10] In the spatial expansion of capital, the capitalists tend to encroach upon each other's territory and become one—the monopolist. As 'hostile brothers', says Marx, the capitalists first 'divide among themselves the loot of other people's labour' and, in course, they become hostile to each other.[11] Unlike corporate players in the accumulation economy, the hawkers do not reproduce capital at an expanded scale, but then, neither do they suffer from sudden economic shocks and exit the market. A hawker leader in Shyambazaar said to me: 'If I am a hawker, I will take all measures to keep my enterprise on, keeping its size intact. Typically, I will not reproduce my enterprise at an expanded scale as Ratan Tata or Mukesh Ambani would do.' Many hawkers proudly told me that they saved India during the recession of 2008–2009. They survived because of their autonomy from the banking sector and the real estate, which bore the brunt of the recession.

---

[10] Kalyan Sanyal, *Rethinking Capitalist Development: Primitive Accumulation, Governmentality and Post-Colonial Capitalism* (Delhi: Routledge, 2007).

[11] Karl Marx, *Theories of Surplus Value*, vol. 2 (Moscow: Progress Publishers, 1968), 29. For an understanding of mutual hostility among the capitalists, see *Capital*, vol. 3. Marx writes: 'The antagonism between each individual capitalist's interests and those of the capitalist class as a whole, then comes to the surface, just as previously the identity of these interests operated in practice through competition.' Karl Marx, *Capital*, vol. 3 (Institute of Marxism-Leninism, USSR, 1959), 178.

Thus, it is not profit but livelihood that governs motive in the profession of hawking. Hawkers become numerous while proliferating spatially, and this helps the hawkers' enterprise because it reproduces and expands via commoning. The capitalist's enterprise, by contrast, reproduces because of expansion via enclosure. Consequently, from the capitalist worldview, hawking appears as an obstruction—albeit one that it seeks to discipline rather than destroy, so that it can function as a sector that enables low wages in the accumulation economy. But obstruction, too, can and does offer a critique of motion while proposing a counter-hegemonic universal. The precarious but continued viability of footpath hawking as a form of livelihood in Calcutta ensured that hawkers served poorer social classes and enabled a low-cost living in the city. Their economic viability also gave footpath hawkers strength to emerge as a political force in the city, despite several eviction operations. In fact, hawkers used the eviction operations to re-group and build a new horizon of solidarity, and further consolidate a durable politics of obstructionism.

Obstructionism as Politics: Organization, Eviction, and Reclamation in the 1970s

The spread of footpath hawking and the hawkers' ability to retain the footpaths, thereby creating a 'durable obstruction' in the city, involved not just agility but the 'force' of organized mobilization. In Calcutta, the history of unionization of the footpath hawkers dates to the early 1950s. In the late 1950s, when hawking emerged as a viable livelihood option for impoverished refugee migrants from East Pakistan, the labour wings of many other Left parties active in Calcutta started footpath hawkers' associations and unions.[12] These associations and unions were the offshoots of the established trade unions associated with the Congress, the Communist Party of India (CPI), the Revolutionary Socialist Party (RSP), the Forward Bloc, and the Communist Party of India (Marxist) (CPI [M]).

Among the Left parties, the CPI(M) especially—after the CPI split in 1964—strengthened their political credibility and organizational structure by mobilizing peasants (through their peasant wing, Krishak Sabha) and the working classes (through their Centre of Indian Trade Unions, or CITU). Other Left-leaning political parties, such as the Workers' Party, the RSP, the CPI, and

---

[12] In 2007, an old trade unionist belonging to the Bengal Hawkers' Association of the Trade Union Coordination Committee of the Forward Bloc recollected the formation of his association with Muslim greengrocers (known as *subzifrosh*).

the Forward Bloc, also developed a significant rural and urban mass base in the 1960s. While the Congress Party had dominated the state legislature until then, in 1967 the first non-Congress alliance, the United Front, came to power with the CPI(M) as one of its major constituents.

However, the years between 1967 and 1972 were politically unstable. Two United Front governments were formed and dismissed, and 'President's Rule'[13] was imposed more than once. By the 1972 Assembly elections, a Congress–CPI alliance decimated the CPI(M), and the Congress once again assumed absolute majority. Siddhartha Shankar Ray became the Chief Minister, and this time a new brand of Youth Congress leaders entered the cabinet. During the 21 months of Emergency imposed by the Congress government at the centre, West Bengal witnessed the severest state crackdown on Naxalite rebels and the mainstream Left led by the CPI(M). Arguably, the youth and student wings of the Congress were at the vanguard of their party's revival and the subsequent witch hunt.

The Youth Congress emerged as an aggressive cadre-based organization centred on local clubs; it took over many governmental functions and invested clubs with these functions. Control over local clubs also became a way for establishing surveillance and espionage over neighbourhoods and garnering volunteers during factional or inter-party skirmishes. Footpath hawkers also entered local economies of power through these clubs and social and cultural events. Prominent Youth Congress leaders like Subrata Mukherjee in Gariahat and Somen Mitra in Sealdah, and their subordinate leader in other places, played a crucial role in forging links between Congress-sponsored club Pujas and the street economy. These clubs maintained strong networks with the street economy, among other reasons, to develop their own financial structures. While many of the funds meant for developmental work started to be channelled through these clubs, the street remained a real source of revenue for such clubs. Since the clubs depended on hawkers to maintain their rent-seeking financial structure, between 1967 and 1972, different political parties and Congress factions competed among themselves to claim important intersections of the city. The dependence on rents from the street allowed hawkers a foothold in various political parties as well as the government.

---

[13] President's rule or central rule in India refers to a constitutional situation when a state legislature is dissolved or suspended, and the state comes directly under federal rule. Article 356 of the Constitution of India enables the central government to impose president's rule if the state government fails to rule the state according to the Constitution.

By the time of the Emergency (1975–1976), the municipal governance of all major metropolitan cities, including Calcutta, came to be controlled by the bureaucracy of either the state or central government. During the Emergency, the Delhi Development Authority (DDA) began demolishing slums and squatter colonies in various parts of Delhi in the name of urban sanitization. At Turkman Gate in Old Delhi, Sanjay Gandhi (the younger son of Indira Gandhi) allegedly 'bulldozed a slum into a wasteland'.[14] But in Calcutta, slum dwellers, squatters, and hawkers managed to resist such sanitization projects because hawkers had successfully inserted themselves into the factional conflicts within the ruling Congress Party. This allowed them spaces of manipulation at the neighbourhood level. Many eviction operations were stalled because these faction leaders wanted to use the opportunity to increase their share of informal rent by first evicting the hawkers and then allowing them to resettle under a new agreement. In fact, as Ashok Ghosh mentioned, settled groups of hawkers were often happy about a raid that they knew of in advance, as periodic evictions thinned out the competition posed by new entrants.

Three significant hawker eviction drives took place between 1969 and 1975. In 1969, the second United Front government evicted refugee hawkers in Gariahat. The hawkers returned under the leadership of the Ballygunge Hawkers' Association, then affiliated to the Workers' Party, which had been a part of the ruling United Front.[15] In 1972, a second eviction drive was carried out in central Calcutta around the Esplanade area, spanning roughly three neighbouring wards of the Calcutta Municipal Corporation: wards 44, 53, and 62.[16] Frequent entries in the 'Daily Notes Register' of the Special Branch of Calcutta Police, made between 5 March 1972 and 11 June 1972, note six hawkers' unions under the subtitle 'West Bengal Hawkers'—the Nationalist Hawkers' Association (Congress-R), Ballygunge Hawkers' Association (Congress-R), Chowringhee Hawkers' Association (Congress-R), Bengal Hawkers' Association (Forward Bloc), Calcutta Hawkers' Congress (Socialist Party), and Jai Hind Calcutta Hawkers' Union (Congress-R). Another file titled 'Copy of SB Secret Report

---

[14] This was the headline of a long report in *The Guardian*, 6 February 1978.

[15] Office of the Deputy Commissioner of Police, Special Branch, Calcutta, Government of West Bengal, Daily Notes of the Special Branch of Calcutta Police, SW 630/71–72, Serial A-4, ORS 4513–518. See also *The Statesman*, 29 November 1969.

[16] For a description of the wards, see http://www.calcuttayellowpages.com/mwards.html (last accessed 20 June 2015).

Dated: 29.7.72 on West Bengal Hawkers' Associations' contained some more documents tracking the political activities of these associations.

It appears that affected hawkers found it more effective to negotiate with the government by expressing allegiance to ruling parties or, at any rate, to a party that was not its staunchest opponent. This is suggested by the complete silence in these police records on the activities of the CITU, the labour union of the CPI(M), which remained in the opposition through this period. In fact, many local hawker associations shifted their allegiance during the eviction drive, using it as a bargaining tool. When the United Front government was in power, the Ballygunge Hawkers' Association operated through the Workers' Party, then part of the ruling front. This association successfully resisted the anti-hawker drive at Gariahat in 1969. However, the Daily Notes of Special Branch in its entry on 8 April 1972 tells us that the leaders of the aforementioned unions met at a '*katra*[17] opposite Gariahat Market on the afternoon of 6.4.72',[18] where they 'decided to merge with the INTUC', the trade union wing of the Congress.[19] Facing differences of opinion within the party, the United Front government decided to take a soft stand, and hawkers returned to their original affiliations. While such shifting allegiances worked as an effective negotiating tactic, it also made hawkers increasingly dependent on unions.

A third eviction drive, codenamed 'Operation Hawker', was conducted a month before Prime Minister Indira Gandhi promulgated the National Emergency in 1975. The hawkers, as in 1972, were organized by street-based hawkers' associations. The associations regularly conducted protest rallies and press conferences and fasted in public spaces. They also submitted letters, memoranda, and proposals of resettlement on behalf of their client hawkers.[20] Finding it difficult to negotiate with an organized state machine hostile to hawkers, many associations soon came together and formed an umbrella organization called the Coordination Committee of Calcutta Hawkers (CCCH). The first entry reporting on the activities of the CCCH in the Daily Notes on 24 March 1975 describes the CCCH as comprising the labour cells of the

---

[17] *Katra* means market.

[18] Office of the Deputy Commissioner of Police, Special Branch, Calcutta. Government of West Bengal, Daily Notes of the Special Branch of Calcutta Police, SW 630/71–72, Serial A-4, ORS 4513–518.

[19] INTUC is the abbreviated form of Indian National Trade Union Congress.

[20] Office of the Deputy Commissioner of Police, Special Branch, Calcutta, Government of West Bengal, Daily Notes of the Special Branch of Calcutta Police, SW 636/75.

West Bengal Pradesh Congress Committee-R and the Socialist Party.[21] The second entry on 2 April 1975 mentions a third organization called the National Federation of Independent Trade Unions.[22] The third entry on 5 April 1975 indicates the further addition of the Muslim League to the Committee.[23]

The political activism of the CCCH suggested growing Marxist inclinations of the unions. The CCCH members started fasting in public below Lenin's statue in Esplanade's old tram *goomty* (depot), which continued for more than two weeks. A Gandhian technique of pressurizing the state machine was thus observed below the statue of Lenin. In the politically explosive environment of Calcutta in 1975, in the context of the Congress-imposed Emergency, such a combination was politically provocative. The use of Marxist references, while simultaneously declaring allegiance to the Congress, was also evident in the two slogans that the CCCH raised in its rallies: *Sara prithbir hawker ek hao* (Hawkers of the world, unite), and *Goriber debi Indira Gandhi amar rahe* (Long live the goddess of the poor, Indira Gandhi). While the first slogan invoked the popular Left jargon of an internationally united struggle of workers against class oppression, the second (paradoxically) declared the committee's conformity to the Congress and Prime Minister Indira Gandhi, who represented the Indian state during the Emergency.

The CCCH further provoked the Indian state under the Congress by critiquing its secularist claim. It openly accused the government of deliberately targeting Muslims and members of the Scheduled Castes during Operation Hawker.[24]

---

[21] Office of the Deputy Commissioner of Police, Special Branch, Calcutta, Government of West Bengal, Daily Notes of the Special Branch of Calcutta Police, SW 636/75, 253, ORS 3988–90.

[22] National Federation of Independent Trade Unions was a breakaway group of Congress trade unionists established by Naren Sen in 1967. Office of the Deputy Commissioner of Police, Special Branch, Calcutta, Government of West Bengal, Daily Notes of the Special Branch of Calcutta Police, SW 636/75, 18, ORS 4398.

[23] Office of the Deputy Commissioner of Police, Special Branch, Calcutta, Government of West Bengal, Daily Notes of the Special Branch of Calcutta Police, SW 636/75, 55, ORS 4679–80.

[24] In a pamphlet issued by the Muslim League titled 'Chowringhee Elakar Hawker Uchchheder Poriprikshete Janasadharaner Nikat Muslim League Er Abedan' (The Submission of the Muslim League to the General Public in the Context of Hawker Eviction in Chowringhee), it was claimed (according to a translation by the police) that the majority of the evicted hawkers belonged to the Muslim and Scheduled Caste communities, among whom the problem of unemployment had been more

On 5 April 1975, addressing a rally organized by the CCCH, prominent Muslim League leader and Member of Legislative Assembly Sikandar Ali Molla asked the hawkers to 'start a crusade (*jihad*) against the government'.[25] On 9 April, the Calcutta District Committee of the Muslim League organized a meeting at the crossing of Tantibagan Lane and Cantopher Lane. In this, the speakers criticized the state government, as the Daily Notes records, for 'allegedly showing step-motherly attitude towards the Muslim hawkers, while other non-Muslim hawkers in Sealdah, Gariahat and Kalighat area were not yet disturbed'.[26]

Nandini Dasgupta's careful observation reveals a pattern in Operation Hawker in 1975. She shows that the eviction was planned in two phases. The first phase would cover Chittaranjan Avenue (from Madan Street Crossing to Lenin Sarani Junction), parts of Bentinck Street (from its crossing with R. N. Mukherjee Road to the junction of Lenin Sarani and Jawaharlal Nehru Road), parts of Jawaharlal Nehru Road (from its crossing with the Lenin Sarani up to its crossing with Lindsay Street), and also certain portions of the Esplanade East (from the crossing of Lenin Sarani to Old Court House Street). The geographic area for eviction in the first phase corresponded to the bulk of the major commercial areas of the city bordering the wholesale markets of Burrabazaar— the Machua Bazaar and New Market area. Most of the hawkers in these areas were 'non-Bengali' Muslims.[27]

It was decided that a second or third phase of the Operation would be undertaken in the Gariahat–Ballygunge and Sealdah and Shyambazaar areas, respectively, which had been the strongholds of Hindu Bengali refugees.[28] In 1972, these three regions had already been targeted, but the government had faced stiff resistance from the hawkers who lobbied through trade unions.[29] The eviction drives of Operation Hawker in 1975 also did not affect the hawkers at

---

acute. SW 636/75, 82, ORS 4679–80 and SW 636/75, ORS 4679–80, 5 April 1975, 33, Office of the Deputy Commissioner of Police, Special Branch, Calcutta, Government of West Bengal, Daily Notes of Special Branch of Calcutta Police.

[25] Office of the Deputy Commissioner of Police, Special Branch, Calcutta, Government of West Bengal, Daily Notes of Special Branch of Calcutta Police, SW 636/75, 82, ORS 4679–80.

[26] Office of the Deputy Commissioner of Police, Special Branch, Calcutta. Government of West Bengal, Secret Report of the Special Branch of Calcutta Police, OR 4982, Communal Groups: Muslim Affairs, 160 Muslim League, 114.

[27] N. Dasgupta, *Petty Trading in the Third World*.

[28] *Anandabazar Patrika*, 24 March 1975.

[29] *Anandabazar Patrika*, 21 April 1972.

the intersections at Shyambazaar in the north and Gariahat in the south. This was because, as mentioned earlier, hawkers managed to exploit the factionalism within the Congress to stay afloat. In these two places, refugee identity did play an emotive role to raise a moral claim in support of footpath hawking. The unions in refugee-dominated areas repeatedly referred to Partition and the refugee influx in Calcutta as the prime cause of encroachments. They promised to move out if they were given a viable scheme of economic rehabilitation.[30] Additionally, it also helped that established garment retailers in these areas had complementary relations with hawkers and did not wish to have them evicted. Thus, the Operation did appear to harbour intolerance towards Muslim hawkers, an allegation repeatedly made by the Muslim League leaders during the Operation.

Footpath hawkers therefore entrenched themselves both in local, informally operating economies of power as well as in formal trade unions affiliated to various political parties. Their success was often regulated by the social and religious background of the hawkers being targeted as well as their relationship with established commercial groups in the locality and trade unions affiliated with political parties. Because of intense conflicts and factionalism that characterized the politics of West Bengal between 1969 and 1975, hawkers found some space to manoeuvre and negotiate for their own interests, while cutting across party lines. They often expressed loyalty to the ruling party or the ruling coalition as a way to have their demands met. In 1969, for example, the Workers' Party leader Jyoti Bhattacharyya claimed that Gariahat hawkers were loyal to the 'Left' and, therefore, a Left-wing government should reconsider its stand on hawker eviction at Gariahat. Similarly, we have seen that during Operation Hawker, the CCCH expressed its allegiance to the Congress and Prime Minister Indira Gandhi.

Irrespective of party affiliations though, hawkers' associations ultimately defended their right to occupy public spaces in the city. Both in 1969 and 1975, the unions claimed that their clients were poor, honest, and industrious. Moreover, they were the victims of Partition, deindustrialization, and rural impoverishment. On these grounds they demanded exceptional treatment from governments. They hardly claimed that their illegal occupation was right. Instead, they professed a readiness to move out if they were given viable rehabilitation.[31]

[30] SW 636/75, 82, ORS 4679–80 and SW 636/75, ORS 4679–80, 5 April 1975, 33, Office of the Deputy Commissioner of Police, Special Branch, Calcutta, Government of West Bengal, Daily Notes of the Special Branch of Calcutta Police.

[31] Partha Chatterjee, *Lineages of Political Society: Studies in Postcolonial Democracy* (Ranikhet: Permanent Black, 2011).

Bulldozing Obstruction, 1996–1997

In 1977, the National Emergency was withdrawn, and the Indian electorate ousted the Congress from power in the Centre and most states. In West Bengal, the CPI(M) won the elections to the Legislative Assembly with a huge mandate. Other Left parties, such as the Forward Bloc, the RSP, and the CPI subsequently joined the government as the constituents of a ruling coalition known as the Left Front. The Left Front would rule the state for close to 35 years and create a record in the annals of Indian democracy. The CPI(M)'s coming to power reactivated many of the dreams of refugees and other marginalized groups who had waited for decades to see their party rule West Bengal.

In the initial years of the Left Front rule, the CPI(M) sought to establish and consolidate incumbency by strengthening and restructuring various patronage networks without further radicalizing the urban poor. The practical step for the party was to consolidate benefit distribution through its affiliated labour unions by restricting new membership after 1977. Consequently, the government declared that no hawkers who had occupied the footpath after 1977 would be given vending licences (which were never issued), the implication being that violators would not be granted resettlement if eviction took place in the future.

In 1983, Chief Minister Jyoti Basu ordered the police to identify hawkers who entered the business after 1977,[32] and CPI(M) leader and Member of Legislative Assembly Saral Deb presented a petition on the situation arising from the 'unauthorised occupation of pavement/streets/roads by hawkers'.[33] Based on this petition, the 'Committee on Petition' formed by the representatives of all parties present in the legislature presented in the ninth Legislative Assembly a 'Report in the Matter of Framing Suitable Laws for Controlling and Regulating the Unauthorised Occupation of Public Lands and Thoroughfares by the Hawkers and Others in This State'.[34]

The Report revealed that the state government wanted to neither evict hawkers completely nor let them proliferate in an uncontrolled manner. The proposal recommended creating hawking and non-hawking zones in the city and the rehabilitation of hawkers in low-cost market complexes. Such recommendations were entirely in accordance with rulings in various high courts and the Supreme Court of India from the mid-1980s. Several hawker unions

---

[32] *The Statesman*, 8 July 1983.

[33] *West Bengal Legislative Assembly Proceedings*, 1986, 50.

[34] Ibid., Annexure 4.

had moved the courts, which had ruled in accordance with Article 19 (1)(g) of the Constitution of India. The article guarantees citizens the right to practice any profession or carry on any occupation, trade, or business. The courts usually suggested some spatial norms of managing hawking and acknowledged the legitimacy of trading licit goods and services as fundamental rights.[35] However, the Left Front government's stand regarding the hawkers became hostile in the 1990s.

In early 1994, the Left Front government published a supplement in the *Financial Times*, London, outlining the forthcoming industrial policy for the state of West Bengal. In the preamble, it declared its agenda:

> The Govt. recognizes the need for improvement in roads, communication and development of Growth Centres. Since these programmes require massive investment, the Govt. proposes to undertake projects to develop industrial infrastructure through the Private Joint Sector also, whenever feasible.[36]

The impact of the supplement on the international business community proved considerable. According to state government sources, the government approved 36.42 per cent more proposals in the first nine months than in the same period in the previous year. The Central Committee of the CPI(M) approved the new industrial policy. It affirmed that trade unions' rights had to be preserved but that the state had to interfere positively in specific core areas. Subsequently, the new industrial policy was debated within the CPI(M); its resolution overrode the discontent of sceptical hardliners within the party, accepted the Central Committee's decision, and called for 'modernizing trade unions'. This stance included an overall rejection of workers' militancy (repeated industrial strikes and blockades) that marked West Bengal's political history

---

[35] See Supreme Court and High Court rulings such as Supreme Court of India, 'Olga Tellis & Ors vs Bombay Municipal Corporation & ... on 10 July, 1985' (1986 AIR 180, 1985 SCR Supl. (2) 51); 'Sodan Singh Etc. Etc. vs New Delhi Municipal Committee & ... on 30 August, 1989' (1989 AIR 1988, 1989 SCR (3)1038); Calcutta High Court, 'South Calcutta Hawkers ... vs Government Of West Bengal And ... on 20 December, 1996', (AIR 1997 Cal 234, (1997) 1 CALLT 453 HC); Supreme Court of India, 'Maharashtra Ekta Hawkers Union & ... vs Municipal Corporation, Greater ... on 9 September, 2013': http://indiankanoon.org/doc/21657117 (last accessed 3 June 2015).

[36] West Bengal Industrial Policy 1994: http://dcmsme.gov.in/policies/state/westbengal/ipwb.htm (accessed 20 June 2015).

since independence.[37] The party maintained its antagonism toward the overall liberalization strategy of the Government of India, and yet agreed to liberalize West Bengal's economy as a matter of 'federal compulsion'. The effect was immediate. The Confederation of Indian Industries launched its centenary celebrations from Calcutta. Several ministers and high-level delegates from the United Kingdom, the United States, and Japan visited Calcutta.[38] The rulers felt it necessary to rebuild Calcutta as an investment-friendly city, mobilizing the *bhadralok* sentiment of 'pristine Calcutta'.[39]

It was in this new zeal of urban renewal that 'Operation Sunshine', another eviction drive, was carried out between the winters of 1996 and 1997. The CPI(M) of the 1990s tried to reverse the tide of urbanization through de-accumulation (and obstruction) of the post-colonial decades, and insert the city into the capitalist circulation network. Hawkers and the squatters were seen as obstructing capital accumulation in urban space. Around 21 major streets in the city were chosen for clearing out through eviction. Operation Sunshine was the Left's attempt to build an investment-friendly entrepreneurial image for the city.

In a well-planned and coordinated operation, undertaken intensely over a month in 1996 and intermittently throughout 1997, the Calcutta Municipal Corporation's bulldozers destroyed thousands of street-side stalls. The eviction operation was led by CPI(M) cadres along with employees of the Calcutta Municipal Corporation and the Public Works Department. After the eviction, they widened the streets in many places by cutting down the width of footpaths. In some other places, they planted trees and reclaimed space. The government and the CPI(M) spokespersons justified Operation Sunshine by drawing a correlation between the concentration of hawkers at busy street crossings, traffic congestion, and 'air pollution'—a relatively new entrant in the sanitization vocabulary. The twin logic of circulation and sanitization was deployed to reclaim the streets from the decadence of quotidian practices, restoring it to its 'proper use'—pedestrians would walk on pavements and automobiles would run relentlessly on streets.

In one instance, on 30 October 1996, in a coordinated operation in the Gariahat–Rashbehari Avenue area, the city Corporation confiscated as many

---

[37] *Times of India*, 10 October 1994.
[38] *Times of India*, 26 July 1995.
[39] Ananya Roy, *City Requiem, Calcutta: Gender and Politics of Poverty* (Minneapolis: University of Minnesota Press, 2002).

as 103 electricity generators from the hawkers of the locality. Justifying the Corporation's move, Councillor Kanti Ganguly (also a key actor of Operation Sunshine) said: 'The hawkers of Gariahat use these generators on every evening to keep their stalls well-lighted, which has increased the level of air pollution in the neighbourhood, making it difficult for the residents to breath properly.' The Hawker Sangram Committee (HSC) activists retaliated by organizing a roadblock in Gariahat, which disrupted the traffic in south Calcutta between 12 noon and 4 p.m.[40] The Corporation charged 1,000 rupees to return each generator. Ultimately, the HSC managed to pay a symbolic penalty of 100 rupees and rescued the generators.[41] Several members of the HSC told me that the successful reclamation of the generators became a turning point in establishing the HSC as the 'true' negotiator on behalf of the city's hawkers.

The intensity of the eviction operation increased in the midnight of 23 November 1996 in the Dalhousie area. Within a few hours, similar operations were carried out simultaneously at Taratala in the west (an important intersection embracing the Diamond Harbour Road), Bowbazaar and Chittaranjan/Central Avenue in central Calcutta, and Hatibagan in the north. At Bowbazaar crossing—a traditional stronghold of the Calcutta Hawker Men's Union—a mob set fire to two of the Corporation's trucks carrying seized goods from Shyambazaar to the Corporation's headquarters in Esplanade. A conservative estimate by *The Statesman* reported that more than 10,000 people, about 200 vehicles, and 10 bulldozers were deployed to conduct this 'surprise' operation. *The Statesman* further reported that Corporation officials, the 'menial staff' of the Corporation's conservancy department, police and Calcutta Electric Supply Corporation Limited (CESC) officials, and thousands of badge-holding CPI(M) cadres from the 24 Parganas were deployed to conduct the operation.[42]

In the Shyambazaar–Hatibagan area, the first deployment of the eviction gang took place at 1:15 a.m., a couple of hours after film shows in local cinemas were over. The gang was heavily guarded by the city police and the elite Rapid Action Force (RAF). As an anticipatory measure, the police barricaded all entries to the stretch of Bidhan Sarani (formerly Cornwallis Street) between the

---

[40] A couple of months before the official declaration of Operation Sunshine in 1996 (precisely on 9 August 1996), the non-Centre of Indian Trade Unions (CITU) hawker unions (at least 24, with an approximate strength of 80,000 hawkers) decided to form the Hawker Sangram Committee.

[41] *Anandabazar Patrika*, 31 October 1996.

[42] 'Operation Sunshine Lunched: Hawkers' Stalls Demolished in CMC Drive', *The Statesman*, 24 November 1996.

Shyambazaar five-point crossing and the Hatibagan junction an hour before the first Corporation vehicle appeared in the area. A large contingent of cops led by a Joint Commissioner oversaw security arrangements. Already in the evening, rooftops of nearby houses were thoroughly searched to avoid brick batting. The forces were divided into two units. One contingent moved towards the Shyambazaar five-point crossing along Vivekananda Road and Bidhan Sarani, and the other towards Radha Cinema on Bidhan Sarani along A. P. C. Road and Aurobindo Sarani.

At this point, a petrol bomb was hurled at the police when they reached the five-point crossing. The RAF (riot police) was deployed to chase the crowd, which drove the hawkers away into nearby lanes. By 11 p.m. (on 23 November), the HSC had issued a public statement, threatening a 'bloodbath' if the hawkers of this area were touched. Much before the operation began, the activists were already present and tension was palpable in the area. A large crowd silently watched the operation from B. T. Road. A large number of them were arrested in the apprehension of trouble. In Dalhousie, Operation Sunshine began at Brabourne Road at 11:40 p.m. (on 23 November). The hawkers burned down a lorry carrying the broken structures of their stalls. At Taratala, the drive began a little after midnight. Heavy police deployments were reported in Brabourne Road, Canning Street, Clive Row, Armenian Street, and Kiran Shankar Roy Road. The demolition was successful in these areas, but when the goods were being transported in two lorries towards Mathurapukur Dhapa Pumping Station, HSC activists stopped them near College Street, dragged out the drivers, beat them up, and eventually set the vehicles on fire.[43] The hawkers and the local people alleged that CPI(M) cadres from Bangur, Baranagar, Kalindi, and other areas of North 24 Parganas helped the government machinery to pull down the stalls.[44]

A little background to these events will help us understand the logistical side of this drive. On 24 November 1996, Operation Sunshine received the green signal from the Chief Minister's office. The core team of the Operation—Home Minister Buddhadeb Bhattacharyya, Transport Minister Subhas Chakrabarty, Minister-in-Charge of Urban Affairs Ashok Bhattacharyya, Mayor-in-Council (conservancy) Kanti Ganguly, the Corporation's Commissioner Asim Barman, and Police Commissioner Dinesh Bajpayee—maintained utmost secrecy so that the plan would not get leaked to the HSC and the powerful opposition leader

---

[43] 'Hawkers Hit back, Torch Buses, Tram', *The Statesman*, 26 November 1996.

[44] 'Operation Sunshine Lunched: Hawkers' Stalls demolished in CMC Drive', *The Statesman*, 24 November 1996.

Mamata Banerjee (now the Chief Minister of West Bengal). From the morning of 23 November, the entire army of demolition workers was mobilized in such a way that the opposition leaders and the HSC became convinced that the operation would start from the south—in Tollygunge, Gariahat, and Hazra—the stronghold of Mamata Banerjee. According to Kanti Ganguly's estimate, eventually carrying out a sudden operation elsewhere wholly baffled the opposition and enabled demolition workers to accomplish their task in relative peace. In a later recollection, Kanti Ganguly did not hesitate to call Operation Sunshine a 'bloodless revolution' to free Calcutta from the hawkers.[45] The HSC's retaliation came in the next few hours after the midnight event. By the morning of 24 November, the hawkers had managed to burn down two state buses, a tramcar, and three vehicles belonging to the city Corporation and damage five state-owned buses as the day progressed.

The incident of 24 November 1996 led to an intense discussion within the city's civil society circles. Media speculations about internal dissension within the CPI(M) regarding the modalities of the operation compelled the senior Left Front leaders to make public statements about the unity within the party. The trade unions associated with smaller stakeholders of the Left Front such as the Forward Bloc, the CPI, and the RSP openly sided with the HSC. At the same time, their senior leaders maintained a cautious public posture on Operation Sunshine as they could not disapprove of the government's decision to carry out the operation.

Around 10 centres were hastily created to rehabilitate hawkers.[46] In many cases, as Ananya Roy reports, evicted hawkers were selected for rehabilitation by mid-ranking functionaries of the CPI(M). While Subhas Chakrabarty, the Transport Minister, was the architect of Operation Sunshine, Kanti Ganguly, an associate, was in charge of rehabilitating the evicted garment hawkers at Gariahat. He chose a plot of land down the Sukanta Setu at Santoshpur (in south Calcutta) and another down the Bijon Setu in Ballygunge, where he had substantial control over the real estate market and squatter colonies. He designed the rehabilitation project to disaggregate the hawkers' resistance into numerous subterranean pockets.[47]

---

[45] Kanti Ganguly, 'Sanshiner Aage o Pore', in *Operation Sunshine*, ed. Soumitra Lahiri (Kolkata: Biswakosh Parishad, 1997), 66–75. This essay contains a 'thick description' of Operation Sunshine from the perspective of the ruling establishment.

[46] 'Hawker Rehabilitation Begins', *The Statesman*, 30 January 1997.

[47] Ananya Roy, *City Requiem, Calcutta*.

During the eviction drive, the distinction between the party and the government dissolved. The media celebrated this new authoritarianism as a much-needed move to rectify a city 'notorious' for its democratic culture and slow pace. On 6 December 1996, *The Telegraph* captioned an exclusive on Operation Sunshine as 'State Resolve Flattens Feeble Defiance of Hawkers'. Noted city intellectuals and successful professionals from various fields too came forward with a trove of nostalgia and aestheticized Operation Sunshine. Soon, an anthology in Bengali titled *Operation Sunshine* came out in which well-known poets, essayists, novelists, journalists, and educationists justified the move to sanitize the city streets and congratulated Subhas Chakrabarty and Kanti Ganguly for their courage to rise above the everyday compulsions of 'party politics'. They set pen to paper to save the pedestrian—the quintessential citizen (*sadharan manush*)—and evoked the utopian city of their childhood dreams: clean, green, and civil. Thus, the moment of Operation Sunshine was also a moment of autobiographical reckoning, of expressing the powerful desire to reclaim Calcutta after the city being captive for so long in the prison of 'stagnation' and obstruction.[48]

Operation Sunshine was the Left's attempt to build an investment-friendly entrepreneurial image of the city—one which was dynamic and already inserted into the global circulation of capital. Predictably, the media celebrated the new move of the Left as a rupture in the city's history. Thus, *Newsweek* wrote of Calcutta:

> It used to be described as India's Black Hole by the British in the 18th Century when the industrial revolution was at its peak in the country.... Things began to change about six months ago, just before the British Prime Minister John Major was due to visit the city. In a rapid-fire campaign, the civic administration and the West Bengal government evicted hundreds of hawkers and roadside shop owners entrenched in several prestigious neighbourhoods.[49]

And yet Operation Sunshine failed. As in most rehabilitation efforts, this time, too, the state functionaries overlooked the restricted space and low economic viability of the resettlement sites as business spots for evicted hawkers. For instance, the

---

[48] See articles and poems compiled in Soumitra Lahiri (ed.), *Operation Sunshine* (Kolkata: Biswakosh Parishad, 1997). Also see Ananya Roy, *City Requiem, Calcutta*, especially ch. 4: 'Dreaming of Tombstones', 133–189.

[49] *Newsweek*, 7 May 1997.

government located a site in Galiff Street to rehabilitate the 1,800 hawkers who were evicted from the Shyambazaar–Hatibagan area. The resettlement site in Galiff street could at best accommodate 816 hawkers. Moreover, it was decided that each hawker would pay 5,000 rupees in two instalments to the government to secure a vending space in the resettlement scheme.

Two years down the line, on 3 January 1999, 816 hawkers occupied the allotted stalls in Galiff street. However, within a couple of weeks, they began to return to Shyambazaar–Hatibagan, as the new location could not give them enough business to meet the basic establishment cost. Santosh Nandi, a hawker who took up a stall in Galiff Street and then returned to Hatibagan, informed me in 2007 that the market the government built for them in the Galiff Street plot lacked the common sense of a successful marketplace. It was built on the lines of a fish market and looked like an FCI (Food Corporation of India) warehouse. The site was enclosed by a wall and had a big courtyard to host the hawkers. Nandi further alleged that the entire area was full of noxious smell and was surrounded by destitute pavement dwellers. 'Such a place', Nandi continued, 'was not conducive to the business' which could 'attract *bhadralok* clients'.

When the tide of Operation Sunshine receded, the resettled hawkers returned to the street crossings.[50] This time though, they were united under the banner of the now stronger HSC—a federation of several local unions. Along with sensational protest rallies—using innovative means, such as carrying 18 coffins to remember the mass suicide of hawkers that followed Operation Sunshine—the HSC leaders exploited the difference of opinion within the Left Front and the top-level bureaucracy to their advantage. It was well known that the city wing of the CPI(M) viewed Operation Sunshine as an unnecessary assertion from the leaders belonging to the District Committees of North and South 24 Parganas,[51] and that the Corporation's Mayor himself did not know its exact blueprint. Despite the difference of opinion within the CPI(M), the party could mobilize its machine and CITU to support the operation. As mentioned earlier, Forward Bloc leader Ashok Ghosh openly supported the hawkers and even led them to reclaim their lost spaces in Shyambazaar. While Asim Barman, the Municipal Commissioner (and Chief Executive of the Calcutta Municipal Corporation), favoured evicting the hawkers, Tushar Talukdar, city Police Commissioner, and

---

[50] 'Hawkers Thrive Under CMC's Nose', *The Statesman*, 10 March 2000.

[51] It is worth mentioning here that Subhas Chakravarty was the leader of the North 24 Parganas District Committee and Kanti Ganguly, who at that time was a member of the Mayor's Council, represented the South 24 Parganas District Committee.

the lower-level workers of the Calcutta Municipal Corporation favoured the regulated continuation of hawking.

The disagreement within the bureaucracy and coalition partners hampered sustained and coordinated action against the hawkers. By June 1997, hawkers started returning to their locations, and the HSC played a significant role in redistributing footpath space among them after Operation Sunshine ended. Four years after Operation Sunshine, on 9 March 2000, *The Statesman* carried out a survey on the footpaths in central Calcutta. Here is what they found:

> Less than a kilometre from the CMC, on either side of the road leading to Globe or the Corporation Place Street leading to New Market, hawkers literally rule curtsey the VIP proximity they enjoy.... The civic authorities claim these areas were on the first list of 21 roads where eviction was slated to be conducted.

When asked how these hawkers returned to the area, an exasperated Kanti Ganguly quipped: 'It is difficult to hurt the hawkers' sentiments who mostly sell their wares during Hindu and Muslim festivals.' 'So, is there no day in the year which can be marked a non-festival day?' asked the naughty reporter. A visibly embarrassed Kanti Ganguly vowed that 'no one will go unscathed'.[52]

In Calcutta, footpath hawkers have been crucial actors in making urban motion a culturally and politically negotiated affair. Through the cycle of eviction, organization, and reclamation over decades, hawkers emerged as a significant player in Calcutta's social and economic developments when the city was experiencing a sustained crisis in the accumulation economy. Operation Hawker of 1975 was a pretext for the playing out of local factionalism. But Operation Sunshine of 1996–1997 was an ideological project that wished to reinstall Calcutta in the network of accumulation. In other words, this drive was designed to 'recover' the inner city from the blight of obstructions. It flushed out obstructions by the force of bulldozers and set the streets in motion once again—a 'sunshine' as the government euphemistically called it.

Yet Operation Sunshine failed in the face of strong resistance from the hawkers.[53] The HSC reversed the narrative and named the drive 'Operation Sunset' that resulted in the loss of livelihood, hunger, and several suicides. The hawkers stood resolute and united, and they foiled large-scale gentrification of the inner city. The sprawling avenues that the Calcutta Improvement Trust

---

[52] 'Hawkers Thrive Under CMC's Nose', *The Statesman*, 8 March 2000.
[53] 'Cat-and-mouse Eviction Game Foxes Targets', *The Telegraph*, 7 December 1996.

had built in the early twentieth century to facilitate the city's capitalization turned finally on their heads just before the century ended. Obstructions metamorphosed into obstructionism, which offered an alternative trajectory of urbanism and urban sociality.

Subsequently, the government tried to get rid of unauthorized colonies along various canals and rail tracks. The HSC—now emboldened by their recent victory—associated themselves with various squatter groups and built a people's movement around livelihood issues. The government failed once again before an organized resistance. These movements kept a vibrant political discourse alive in the city around livelihood and the 'right to the city'.[54] Obstructionism was the manifesto of this new culture of solidarity. Facing repeated resistance from these organized groups ever since the Emergency era, the private capital–government nexus finally 'bypassed' the inner city and opened new avenues of accumulation in the frontiers.[55] Frontier urbanization of the 1990s and the 2000s occurred along the eastern side of the Eastern Metropolitan Bypass and in Rajarhat.[56]

A New Strategy of Trade Unionism

Internal dissensions within the government after Operation Sunshine forced the government to come to the negotiating table with the HSC representing the hawkers. Since then, the HSC evolved a long-term political support structure of Calcutta's footpath hawkers with a view to institutionalizing footpath hawking. It developed a federal approach in its trade unionism in keeping several smaller unions united on a platform. When hawkers had to negotiate with questions of representation in the governmental space, and at times of protest against issues of national and global dimensions (such as protests against foreign direct

---

[54] In 2005, the National Hawker Federation (NHF)—the national-level platform of the hawkers (HSC is a part of the NHF since 2000)—formally adapted the World Charter on the Right to the City. See the Charter's Preamble here: https://www.hlrn.org.in/documents/World_Charter_on_the_Right_to_the_City.htm, accessed 22 November 2021.

[55] Rajesh Bhattacharya and Kalyan Sanyal, 'Bypassing the Squalor: New Towns, Immaterial Labour and Exclusion in Post-colonial Urbanisation', *Economic and Political Weekly*, 46, no. 31 (2011): 41-48.

[56] Ananya Roy, *City Requiem, Calcutta*; Ishita Dey, Ranabir Samaddar, and Suhit Sen, *Beyond Kolkata: Rajarhat and the Dystopia of Urban Imagination* (London: Routledge, 2013).

investment in the retail sector), the identity of the HSC as a strong organization prevailed. Individual associations and unions of hawkers used their own identities to deal with the local state, maintain relations with political parties, and recruit and expel individual candidates at the local level. This way the HSC could become an organization where conflicting party interests converged.

The HSC does not micromanage its federation members, and in return its member units adhere to some prescriptions of the HSC. For example, they maintain spatial norms as imposed by the government and upheld by the HSC, as agreed through negotiations. Hawkers are usually allowed to occupy one-third of the footpath in a single row facing the established shops. Also, members of the HSC do not use party banners if the latter organizes the event. The HSC seems to keep them united and retains its political legitimacy through the logic of an unceasing *sangram* (struggle) against the state and the corporate capital. It commemorates the *sangram* through events, actions, and rallies where the federation members supply the viewers and listeners.

Operation Sunshine took place at a time when the outcomes of neoliberal globalization were still uncertain. The first decade (the 1990s) of globalization opened with a new promise of motion—that it would bring more employment and prosperity to cities like Calcutta, long under the grip of militant trade unionism. But, as the decade progressed, this dream met with the reality of growing inequality, unemployment, blight, and informalization even in the 'formal sector' of the economy. All over urban India, industrial centres shut down. Ex-industrial workers, too, took recourse to the informal economy. Thousands of them erected stalls outside the factory premises to eke out a living. The state began to propagate the new mantra of self-reliance and entrepreneurialism when its welfare programmes ran dry. In this context, footpath hawking appropriated the new language of entrepreneurialism both to justify their encroachment in market terms and to reinvent itself as the last vestige for the newly unemployed workers. As Saktiman Ghosh (of the HSC) told me in 2008 (and repeatedly since then):

> We are an important market force when the majority of India's population are relegated to abject poverty. We do not depend on an impoverished state. We make our own business without state support and serve the society. What we demand is the end of eviction and extortion through a new central legislation legalizing footpath hawking.

During Operation Sunshine, the government evicted hawkers citing traffic congestion and pollution, in an attempt to make Calcutta appear attractive to potential investments. But now that hawkers face the threat of destruction from the expanding market control of large corporations, they turn back on the state with a critique of neoliberal trends in the state and the economy. In fact, the HSC produces a certain kind of self-discipline among its adherents while enabling them to navigate the difficult spaces of everyday government and the market. The calculus of self-discipline is structured by the hawkers' claim to entrepreneurialism, coupled with civic responsibility. The entrepreneur (the hawker) has had to refashion himself or herself as more of a consummate claim-maker on the state than a recipient of welfare such as pavement dwellers.

Another interesting political manoeuvre by the HSC in the post–Operation Sunshine era was founded upon a sustained and self-conscious archival function aimed at influencing policy and academic discourse on footpath hawking. By arrogating to itself the task of producing and recording information—a function that is conventionally associated with the state—the HSC succeeded in opening up a shared space of negotiation with the government. After Foucault's discussion of 'governmentality', it has become common knowledge that modern governmental states manage populations by mapping them in every possible way. Organizations such as the HSC replicate this task in their own right to be able to intervene in the state's process, thus inserting themselves as crucial actors in this politics of archiving. Let me present three instances of the HSC's various archival motivations.

In April 2005, I visited the office of the HSC on College Street for the first time. The in-charge of the office, Murad Hussain, assured me partial access to their archive, adding that some sensitive records would remain secret. Otherwise, they would reveal the 'internal contradictions of the HSC'. Murad said that those documents could be made public only if the HSC resolved to document their own history in the future. Murad was acutely aware of the public nature of the act of writing history, and he was not willing to allow me authorship of the HSC story. His ability to mark the border between secrets and revelation sparked my imagination on the meaning of secrecy in the life of records. Notably, when Murad denied my request to see the secret archive, he revealed a tension, or discomfort, with those records. Perhaps Murad sensed that those documents might contradict the official position of the HSC. Thus, the HSC reserved the right to write its autobiography and disclose its own 'secrets'. It took me years to get access to the HSC's regular process of organizational documentation.

In another instance, in December 2005, the Calcutta Municipal Corporation decided to 'identify and quantify' hawkers on the streets and footpaths of the municipal area of Calcutta so that they could implement the rule to evict hawkers who joined the trade after 1977—the year the Left Front captured the Writers' Building. The HSC made two interventions at this time. First, its members began to follow the surveyors around and eventually challenged the accuracy of their assessment. If, for example, a stall was found vacant, and the Corporation surveyor was on the verge of omitting it from the survey register, HSC workers told them who the owner of the stall was and how long he or she had been trading there. The surveyor was dependent on local knowledge. Second, the HSC undertook a counter-survey, including a sample of 2,350 hawkers distributed along the 21 intersections. This pilot self-survey became the seed for all subsequent surveys on hawkers in Calcutta. Using its own survey, the HSC rendered visible the benefits of the 'low-circuit economy'[57] in Calcutta by documenting how hawkers sell the products of small primary producers and thereby sustain the small economy of the poor.

The final instance of the archival activities of the HSC that I shall cite here also occurred in 2005, when the Mayor of the Calcutta Municipal Corporation formed a municipal consultative committee. The HSC was a member of this committee. Between 2005 and 2009, the committee met five times in the Mayor's office. On each occasion, I found Saktiman Ghosh, the HSC leader, at the meeting. Ghosh had files and papers containing some sort of database of hawkers, the earliest court orders in favour of hawkers, as well as the latest court order. He claimed that he had many other paper documents that he had picked up from the office of an important government official in New Delhi or even a cabinet minister. Though suspicious of the government, he never forgot to disclose his intimacy with its functionaries in the upper echelons, who, he claimed, often updated him about new government secrets.

When the Corporation decided to evict hawkers from Park Street, Saktiman Ghosh presented a map showing the exact location of the HSC's affiliate hawkers in the area and claimed that his clients had been operating there since the early

---

[57] The genealogy of 'low-circuit economy' can be found in the 'dualistic' phase of the intellectual history of the informal economy in the early 1970s. Broadly, it refers to the labour-intensive, family-based, resource- and capital-anaemic, and non-contractual relations of production in the petty commodity sector structurally connected to the capital-intensive 'upper circuit' by providing 'wage subsidy' to the rest of the economy. The concept comes from the work of T. G. McGee. For a discussion of the features of the lower circuit, see T. G. McGee, 'In Praise of Tradition: Towards a Geography of Anti-development', *Antipode* 6, no. 3 (1974): 30–47.

1970s. He presented the past eviction records—attested by the Corporation—and records of police raids and the confiscation of hawkers' wares. A police official told me that the police department kept records of confiscation, release, and 'minor crimes' for five years and then destroyed them. These counterfoils of the old records, now preserved with the HSC, keep the government accountable as its functionaries cannot produce those documents but cannot ignore them either, given that they contain the signatures of officials.

Often these records change hands along with the vending site, which suggests that the HSC's archive is not a frozen entity awaiting a historian; rather, it is an archive in constant circulation, enabling the HSC to both function with greater agency in the governmental space and in the process craft its own history. For instance, in the post–Operation Sunshine era, the HSC became a part of a regulatory framework pertaining to sidewalks. Since the government did not have a robust database on the hawkers, the HSC archive and enumerations were deemed to be the most authoritative source of information on footpath hawking. The academics, too, had to work with this database. Subsequently—in the early 2000s—the HSC spearheaded a nation-wide campaign for a central legislation on street hawkers. It was during this time that a new federal platform for the hawkers came into being—the National Hawker Federation (NHF). By the mid-2000s, the NHF became the largest body of the hawkers that replicated the archival function of the HSC in various other cities and produced a robust national archive on hawking.

By the mid-2000s, the NHF emerged as a major constituent of the techniques of the government. It made the post–Operation Sunshine *sangram* a public memory by repeated recollections. It 'civilized' hawkers, 'trained' them to observe civic virtue, and built a populist infrastructure of *sangram* that was entangled with techniques of governing. The HSC's archival function, or its capacity to frame a narrative, enabled it to convert what was a record of transgression into a record of legitimation. The archive authorized the union to offer an alternative trajectory of urbanism for Calcutta in the twenty-first century in which obstruction could be viewed as generative of urban motion.

The instance of this government–union complex unravels conditions whereby information accumulated by the poor about themselves comes to be recognized by the government as 'legitimate', and where archiving by the poor comes to stand alongside government-produced knowledge. In so doing, this complex also shows how battles over the politics of knowledge can ensure that collectives of poor people are able to define the terms by which the government 'recognizes' them.

Pedestrianism versus Obstructionism

The operation of footpath hawking at such a scale required consensus-building exercise on the part of hawkers. This exercise—the hawkers' bid towards a consensus—involved a sustained critique of the pedestrian- or mobility-centric understanding of the sidewalk and the street, and offered an alternative framework to think of urban sociality.

Footpath hawkers often face eviction as they are deemed as obstructing pedestrian flow. The sidewalk or footpath, as we have seen in Chapter 1, is engineered as a clearly marked-out zone for the pedestrian, whose right of passage has been a stable modern legal axiom. Often, the pedestrian becomes the symbol of the urban everyman being increasingly run off the sidewalk by automobile traffic and by different forms of 'encroachment' on pedestrian spaces.[58] Moreover, the sidewalk is supposed to be protected from private appropriations. Any kind of formal-legal recognition of stationary hawkers on the sidewalks must then deal with both the pedestrian's inviolable right of passage as well as the distribution of property between public and private domains. It will have to justify obstruction, which is mainly imagined as the negation of motion.

Unlike the abstract pedestrian's rights, which are fundamental to the law of public space in a city, the street vendor's 'rights' have usually been founded on a series of exceptions and contingent legality. The Street Vendors (Protection of Livelihood and Regulation of Street Vending) Act, 2014[59] (SVA), in India came out as a legal 'formalization' of the hawkers' right to livelihood that does attempt a reversal of some of this contingency.[60] The SVA enacts a mechanism to

---

[58] It is often argued that the conceptualization of the pedestrian as an abstract and liberal right-bearing subject is a 'western' concept, and that the figure did not emerge significantly in non-western contexts. However, some of the historical evidence can also be at odds with such an argument. Jonathan Anjaria has tracked how from the 1920s, a new band of middle-class newspaper columnists in Bombay would start arguing that the pedestrian's rights were increasingly being squeezed by the 'wealth and clout of the elite and the populism of the poor'. Jonathan Anjaria, *The Slow Boil: Street Food, Rights and Public Space in Mumbai* (Stanford: Stanford University Press, 2016), 58.

[59] 'The Street Vendors (Protection of Livelihood and Regulation of Street Vending) Act, 2014': https://legislative.gov.in/sites/default/files/A2014-7.pdf, accessed 23 November 2021.

[60] This is one of those Acts that came up as a result of decades of popular movements. The Calcutta chapter was perhaps the most unionized phase of this struggle. Cities

protect the livelihood of hawkers by regulating the very means of their livelihood (which is their access to the sidewalk).

The SVA manifests the position stated earlier—that the unregulated growth of sedentary hawkers in our cities will eventually displace pedestrians from the sidewalk. Hence, the act of vending must be regulated on the sidewalk to retain the pedestrian's right of passage. Thus, the SVA regulates vending by partitioning the entire city into vending and non-vending zones.[61] Only a limited number of street vendors are allowed to operate in vending zones. The SVA the promulgates the disciplinary technology of zoning to identify every single hawker at a proper place. The SVA appears to be sympathetic to peripatetic or mobile hawkers—if they are registered in the municipal notebook. However, it is anxious about sedentary or stationary hawkers—'objects' that can potentially obstruct pedestrian flow.

Several municipal legislations before the SVA have for long forbidden 'structure or fixture' or even moving vehicles related to vending, having cast them as obstructions to bodies and movement on streets. The SVA modifies this approach by allowing vending materials that are collapsible. This includes folding tables and chairs made of metal and plastic as opposed to the traditional wooden *chowki*s used to display merchandise previously, and pushcarts and umbrellas rather than bamboo structures and corrugated roofing. They also tolerate the use of removable plastic racks, shelves, and cardboard boxes. These stipulations betray a governmental urban rationality founded upon a clear distinction between static objects on the one hand and channels of circulation on the other, like the street, the pedestrian zone, and the sewerage channel. The static objects are viewed as obstructing the free circulation, not just of pedestrians but also of air and water. In this sense, the footpath hawker is nothing more than an urban object legitimate only insofar as he or she does not obstruct the pedestrian flow.

---

such as Bombay, Delhi, and Bangalore, too, witnessed struggles. In 2004, the Government of India came up with a National Policy on Urban Street Vendors whose much modified version is the SVA. For an analysis of the 'movement perspective' of the SVA and the nationalization of the hawkers' question via the NHF, see Ritajyoti Bandyopadhyay, 'Institutionalizing Informality: The Hawkers' Question in Postcolonial Calcutta', *Modern Asian Studies* 50, no. 2 (2016): 675–717.

[61] But there is also a clause of 'public purpose', for which a vending zone can be made a non-vending zone for 'greater public good'.

Measures like the SVA then continue to pronounce law, in howsoever modified ways, upon the conditions of eviction rather than means of inclusion or facilitation of livelihood on streets. The proto-legal entity of the abstract pedestrian (and his or her 'rights') could very well be a necessary medium for the playing out of a powerful yet little recognized governing principle of disciplining bodies and objects on modern streets. This principle, drawing from Nicholas Blomley, could be termed 'pedestrianism'—a rationality that 'structures the ways in which state agents think about and act upon the spaces of the city.'[62]

Pedestrianism focuses on concerns such as flow, placement, and circulation of bodies and things, and as Blomley explains, 'pedestrianism can treat the human subject as essentially "an object", either in motion or at rest'.[63] Several arguments are frequently made against hawkers from the point of view of pedestrianism. First, hawkers tend to concentrate densely in locations with higher pedestrian and vehicular convergence. The hawkers concentrate near the congestion because that is where they expect they would find their customers. As a result, street sales and congestion constitute and reinforce each other. Second, it is argued that by obstructing traffic, hawkers are responsible for traffic accidents. Third, it is also said that they block important building sites and impede the access of emergency vehicles to those sites in moments of crisis and mass hysteria. Even a cursory look at popular newspapers would give us an understanding of how the opposition between the pedestrian and the hawker is almost naturalized in urban discourses.[64]

Blomley is convinced that opposition to pedestrianism cannot come from the humanist perspective long upheld by activists and academics who treat 'public space as space, first and foremost, of [the] people'.[65] He thus considers the 'civic humanist' perspective of human rights as always already superseded by the apparently banal 'post-humanist' perspective of pedestrianism. The

---

[62] Nicholas Blomley, *Rights of Passage: Sidewalks and the Regulation of Public Flow* (London: Routledge, 2011), 106.

[63] Ibid., 9.

[64] Roy Bromley, 'Street Vending and Public Policy: A Global Review', *International Journal of Sociology and Social Policy* 20, nos. 1–2 (2000): 1–28; Aniruddha Dutta, 'Space, Sanitization and the Press: The Coverage of Street Vending in Kolkata': http://development-dialogues.blogspot.com/2007_05_01_archive.html, accessed 23 November 2021.

[65] Blomley, *Rights of Passage*, 8.

alternative, for him, should then emerge from 'within pedestrianism'.⁶⁶ In dealing with pedestrianism we then perhaps need a radical but also practical critique of the pedestrian-centric understanding of the sidewalk in law and policy—one founded upon what I call the ethics of creative obstructionism and collective appropriation of the sidewalk.

Ironically, the SVA marks the founding instance of both legal recognition and strategic manoeuvring of the hawkers by the government. But even though it enables hawkers to practise their trade, it is erected on ideas of legitimacy that were crafted prior to explicit legal sanction for hawkers. The latter in fact has been achieved through engaged public action. One such initiative was that of the HSC. I propose that the HSC has sought to devise a world of what might be referred to as *counter-pedestrianism*, which is also a form of obstructionism.

In March 2009, the HSC leadership decided to organize a mass contact drive to counter a spell of devastating media attack on hawkers.⁶⁷ The HSC formed a team that visited hawkers' stalls, interacted with hawkers, and documented pedestrian behaviour. The idea was to reaffirm the intimacy of the hawkers' connection with the rest of society and establish that hawking was not the primary cause of congestion, accidents, or pedestrian immobility. As a member of that team, I was asked to demonstrate that the notion of a conflict of interest between pedestrians and hawkers was premised on factually wrong assumptions. The investigating team, which comprised hawkers and activists, visited as many as 22 busy street intersections of the city, observing transactions and talking to all willing participants. The team interacted with shop owners, traffic police, shopping mall employees, transport sector workers, office goers, pavement dwellers, hospital visitors, and daily commuters.

---

⁶⁶ Ibid., 111.

⁶⁷ From the time of Operation Sunshine, the 'hawker problem' began to attract media coverage more than ever. The local English print media often targeted hawkers invoking a liberal-democratic discourse of citizenship: the rights of the 'common man' or the 'pedestrian' to public space, the common man being a politically innocent, classless, neutral entity. The local press took sides with this abstract citizen figure who was also the 'taxpayer' and hence has the legitimate claim over the sidewalk, as against the 'hawker'—epitomizing the usurper of urban space. For a powerful analysis of the English-language print media on Calcutta's hawkers in the mid-2000s, see Aniruddha Dutta, 'Space, Sanitization and the Press: The Coverage of Street Vending in Kolkata': http://development-dialogues.blogspot.com/2007_05_01_archive.html, accessed 23 November 2021.

Our survey continued for two months. We asked hawkers about pedestrians and vice versa, but we spent more time observing how pedestrians and hawkers engaged with each other. We thus could not but note how human relations on the street were framed and mediated by the street apparatus—benches, traffic barriers, bollards, streetlamps, traffic lights and signs, bus and tram stops, taxi and auto-rickshaw stands, public lavatories, municipal water taps, tree protectors, memorials, public sculptures, waste receptacles, and so on. Ultimately, we learnt how street actors developed their own theories of association.

The 'evidence' we collected also enabled the HSC, in certain ways, to frame its official position regarding pedestrianism. Subsequently, the HSC organized a roadshow of photographs that demonstrated how hawkers and pedestrians inhabit a kind of shared network in which categories continuously overreach their assigned labels. Pedestrians were classed or grouped into categories like the occasional visitor, the regular, the office worker, and so on; the hawker at times became a pedestrian and at other times a customer; and the tree protector and lamp post turned out to be ideal supports for a tarpaulin sheet. Many of our pedestrian respondents pointed out that in congested hawking areas, such as in Shyambazaar and Gariahat, the long continuum of tarpaulin roofs protected them from sunburn and rain. Some mentioned how in the late evening the city was illuminated thanks to the abundance of electricity hook-ups at hawkers' stalls.

The more one follows these arrangements in particular situations, the more clearly one understands how the destiny of an 'object', human or non-human, acquires infinite dimensions in association with other objects. In the course of a number of street demonstrations, the HSC revealed the complex inner workings of these dense associations. For instance, they showed how the demolition of one stall in a particular area could lead to the destruction of a network of small economies that sustained the 'poor', the 'daily commuter', and the 'lower middle class', and severely affect the way other hawkers carried out business.

The demonstrations of the HSC further exhibited how the pedestrian's right of passage at a busy street intersection was hampered usually by factors other than hawkers. These included illegal extensions of shops, potholes, intermittent enclosures, and diversions necessitated by work being done on roads, drainage systems, and telephone and power lines; parking spaces, both legal and illegal; and illegal shrines on streets and sidewalks. For instance, we observed that the sidewalks were often broken, and manholes adjacent to the sidewalks were open, threatening commuters with serious accidents. We also found that road repair was going on near several of the city's major crossings, suspending the normal flow of traffic. A lack of coordination between different state departments was evident. In one instance, it was found that at a busy street intersection where a new flyover was planned, the condition of the sidewalk was unfriendly to pedestrian passage. Once the roads were repaired by the PWD, Kolkata Telephones started digging up the land. When Kolkata Telephones ended its job in late 2007, the Corporation Water Department felt it necessary to repair the underground water channels. Once the Water Department repaired the sidewalks, the Conservancy Department started addressing the long-standing public demand to have a better sewerage system in the area, especially during the rainy season. Consequently, the streets and sidewalks remained in a state of constant disrepair between 2006 and 2010, indefinitely suspending 'normal' life on the streets. Since most public utilities run under the sidewalks, sidewalks are the prime sites of such development and maintenance projects. Much of the city's traffic obstruction is caused by the fact that pedestrians are forced to walk on the streets due to the interruptions on the sidewalks caused by repair works.

In another instance, we interviewed three traffic sergeants and consulted the Deputy Commissioner of Police in charge of traffic in the central part of the city. All of them attested to the fact that most reports of road accidents in their jurisdictions would occur between 11 p.m. and 8 a.m. We then interviewed the Superintendent of Bangur Hospital in Tollygunge, who corroborated that the largest number of accident victims arrived between late night and early morning. This is the time when hawkers are not present on the sidewalks to potentially obstruct pedestrian mobility. This piece of information was important for the hawkers to contest the view that accidents happen because pedestrians leave safe and secure sidewalks to walk on the carriageways on account of obstructions put forth by the hawkers.

To verify whether pedestrians thought that hawkers acted as an impediment to their mobility, forcing them to risk their lives on the streets, we interviewed five pedestrians at each of the 22 crossings. Our pedestrian sample size was, thus, 110. Though it was hard for us to determine the class background of each of our respondents, we could discern from their clothes, bags, cell phones, wristwatches, and other accessories that an overwhelming proportion (94.5 per cent) of the sample came from middle- to lower-middle-class backgrounds (we also deliberately chose people from this background anticipating that they would demonstrate a strong anti-hawker feeling). Intending to ensure that we had equitable gender representation, we had 54 female respondents (49.1 per cent) (between ages 21 and 65 years) and 56 male respondents (50.9 per cent) (between ages 20 and 75 years). We asked each of our respondents three sets of questions: (*a*) whether they thought that street hawkers cause an obstruction to their mobility and whether they thought that evicting all hawkers from crossings would solve the problem of obstruction; (*b*) whether they were frequent visitors to the street stalls; (*c*) whether some regulation would add value to street hawking and improve traffic conditions.

From Table 5.1, it can be observed that 10 respondents said that street hawkers do not cause any impediment to their mobility on the sidewalks. 81 respondents claimed that sidewalks become inaccessible during the festive season or cyclically. However, they believed even the seasonal or cyclic congestions could not be enough reason to evict hawkers from crossings. They did not believe that there could be an immediate solution either to the hawker problem or to the problems of traffic or to the mass hysteria of shopping associated with festive seasons. Of the total respondents, 19 found a strong correlation between congestion and street hawking, out of which 7 accepted that the positives of hawking outnumber the negatives, while 12 respondents were in favour of complete eviction of hawkers from important crossings to facilitate pedestrian and vehicular traffic.

If we look at the number of respondents who wanted hawkers to be evicted, 98 respondents felt that there was no need to evict hawkers, while only 12 were of the opinion that hawkers should be evicted. While addressing the second question, all the respondents (110 out of 110) said that they bought wares and services from hawkers. Street food was preferred by 103 respondents

Table 5.1 Pedestrian survey on 'Do hawkers cause obstruction to your passage?'

Do Hawkers Cause Obstruction?	No. of Responses
Yes	19
At times	81
No	10

Table 5.2 Pedestrian survey on 'Should hawkers be evicted for your passage?'

Should Hawkers Be Evicted?	No. of Responses
No	98
Yes	12

(93.6 per cent). While 45 of them (43.7 per cent) expressed concerns over public health issues associated with street food vending, they also justified their street eating on grounds of price, convenience, and variety. We found that all the respondents were in support of some form of regulation of street hawking. However, a significant majority of the sample (107 out of 110) said that there were several other reasons for the obstruction of the free flow of traffic. Political rallies, *dharna*, strikes, inefficiency of the traffic police, road repair works, and car parking appeared to top the list. A significant enough number, 100 of our respondents, strongly felt that the growing demand for parking of vehicles was leading to the problem of encroachment on sidewalks and open spaces and, consequently, congestion. None of our respondents had a clear idea of the nature and mandate of the regulations to be implemented on hawking. The limited sampling and class homogeneity of the sample do not allow us to discern a general trend in the hawker–pedestrian–consumer relation. Yet the sample simply shows the falsity of the assumption that sidewalk hawking is responsible for pedestrian flight from the sidewalk.

In their explanation to the public of the many causes of pedestrians' flight from sidewalks, the HSC demonstrations actually admitted to hawkers' stalls being potential impediments to pedestrian mobility, but only as one of numerous such obstructions. The demonstrations asserted that despite their 'encroachment', hawkers merited a grant of immunity, as they provided the poorer social classes with 'services' at a remarkably low cost and thus contributed to the country's economy. As one of the HSC leaders said, 'We keep the city affordable and accessible to the poor. We are here as poor pedestrians require us to be here. We are also here to create the pedestrian.' At this precise moment, the HSC perhaps invented an entire cosmos where the hawker's claim to space became a claim to enter society's structures of obligation. In fact, as he mentioned, as a sale strategy, hawkers encouraged pedestrians to walk on sidewalks rather than on the streets.

The HSC leader's comment also encapsulated, of course, the political economy of hawking in cities such as Calcutta. The leader reminded the city that hawkers survive but also contribute to the circulation (the hallmark of pedestrianism) of commodities, money, and bodies. While the apparent conflict of interest between the 'mobile' pedestrian and the 'immobile' hawker could continue to frame conceptions and decisions governing urban street life, the HSC's campaign throws light upon the much deeper structural connections between diverse elements of the street. These elements implicate each other in mutual creation and often exceed their intended utility to create multiple publics around them. Thus, like pedestrianism, counter-pedestrianism attaches as much significance to and is in fact premised on the relationality among bodies, spaces, and objects.

The preceding discussion indicates the ways in which the facts of complex interdependencies continually haunt and bring into crisis our current conceptual frameworks. Counter-pedestrianism is an effort to forge alliances among users of the street and re-imagine a space of sociability to fight legal and governmental exclusions. It first asserts that we cannot act without the infrastructures and material means of action. It then suggests we should also emerge as a collective—as commoners—to struggle to establish and preserve those very infrastructures of action. Counter-pedestrianism thus does not take a preordained role of the sidewalk for granted. Rather, through everyday negotiations with pedestrians, shopkeepers, property owners, the state, and themselves, the hawkers create, reconfigure, and 're-function' the materiality of infrastructures. The instance of Calcutta's footpath hawkers shows that streets can accommodate creative obstructions that actually enable and spatialize motion in inclusive and, hence, constructive ways. Such obstructions as that caused by hawkers punctuate motion, give it a 'grip' on the ground, and provide a terrain for exchange between bodies and things over space.

Exclusions

Thus, counter-pedestrianism serves a significant role in bringing into being a cosmos of urban sociality. It has brought the sidewalk back to the lifeworld of the city, justified its multifunctionality, and included a host of sidewalk users in the frame of the public. However, counter-pedestrianism, too, has its constitutive exclusions. Let me cite two instances—wage-earning hawkers and pavement dwellers—to substantiate this point.[68]

In the mid-1980s, Nandini Dasgupta found that each stall employed two to six persons in employment. Therefore, a sizeable section of labourers in the sector were the ones who the 'owner'-hawkers employed. When I started my research on hawkers in Calcutta in the mid-2000s, I found that there existed

[68] Here, I am not talking about how the HSC's narrative of *sangram* silenced women's voice and leadership in the movement. An excellent PhD thesis is on its way to accomplish this task. See Rimpa Ghosh, 'Gendered Informality: Life, Work and the Politics of Livelihood in Kolkata's Street Economy' (PhD dissertation to be submitted to the Faculty of Arts, Jadavpur University).

an employment cycle in the sector. During two festive seasons (one during the Pujas between August and November, and another during the Chaitra Sankranti–Bengali new year between April and May), hawkers tend to employ a significant number of labourers, especially in the stalls selling garments, to attract and manage buyers by means of an aggressive and competitive use of 'lung power'. I also found that a significant portion of these labourers were not related to the owner-hawkers through blood and family relations. This implied the existence of a wage relation among those who sell on the sidewalk. The stall, then, was not simply an extension of the hawkers' 'family enterprise', in which the employers collapsed into the employee in the figure of the hawker.

These wage earners are invisible in the organizational structure of the hawkers' union. The union appears to be a cartel of the employer-hawkers. It aggregates thousands of petty employers and sellers to function in the competitive market and to operate within the governmental space. The labourer-hawkers were left out of the political public that the HSC's counter-pedestrianism constructed. Moreover, even the SVA excludes the wage earners when it designates street vending as a family affair.[69] It asserts that if a hawker makes use of another's labour, then that person should be related to him or her by blood relation or by marriage. This is where, I think, the enterprise of the union and the state have arrived at a consensus.

The consensus is that, in the 'informal' economy, wage relations and profit motive, while not irrelevant, do not play a dominant role. And, hence, it is believed that wage relations do not exist, at least to a significant extent, beyond the confines of the hawker's 'family'. The SVA-created norm has effectively derecognized wage workers in this sector. The law requires the practising hawker to give an undertaking to the regulating body—the Town Vending Committee (TVC)[70]—that 'he shall carry on the business himself or through any of his

---

[69] Chapter II, Clause 5 of the SVA 2014.

[70] The Town Vending Committee (TVC) is the participatory body and is supposed to mediate between the local state and the civil society. It has representatives of the state, street vendors, banking sector, non-governmental organizations, and citizens' bodies (like the resident welfare associations and the Consumers' Forum). The TVC is mandated to recruit at least 40 per cent of its members from among registered street vendors; they are to have voting rights to elect their representatives. Thus, street vendors have the right to elect only a section of the members in the TVC, a crucial decision-making body, and that section does not even constitute the majority of its members.

family member'. Further, to make hawking more familial, the SVA instructs that if the incumbent vendor dies or suffers from permanent injuries, his stall shall pass on to the spouse and the dependent child in order of priority. Such clear attempts to reduce street hawking to a family affair make it difficult for wage workers among hawkers to claim even the 'right to have rights'. The unions have not so far raised any voice to acknowledge their existence either. Perhaps this is one of the many 'constitutive exclusions' on which counter-pedestrianism's or obstructionism's notion of inclusion is founded and demarcated.

The counter-pedestrianism worldview was successful in creating a public discourse about the sidewalk as a site of negotiation 'only' between the hawkers and the pedestrians. It did little to include other constituencies such as pavement dwellers in a common forum of livelihood struggles. Pavement dwellers are still an empirical reality in Calcutta, but they do not anymore exist in public discourse in the way they did until the 1980s, when the hawkers' archive was not in existence. They existed in governmental enumeration, in Mother Teresa's charity initiatives, in urban poetry,[71] as well as in the 1992 movie *City of Joy*. Moreover, for the western 'poverty tourists' of the 1970s and the 1980s, the indigent bodies on the footpath were the much sought-after visual proof of the post-colonial urban predicament. Calcutta's pavement dwellers never organized as a political constituency in the city and remained an object of archiving from above. They gradually exited public memory when the sidewalk began to be seen as a site of conflict between the pedestrians and the hawkers.

In the post–Operation Sunshine flash flood, when hawkers returned, they not only regained their lost land, but they also occupied some more 'valuable' sites where pavement dwellers used to live. The pavement dwellers also returned slowly, but they did not necessarily occupy all the old points of dwelling. Nor did they return as an organized group. They occupied places in whose vicinity no vehicle was allowed to stop. Thus, there emerged an interesting spatial distribution of hawkers and pavement dwellers: hawkers in the busy intersections and pavement dwellers in the in-between spaces of the sidewalks. In this way, a movement to interrogate spatial zoning by the state (that is, sidewalks only for pedestrians) ended up creating new margins, boundaries, and territories. The success of the HSC and the NHF in pursuing a radical democratic politics

---

[71] Debjani Sengupta, 'The Refugee City: Partition and Kolkata's Postcolonial Landscape': http://bangalnama.wordpress.com/2009/08/31/the-refugee-city-partition-and-kolkata%E2%80%99s-postcolonial-landscape/, accessed 23 November 2021.

will depend in the future on how they address the frontiers of inclusion such as other marginalized groups, and the issues of wage relations, profitability, accumulation, and scale as footpath hawking increasingly becomes subject to an anonymous market process and governmental procedures.

Conclusion

The hawkers began to consolidate themselves in Calcutta's sidewalks in the 1950s alongside the *jabardakhal* movement. *Jabardakhal*—as we have previously seen—had an electrifying impact on urban space and politics in that decade. The hawkers learned to attribute their precarious existence to *desh bhaag* (partition) and the inability of the post-colonial state to conduct economic rehabilitation. However, the trajectories of the hawkers' movement both diverged and exceeded the scope of the *jabardakhal* movement which gave the hawkers a political context as well as the initial vocabulary of a struggle. We may remember that the *jabardakhal* movement was purely a province of the refugees and it was primarily targeted at ensuring housing rights via property titles to each household. It was a collective action to redistribute private and public properties to meet housing demands.

The hawkers' movement—on the other hand—was a struggle for livelihood and its participants came from diverse demographic backgrounds. Refugees were only one of the many constituencies that took up hawking in those tumultuous days of the mid-twentieth century (in fact, the refugee population among the hawkers declined from the 1970s onwards). The hawkers gathered *only* on public property and developed a vocabulary around the collective appropriation of public property to meet livelihood necessities. In doing so, they periodically sidestepped the bourgeois law of property, appropriated sidewalks, and made sidewalks the focus of a collective existence. Often, they demanded concessions from the government as a matter of right to livelihood in the city. They placed such claims not as a matter of rule, but as acceptable exceptions to the rule of property.[72] It was a story of slow but continuous and incremental growth. The hawkers attained some tenurial stability much later, only after a discussion of legalizing hawking began in the early 2000s. In this, the HSC's clever political manoeuvres played a crucial role. The HSC never fought for a right to private property on the sidewalks. They fought for a collective right to life and livelihood and compelled the democratically elected regimes to remain

---

[72] P. Chatterjee, *Politics of the Governed*.

committed to this basic constitutional mandate upon which India's popular sovereignty is founded. This was how the hawkers attempted to 'common' infrastructures and public spaces. It was only in the context of a mass democracy that hawking on the sidewalks gained legitimacy in the postcolonial city's public discourse. We have seen that even such a cause had its constitutive exclusions and internal boundaries.

Nonetheless, the hawkers' obstructionism in Calcutta gives us an avenue to think of inclusive urbanism. Their engagement with the city shows that the 'public' of the present and the future must 'enrol' more of such 'obstructions' to enable both its material and political existence. This is even more necessary at a time when not only livelihood but also politics seems to be increasingly a matter of zoning. Zoning is an imposed control over both the 'politics of the street' and the 'politics on the street'.[73] In existing urban studies frameworks, the former pertains to a referential frame of the 'everyday', while the latter invariably becomes the site of the spectacular and increasingly mediatized forms of public protest in various urban centres. If the hawkers' demonstration yields any lessons, it is really one that points towards the necessity of connecting the politics *on* and *of* the streets.

5.1 Demolition drive in Gariahat, 1996

Source: From the archives of the Hawker Sangram Committee, Kolkata, reproduced with permission.

[73] Jennifer Robinson, *Ordinary Cities: Between Modernity and Development* (London: Routledge, 2006).

5.2 Post–Operation Sunshine look of Sealdah

Source: From the archives of the Hawker Sangram Committee, Kolkata, reproduced with permission.

5.3 An image of a demolished stall, 1996

Source: From the archives of the Hawker Sangram Committee, Kolkata, reproduced with permission.

5.4 Having lost his stall due to demolition, a hawker trying to find his belongings among rubble being aided by a co-worker and a sympathetic policeman, 1996

Source: From the archives of the Hawker Sangram Committee, Kolkata, reproduced with permission.

5.5 Hawkers marked their stall locations after demolition with emotive appeals written in placards; this one was by one Badal Debnath who wrote, 'We want to live'

Source: From the archives of the Hawker Sangram Committee, Kolkata, reproduced with permission.

5.6 Hawkers and activists put a police traffic post on fire, 1996

Source: From the archives of the Hawker Sangram Committee, Kolkata, reproduced with permission.

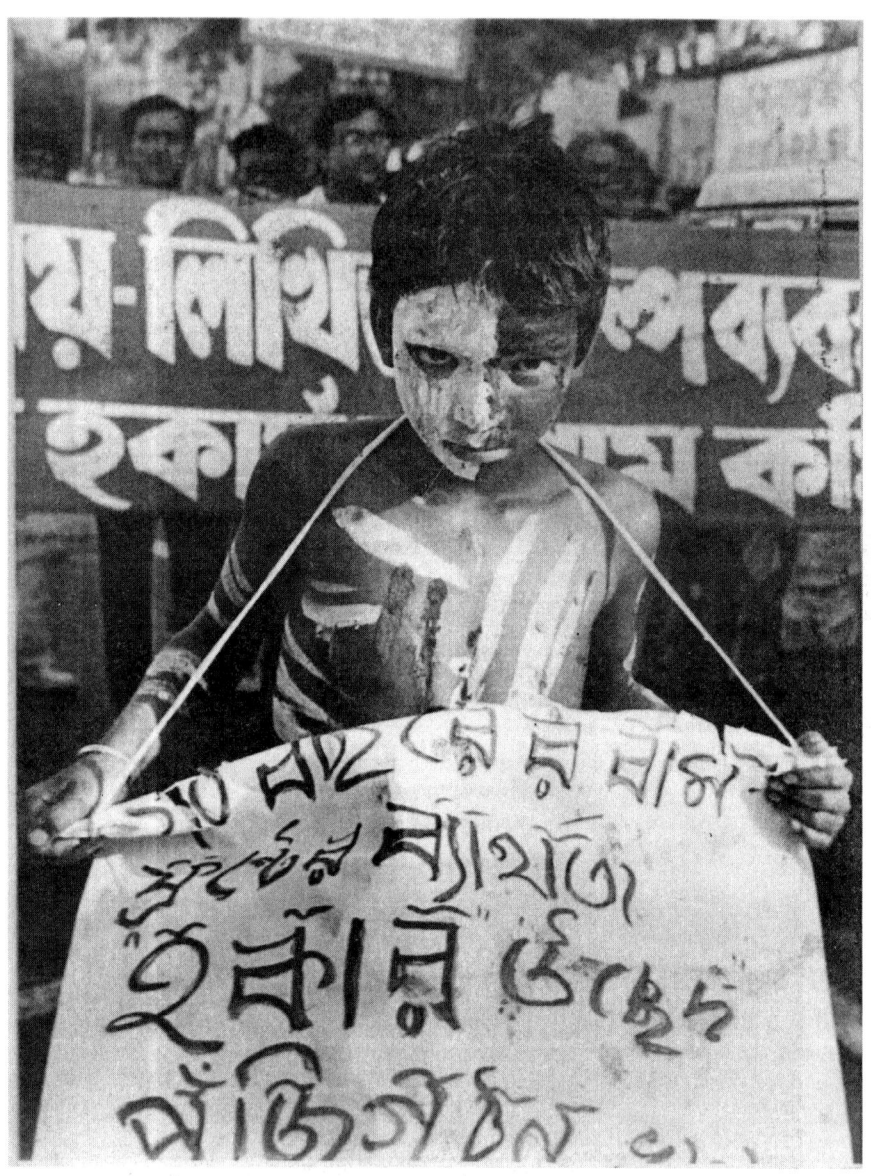

5.7 A protest scene: a child hawker expresses his dissent, 1996

Source: From the archives of the Hawker Sangram Committee, Kolkata, reproduced with permission.

5.8 Hawkers trying to dismantle their shops before being bulldozed by the authorities, 1996

Source: From the archives of the Hawker Sangram Committee, Kolkata, reproduced with permission.

5.9 Opposition leader Mamata Banerjee (now Chief Minister of West Bengal) addressing citizens in a protest rally

Source: From the archives of the Hawker Sangram Committee, Kolkata, reproduced with permission.

5.10 A poster proclaiming how Bulu Poddar committed suicide having lost his job after Operation Sunshine, 1996

Source: From the archives of the Hawker Sangram Committee, Kolkata, reproduced with permission.

5.11 Hawkers trying to rescue their wares while the municipal payloader is about to demolish their stalls, 1996

Source: From the archives of the Hawker Sangram Committee, Kolkata, reproduced with permission.

5.12 Mamata Banerjee and her colleagues in the opposition selling garments in Gariahat while encouraging hawkers to reclaim their spaces

Source: From the archives of the Hawker Sangram Committee, Kolkata, reproduced with permission.

Epilogue

Every true history is contemporary history

—Benedetto Croce[1]

We are coming to the end of one tradition, and the new tradition has scarcely emerged

—E. P. Thompson[2]

In this book, I have tried to demystify the ideology of motion in the twentieth century's capitalist urban context by narrating the making of Calcutta through its streets. Drawing on specific instances from Calcutta's twentieth-century archives, the book reveals that the street is not a mere engineering object outside the realms of ideology and politics (in fact, no engineering object is ever outside the realms of ideology and politics). In our story, the street is not just a metaphor or a vehicle for politics. Neither is the street merely the setting for politics, existing outside of and separate from it. Here the street itself is the product of politics and politics, in turn, a product of the street. In fact, I have argued that the street *is* politics inasmuch as politics is the production of space—whether by states or their subjects, whether in pursuit of capitalist accumulation or not. I historicized and theorized the street as a framing device of my story and an apparatus of city-making—a master infrastructure. In this journey, we met some remarkable urban craftsmen—agitators, rioters, commoners, raiders, hawkers, cops, and engineers—and wrote a local history of Calcutta from their perspectives. I read their diverse crafts of city-making through the 'dialectical twining' of capital's spatial mobilization and the everyday struggles of city dwellers—structure and agency.

---

1 Benedetto Croce, *History: Its Theory and Practice*, trans. Douglas Ainslie (New York: Harcourt Brace and Company, 1921), 12.

2 E. P. Thompson, 'The Moral Economy of the English Crowd in the Eighteenth Century', *Past and Present* 50, no. 2 (1971): 76–136, see 107–108.

Together, these five chapters tell us a story. At once mundane and monumental, the streets are matters that move matters and thus enable motion's distribution in space.[3] The violence of planned street and infrastructure building valorized urban land as it became the prime outlet of capital in the interwar years. Ultimately it produced an indistinction between rent and interest, with interest rate becoming crucial for both the Calcutta Improvement Trust and developers. In short, rent became the prime count of wealth and a new image of profit as surplus profit transformed into ground rent.[4]

This process unfolded in the separation of the urban poor from their sites of production and social reproduction as 'congested' neighbourhoods and *bustees* in the inner city made way for viable neighbourhoods as 'land' in the market. The Calcutta Improvement Trust was at the helm of this primitive process in the inner city. The Trust recovered the cost of renewal through the sale of surplus land in the open market, usually to the highest bidder. This led to speculation in empty land and gentrification along the axes of class, religious communities, and ethnicity. Simultaneously, dwelling spaces were converted into commercial spaces. Because of speculation, gentrification, and commercialization, a housing crisis arose in the interwar period.

During the interwar years, Calcutta also bled into its rural and semi-urban frontiers as the Improvement Trust acquired land and built infrastructures for 'suburban expansion' of Calcutta. Yet the vision of graded dispersal of population (from the inner city) towards the newly created suburbs failed, as land speculation reached these places before the inner-city displaced populations could be resettled. Class and communal tensions made their way through this demographic churning and produced intermittent communal riots between 1910 and 1926. These forces culminated in a communal civil war in 1946. The civil war enforced the territorial division of the city into a Hindu city and its Muslim ghettos.

Ghettoization took place along with the Partition's demographic shock. *Jabardakhal* became a new force of frontier urbanization beyond the planned suburbs of the Improvement Trust. The protagonists of *jabardakhal* were newly dispossessed people—the victims of the foundational violence of the two nation states. *Jabardakhal* was a combination of encroachment-as-class and

---

[3] 'Logistical Worlds: Infrastructure, Software, Labour', *Logistical Worlds*: https://logisticalworlds.org/concepts, accessed 3 December 2021.

[4] I am thankful to Ranabir Samaddar for drawing my attention to the metamorphosis of the rent question in infrastructure-driven urbanization.

encroachment-as-community. As encroachment-as-class, it snatched property from the wealthy owners and the state. As encroachment-as-community, it dispossessed and displaced petty Muslim property owners, becoming an electrifying agent of Hinduization of the urban space. *Jabardakhal* led to the fragmentation of capital sunk in land, especially in the emerging frontiers of the city. As a result, the connection between urbanization and capital accumulation, as we found in the interwar era, collapsed for many years in the post-colonial metropolis.

After this, one encounters urbanization *without* accumulation in Calcutta's frontiers. A massive fringe economy developed in the city as well as in its frontiers. This is the story of footpath hawking from the late 1960s to the 1990s. In the initial years after Independence, the displaced upper-caste population participated substantially in the fringe economy and gradually moved up to more stable employment, leaving the sector to Dalit refugees and Dalit and land-deprived lower-caste economic migrants from various rural districts of West Bengal.

In the late 1990s, the Communist government unleashed a massive innercity renewal drive and a peri-urban expansion project. The former manifested in a major hawker eviction drive called Operation Sunshine (1996–1997). The drive failed terribly in the face of resistance by hawkers and squatter groups. Having failed to decisively transform Calcutta into a 'bourgeois city' of its twenty-first-century vintage,[5] corporate capital deserted the city and migrated to the peri-urban frontiers. There it produced massive urbanization beyond the Eastern Metropolitan Bypass and Salt Lake in the 1990s and the early 2000s, converging with the IT boom in urban India.[6]

This book thus traces the history of how the urban poor have continued to possess and repossess city spaces. Their actions and struggles over the city enable us to gauge 'more effective narratives of human belonging'.[7] These are

---

[5] Partha Chatterjee, 'Are Indian Cities Becoming Bourgeois At Last?', in Partha Chatterjee, *The Politics of the Governed: Reflections on Popular Politics in Most of the World* (Ranikhet: Permanent Black, 2004), 131–148.

[6] Ananya Roy, *City Requiem, Calcutta*; Kalyan Sanyal and Rajesh Bhattacharya, 'Bypassing the Squalor: New Towns, Immaterial Labour and Exclusion in Postcolonial Urbanisation', *Economic and Political Weekly* 46, no. 31 (2011): 41–48; Ishita Dey, Ranabir Samaddar, and Suhit Sen, *Beyond Kolkata: Rajarhat and the Dystopia of Urban Imagination* (New Delhi: Routledge, 2013).

[7] D. Chakrabarty, 'Two Histories of Capital', 71.

narratives of human belonging that counter narratives of dispossession induced by primitive accumulation of capital. Calcutta managed to remain a city of de-accumulation, protest, agitation, and popular resistance when the twenty-first century arrived.

However, it also became clear to 'us'—the city dwellers—that Calcutta was at the brink of a new horizon of motion and obstruction—a twenty-first-century revolution. But I was and still am uncertain about its trajectories. The second quote by E. P. Thompson that opens this epilogue captures my intellectual struggle with the new century. It is out of this consciousness that I began writing this book about the twentieth-century city. After all, as the opening quote by Benedetto Croce suggests, all history is crafted from the point of view of contemporary concerns. We discover the past from the perspective of the present. Like any products of human labour, this book, too, bears the mark of its time in the 2020s.

A New Horizon of Motion and Obstruction

A decade ago, fellow urban scholar Curt Gambetta and I put together a *Seminar* symposium on the 'future of the street' in Indian cities. In the 'problem statement', we wrote that our experience in the 'last decade' (that is, 2000–2010) appears only to confirm the fact that the street as a 'conduit' of social and political life is 'a vestige of the past'. In that decade, we witnessed multiple changes in the streetscape.[8] New infrastructures of mobility such as airconditioned vehicles, single occupancy cars, new 'bypass transit corridors', flyovers, and so on, tended to abstract traffic from the 'discontinuous ebb and flow' of street congestion. Retail and leisure had increasingly been taken out of the streets and given new interior contexts in the shopping malls and plazas, while street hawkers were subjected to follow rigorous zoning norms. The Street Vendors Act came in force in 2014, which significantly transformed the tactics and strategies of the hawkers' engagement with the state in most of the cities, as the street fights increasingly gave way to litigations in courts and advocacy at higher policy circles.

Other technological transformations, with the introduction of GIS (geographic information system) and CCTV cameras, have transformed the omni-optical field of the street into the invisible eye of the surveillant state. With the mediation of the internet, streets have become 'real-time flows' of the huge cache of unstructured data such as photos and videos circulating in social

---

[8] Gambetta and Bandyopadhyay, 'The Problem' (2012).

networks such as Facebook, the reams of information from numerous CCTV footages, the information generated by cell phones, GPS devices, sensors tagged with most of the commodities we use, and by various app-based platforms, such as Uber, Ola, and Zomato. When Gambetta and I wrote the *Seminar* problem statement, Indian streets were still not under the radar of these app-based platforms. They became ubiquitous in the next decade and quickly took over various everyday activities.[9]

These digital platforms have become a necessary mediator in capital's motion at every level—production, circulation, and consumption.[10] The owners of these platforms—usually the corporate venture capitalists—exert their control over access to their licensed products to let production and consumption take place on their platforms and, in return, extract tributes from the users. Many formerly analogue devices now have software, sensors, and network connections. The digital interface has become the 'default way that technologies are designed and sold'.[11] As a consequence, software corporations and app owners have accomplished 'a form of micro-enclosure', claiming 'ownership' over the digital components of the physical devices.[12]

Further, it has increasingly been the case that big real estate players take data services from these platforms to exchange and manage real estate as a 'financial asset'.[13] Our twentieth-century street is now increasingly subjected to the control of this 'real estate/financial/technology complex of the twenty first century'. As the internet and data scholars have repeatedly argued, technology-driven data mining from our everyday activities is one of the significant 'frontiers of extraction' in contemporary capitalism. This new internet-driven order reinvents rent and subjects the streets to a new mining regime involving the corporate landlords, miners, plunderers, and the state.[14]

The pedestrian's movement, or the movement of the app-governed gig workers, becomes a 'site of translation through which complex urban

---

[9] Jathan Sadowski, 'The Internet of Landlords: Digital Platforms and New Mechanisms of Rentier Capitalism', *Antipode* 52, no. 2 (2020): 562–580.

[10] Ibid.

[11] Ibid., 572.

[12] Ibid., 573.

[13] Jathan Sadowski, *Too Smart: How Digital Capitalism Is Extracting Data, Controlling Our Lives, and Taking Over the World* (Cambridge: MIT Press, 2020), 63.

[14] Ranabir Samaddar, 'The Logistical City', *IIC Quarterly* 43, nos. 3–4 (2017): 104–115.

environments are formatted into machine-readable data streams'.[15] The information that flows from the streets to these platforms hardly returns for a common and unenclosed consumption, after their algorithmic processing. Thus, 'the street', argues Sumandro Chattopadhyay, 'is reduced to an abstract geo-locational identifier' for the data sets generated by the 'Internet of Things', controlled by a set of neo-landlords.[16] In the new rental economy, 'the street acts as material context and as a socio-emotional setting' for data mining, 'but does not retain any of the produced data'.[17] Platforms 'enact their programmability to decentralize data production and recentralize data collection'.[18] As Jakob Rigi and Robert Prey tell us, 'a price on data can best be understood as a form of monopoly rent (tribute)'.[19]

If in the twentieth century, street reforms made automobility, sanitation, security, and the real estate as their primary objectives, in the twenty-first century, urban streets are being 'reformed' and restructured to become the 'sources and the contexts of data collection'—as a site of extraction. Such initiatives render the streets 'more visible, predictable, and administrable by approaching them in terms of various sets of numerical representations offered by human and non-human actors occupying these spaces'.[20]

This new rental economy of the twenty-first-century street emerges along with and as a result of the network of the information technology (IT) mediated globally connected logistical practices as capital's focus tilts toward circulation (from industrial production), borne by a combined effect of containerization, Toyotization, IT, and finance.[21] In *Grundrisse*, Marx says, 'continuity of

[15] Niels van Doorn and Adam Badger, 'Platform Capitalism's Hidden Abode: Producing Data Assets in the Gig Economy', *Antipode* 52, no. 5 (2020): 1475–1495, quoted from 1478.

[16] Sumandro Chattopadhyay, 'Smart Cities as Urbanisation of Data: Towards a Critique of Urban Informatics', 2013 (unpublished paper).

[17] Ibid. Data turn into commodities when access to them is restricted through enclosures, copyrights, patents, and other kinds of property laws.

[18] Anne Helmond, 'The Platformization of the Web: Making Web Data Platform Ready', *Social Media + Society*, July–December (2015): 1–11, quoted from 5.

[19] Jakob Rigi and Robert Prey, 'Value, Rent, and the Political Economy of Social Media', *Information Society* 31, no. 5 (2015), 392–406, quoted from 398.

[20] Sumandro Chattopadhyay, 'Smart Cities'.

[21] Joshua Clover, *Riot. Strike. Riot: The New Era of Uprisings* (London and New York: Verso, 2016), 23.

production presupposes the suspension of circulation time', while the nature of capital presupposes that it travels through different phases of circulation and situations separate in time. The globally connected cities stand at the crossroad of these two contradictory impulses with physical, legal, social, and financial infrastructures to synchronize the gap between production and consumption which ultimately leads to the erosion of distinction between production and circulation.[22]

The informatized logistical cities in the post-colonial world keep a large assemblage of establishments of petty capitalist production units partially or fully immersed to global production and supply chains. Think of a familiar South Asian *karkhana* set up on the fringes of the Delhi National Capital Region (NCR) or in the hinterlands of Howrah—with shed, workshop, at times factory, but not in the sense of a modern mill with *karigar*s (artisans), *mistri*s (chief craftsmen, foremen), and head-*mistri*s (some of them jobbers). The entire setup makes sense only when we take into account a particular environ of production marked by proximity, small and closed space with very little room for stock-keeping, housing quarters, and so on, caste and clan ties. Here, one would inevitably find a master mechanic who knows how to prolong the lifespan of a machine, or how to assemble one from scrap materials rejected by larger mills. These mechanics came to the forefront of commodity production in South Asia, or the colonial world, along with industrial capitalism—a history of which is utterly incomplete without these *karkhana*s and their remarkable craftsmen. What happens in a *karkhana* setup is slow depreciation of machinery and their longer and diverse lives. The repair-work adds to the original value-stock in the machinery which gets transferred to a surprisingly diverse range of commodities.

These *karkhana*s are flexible production units. Their products change from season to season, according to the demand for commodities, and are immersed both to 'local' and 'global' demands. Thus, *karkhana*s and workshops in NCR Delhi's Bawana and Narela may commence with plastic goods manufacturing and end up producing 'enough' relative to demand and price. They will now consider switching to other products using the same set of workers and the same basic machinery. Thus, a factory, making plastic goods, may switch to making firecrackers during Diwali, *gulal* during Holi, *rakhi* during Rakshabandhan, or

---

[22] Samaddar, 'The Logistical City'. A logistical city is also an informatized smart city that thrives on information-driven algorithmic solutions to the problem of utility and service delivery.

packaging goods set to go to container ships as packing machines are already available in these units.[23]

Thus, on the frontiers of the logistical cities of the post-colonial world, informal factory production of commodities reinvents itself and increasingly resembles the crop-production cycles in the fields. These units do not even 'exist legally' in the government's archives, and constitute the flipside of the data avalanche of the informatized city. The value that these highly labour-intensive and exploitative petty capitalist units pump into the accumulation economy rescues global capital from falling into a permanent trap of falling rate of profit. Thus, twenty-first-century (neoliberal) capitalism comes to be conditioned by a post-colonial context of petty capital accumulation that acts as an agent of capital's historical transformation.

Every major city of the post-colonial world witnessed mega urbanization since the 1990s, as the bourgeois economy sought to compensate the loss in industrial investment via urban rent trudging its way along 'the lanes laid out by global logistical networks'.[24] These regimes thrived on the exploitation of the migrant 'transit labour' involved in construction, transport, and gig jobs in shopping malls, hospitals, airports, restaurants, call centres, softwire hubs, and the petty capitalist sector (described earlier).

Calcutta, too, witnessed transformations. Already by the mid-1990s, Calcutta presented itself as a junction city of a multimodal transport network consisting of a vast already existing port installation, railway and highway networks, and at least two proposed trans-regional corridors as part of India's 'Look East Policy'. Such a repositioning of the city in the global networks of circulation necessitated a policy shift to aggressively facilitate mobility of humans, commodities, money, credit, and information. This 'infrastructuration' of the city under the public–private partnership (PPP) mode occasioned internal displacement of certain population groups such as squatter colony dwellers, hawkers, and working-class groups in and around the city. The decade between 1996–1997

---

[23] For a more detailed discussion of these units, see Rajan Pandey and Ritajyoti Bandyopadhyay, 'Covid-19: Migration, Informality and Postcolonial Capitalist Development', in Ritajyoti Bandyopadhyay, Paula Banerjee, and Ranabir Samaddar (eds.), *India's Migrant Workers and the Pandemic* (London: Routledge, 2021), 99–114. The description in this paragraph is from Pandey's fieldwork in NCR Delhi in 2020.

[24] Ibid., 24.

('Operation Sunshine') and 2007–2009 (the Singur–Nandigram struggle) remained particularly violent for the urban poor and an intense moment of primitive accumulation of capital both in the inner city and in the rural and peri-urban frontiers.

Many of these drives were also met with popular resistance, leading to the defeat of the Left Front government in 2011 by a political party that had acquired popular legitimacy during this era of resistance. During its rule, Calcutta witnessed another wave of mass encroachment on sidewalks by hawkers. This time, hawking pushed its boundaries to New Town and Rajarhaat—the satellite cities that once rehabilitated corporate capital facing obstructions in the inner city in the late 1990s and the early 2000s. Calcutta remained a 'living city' despite several decades of deindustrialization and de-accumulation.

A New Vocabulary of Obstructionism

Collective action in an informatized, mediatized, and logistical city also underwent some major transformations. The twenty-first-century cities witnessed the eruption of new kinds of public emotions in the social media space that informed everyday life and collective action on the streets. For much of the twentieth century, we knew about events such as crowd action via the print media, and the state-controlled All India Radio and Doordarshan. There was always a time gap between the actual event, the 'news formation', and its consumption by the virtual public via these media. In other words, the relation between the crowd and the virtual public was rather muted, as the passage of information between the street and the drawing room took time. Also, there was no steady feedback loop available for the 'just-in-time' communication of emotions, sentiments, and opinions between the crowd-in-action and the larger public—between the concrete and the abstract.

Empowered by digital technology, the new camera has more access to the cityscape, its visual embodiments and its noise which can be programmed to information and be transmitted immediately to the virtual public that consumes the news as entertainment via 24x7 news channels and then circulates among individuals immediately via social media platforms. Through Twitter and Facebook, 'storms' of opinion can be generated and communicated, which would immediately inform the physical crowd on the street. Calls for protest can be circulated via social media, which would end up producing remarkable crowd formation in public squares. We have seen this during the Occupy movements, the Arab Spring, the Shahbag Protest in Dhaka, the Nirbhaya Protest in Delhi, and the recent anti-CAA campaign in Indian cities.

The students and the youth of the twenty-first century are learning to use technology in subversive ways. During the recent pro-democracy protests in Hong Kong in October–November 2019, the students used easily procurable laser pointers to blind police cameras. They sprayed paint or put black tapes over CCTV cameras and secured their march routes from police surveillance. They took recourse to hard cash for their subway rides to avoid passage information being recorded. They uniformly wore black clothes and those at the frontlines had their faces completely hidden behind gas masks, helmets, and goggles. The protesting students took utmost care while transmitting information among crowd members. They used the encrypted messaging app Telegram for communication.[25]

Months before the protests started in Hong Kong, the city authority installed about 100 smart lampposts in various important streets. The official justification was that the smart lampposts would measure the city's air quality more accurately and manage traffic more efficiently. The administration denied the allegation that those devices would also collect facial and personal data of the street users. The protestors used surgical masks and carried umbrellas to hide themselves from these sensors. Some among them were the twenty-first-century luddites. They were seen to have used some rudimentary technologies such as a handheld saw and a rope to strike a smart lamppost. As the lamppost began to fall, the crowd cheered. Of course, the fall of one such lamppost did not end the 'smart city'. Like the barricade of the mid-nineteenth-century Paris, this too had 'a moral than a material effect'.[26] Such engagements with the new technologies of control are not going to be limited to Hong Kong. Agitators, too, inform each other through exchange across spaces.

The digital infrastructure of the logistical smart city is also vulnerable to virus, leakage, loss of data, breakdown, internet shutdown (often committed by governments in the name of public order), 'digital exclusion',[27] online robbery,

---

[25] 'The Hong Kong Protestor's Toolkit for a Cat-and-Mouse Game with Authorities', *Wall Street Journal*, 16 September 2019: https://www.wsj.com/articles/the-hong-kong-protesters-toolkit-for-a-cat-and-mouse-game-with-authorities-11568628648 (last accessed on 1 September 2020).

[26] Engels, 'Introduction to Karl Marx's *Class Struggles in France, 1848–1850*'.

[27] As Mathhew Zook reminds us, 'simple expectations of uniform geography or ubiquitous access are simply unreflective of the reality of the Internet', which

hacking, and sabotage. In February 2019, in a bid to 'attack and destroy', hackers breached the servers of a US-based email provider. This incident erased data from their US servers. The backup measures of the affected agency were not sufficient to avert the rebels from invading their backup servers. It was just an act of vandalism that pauperized the agency overnight.[28] The attackers did not seek a ransom to release confiscated assets.

The causes of a data centre and data infrastructure to crumble can range from a 'cyber incident'—such as the aforementioned—to classic damage caused, for example, by fire, flood, climate change, and earthquakes. Much like the nineteenth-century cities of riots and insurrections, and twentieth-century cities of industrial strikes and blockades, the logistical city of the twenty-first century is also vulnerable to exclusions, riots, sabotages, and disasters—a city of obstructed motion.

The more the cities get globally connected with mobile humans, commodities, and livestock, the greater is the risk of pandemics. In a powerful recent essay, Rob Wallace and his interlocutors argued that pandemics such as Covid-19 must indeed be viewed as the outcome of the frictionless circulation of bodies and things under supply-chain capitalism. As commodities transcend boundaries of ecological zones, they destroy local ecological specificities that could otherwise have checked the proliferation of virulent pathogen population. The growing travel of humans and global livestock trade networks 'deliver' the pathogens from one socio-ecological context to another in 'record time'. The networks between logistical hubs and their global hinterlands 'lower transmission friction, selecting for the evolution of greater pathogen deadliness in both livestock and people'.[29]

---

follows and thrives on pre-existing social hierarchies and older trajectories of the nature of ownership and investment to infrastructure. Hence, the logistical city is far from being an inclusive city. The digital divide became very clear across the world during the recent pandemic which gave a boost to online work, transactions, and learning. Matthew Zook, 'The Geographies of the Internet', *Annual Review of Information Science and Technology* 40: 1 (2006), 53–78.

[28] 'Theft, Ransom and Vandalism: Securing Your Data Is Getting Tougher', *ITProPortal*, 1 April 2019: https://www.itproportal.com/features/theft-ransomware-and-vandalism-securing-your-data-is-getting-tougher/, accessed 3 December 2021. Rob Wallace, Alex Liebman, Luis Fernando Chaves, and Rodrick Wallace, 'Covid-19 and the Circuits of Capital', *Monthly Review* 72, no. 1 (2020): https://monthlyreview.org/2020/05/01/covid-19-and-circuits-of-capital/, accessed 3 December 2021.

[29] Wallace, Liebman, Chaves, and Wallace, 'Covid-19 and the Circuits of Capital'.

Thus, the logistical city thrives on fragile infrastructures. This became clear to us during the recent pandemic, when nation-states promulgated 'lockdown' on the movement of labour and supply chains. For many months, the lockdown continued to disrupt the flow of capital and the supply chain of commodities.[30] As a result, commodities could not be sold 'just-in-time', causing the onset of devaluation. The pandemic thus reminded us that capital as the valorization of value is far from being 'self-subsistent', and it is more so when capital hits the zenith of a systemic crisis. Admittedly, these reminders came not because of a world-encompassing general strike of the workers, but because of a lockdown imposed from the above but unwillingly by governments that would prefer to maintain 'business-as-usual'.

'Lockdown' was an obstruction enforced from above by the nation-states. In India, this measure was addressed by the mass of unorganized migrant labourers through an exodus from the logistical cities that provided them with no tangible social security to withstand the loss of daily wage. The disturbing image of thousands of men, women, and children walking along highways under the scorching sun and with bleeding feet became a standard and a familiar image of the national lockdown. This image resembled primitive on-foot mass exodus which destroyed the self-image of modernity in the twenty-first century.

Devoid of voting rights in the 'host' city and unionization, the migrant workers were a rather unexpected political constituency to voice dissent. The visibility of the exodus made it so powerful that even the most ignorant of the urban middle class began to identify internal migration and transit labour as a massive phenomenon. As they moved in large numbers from the host states to their homes, they became the vehicles for spreading the horror stories of lockdown, contagion, looming unemployment, and hunger. Their sheer mobility on foot threatened society. Will they bring disease to newer places? Which sector of the economy will absorb them? How are they going to be received in their villages? When they took to the streets, the migrants' question became a social question.

The national lockdown unfolded as a massive paradox. The act of immobilization and obstruction from above entailed an act of unimaginable mobility of labouring bodies across the nation, leading to the absolute breakdown of lockdown. A policy to immobilize led to an unforeseen mobility of people

---

[30] David Harvey, 'Anti-Capitalist Politics in the Time of Covid-19', *Jacobin*, 20 March 2020: https://jacobinmag.com/2020/03/david-harvey-coronavirus-political-economy-disruptions, accessed 3 December 2021.

that the country had never witnessed after the refugee exodus in 1947–1948. If lockdown was a gigantic boundary-making exercise, the migrants' exodus was its mass political response as it broke those boundaries. Mass walking along streets and highways became the language of the unheard. The migrant labourers turned and did something and not merely return to their villages. What were they turning from and turning towards?

Cities such as Surat, Ahmedabad, Mumbai, Delhi, Jaipur, and Lucknow witnessed serious law and order problems as migrants and the urban underclass transgressed lockdown protocols, again and again, demanding rations, wages, and safe passage home.[31] The police found it extremely difficult to contain these crowds as the usual methods of crowd control proved too dangerous from a public-health standpoint. Beating up and dispersing the crowd involved the police in close contact with alien bodies, breaking social distancing protocols. Shelling teargas meant that the crowd would start collectively sneezing and coughing, which would inevitably spread the disease.[32] Taking the protestors into police custody meant a further concentration of bodies in already crowded prisons. Thus, the street under lockdown became a stage for a new kind of protest and collective action by the 'unorganized' masses—the migrant transit labourers who made the infrastructural and rental transformation of these cities possible in the last three decades.

In an age of neoliberal economy, these masses devoid of a strong concept of organization will write the history of democracy in a new way and reclaim the streets and the sidewalks of the post-colony. In this new chapter of apparatus and subject formation, perhaps the old chronicles of solidarity, befriending, camaraderie, and barricades will appear in a new way. In that sense the street may have passed its 'golden age' of organized mass action, which is why the historian can think aloud on the twentieth-century streets.

Contemporary histories of protest in Hong Kong, Beirut, Bombay, Calcutta, Cairo, or Delhi's Singhu border offer faint sketches of the likely nature of that new chapter of street politics.[33] If motion defines authoritarian regimes, obstructions set the terms and the tenures of everyday democratic politics.

---

[31] 'Migrant Workers' Resistance Map: Documenting Migrant Workers' Resistance across India', MWSN: https://www.mwsn.in/resistancemap/.

[32] Nonetheless, teargas was used with bleach and other lethal disinfectants.

[33] Alain Badiou, *The Rebirth of History: Times of Riots and Uprisings*, trans. Gregory Elliot (New York: Verso, 2012); Clover, *Riot. Strike. Riot.*

Imagined differently, authoritarian regimes can also feel still and immobile, which democratic politics shakes up into activity. The street can occasion the move from one to the other very quickly. A heavily guarded and surveilled city square can erupt into a rebellion like the one we saw in the Tahrir Square protests in Cairo. At the same time, a pulsating protest site can swiftly be supplanted by smooth, uninterrupted traffic flows or shut down by the imposition of a curfew, like in the case of Shaheen Bagh in Delhi. The street then embodies the messy nature of politics itself. The street aligns with capital and authoritarian regimes, but the street is also invaluable for democratic upsurges. The street and its practices are fundamentally constitutive of the malleable substance of both authoritarian politics and democratic politics.

The twenty-first-century street requires a new political vocabulary. Vocabulary is immanent in struggles. It will emerge from its lived contradictions. The twentieth-century's owl of Minerva that brought wisdom has flown out at dusk.[34] The twentieth-century street is dead. Long live the street!

---

[34] Note the last two epic lines of Eric J. Hobsbawm's *Nations and Nationalism since 1780* (Cambridge: Cambridge University Press, 1990), 192.

Glossary

adda	informal conversations
akhara	gymnasium
bazaar	market, marketplace
bede	a Bengali marginalized nomadic community who make a living by snake catching and snake charming
bhadralok	Bengali gentlemen
bharatiya	tenant
bigha	a measure of land equal to a quarter of a hectare
bustee	slum, usually made without the use of cement concrete
chatak	a land measurement unit, approximately 180 square feet
chawk	a quadrangle surrounded by buildings
chawl	tenement-like row houses
chowdhuri	up-country cart owners in early twentieth-century Calcutta
chowki	a wooden slab with four legs
coolie	labourer
Dalit	the formerly untouchable castes
darwan	doorkeeper
debi	goddess
debuttar	property in the name of a deity
dhangar	referred to municipal sanitary workers in early-twentieth-century Calcutta
Diwali	a Hindu festival of lights that takes place every year in October–November
Durga Puja	the annual autumnal Bengali festival of worshipping Goddess Durga

Glossary

garib	poor
ghat	embankment of a river or a static waterbody
gherao	encirclement of important seats of power
goli/gulley	lane
goomty	depot
goonda	ruffian
gulal	brightly coloured powder of a type thrown into the air and on to others in celebration of the Hindu festival of Holi
haat	weekly market
hartal	a closure of marketplaces and offices as a protest or a mark of sorrow
jabardakhal	forcible collective occupation of space by people
jaltungi	water pavilion
karigar	artisan
karkhana	commodity production unit, workshop, factory
kottah/cottah	a land measurement unit, usually 720 square feet
krishak	peasant
kutcha	mud-built
mahajan	moneylender
Maidans	an open ground between Jawaharlal Nehru Road and Red Road in Calcutta
mashal	a long stick with burning material at one end, used to provide light or to set things on fire
mistri	mechanic, chief craftsman, foreman
moholla	neighbourhood
momin	believer
mor	intersection
mulla	Islamic theologist
nagarik	citizen
ostagar	master tailor
paan	betel leaf
para	neighbourhood community
pukka	brick-built

rajpath	main street
Rakhibandhan/ Rakshabandhan	a Hindu festival celebrating brotherhood and love
saak	leafy vegetables
sal	Shorea robusta (scientific name), a species of tree
samaj	caste-based Hindu community
sangram	struggle
sarkar	government
satyagraha	passive political resistance deployed widely by Gandhi
setu	bridge
sonajhuri	Acacia auriculiformis (scientific name), a species of tree
swaraj	self-government
taktaposh	wooden platform with four legs
telebhaja	fried food
thana	police station
thika	leasehold
udbastu	refugee
up-country	referred to north Indian migrants in early-twentieth-century Calcutta
waqf	religious endowment by a Muslim
zamindar	landlord

Bibliography

Manuscript and Archival Sources

Calcutta Improvement Trust Records, Kolkata, India

Deed and charge registers of properties acquired and sold by the Improvement Trust (1912–1946)

Historic images of the city taken during the roll out of various Street Schemes

Maps of various Street Schemes

Private files of some Trust Members

Proceedings of the Meetings of the Board of Trustees of the Calcutta Improvement Trust (Valuation Department and Record Room copies), (1912–1962) and attached Documents, Notes, Contracts, and Letters

Calcutta Police Records, Kolkata, India

Special Branch (SB), Daily Notes (SW630 series) Files (1955–1997)

Hawker Sangram Committee Archive, Kolkata, India

Audio files of interviews of various HSC leaders, activists, and human rights workers taken by the author between 2005 and 2015 (a total of 250 hours)

Audio files of interviews of footpath hawkers taken by the author between 2006 and 2014 (a total of 501 hours)

Images of protests, demonstrations and evictions (1996–2015)

Letters to and received from various organizations and government agencies (1996–2015)

Proceedings of various organizational meetings, conferences, and workshops (1996–2015)

India Office Records, British Library, London, UK

Legislative, Political and Judicial (L/P&J) Records

National Archives of India, New Delhi, India

Digitized Public Records, Home Affairs
Digitized Public Records, Sardar Patel
Home (Municipalities) Proceedings
Home (Political) Proceedings
Ministry of Rehabilitation, Government of India (RHB Branch) Files

School of Cultural Texts and Records, Jadavpur University, Kolkata, India

Ashoka Gupta Papers
Bengal Chamber of Commerce and Industries Collection (Online)

South Asia Archive (Online)

Proceedings of the Bengal Legislative Council (various volumes)

Town Hall, Kolkata, India

Proceedings of the Calcutta Municipal Corporation (1880–1947)

West Bengal State Archives, Kolkata, India

Government of Bengal (Political Confidential)
Home (Political) Proceedings
Intelligence Branch Records
Municipal (Municipal), Proceeding
Public Works Department (Miscellaneous Public Improvement Branch) Files

Periodicals and Newspapers

Amrita Bazar Patrika
Anandabazar Patrika

Bengalee
Calcutta Law Journal
Calcutta Municipal Gazette
Hindustan Times
The Statesman
Times of India
Wall Street Journal

Printed Reports

Annual Report on the Police Administration of the Town of Calcutta and Its Suburbs, various years.
Annual Report on the Operations of the Calcutta Improvement Trust, various years.
Annual Report of the Municipal Administration of Calcutta, various years.
Bengal (India), Calcutta Rent Enquiry Committee. *Report of the Committee Appointed to Enquire into Land Values and Rents in Calcutta*. Calcutta, 1920.
Calcutta Building Commission. *Annual Reports*, 1897–1898.
Calcutta Disturbances Commission of Enquiry, Government of Bengal, Volumes I–X.
Calcutta Improvement Act and Allied Matters, Calcutta Improvement Trust, Calcutta, 1912.
Census of India, various years and volumes.
Chatterjee, C. C. *Calcutta Drainage Works: A Brief History*. Calcutta: The Corporation Press, 1921.
Crake, H. M. *The Calcutta Plague 1896–1907*. Calcutta: Criterion Printing Works, 1908.
General Report of the Commissioners for the Improvement of the Town of Calcutta for the Year 1857. Calcutta: Military Orphan Press, 1858.
Hawker Sangram Committee (by Subhendu Dasgupta and Dipankar Dey). *A Survey of the Socio-Economic Condition of Footpath Hawkers of Kolkata, 2004*. Kolkata: Hawker Sangram Committee, 2004.
Hawker Sangram Committee. *A Chronology of Events, 1994–2015*. Kolkata: Hawker Sangram Committee, 2015.
Kolikata Street Directory, 1915. Edited by Samik Bandyopadhyay and Debasis Bose. Calcutta: P. M. Bagchi and Company Private Limited, 2017.
Maden James and Albert de Bois Shrosbree. *City and Suburban Main Road Projects, Joint Report, 1st July 1913*. Calcutta: Calcutta Improvement Trust, 1913.

N. Vijay Jagannathan and Animesh Halder. *Pavement Dwellers of Calcutta-1987: A Socio-Economic Study, April-1988*. Calcutta: Economic Planning Cell, Calcutta Metropolitan Development Authority, collated in *Metropolitan Kolkata: An Anthology of Socio-Economic Studies and Survey Reports of KMDA, 1970–2004* (Vol. IV: *1986–1992*) (Kolkata: Socio-Economic Planning Unit, Directorate of Planning and Development, Kolkata Metropolitan Development Authority, 1988), 109–171.

Report of the Calcutta University Commission. Calcutta: Superintendent of Government Printing, 1919.

Report of the Indian Tariff Board on the Sewing Machine Industry. Bombay: Government Central Press, 1947.

Richards, E. P. *Report by Request of the Trust on the Condition, Improvement and Town Planning of the City of Calcutta and Contiguous Areas: The Richards Report*. Ware, Hertfordshire, 1914.

Sarabhai Mridula. 'Report on the Communal Situation and Riots in Calcutta in 1950'. In *The Trauma and Triumph: Gender and Partition in Eastern India*, Vol. 2, edited by Jasodhara Bagchi and Subharanjan Dasgupta, 260–267. Kolkata: Stree, 2009.

Sudhendu Mukherjee, *A Report on the Survey of 10,000 Pavement-Dwellers in Calcutta, February 1975, Under the Shadow of the Metropolis: They are Citizens Too*. Calcutta: CMDA, 1975, collected in *Metropolitan Kolkata: An Anthology of Socio-Economic Studies and Survey Reports of KMDA, 1970–2004* (Vol. 1: *1970–1979*) (Kolkata: Socio-Economic Planning Unit, Directorate of Planning and Development, Kolkata Metropolitan Development Authority, 1988), 183–330.

Squatters' Colonies, by a Correspondent, *Economic Weekly*, 5 June 1954: 631–634.

Thacker's Indian Directory: Embracing the Whole of the Indian Empire for the Years 1910, 1918, 1933, 1945. Calcutta: Thacker, Spink & Co.

The Indian Annual Register: Chronicle of Events, 1921–22. Sibpur: The Annual Register Office, 1923.

India Department of Statistics. *War Prices and House Rents*. Calcutta: Superintendent Government Printing, India, 1918.

West Bengal Legislative Assembly Debates, 1986–1997. Calcutta: Government of West Bengal.

Printed Secondary Sources

Adey, Peter. 'If Mobility Is Everything Then It Is Nothing: Towards a Relational Politics of (Im)mobilities'. *Mobilities* 1, no. 1 (2006): 75–94.

Bibliography

Agrawal, Amol. 'When Bombay Overtook Calcutta: A History of India's Financial Geography'. *Mint*, 24 June 2017.

Ahuja, Sarayu. *Where the Streets Lead.* New Delhi: Penguin, 1997.

Anjaria, Jonathan S. 'Unruly Streets: Everyday Practices and Promises of Globality in Mumbai'. PhD dissertation, Department of Anthropology, University of California, Santa Cruz, 2008.

Anjaria, Jonathan. S. 'Is There a Culture of the Indian Street?' *Seminar* 636 (2012): https://www.india-seminar.com/2012/636/636_jonathan_s_anjaria.htm, accessed 24 February 2022.

———. *The Slow Boil: Street Food, Rights and Public Space in Mumbai.* Stanford: Stanford University Press, 2016.

Appadurai, Arjun. 'Street Culture'. *India Magazine* 8, no. 1 (1987): 12–22.

Arendt, Hannah. *The Human Condition.* Chicago: University of Chicago Press, 1958.

Arnold, David. 'Subaltern Streets: India, 1870–1947'. In *Subaltern Geographies*, edited by David Arnold, Sharad Chari, David Featherstone, Vinay Gidwani, Mukul Kumar, and Sunil Kumar, 36–56. Georgia: University of Georgia Press, 2019.

———. 'The Problem of Traffic: The Street-Life of Modernity in Late-Colonial India'. *Modern Asian Studies* 46, no. 1 (2012):119–141.

Badiou, Alain. *The Rebirth of History: Times of Riots and Uprisings.* Translated by Gregory Elliot. New York: Verso, 2012.

Bagchi, Amiya K. 'Studies on the Economy of West Bengal since Independence'. *Economic and Political Weekly* 33, nos. 47–48 (1998): 2973–2978.

———. *Private Investment in India, 1900–1940.* Cambridge: Cambridge University Press, 1973.

Balakrishnan, Sai. *Stakeholder Cities: Land Transformations along Urban Corridors in India.* Philadelphia: University of Pennsylvania Press, 2019.

Bandyopadhyay, Ritajyoti. 'Institutionalizing Informality: The Hawkers' Question in Postcolonial Calcutta'. *Modern Asian Studies* 50, no. 2 (2016): 675–717.

———. 'Negotiating Informality: Changing Faces of Kolkata's Footpaths, 1975–2005'. PhD dissertation, Faculty of Arts, Jadavpur University, 2010: http://hdl.handle.net/10603/146584, accessed 24 February 2022.

Bandyopadhyay Ritajyoti and Ranabir Samaddar. 'Caste and the Frontiers of Postcolonial Accumulation'. In *Accumulation in Post-colonial Capitalism*, edited by Iman. K. Mitra, Ranabir Samaddar, and Samita Sen, 189–214. Singapore: Springer, 2017.

Bandyopadhyay, Sandip. 'The Riddles of Partition: Memories of the Bengali Hindus'. In *Reflections of the Partition in the East*, edited by Ranabir Samaddar, 59–72. Delhi: Vikas, 1997.

Bandyopadhyay, Sekhar. 'Partition and the Ruptures in Dalit Identity Politics in Bengal'. *Asian Studies Review* 33, no. 4 (2009): 455–467.

———. *Decolonization in South Asia: Meanings of Freedom in Post-independence West Bengal, 1947–52*. London: Routledge, 2009.

Banerjee, Sarbani. 'Different Identity Formation in Bengal Partition Narratives by Dalit Refugees'. *Interventions* 19, no. 4 (2007): 550–565.

Banerjee, Sumanta. *The Memoirs of the Roads: Calcutta from Colonial Urbanization to Global Modernization*. Delhi: Oxford University Press, 2016.

Basu, Ajit Kumar. *Kolikatar Rajpath: Samaje O Sanskritite*. Calcutta: Ananda Publishers: 1996.

Basu, Pratibha. *Jiboner Jalchhabi*. Kolkata: Ananda, 2011.

Baviskar, Amita. 'Between Violence and Desire: Space, Power, and Identity in the Making of Metropolitan Delhi'. *International Social Science Journal* 55, no. 1 (2003): 89–98.

Bayat, Asef. *Life as Politics: How Ordinary People Change the Middle East*, 2nd ed. Stanford: Stanford University Press, 2013.

Bhan, Gautam. *In the Public's Interest: Evictions, Citizenship and Inequality in Contemporary Delhi*. Athens: University of Georgia Press, 2016.

Bhattacharya, Rajesh and Kalyan Sanyal. 'Bypassing the Squalor: New Towns, Immaterial Labour and Exclusion in Post-colonial Urbanisation'. *Economic and Political Weekly* 46, no. 31 (2011): 41–48.

Bhattacharyya, Debjani. 'Provincializing the History of Speculation from Colonial South Asia'. *History Compass* 17, no. 1 (2019): 1–11.

———. 'Speculation'. *Comparative Studies of South Asia, Africa and the Middle East* 40, no. 1 (2020): 51–56.

———. *Empire and Ecology in the Bengal Delta: The Making of Calcutta*. Cambridge: Cambridge University Press, 2018.

———. 'Hoarding Land': Interwar Housing Speculation and Rent Profiteering in Colonial Calcutta'. *Comparative Studies of South Asia, Africa and the Middle East* 36, no. 3 (2016): 465–482.

Birla, Ritu. *Stages of Capital: Law, Culture, and Market Governance in Late Colonial India*. Durham: Duke University Press, 2009.

Blomley, Nicholas. 'The Territory of Property'. *Progress in Human Geography* 40 no. 5 (2016): 593–609.

Blomley, Nicholas. *Rights of Passage: Sidewalks and the Regulation of Public Flow*. New York and London: Routledge, 2011.

Bompas, C. H. 'The Work of the Calcutta Improvement Trust'. *Journal of the Royal Society of Arts* 75, no. 3868 (1927): 199–219.

Bose, Buddhadeva. *Amar Jouban*. Kolkata: M. C. Sarkar & Sons, 1967.

Bose, Nirmal Kumar. 'Calcutta: A Premature Metropolis'. *Scientific American* 213, no. 3 (1965): 90–102.

———. *Calcutta 1964: A Social Survey*. Bombay: Lalvani Publishing House, 1968.

Brighenti, Andera M. 'On Territory as Relationship and Law as Territory'. *Canadian Journal of Law and Society* 21, no. 2 (2006): 65–86.

Bromley, Roy. 'Street Vending and Public Policy: A Global Review'. *International Journal of Social Policy* 20, nos. 1–2 (2000): 1–28.

Broom, Alastair. 'Theft, Ransom and Vandalism: Securing Your Data Is Getting Tougher'. *ITProPortal*, 1 April 2019. https://www.itproportal.com/features/theftransomware-and-vandalism-securing-your-data-is-getting-tougher/, accessed 3 December 2021.

Brukett, John. P. 'Marx's Concept of an Economic Law of Motion'. *History of Political Economy* 32, no. 2 (2000): 381–394.

Chakrabarti, Prafulla. *The Marginal Men: The Refugees and the Left Political Syndrome in West Bengal*. Kolkata: Naya Udyog Edition, 1999.

Chakrabarty, Dipesh. '"In the Name of Politics": Sovereignty, Democracy and the Multitude in India'. *Economic and Political Weekly* 40, no. 30 (2005): 3293–3301.

———. 'Two Histories of Capital'. In *Provincializing Europe: Postcolonial Thought and Historical Difference*, 47–71. Princeton: Princeton University Press, 2000.

Chandavarkar, Rajnarayan. *The Origins of Industrial Capitalism in India: Business Strategies and the Working Classes in Bombay, 1900–1940*. Cambridge: Cambridge University Press, 1994.

Chatterjee, Anasuya. *Margins of Citizenship: Muslims in Urban India*. New York and London: Routledge 2017.

Chatterjee, Himadri. 'Partitioned Urbanity: A Refugee Village Bordering Kolkata'. *Economic and Political Weekly* 53, no. 12 (2018): 93–100.

Chatterjee, Nilanjana. *Midnight's Unwanted Children: East Bengali Refugees and the Politics of Rehabilitation*. PhD Dissertation: Brown University, 1994.

Chatterjee, Partha. *A Princely Impostor? The Kumar of Bhawal and the Secret History of Indian Nationalism*. Ranikhet: Permanent Black, 2002.

———. 'Are Indian Cities Becoming Bourgeois At Last?', in Partha Chatterjee, *The Politics of the Governed: Reflections on Popular Politics in Most of the World* (Ranikhet: Permanent Black, 2004), 131–148.

Chatterjee, Partha. 'The Political Culture of Calcutta'. In *Calcutta: The Living City, Vol II: The Present and Future*, edited by Sukanta Chaudhuri, 27–33. New Delhi: Oxford University Press, 1990.

———. *The Politics of the Governed: Reflections on Popular Politics in Most of the World*. Ranikhet: Permanent Black, 2004.

Chatterji, Joya. 'Of Graveyards and Ghettos: Muslims in Partitioned West Bengal, 1947–67'. In *Living Together Separately: Cultural India in History and Politics*, edited by M. Hasan and A. Roy, 222–249. New Delhi, Oxford University Press, 2005.

———. *Bengal Divided: Hindu communalism and Partition, 1932–1947*. Cambridge: Cambridge University Press, 1995.

———. *The Spoils of Partition: Bengal and India, 1947–67*. Cambridge: Cambridge University Press, 2007.

Chatterji, Neha. 'Sacred Calling, Worldly Bargain: Caste, Self-cultivation and Mobilisation in Late Colonial Bengal'. PhD dissertation, Centre for Historical Studies, Jawaharlal Nehru University, 2017.

Chattopadhyay, Sumandro. 'Smart Cities as Urbanisation of Data: Towards a Critique of Urban Informatics'. 2013 (unpublished paper).

Chattopadhyay, Swati. 'Cities of Power and Protest: Spatial Legibility and the Colonial State in Early Twentieth-Century India'. *International Journal of Urban Sciences* 19 no. 1 (2015): 40–52.

———. *Representing Calcutta: Modernity, Nationalism and the Colonial Uncanny*. New York: Routledge, 2005.

Choudhury, Ahindra, *Nijere Haraye Khunji*, vol. I. Kolkata: Saptarshi Prakashan, 2011.

Clark, William. 'The Drainage of Calcutta'. Paper read at the Bengal Social Science Congress, held at the Town Hall, Calcutta, on 2 February 1871. The Town Hall Library, Kolkata.

Clover, Joshua. *Riot. Strike. Riot: The New Era of Uprisings*. London and New York: Verso, 2016.

Cowan, Tom. 'The Urban Village, Agrarian Transformation, and Rentier Capitalism in Gurgaon, India'. *Antipode* 50, no. 5 (2018): 1244–1266.

Croce, Benedetto. *History: Its Theory and Practice*. Translated by Douglas Ainslie. New York: Harcourt Brace and Company, 1921.

Das, Alamohan. *Amar Jiban*. Dash Nagar, 1949.

Das, Suranjan. 'The 1992 Calcutta Riot in Historical Continuum: A Relapse into "Communal Fury"?' *Modern Asian Studies* 34, no. 2 (2000): 281–306.

Das, Suranjan. 'The Calcutta Riots of 1907: An Investigation into Crowd Behaviour'. *Proceedings of the Indian History Congress* 40 (1979): 587–603.

———. *Communal Riots in Bengal, 1905–1947*. Delhi: Oxford University Press, 1993.

Dasgupta, Keya. 'Genesis of a Neighbourhood: The Mapping of Bhavanipur'. Occasional Paper 175, Centre for Studies in Social Sciences, March 2003.

Dasgupta, Nandini. *Petty Trading in the Third World: The Case of Calcutta*. Aldershot: Avebury, 1992.

Datta, Partho. 'Calcutta on the Threshold of 1940s'. In *The Stormy Decades: Calcutta*, edited by Tanika Sarkar and Sekhar Bandyopadhyay, 18–41. Delhi: Social Science Press, 2015.

———. *Planning the City: Urbanization and Reform in Calcutta; c. 1800–c. 1940*. New Delhi: Tulika Books, 2012.

Dey, Ishita, Ranabir Samaddar, and Suhit Sen. *Beyond Kolkata: Rajarhat and the Dystopia of Urban Imagination*. London: Routledge, 2013.

Doorn, Niels van and Adam Badger. 'Platform Capitalism's Hidden Abode: Producing Data Assets in the Gig Economy'. *Antipode* 52, no. 5 (2020): 1475–1495.

Dunbar, S. Chas. *Buses, Trolleys and Trams*. London: Hamlyn, 1967.

Dutta, Aniruddha. 'Space, Sanitization and the Press: The Coverage of Street Vending in Kolkata': http://development-dialogues. blogspot.com/2007_05_01_archive.html, accessed 2 September 2011.

Ehrenfeucht, Renia and Anastasia Loukaitou-Sideris. 'Constructing the Sidewalks: Municipal Government and the Production of Public Space in Los Angeles, California, 1880–1920'. *Journal of Historical Geography* 33, no. 1 (2007): 104–124.

Elden, Stuart. *The Birth of Territory*. Chicago: University of Chicago Press, 2013.

Engels, Friedrich. 'Introduction to Karl Marx's *Class Struggle in France, 1848–1850*'. In *Selected Works of Karl Marx and Friedrich Engels*, vol. 1, 1–14. Moscow: Progress Publishers, 1969.

———. *The Housing Question* (1872). Published: (and re-published) as a pamphlet. Reprinted by the Co-operative Publishing Society of Foreign Workers. Transcribed: Zodiac, June 1995.

Feldman, Leslie. D. 'Freedom as Motion: Thomas Hobbes and the Images of Liberalism'. *Journal of Philosophical Research* 22 (1997): 229–243.

Foucault, Michel. *Power/Knowledge: Selected Interviews and Other Writings, 1972–77*. Brighton, England: Harvester, 1980.

———. *Security, Territory, Population: Lectures at the Collège de France 1977–1978*. Translated by Graham Burchell. London: Palgrave Macmillan, 2007.

Fraser, Nancy. *The Old Is Dying and the New Cannot Be Born: From Progressive Neoliberalism to Trump and Beyond*. London: Verso, 2019.

Freitag, Sandria B. *Collective Action and Community: Public Arenas and the Emergence of Communalism in North India*. Berkeley and Los Angeles: University of California Press, 1989.

Gambetta, Curt and Ritajyoti Bandyopadhyay, 'The Problem'. In *Streetscapes: A Symposium on the Future of the Street*, edited by Curt Gambetta and Ritajyoti Bandyopadhyay. *Seminar*, 636 (2012).

Ganguly, Kanti. 'Sanshiner Aage o Pore'. In *Operation Sunshine*, edited by Soumitra Lahiri, 66–75. Kolkata: Biswakosh Parishad, 1997.

Ghertner, Asher D. *Rule by Aesthetics: World-class City Making in Delhi*. New York: Oxford University Press, 2015.

Ghose, Bimal, C. *A Study of Indian Money Market*. Calcutta, Baptist Mission Press: 1943.

Ghosh, Anindita. *Claiming the City: Protest, Crime, and Scandals in Colonial Calcutta, c. 1860–1920*. Delhi: Oxford University Press, 2016.

Ghosh, Nabaparna. *A Hygienic City-Nation: Space, Community, and Everyday Life in Colonial Calcutta*. Cambridge: Cambridge University Press, 2020.

Gidwani, Vinay. 'Six Theses on Waste Value and Commons'. *Social and Cultural Geography* 14, no. 7 (2013): 773–783.

Goldman, Michael. 'Speculative Urbanism and the Making of the Next World City'. *International Journal of Urban and Regional Research* 35, no. 3 (2011): 555–581.

Goode, S. W. *Municipal Calcutta: Its Institutions in their Origin and Growth*. Calcutta: Corporation of Calcutta, 1916.

Gooptu, Nandini. *The Politics of the Urban Poor in Early Twentieth Century India*. Cambridge: Cambridge University Press, 2001.

Guha-Thakurta, Tapati. *In the Name of the Goddess: The Durga Pujas of Contemporary Kolkata*. New Delhi: Primus, 2017.

Gururani, Shubhra. 'Cities in the World of Villages: Agrarian Urbanism and the Making of India's Urbanising Frontiers'. *Urban Geography* 41, no. 7 (2020): 971–989.

Gururani, Subhra and Rajarshi Dasgupta. 'Frontier Urbanism: Urbanization beyond Cities in South Asia'. *Economic and Political Weekly* 53, no. 12 (2018): 41–45.

Haila, Anne. *Urban Land Rent: Singapore as a Property State*. Oxford: Wiley-Blackwell, 2015.

Hannam, Kevin, Mimi Sheller, and John Urry. 'Editorial: Mobilities, Immobilities and Moorings'. *Mobilities* 1, no. 1 (2006): 1–22.

Hansen, Thomas B. 'Democracy Against the Law: Reflections on India's Illiberal Democracy'. In *Majoritarian State: How Hindu Nationalism is Changing India*, edited by Angana. P. Chatterji, Thomas. B. Hansen, and Christophe Jaffrelot, 19–40. Noida: HarperCollins, 2019.

Hardgrove, Anne. *Community and Public Culture: The Marwaris in Calcutta*. New Delhi: Oxford University Press, 2004.

Harris, Richard and Robert Lewis, 'Introduction'. In *The Condition, Improvement and Town Planning of the City of Calcutta and Contiguous Areas*, edited by Richard Harris and Robert Lewis, VII–XXII. London: Routledge, 2015.

Harvey, David. 'Anti-Capitalist Politics in the Time of Covid-19'. *Jacobin*, 20 March 2020. https://jacobinmag.com/2020/03/david-harvey-coronavirus-politicaleconomy-disruptions, accessed 3 December 2021.

———. *Limits to Capital*. Oxford: Blackwell, 1982.

Haynes, Douglas E. and Nikhil Rao, 'Beyond the Colonial City: Re-Evaluating the Urban History of India: 1920–1970'. *South Asia: Journal of South Asian Studies* 36 no. 3 (2013): 317–335.

Heidegger, Martin. *Poetry, Language, Thought*. Translated by Albert Hofstadter. New York: Harper & Row, 1971.

Heitler, Richard. 'The Varanasi House Tax Hartal of 1810–11'. *Indian Economic and Social History Review*, 9, no. 3 (1972): 239–257.

Helmond, Anne. 'The Platformization of the Web: Making Web Data Platform Ready'. *Social Media + Society* 1, no. 2 (2015): 1–11.

Hobsbawm, Eric J. *Nations and Nationalism since 1780*. Cambridge: Cambridge University Press, 1990.

Jefferson, C. and J. Skinner, 'The Evolution of Urban Public Transport'. *WIT Transactions on the Built Environment* 77 (2005): 75–84.

Joshi, Chitra. *Lost Worlds: Indian Labour and Its Forgotten Histories*. Ranikhet: Permanent Black, 2005.

Kalia, Ravi. *Chandigarh: The Making of an Indian City*. New Delhi: Oxford University Press, 1998.

Kamtekar, Indivar. 'The Shiver of 1942'. *Studies in History* 18, no. 1 (2002): 81–102.

Kar, Bodhisattva. 'Chatro Andaloner Itihaas Likhte Jaoyar Aage'. Gautam Chattopadhyay Smarak Baktrita, Kolkata, 2017.

Kaviraj, Sudipta. 'Filth and the Public Sphere: Concepts and Practices about Space in Calcutta'. *Public Culture* 10, no. 1 (1997): 83–113.

Kidambi, Prashant. 'South Asia'. In *Oxford Handbook of Cities in World History*, edited by Peter Clark, 561–580. Corby: Oxford University Press, 2013.

Kidambi, Prashant. 'Housing the Poor in a Colonial City: The Bombay Improvement Trust'. *Studies in History* 17, no. 1 (2001): 57–79.

———. *The Making of an Indian Metropolis: Colonial Governance and Public Culture in Bombay, 1890–1920*. Aldershot: Ashgate, 2007.

Kindleberger, Charles P. 'The Formation of Financial Centers: A Study in Comparative Economic History'. *Princeton Studies in International Finance* 36 (1974).

Lahiri, Koyel. '"Aachhi aar thhakbo": Towards a Reading of the Politics of the Hawker Sangram Committee'. M. Phil dissertation, Centre for Studies in Social Sciences, Calcutta, 2013.

Lefebvre, Henri. *Marxist Thought and the City*. Translated by Robert Bononno. Minneapolis: University of Minnesota Press, 2016.

———. *The Production of Space*. Translated by Donald Nicholson-Smith. Oxford: Basil Blackwell, 1991.

Legg, Stephen. 'Postcolonial Developmentalities: From the Delhi Improvement Trust to the Delhi Development Authority', In *Colonial and Postcolonial Indian Geographies*, edited by Stuart Corbridge, Satish Kumar, and Saraswati Raju, 182–204. London: Sage, 2006.

Linebaugh, Peter. 'Police and the Wealth of Nations: Déjà Vu or Unfinished Business?' *Counter Punch*, 3 July 2020.

Low, Sidney. *A Vision of India*. New York: E.P. Dutton and Company, 1907.

Lubell, Harold, *Urban Development and Employment: The Prospects for Calcutta*. Geneva: International Labour Office, 1971.

Mani, Lata. 'Urban Triptych'. *Seminar* 636 (2012).

Markovits, Claude. 'Bombay as a Business Centre in the Colonial Period: A Comparison with Calcutta'. In *Bombay: Metaphor for Modern India*, edited by Sujata Patel and Alice Thorner, 26–46. Delhi: Oxford University Press, 1995.

———. 'The Calcutta Riots of 1946'. *Online Encyclopaedia of Mass Violence*, 5 November 2007: http://www.sciencespo.fr/ceri/en/ouvrage/oemv, accessed 11 July 2020.

Marx, Karl. *Das Capital*, vol. 1. Moscow, Progress Publishers, 1887.

———. *Das Capital*, vol. 3. Institute of Marxism-Leninism, USSR, 1959.

———. *Economic and Philosophical Manuscript of 1844*. Moscow: Progress Publishers, 1959.

———. *Theories of Surplus Value*, vol. 2. Moscow: Progress Publishers, 1968.

Massey, Doreen. 'A Global Sense of Place'. In *Exploring Human Geography: A Reader*, edited by S. Daniels and R. Lee, 237–245. London: Routledge, 1996.

Mazumder, Soumita. 'The Clique of the Club: A Small History of Nationalism in Calcutta, 1920–1946'. M.Phil. dissertation, Centre for Studies in Social Sciences, Calcutta, 2016.

McGee, T. G. 'In Praise of Tradition: Towards a Geography of Anti-development'. *Antipode* 6, no. 3 (1974): 30–47.

Mehta, Deepak. 'Crowds, Mob and the Law: The Delhi Rape Case'. *Contributions to Indian Sociology* 53, no. 1 (2019): 158–183.

Mitra, Bimal. *Saheb Bibi Golam*. Calcutta: Mitra O Ghosh, 1953.

Mitra, Iman. 'Towards a Rental Economy of the City: Calcutta Improvement Trust and Urbanisation in Calcutta in the Early Twentieth Century'. Paper presented at the 'Sixth Critical Studies Workshop' at the Mahanirban Calcutta Research Group (2015), 6: http://www.mcrg.ac.in/6thCSC/6thCSC_Full_Papers/Iman.pdf, accessed 3 September 2020.

Mitra, Premendra. *Agamikal*. Kolkata: Indian Associated Publishing Co. Ltd., 1953.

Mittra Bahadur, Rai S. C. 'Modern Road Making and Maintenance-1'. *Calcutta Municipal Gazette*, 28 November 1925.

Mom, Gjis. 'Inter-artifactual Technology Transfer'. *History and Technology* 20, no. 1 (2004): 75–96.

Moncrieff-Smith, Henry. 'British Empire: British India'. *Journal of Comparative Legislation and International Law* 10, no. 3 (1928): 141–149.

Mukherjee, Janam. *Hungry Bengal: War, Famine and the End of Empire*. Noida: HarperCollins: 2015.

Mukhopadhyaya, Harisadhan. *Kolikata: Sekaler O Ekaler*. Calcutta: P. M. Bagchi, 1915, reprint in 1985.

Nail, Thomas. *Marx in Motion: A New Materialist Marxism*. Oxford: Oxford University Press, 2020.

Nair, Janaki. *The Promise of the Metropolis: Bangalore's Twentieth Century*. Delhi: Oxford University Press, 2005.

Nair, P. T. *A History of Calcutta's Streets*. Calcutta: Firma KLM, 1987.

Nakazato, Nariaki. 'The Role of Colonial Administration: "Riot Systems" and Local Networks during the Calcutta Disturbances of August 1946'. In *The Stormy Decades: Calcutta*, edited by Tanika Sarkar and Sekhar Bandyopadhyay, 267–319. London: Routledge, 2015.

Nandy, Jyotirindra. *Baro Ghar Ek Uthan*. Kolkata: Dey's Publishing, 1955.

Otter, Chris. *The Victorian Eye: A Political History of Light and Vision in Britain, 1800–1910*. Chicago: University of Chicago Press, 2008.

Prakash, Gyan. 'The Urban Turn'. In *Sarai Reader 02: The Cities of Everyday Life*, edited by Ravi Vasudevan, Ravi Sundaram, Jeebesh Bagchi, Monica Narula, Geert Lovink and Shuddhabrata Sengupta, 2–7. Delhi: CSDS, 2002.

Prakash, Vikramaditya. *Chandigarh's Le Corbusier: The Struggle for Modernity in Postcolonial India*. Seattle: University of Washington Press, 2002.

Pullan, Wendy. 'Frontier Urbanism: The Periphery at the Centre of the Contested Cities'. *Journal of Architecture* 16, no. 1 (2011): 15–35.

Rajagopal, Arvind. 2001. 'The Violence of Commodity Aesthetics: Hawkers, Demolition Raids, and a New Regime of Consumption'. *Social Text* 19, no. 3: 91–113.

Rao, Nikhil. 'Space in Motion: An Uneven Narrative of Urban Private Property in Bombay'. In *Rethinking Markets in Modern India: Embedded Exchange and Contested Jurisdiction*, edited by A. Gandhi, B. Harris-White, D. Haynes, and S. Schwecke, 54–84. Cambridge: Cambridge University Press, 2020.

———. *House, but No Garden: Apartment Living in Bombay's Suburbs, 1898–1964*. Minneapolis: University of Minnesota Press, 2013.

Ray, Rajat Kanta. 'The Bazaar: Changing Structural Characteristics of the Indigenous Sections of the Indian Economy before and after the Great Depression'. *Indian Economic and Social History Review* 25, no. 3 (1988): 263–381.

———. *Social Conflict and Political Unrest in Bengal, 1875–1927*. Delhi: Oxford University Press, 1984.

———. Urban Roots of Indian Nationalism (New Delhi: Vikas Publishing House Pvt Ltd, 1980).

Rigi, Jakob and Robert Prey. 'Value, Rent, and the Political Economy of Social Media'. *Information Society* 31, no. 5 (2015): 392–406.

Robinson, Jennifer. *Ordinary Cities: Between Modernity and Development*. London: Routledge, 2006.

Roy, Ananya. *City Requiem, Calcutta: Gender and the Politics of Poverty*. Minneapolis: University of Minnesota Press, 2002.

Roy, Arundhati. 'The Pandemic Is a Portal'. *Financial Times*, 3 April 2020.

Rumbach, Andrew. '"Between the Devil and the Bay of Bengal": The Ford Foundation and the Politics of Planning in Post-independence Calcutta'. *Planning Perspectives* 36, no. 5 (2021): 1025–1051.

Sadowski, Jathan. 'The Internet of Landlords: Digital Platforms and New Mechanisms of Rentier Capitalism'. *Antipode* 52, no. 2 (2020): 562–580.

———. *Too Smart: How Digital Capitalism Is Extracting Data, Controlling Our Lives, and Taking Over the World*. Cambridge: MIT Press, 2020.

Samaddar, Ranabir, ed. *From Popular Movements to Rebellion: The Naxalite Decade*. London: Routledge, 2018.

———. 'Policing a Riot-Torn City: Kolkata, 16–18 August 1946'. *Journal of Genocide Research* 19, no. 1 (2017): 39–60.

Samaddar, Ranabir, ed. *Ideas and Frameworks of Governing India*. New York and London: Routledge, 2016.

Sanyal, Kalyan. *Rethinking Capitalist Development: Primitive Accumulation, Governmentality and Post-Colonial Capitalism*. Delhi: Routledge, 2007.

Sanyal, Romola. 'Contesting Refugeehood: Squatting as Survival in Post-Partition Calcutta'. *Social Identities* 15, no. 1 (2009): 67–84.

———. 'Hindu Space: Urban Dislocations in Post-Partition Calcutta'. *Transactions of the British Institute of Geographers* 39, no. 1(2014): 38–49.

Saran, Awadhendra. *In the City, Out of Place: Nuisance, Pollution and Dwelling in Delhi, 1850–2000*. Delhi: Oxford University Press, 2014.

Sarin, Madhu: *Urban Planning in the Third World: The Chandigarh Experience*. London: Mansell Publishing Limited, 1982.

Sarkar, Aditya. *Trouble at the Mill: Factory Law and the Emergence of the Labour Question in Late Nineteenth-Century Bombay*. Delhi: Oxford University Press, 2018.

Sarkar, Sumit. 'The City Imagined: Calcutta of the Nineteenth and Early Twentieth Centuries'. In *Writing Social History*, 159–185. Delhi: Oxford University Press.

———. *Modern India, 1885–1947*. New Delhi: Macmillan, 1983.

———. *The Swadeshi Movement in Bengal, 1903–1908*. Delhi: People's Publishing House, 1973.

Sarkar, Tanika. 'Intimate Violence in Colonial Bengal: A Death, a Trial and a Law, 1889–1891'. *Law and History Review* 38, no. 1 (2020): 177–200.

———. *Bengal 1928–1934: The Politics of Protest*. Delhi: Oxford University Press, 1987.

Sarkar, Tanika and Sekhar Bandyopadhyay, eds. *Calcutta: The Stormy Decades*. New Delhi: Social Science Press, 2015.

Scott, James C. *Two Cheers for Anarchism: Six Easy Pieces on Autonomy, Dignity, and Meaningful Work and Play*. Princeton and Oxford, Princeton University Press, 2012.

Seabrook, Jeremy and Imran Ahmed Siddiqui, People without History: India's Muslim Ghettos (London: Pluto Press, 2011).

Searle, Llerena Guiu. *Landscapes of Accumulation: Real Estate and the Neoliberal Imagination in Contemporary India*. Chicago: University of Chicago Press 2016.

Sen, Asok. 'Life and Labour in a Squatters' Colony'. Occasional Paper 138, Centre for Studies in Social Sciences, Calcutta, October 1992.

Sen, Uditi. *Citizen Refugee: Forging the Indian Nation after Partition*. Cambridge: Cambridge University Press, 2018.

Sengupta, Anwesha. 'Anti-Tram Fare Rise and Teachers' Movement in Calcutta, 1953–54'. In *From Popular Movements to Rebellion: The Naxalite Decade*, edited by Ranabir Samaddar, 48–84. London Routledge, 2019.

———. 'Becoming a Minority Community: Calcutta's Muslims after Partition'. In *The Stormy Decades: Calcutta*, edited by Tanika Sarkar and Sekhar Bandyopadhyay, 434–458. London: Routledge, 2015.

———. 'Political History of Calcutta: 1947–1977': https://www.sahapedia.org/refugee-colonies-kolkata-history-politics-and-memory, accessed 14 September 2020.

———. 'The Railway Refugees: Sealdah, the 1950s–1960s'. IDSK Working Paper Series, id:117592020.

Sengupta, Debjani. 'A City Feeding on Itself: Testimonies and Histories of "Direct Action" Day'. In *Sarai Reader 06: Turbulence*, edited by Monica Naurala, 288–295. New Delhi: CSDS.

———. 'The Refugee City: Partition and Kolkata's Postcolonial landscape'. 2007: http://bangalnama.wordpress.com/2009/08/31/the-refugee-city-partition-and-kolkata%E2%80%99s-postcolonial-lands cape/, accessed 15 June 2021.

Sengupta, Kaustubh Mani. 'Community and Neighbourhood in a Colonial City: Calcutta's Para'. *South Asia Research* 38, no. 1 (2018): 40–56.

———. 'Infrastructural Development and the Issue of Compensation in Colonial Calcutta': http://www.mcrg.ac.in/6thCSC/6thCSC_Full_Papers/Kaustubh.pdf, accessed 16 June 2021.

Sennett, Richard. *The Fall of Public Man*. London and Boston, MA: Faber and Faber, 1977.

Shah, Ghanshyam. 'The 1969 Communal Riots in Ahmedabad: A Case Study'. In *Communal Riots in Post-independence India*, edited by Asghar Ali Engineer, 175–208. Hyderabad: Sangam Books, 1984.

Shani, Ornit. *Communalism, Caste, and Hindu Nationalism: The Violence in Gujarat*. Cambridge: Cambridge University Press, 2007.

———. *How India Became Democratic*. Cambridge: Cambridge University Press, 2018.

Siddiqui, M. K. A. *Muslims of Calcutta: A Study of Their Social Organization*. Calcutta: Anthropological Survey of India, 1974.

Sinha, Surendranath. 'The Central Avenue: Calcutta's New Thoroughfare'. *Bengal Past and Present* 35 (1916).

Skeggs, Beverley. *Class, Self, Culture*. London: Routledge, 2004.

Sur, Prasanta. 'Foreword'. In Shivaprasad Samaddar, *Calcutta Is*. Calcutta: CMC Publications, 1978.

Tagore, Abanindranath. *Raj Kahini*. Translated from Bangla by Ratan Jha. New Delhi: Ankita Printers, 2014.

Tagore, Rabindranath. 'The Runaway City'. In *Rabindranath Tagore: Selected Writings for Children*, edited by Sukanta Chaudhuri, translated by Sukhendu Ray, 25–26. New Delhi: Oxford University Press, 2002.

Tarlo, Emma. *Unceasing Memories: Narratives of Emergency in India*. Berkeley: University of California Press, 2003.

Tejani, Shabnum. 'Disputing "Market Value": The Bombay Improvement Trust and the Reshaping of a Speculative Land Market in Early Twentieth-century Bombay'. *Urban History* 48, no. 3 (2021): 572–589.

Thompson, E. P. *The Making of the English Working Class*. New York: Vintage Books, 1963.

———. 'The Moral Economy of the English Crowd in the Eighteenth Century'. *Past and Present* 50, no. 2 (1971): 76–136.

Tsing, Anna. T. *Friction: An Ethnography of Global Connection*. Princeton: Princeton University Press, 2005.

Tuker, Francis. *While Memory Serves*. London: Cassell, 1950.

Upadhyay, Surya P. and Rowena Robinson. 'Revising Communalism and Fundamentalism in India'. *Economic and Political Weekly* 47, no. 36 (2012): 35–57.

Urry, John. *Societies Beyond the Social: Mobilities for the Twenty First Century*. London: Routledge, 2000.

———. 'The "System" of Automobility'. *Theory, Culture and Society* 21, nos. 4–5 (2004): 25–39.

———. *Global Complexity*. Cambridge: Polity, 2003.

Vanaik, Anish. *Possessing the City: Property and Politics in Delhi, 1911–1947*. Oxford: Oxford University Press, 2020.

Vidler, Anthony. *The Scenes of the Street and Other Essays*. New York: The Monacelli Press, 2011.

Wall Street Journal. 'The Hong Kong Protestor's Toolkit for a Cat-and-Mouse Game with Authorities'. 16 September 2019: https://www.wsj.com/articles/the-hong-kong-protesters-toolkit-for-a-cat-and-mouse-game-with-authorities-11568628648, accessed 1 September 2020.

Wallace, Rob, Alex Liebman, Luis Fernando Chaves, and Rodrick Wallace. 'Covid-19 and the Circuits of Capital'. *Monthly Review* 72, no. 1 (2020). https://monthlyreview.org/2020/05/01/covid-19-and-circuits-of-capital/, accessed 3 December 2021.

Winter, James. *London's Teeming Streets: 1830–1914*. Routledge, London, 1993.

Wohlfarth, Irving. 'Et Cetra? The Historian as Chiffonnier'. In *Walter Benjamin and The Arcades Project*, edited by Beatrice Hanssen, 12–32. London and New York: Continuum, 2006.

Zook, Matthew. 'The Geographies of the Internet'. *Annual Review of Information Science and Technology* 40: 1 (2006), 53–78.

Index

Aadhaar registration centres, 155–156
Abercrombie, Lieutenant, 57
accumulation economy, 59, 212–213, 228, 261
Addi, Amulya Dhan, 170, 178
Agamikal (1934), 174
agents of liaison, 42
Age of Consent Act (Act X of 1891), 61n81
akharas (gymnasiums), 12, 139–140, 143
Alipore Bomb Trial of 1909, 12
All India Forward Bloc, 208
Amar Jiban, 22n52
Amar Jouban, 169
Ambani, Mukesh, 212
Amrita Bazar Patrika, 84n23
Ananda Margi sect, 191
animal-driven locomotion, 42
Annual Report of the Calcutta Municipal Administration, 58
Annual Report of the Trust for 1915–16, 173
Ansari, Aftab Alam, 154
anti-CAA campaign, in Indian cities, 263
anti-colonial mass mobilizations, 60
anti-cow-slaughter agitations, 75–76
anti-eviction movement, 26
anti-landlord sloganeering, 183
anti-Partition agitation, 29
anti-tram-fare-hike movement (1953), 70
Arab Spring, 263
Arcades Project, The (Walter Benjamin), 13
Arendt, Hanna, 31n79

Armenian Street, 74–76, 82, 85, 89, 224
Armstrong, J. E., 123
Arnold, David, 50n51, 55
art of presence, 57
Arya Samaj, 139
Ashutosh Dey Lane, 102
Asian *karkhana*, 260
asphalt
    Age of Asphalt, 48
    discovery of deposits, 46
    importance in the construction industry, 47
    liquid bituminous asphalt, 47
    market in India, 46n38
Asutosh Mookerjee Road, 161
attacks on religious institutions, 140
automobiles, within urban space, 51
automobile traffic, 48–49, 51, 234
avenues with sidewalks, emergence of, 50–54

Babri Mosque demolitions, 154
Badger, Adam, 259n15
Bagbazaar, 52, 89
Bagchee, S., 176
Bagchi, Amiya, 111n90
Bahadur, Rai Radha Charan Pal, 98n54, 109n83
Bahadur, Rai Ramdev Chokhani, 115
Bahadur, Rai S. C. Mittra, 47
Bakr-Id festival, 74
    riot of December 1910, 76–77, 120
Ballygunge Avenue, 167

Ballygunge Hawkers' Association (Congress-R), 215
Ballygunge Rail Station, 150, 165, 166, 189, 191
Banamali Sarkar Lane, 90
Bandyopadhyay, Sekhar, 69, 148
Banerjee, Canon, 164
Banerjee, Mamata, 225, 251, 253
Banerjee, Nanda Lal, 12n24
Banerjee, S. C., 141n51
Banerjee, Sudhir Kumar, 185
Banerjee, Sumanta, 176
Banerjee, Surendranath, 61n81
Bangladesh War of Independence, 209
Barman, Asim, 227
Basu, Bijon, 191n97
Basu, Jyoti, 220
Basu, M. N., 169
Basu, Pratibha, 168
Beadon Square, 60
Beadon Street, 89, 93, 114, 130–131, 133, 144, 146
Bengal Act III of 1926. *See* Presidency Area (Emergency) Security Bill (1926)
Bengal Act I of 1923, 124
Bengal Belting Works Limited, 176–177
Bengal Chamber of Commerce (BCC), 42n19, 48
Bengal Council, 124
Bengalee, The, 64
Bengal Famine (1943), 7
Bengal Hawkers' Association (Forward Bloc), 215
Bengali *bhadralok* (gentlemanly) class, 29, 125
Bengali Hindus, 7, 81, 163
Bengal Legislative Council, 108n76, 170
Bengal, partition of (16 October 1905), 60
Bengal Presidency, 46
Bengal Provincial Congress Committees, 141n52
Bengal Provincial Khilafat Committee, 141

Bengal Provincial Muslim League, disbandment of, 145
Bengal Young Men's Association, 141
bhadralok, 103, 136, 144, 167, 169, 227
  network of *jabardakhal* colonies, 210
  resettlement of the displaced, 104–105
  sentiment of 'pristine Calcutta,' 222
Bharat Sevasram Sangh, 144n62
Bhattacharyya, Ananda, 67
Bhattacharyya, Jyoti, 219
Bhattacharyya, Srimat Ananta, 91
Bhawani Charan Dutt Lane, 93, 94–97, 98
Bhowanipore, 103–105, 141n53, 160–161, 163–165, 198–203, 208n6
Bidhan Sarana, 223–224. *See also* Cornwallis Street
Bidyadhari River, 165
*bigha*s, 85, 164, 172
Bijon Setu massacre (1982), 191
Bikramgarh refugee colony, 209
Birla, G. D., 111
Biswanand, Swami, 62
Blomley, Nicholas, 25n61–62, 26, 51n54, 116n105, 236
Bolshevik Revolution, 108
Bombay Improvement Trust, 3n7, 20n48, 76n10, 111n91
Bompas, C. H., 51, 54, 85n27, 160, 171
Bose, Biren, 209
Bose Brothers, story of, 210
Bose, Buddhadeva, 168–169, 187–188
Bose, Nirmal Kumar, 149
Bose, Sarat Chandra, 180
Boulevards of Paris, 103
bourgeois city, 256
Bowbazaar Street, 90, 104–105, 114
Brabourne Road, 73, 120, 224
Bray Club, 140
British Consulate, 148
British Empire, 4n9, 126
bulldozing obstruction (1996–1997), 220–229
bullock-cart era, 48

Index 291

bullock-cart traffic, 45
Burrabazaar, 4n9, 65, 74, 77, 93, 116, 184
   Mahomedan worker in, 117
   Marwari quarters in, 75
   Marwari residents of, 115
bustee dwellers, 31, 106, 114, 204
Bustee Improvement Programme (BIP), 31–32
bustee lands, private ownership of, 31n80
*bustee*s, 3, 3n8, 11, 31, 40, 63, 73, 100, 131, 147, 164, 204, 255
   decline of population density in, 92
   demolition of, 92
   displacement of working class occupying, 86
   inner-city, 113
   Kalabagan *bustee*, 77
   of poor Muslim tenants, 74, 81
   social composition of, 99n59
   working-class tenants of, 107
bypass transit corridors, 257

Calcutta
   as city of hawkers, 33
   communal mobilization and territorial warfare in, 29
   decline of economic fortune of, 27–28
   as dying city, 32
   economic dependence on European capital, 27
   economic prosperity of, 27
   as Empire's Indian capital, 27
   expansion in Salt Lake, 176n59
   export-oriented economy, 28
   hegemonic representation of, 5
   Hindu Bengali landed elite of, 100
   Hinduization of, 89
   as Hindu-majority city, 119
   inner-city areas, 112
   inter-communal sharing of space, 150
   late colonial period (the 1920s–1940s), 31
   loss of jute-producing agricultural lands to East Pakistan, 28
   prime export commodities, 27
   radical labour agitation, 32
   refugee encroachment of properties in, 180
   settlement with India, 145
   share in industrial employment, 28
   suburban lands, 112
   territorial consolidation of, 189
   tradition of street protest in, 61n81
   transfer of the capital from, 7n13
   urban life, 7
Calcutta Club, 164
Calcutta Disturbances Commission of Enquiry, 127, 128n24
   session with Khundkar, 138–139
Calcutta Electric Supply Corporation Limited (CESC), 223
Calcutta Engineering Society (CES), 175, 176
Calcutta Gazette, 109n80
Calcutta Hawker Sangram Committee (HSC), 34
Calcutta Hawkers' Congress (Socialist Party), 215
Calcutta Improvement Act (1911), 42, 83, 83n19, 100
Calcutta Improvement Trust (CIT), 1–2, 11–12, 19, 34, 38, 42, 47, 64, 72, 115, 255
   Annual Reports of, 111, 167
   building of new avenue over the old Russa Road, 52
   Central Avenue Scheme (Scheme VII), 82
   contractors, 198–202
   decline of, 194
   demolition of *bustee*s, 164
   development of parks in northern Calcutta, 59
   expedition in the southern frontiers of Calcutta, 178
   income through the sale of the recouped land, 83

Index

inner-city schemes, 159
legal notice to Bancharam's shop, 92
neighbourhoods 'beyond recognition,' 99
proposal for land acquisition for excavation, 173
rehousing scheme of, 106
right to recoup land, 83
Russa Road Widening Scheme (Scheme IV), 82
strategy for a layered population displacement, 86–89
street-building initiatives, 77
street schemes, 109–110, 112
urbanization schemes of the late colonial era, 160
vision of graded population dispersal, 113
widening of Russa Road, 160
work of, 41
Calcutta Metropolitan Development Authority (CMDA), 150, 193
Calcutta Metropolitan Planning Organization (CMPO), 31
Calcutta Muhammadan Committee, 141
Calcutta Municipal Act (1899), 83n19
Calcutta Municipal Act (1951), 185
Calcutta Municipal Act VI of 1863, 79
Calcutta Municipal Corporation, 215, 222
    'identify and quantify' hawkers on the streets, 232
Calcutta Municipal Gazette, 167
Calcutta Race Course, 61n81
Calcutta Rent Bill (1920), 108n76
capital accumulation, 4, 12, 16, 17n37, 18n37, 26, 40, 170
    city-associated, 33
    global network of, 33
    mobilization of space for, 26
capitalist circulation network, 222
capital's motion, Marx's notion of, 15
Census of 1951, 145
Central Avenue, 3, 52, 64, 66, 98, 104–105, 108, 110, 113, 117, 132, 137, 163n13, 168, 193, 198, 200, 202, 223. *See also* Chittaranjan Avenue
Central Avenue Scheme, 82, 89–90, 92–93, 103, 107, 142n51
    displacement of residential property owners under, 102
    prime land acquired for, 102
    north–south, 3, 52
    planned layout of, 91
    readjustment of properties on, 99
Centre of Indian Trade Unions (CITU), 213, 216, 223n40, 227
Chaitra Sankranti–Bengali new year, 243
Chakrabarti, Prafulla, 7n14, 179, 182, 183
Chakrabarty, Dipesh, 57n72, 71
Chakrabarty, Prafulla, 22n53
Chakrabarty, Subhas, 225–226
Chandavarkar, Rajnarayan, 55, 56n69
*chandimandap*s, 126n19
Chandra, Prafulla, 144n62
*chatak*s of land, 85
Chatterjee, Partha, 32n82, 33n84, 65n97, 140, 162n8, 219n31, 256n5
Chatterji, Joya, 146, 148
Chattopadhyay, Sumandro, 259, 259n16
Chattopadhyay, Swati, 61n80, 92n43, 126
*chawl*s, 106
Chetla, 105, 160, 164–166, 170, 176, 195
China Town, 146n68
Chitpore Road, 39, 64, 76–77, 80, 82, 89, 99, 122, 131, 134
Chittaranjan Avenue, 218, 223. *See also* Central Avenue
Chora Bagan Lane, 102
Choudhury, Ahindra, 164–165, 173–174
*chowdhuri*s, 63n87
Chowringhee Hawkers' Association (Congress-R), 215
Citizenship Amendment Act, 2019 (CAA), 155
City of Joy (1992), 244
city-rebuilding project, 88

Civil Disobedience Movement, 63
civil war of 1946, 144
Clark, William, 47n41, 50, 89
class-based dispersal of the population, 89
'The Clique of the Club', 140n50, 141n52–54, 144n62
Clover, Joshua, 259n21, 266n33
clubs, 214
coal tar, 43, 45–47
College Square, 60
College Street, 44, 60, 77, 80–82, 89, 93, 98n53, 114, 121, 142, 148, 152, 208, 224, 231
   sidewalks, 61
colonial bureaucracy, 23n55, 27, 99, 99n59, 193
colonialism in India, 27
Colootola–Tiretta Bazaar area, 113
Commissioner of Police, 34, 67, 74, 76, 116, 120n1, 185–186
commodification of land, 117, 159–160
communal aggregation of neighbourhoods, 23
communal civil war, 119, 255
communal cleansing, of ethnic or religious minorities, 23
communal mobilization, 23n54, 29, 118–119, 139–140
communal polarization, 75, 114, 118, 139
communal riots, 7, 22, 25n64, 56, 62, 89, 139, 151, 255
communal territorial warfare, 127
communal violence, 25, 118, 146, 152, 156
Communist Party of India (CPI), 190, 213
Communist Party of India (Marxist) (CPI [M]), 190, 213, 216
   Central Committee of, 221
compensation and rehousing, issue of, 100–107
Condition, Improvement and Town Planning of the City of Calcutta and Contiguous Areas (1914), 38
Congress–CPI alliance, 214
Congress Party, 62, 65, 67, 147, 214
   club Pujas, 214
   Muslim leadership within, 145
   Seva Dals, 143
Constitution of India
   Article 19 (1)(g) of, 221
   Article 356 of, 214
Coordination Committee of Calcutta Hawkers (CCCH), 216
Cornwallis Street, 39, 60, 64, 89, 131, 133–134, 142, 198, 223. *See also* Bidhan Sarani
corporate capital, 230, 256, 262
corporation budget, 51
Corporation of Calcutta, 185
Corporation Water Department, 239
*cottah*s, 85
Cotton Street, 73, 76, 79–80, 120
   expansion of, 79
   widening of, 81
counter-pedestrianism, 237, 242
   and urban sociality, 242
court-martial, of the INA soldier, 68
cow slaughter, at Din Mohamed's Mosque, 74–76
crisis of comprehensibility, 129
crowd–police dialectic, 66–67, 119, 120–127, 137
crude oil, 47
cultural history, dialectics of, 13
culture of accumulation, 33, 59
cyber incident, 264

'Daily Notes Register' of the Special Branch of Calcutta Police, 215–216
daily wage, loss of, 265
Dalhousie Square, 44, 48, 59, 65–69, 223–224
Dalits, 151
Dalmiya, M. L., 175n58

Das, Chittaranjan, 62, 141
Dasgupta, Nandini, 208n6, 218, 242
Das, S., 76n10, 114
Datta, Partho, 1n3, 11n23, 34n85, 41, 83n18, 90n42
data production, 259
de Bois Shrosbree, Albert, 87, 87n32–33, 88, 100, 159
Deb, Saral, 220
Delhi Development Authority (DDA), 215
Delhi National Capital Region (NCR), 260
Deshapriya Park, 175, 183, 187, 203
desh bhaag (partition), 245
Dhakurer Rasta, 165
Dhakuria bazaar, 192
Dhakuria Bridge, 189–190
dhangars, 125
Dharmatala Street, 65–68
Diamond Harbour Road, 106, 176n58, 223
digital technology, 262
Direct Action Day, 138n46
displaced people, movement to the suburbs, 113
Duke of Connaught, 62
Durga Puja, 92n43, 185, 214, 243
Dutta & Company, 176

East Calcutta Wetlands area, urbanization of, 150
Eastern Bengal Railway Lines, 166
Eastern Metropolitan Bypass project, 150, 191, 256
East Pakistan, 186, 208
East Pakistani Press, 148
E. B. Railway lines, 161, 177
economic rehabilitation, 219, 245
Economic Weekly, 204
economies of power, 214, 219
economy, liberalization of, 6, 32
Election Commission, 33n84
electoral politics, 180

electricity hook-ups, at hawkers' stalls, 238
electric trams, 49
encroached-upon properties, decommodification of, 160
encroachment-as-community, 256
encroachment, politicization of, 181
Engels, Friedrich, 1, 1n1, 2, 9–10, 11n20–21, 12, 263n26
engineers, 38–43
Enlightenment, 9
episodic mob violence, 139
European Association, in Calcutta, 47
European pavement, 53

fair pricing mechanism, of property, 182
family and social networks, 210
Famine of 1943, 205
fight for freedom, 149
Financial Times, 221
Food Corporation of India (FCI), 227
footpath hawking, 206. *See also* refugee hawkers; street hawkers
  Bengali-Hinduization of, 209
  expansion of, 207
  institutionalizing of, 229
  legalization of, 230
  moral claim in support of, 219
  operation of, 234
  political economy of, 241
  profession of, 213
  proliferation of, 207–213
  unionization of, 213
Ford Foundation, 31–32
'formal sector' of the economy, 230
Forward Bloc, 213, 225
  rural and urban mass base, 214
  Trade Union Coordination Committee of, 213n12
freedom-as-motion, Hobbes' notion of, 14n27
French Revolution of 1848, 10
fringe economies, 256
  creation of, 177
  proliferation of, 26, 188

Index

frontier urbanization, 171–178
    of the 1990s and the 2000s, 229
fruit trade, 114
'future of the street' in Indian cities, 257

Gait, Edward, 125
Gambetta, Curt, 9n16, n19, 257, 257n8, 258
Gandhian agitation
    in the interwar period, 29
    spread of, 30
Gandhi, Indira, 190, 215–217, 219
Gandhi, Mahatma, 62, 69, 168n32
    technique of pressurizing the state machine, 217
Gandhi, Sanjay, 215
Gandhian agitation, 29–30, 62n84, 217
Ganguly, Kanti, 223, 225–226, 228
garden houses, 159
Gariahat, 167, 179, 186–188, 193, 208–211, 214–216, 218–219, 222–223, 225, 238, 253
    demolition drive in, 246
    frontiers of, 189–192
Gariahat Boulevard, 187
Gariahat Crossing, 186
Gariahat Market, 216
Gariahat Road, 165–167, 172, 186, 189, 203
gated communities, 23, 59
Geddes, Patrick, 51, 53–54, 160
gentrification
    of central Calcutta, 107
    of Indian cities, 32n82
geographic information system (GIS), 257
geo-locational identifier, 259
Geological Survey of India (GSI), 46
gherao, 32–33
ghettoization of Muslims, 209, 255
ghettos, 23, 119, 146, 150, 152, 155, 157–158, 209, 255
Ghosh, Achintya Kumar, 144n62
Ghosh, Anindita, 60

Ghosh, Ashok, 208–209, 227
Ghosh, Nabaparna, 20n48, 34n85, 103
Ghosh, Prafulla, 69
Ghosh, Rashbehari, 168
Ghosh, Rimpa, 210n9
Ghosh, Saktiman, 230, 232
Gladwell system, 44
global logistical networks, 261
'golden age' of organized mass action, 266
Goode, S. W., 43–44
Goonda Act. *See* Bengal Act I of 1923
goondas, 125, 137, 144
governing the city, colonial mode of, 193
Government House (Rajbhavan), 183
Government of India (GOI), 46, 78n13, 143
    liberalization strategy of, 222
Government of India Act of 1919, 23n55
Government of West Bengal, 181, 189
graded population dispersal, strategy for, 86–89
Growth Centres, development of, 221

Haldar, S. N., 140
Halder, Animesh, 205n3, n5
Halliday, F. L., 55, 120–123
Halliday Park, 64
Halliday Street, 52, 73, 76, 85, 93–94, 96, 98, 104, 113, 120
Hansen, Thomas Blom, 154
Harish Mukherjee Road, 162–163
Harrison Road, 1, 12, 39, 64, 75, 78, 80, 82, 90, 117, 120–123, 142, 163n13
    building of (north)western segment, 81
    construction of, 73–74
    cost of building, 79
    east–west diagonal of, 89
    Hindu–Muslim riots on, 76
    inauguration of, 74
    mosque near, 73–77
    properties owned by Marwaris, 82

Harrison Road Protection Scheme,
    73–74, 79, 90, 121n4
  areas affected by, 120
  Chitpore Road–College Street
    segment of, 89
Hartaki Bagan Lane, 144
hartal, 62, 65, 138n46
Hatkhola Bazaar, 184
hawker–pedestrian–consumer relation,
    241
hawkers and pavement dwellers,
    distribution of, 244
Hawker Sangram Committee (HSC),
    34, 208n7, 223–225, 227–233,
    237–238, 241, 243–245
  narrative of *sangram*, 242n68
hawkers' union, organizational structure
    of, 243
Haynes, Douglas E., 6
Hazra Road, 161–162, 166
Hegel, G. W. Friedrich, 15
Helmond, Anne, 259n18
Hindu
  Bengali entrepreneurs, 175
  Bengali landlords, 76, 82, 83n19, 89
  in East Pakistan, 145
  *goonda*s, 120, 122
  paras, 139
  refugees, 145
  temples, protection of, 140
  volunteer organizations, 143
Hindu Mahasabha, 143, 146
  Hindustan National Guard, 144
Hindu–Muslim relationship
  in a Hindu-majority capital, 114
  population ratio in Calcutta, 145
Hindu–Muslim Riot
  of 1907, 125–126
  of 1910, 76, 89, 120
  of 1918, 114
  of 1926, 62, 114, 117
  of 1946, 29, 127–133, 145
  of 1950, 146–149
  of 1964, 149
  of 1992, 154

attack on Hindu Bengali *bhadralok*
    properties, 114
  on Harrison Road, 76
  latent violence, 150–156
  mob lynching of Muslims inside
    Muslim *mohalla*s, 147
  role of the police in, 147
  social infrastructure of violence,
    139–144
Hobbes, Thomas, 13–14n27
house famine, in Calcutta, 111
Howrah Bridge, 1, 39, 64–65, 121
Hukumchand, Swarupchand, 111
human freedom, notion of, 36n3
Hussain, Murad, 231
Hygienic City Nation, The (Nabaparna
    Ghosh), 92n43

Improvement Trust Act, 114
INA Day, 65
Indian Civil Service (ICS), 27, 168n32
Indian crowds, social and cultural
    specificities of, 53
Indian National Army (INA), 65
industrial capitalism, 9, 260
industrial production, 63, 259
industrial townships, 148
'informal sector' of the economy, 26, 204,
    230, 243
  caste-based demographic
    reorganization of, 210
information technology (IT), 259
inner-city, 42
  congestion, 158
  gentrification, 4
  renewal schemes, 159
  slums (*bustee*s), 113, 194, 204, 255
Intelligence Bureau, 65, 114, 141n52, 155
inter-communal sharing, of
    neighbourhoods, 119
inter-communal tensions, 20
inter-district trading channels, 186n85
International Labour Organization
    (ILO), 204

Index

Internet of Things, 259
Ishabhai, A. M., 74
IT boom, in urban India, 256

jabardakhal (forcible collective occupation of space by people), 6, 159, 192–194, 209, 245, 255
  anti-eviction agitations, 183
  bhadralok network of, 210
  de-commodification of private and public properties, 181
  effects of, 182
  forcible colonization by refugees, 181
  as form of claiming space, 178
  proliferation of unorganized retail, 184
  in Rashbehari Avenue, 183
  settlements, 204
  as (sub)urbanization *without* accumulation, 178–183
Jai Hind Calcutta Hawkers' Union (Congress-R), 215
'Jai Hind' slogan, 69
Jamiat-i-Ulema, 140
Jay Engineering Works factory, 211
Jay Engineering Works Ltd, 177
Jiboner Jalchhabi (Pratibha Basu), 169
jihad, 218
joint stock initiatives, 175
Joshi, P. B., 111n91
Jugantar report (1953), 70
just-in-time
  communication, 262
  delivery, 17n34
jute
  global demand for, 27
  mills, 22, 111, 148
    in West Bengal, 28
  trade, 111

Kabita Bhavan, 168–169
Kabuli merchants, 90, 115

Kalabagan *bustee*, 77
*kalibari*s, 126n19
Kalighat, 48, 105, 141, 160, 162, 164, 166, 208n6, 218
Kalighat Road, 161
Kalighat Tram Depot, 165
Kamtekar, Indivar, 7n14
*karigar*s (artisans), 260
Kaviraj, Sudipta, 187
Kepler, Johannes, 15
Khilafat Committee, 141
Khundkar, N. H., 128, 130–132
  sessions with the Commission, 137–138
Kidambi, Prashant, 54n61, 55
Kolkata Telephones, 239
Krishak Sabha, 213

labour officer, 64
labour-saving automation (dead labour), 18
Lal, Awadh Behari (Nitya Nandaji), 75
Lallbagan Seva Samiti, 147
Lal, Panna, 123
land acquisition, 112, 179n70
  under Calcutta Municipal Act (1899), 83n19
  cost of, 79
  Dhakuria Bridge Scheme, 189
  laws, 79
Land Acquisition Act IV of 1876, 79
Land Acquisition Act VI of 1870, 79
land ownership, 20
land prices per *cottah*, 112
land reclamation, 20n48
land use transformation, 4
Lathan, Baldwin
  Report on the Drainage and Conservancy of Calcutta (1891), 58
lathi training, 141
Lefebvre, Henri, 16n32, 17n36, 18–19, 26, 158, 158n1
Left Front government, 32–33, 225

regime in West Bengal (1977–2011), 150
Writers' Building, 232
Legislative Assembly, 110n86, 183, 218, 220
legitimacy of trading licit goods and services, 221
Lieutenant Governor of Bengal, 76, 79
lithofalt, 44
Lockean logic of individual labour, 204
Look East Policy, 261
low-circuit economy, 232
   genealogy of, 232n57
Lower Chitpore Road, 76, 99
lower income group (LIG), 106
low-income urban population, 206

MacCabe, W. B., 45, 47–48
Machooa Bazaar Street, 79, 85, 93
   widening of, 81
Machua Bazaar, 115, 122–123, 218
Maden, James, 87, 88, 159, 171–172
Maharaja of Burdwan, 110
Mahatab, Bijoy Chand, 108
Mahomedan, 116, 120, 122
   properties, 74
   shops, 120
   worker, 117
Mahomed, Din, 73
Major, John, 226
Mandal, Bimal, 209
Mandal, Ratan, 188n88
marshland, conversion into the city, 160–165
Martin, James Ranald, 160–161
Marwari Association, 74–75, 85
   policing of central Calcutta by, 116n104
Marwari businessmen, 98
Marwari mercantile community, 80
Marwari trading community, 3, 111
Marx, Karl, 14n28, 14–15n30, 17, 18n38–39, 19, 20n45, 21n41, 37, 57n72, 190, 212, 212n11, 213, 217, 259

mass agitation, in the streets, 30
mass democracy, 4n10, 6, 26, 30–31, 58, 178, 193, 209, 246
mass meeting, of Police constables, 62
mass mobilization, 60
   infrastructure of, 29
mass nationalism, rise of, 7
Mazumder, Soumita, 140n50, 143
McAdam, John Loudon, 43
Medical College Hospital, 93
mess-bari, 98n53
Messrs Bird and Co., 44
militant trade unionism, 230
minimum wage, government-mandated, 212
*mistri*s (chief craftsmen, foremen), 260
Mitra, Bimal, 92n43
Mitra, Iman, 86
Mittar, Ashutosh, 141n51
Mitter, Nirmal Chandra, 106
M. L. Dalmiya & Co., 175, 176n58, 203
mob–cop dialectic. *See* crowd–police dialectic
mobile subjectivities, politics in generating, 2
mobilization of space, 158
mob lynching, of Muslims inside Muslim *mohalla*s, 147
Mohamedan slaughterhouse, 113
Montague–Chelmsford Reforms, 140
Mookerjee, Asutosh, 83, 84n22
Mookerjee, R. N., 115, 116n104
mosque near Harrison Road, story of, 73–77
motion
   city of obstructed motion, 33
   interplay with obstruction, 17
   people's relationship with, 2
   social production of, 2
motion and obstruction
   dialectic of, 14
   new horizon of, 257–262
motion-oriented urban imaginary, 37
Motor Vehicle Branch, 49
Motor Vehicles Act, 48

Mukherjea, J. C., 168
Mukherjee, Janam, 139
Mukherjee, Subrata, 214
Mukherjee, Sudhendu, 205n4
Mullick, Kumar Nagendra Nath, 102
Municipal Corporation, 72, 74, 100
  construction of Harrison Road, 73
municipal engineers, 43
Muslim community
  bustee dwellers, displacement of, 75
  cleansing of, 149
  greengrocers (*subzifrosh*), 213n12
  literacy rate of, 151
  non-Bengali, 218
  Peshawari traders, 114
  population, in Calcutta, 145–146
  proprietors, 81
  territorial marginalization in Calcutta, 145
  in West Bengal, 145
  working-class, 114
Muslim League, 65, 67, 136, 144, 217, 217n24
  Calcutta District Committee of, 218
  call for 'Direct Action', 138n46
  National Guards, 144
Muzaffarpur bombing incident, 12n24

Nair, Janaki, 6n13
Nair, P. T., 22n53
Nakhodka Mosque, 73n1
namasudra (Dalit) refugees, 209–210
National Emergency (1975–1977), 190, 215–216, 220
  Congress-imposed, 217
National Federation of Independent Trade Unions, 217, 217n22
National Hawker Federation (NHF), 229n54, 233
Nationalist Hawkers' Association (Congress-R), 215
nationalist movements, rise of, 3n7
Natiram Sagarmal & Co., 175
Nehru, Jawaharlal

  'Tryst with Destiny' speech, 69
  visit to the refugee city, 149
neoliberal economy, 266
New Ballygunge, 169
new 'inner city', making of, 165–171
Newsweek, 226
Nirbhaya Protest, in Delhi, 263
'non-Bengali' Muslims, 218
non-collective actors, 57
non-Congress alliance, 214
Non-Cooperation–Khilafat Movement, 30, 61–62, 140–141
obstructed motion
  city of, 33
  topology of, 159
obstructionism
  culture of, 207
  hawkers' obstructionism in Calcutta, 246
  new vocabulary of, 262–267
  pedestrianism *versus*, 234–242
  politics of, 213–219
Ochterlony Monument, 60, 89
offences against public tranquillity, 71
Officer in-Charge (OC), 185
old dwellings, destruction of, 3
Operation Hawker (1975), 216–218, 228
Operation Sunset, 228
Operation Sunshine (1996–1997), 33n84, 222–231, 233, 244, 247, 252, 256, 262
  as 'bloodless revolution' to free Calcutta from the hawkers, 225
  end of, 228
  failure of, 226, 228
  mass suicide of hawkers following, 227
  media coverage of, 237n67
  as State Resolve Flattens Feeble Defiance of Hawkers, 226
organized mobilization, 213
organized street agitation, beginning of, 59–63

Pakistan, creation of, 145
Pal, Radha Charan, 102
Panchanantala *bustee*, 192
Park Circus Maidan, 183
Partition of British India (1947), 7
Partition-related political developments, 28
pavement dwellers, 205, 244
paving experiments, in Calcutta, 43–46
Payne, C. F., 86, 112n93
P. C. Coomar & Co., 176
People's Age, 67
'perfect' city, bourgeois utopia of, 17
Peterson, J. C. K., 100n60
Phaeton carriage, 48
plague crisis, in Bombay (1897), 125n15
Plague of 1898, 75
planned urbanization, 4, 159
police action, against protestors, 64–67
political mobilizations, 22, 140
politics of the street, 246
politics on the street, 246
Porabazaarer
    bustee, 164
    math, 164
Posta Bazaar, 184
poverty tourists, 244
Presidency Area, 124
Presidency Area (Emergency) Security Bill (1926), 124
Presidency College, 93, 97
President's Rule, 214
Prey, Robert, 259n19
Primitive Accumulation of Capital, 57n72
Prince Anwar Shah Road, 160, 178, 211
private property, 19–20, 22–23, 84, 160, 179, 181, 186, 245
production, capitalist mode of, 2, 18
prohibited zones, of white privilege, 67
property distribution, along ethno-religious lines, 82
property prices, redistribution of, 88
public agitation, in Calcutta, 32

public and private property, defacement of, 33n84
public nuisance, 58
public–private partnership (PPP), 59, 261
public property, appropriation of, 245
public, rights of, 56
public space in a city, law of, 234
public violence, on government property, 70
Public Works Department (PWD), 47–48
Puja season of 1955, 185

quintessential citizen (*sadharan manush*), 226

Rabindra Sarovar, 193
race of life, 14n26
racial segregation, 11, 61
Rafiq, S. K., 148
Rajagopalachari, C., 69
Raja Reshee Case Law, 83n19
Ramakrishna Mission, 144n62
Rao, Nikhil, 6
Rapid Action Force (RAF), 223–224
Rashbehari Avenue, 67, 160, 165–171, 174, 177, 179, 189, 191, 193, 202–203, 210, 222
    Basanti Devi College, 186
    and city's underground drainage system, 165
    encroachments in, 185
    hawkers' corner, 186
    jabardakhal movement, 183
    proliferation of the people's economy, 184–188
    residential and commercial properties, 168
    Scheme XV: The Main Sewer Road, 166
Rashid, Abdul, 68
'ratepayers' associations, 49, 93
Ray, Rajat Kanta, 22n53

Ray, Siddhartha Shankar, 214
real estate developments, 32n82
real estate market, 16, 73, 77, 151, 157, 166, 182, 225
rebellion reconstruction, post-1857, 11
recoupment, principle of, 78, 83
Refugee Central Rehabilitation Council (RCRC), 183
refugee encroachment, of properties in south Calcutta, 180
refugee hawkers, 184, 186n85. *See also* footpath hawking
    college-educated, 209
    disappearance of refugee identity, 210
    loans from moneylenders, 211
    migration from Bihar and Uttar Pradesh, 211
    social dynamism among, 211
    survival on Calcutta streets, 211
    upper-caste, 210–211
refugees
    due to economic distress, 211
    interstate migrants, 211
    namasudra (Dalit), 209
    Partition-linked migration, 211
    weavers, 186n85
regime of low intensity terror, 155
Registration Department's Annual Report (1917–18), 111n91
Rehabilitation of Displaced Persons and Eviction of Persons in Unauthorised Occupation of Land Act (1951), 182
rental economy, 259
    principle of, 87
Rent Committee, 109, 110n86
rents
    Calcutta Rent Bill (1920), 108n76
    profiteering by landlords, 21n49, 109
    'rent storm' in the housing market, 107, 109–110
    and riots, 107–117
    rise in house rent and property prices in Calcutta, 108
    theory of, 87
    variations in house rents, 107
    War prices and house rents, 108
rent storm
    in housing market, 107, 109–110
    in industrial jute production market, 111
Report of the Committee Appointed to Enquire into Land Values and Rents in Calcutta (1920), 109n80
residents' welfare association (RWA), 59
Revolutionary Socialist Party (RSP), 153, 213
rice mills, 195–197
Richards, E. P., 38–40, 42–43, 54
right to the city, 229
Rigi, Jakob, 259n19
Risley, H. H., 82
road construction
    coating of coal tar, 43, 46
    discourses of, 43
    paving experiments, 43–46
    relation with land-pricing, 80
    standardization of methods for, 48
    use of bitumen in, 45
road electrification, 12
roads and street alignments, 42
Rockefeller's Standard Oil Company, 47
Rowlatt Bill (1919), 62
Roy, Ananya, 150n86, 222n39, 225, 225n47, 226n48, 229n56, 256n6
Roy, Tapan, 209
RSS, 146
Russa Road, 160, 166–167, 172, 174
    Asutosh Mookerjee Road, 161
    changing world of, 160–165
    holdings along, 162
    between Lower Circular Road and Hazra Road, 161
    Tram Company facility, 164
    transformation of, 164
    widening of, 164

sabotage of public infrastructures, by citizens, 68–71
Sabuj Sangha (a clubhouse), 91
Sachar Committee Report (2006), 151
Saheb Bibi Golam, 90, 92n43
Salt Lake, 256
Samaddar, Ranabir, 7n14, 22n52, 25n64, 70n111, 128n23, 229n56, 255n4, 256n6, 258n14, 261n23
Sambhunath Pandit Street, 164
Sandhya (evening daily), 60, 126n19
sangram (struggle), against the state, 230, 233
    HSC's narrative of, 242n68
Sanyal, Kalyan, 212n10, 229n55, 256n6
Sarabhai, Mridula, 147
    Report on the Communal Situation and Riots in Calcutta (1950), 147n72
Sardar, Ajijur Rahaman, 154
Sarkar, Aditya, 56n69
Sarkar, Banamali, 92
Sarkar, Sumit, 27n67–68, 30n77, 60, 60n78, 107n73, 111n89
Sarkar, Tanika, 7n14, 29n75, 30n76–77, 41, 61n81, 62n85, 64n89, 65n92, 127n22, 146n67
*satyagraha*s, 62, 62n84, 64
Scheduled Castes, 217
self-destruction of spaces old and new, 19
self-improvement and individual labour, Lockean notion of, 24
'self-propelled movement' of capital, 14, 14n29
Sen, Keshab Chandra, 97
Sengupta, Anwesha, 7n14, 70n111, 146, 146n67, 147n70–71, 148n74, 149n81, 188n89
Sengupta, Kaustubh Mani, 78n13, 92n43, 174n52
Sennett, Richard, 37
seva samitis, 141n52
Shahbag Protest, in Dhaka, 263
Shaheen Bagh protest, in Delhi, 267

Sharan, Awadhendra, 7n13
Shimla Byayam Samiti, 140n51, 141
    involvement in expelling Muslim *bustee*, 144
    salishi sabha (arbitration meeting), 141n51
sidewalk hawking, proliferation of, 186–187
sidewalks, 53
    College Street sidewalks, 61
    construction of, 50
    encroachment on, 58
    formal-legal recognition of stationary hawkers on, 234
    hawker–pedestrian–consumer relation, 241
    pedestrian-centric understanding of, 237
    pedestrian's rights, 234
    problem of encroachment on, 241
    proliferation of hawking units on, 208
    public discourse about, 244
Sikh Cavalry, 123
Simon Commission (1927), 62
'Simon go back' agitation (1927), 62
Singur–Nandigram struggle (2007–2009), 262
Sitaramayya, Pattabhi, 180n71
slum-based production, 26
slum dwellers, 191
slum redevelopment programme, 31
Smith, Adam, 14n26
Snow, P. C. H., 125n15
social conflicts, 73
social infrastructure, of obstruction, 211
Socialist Party, 217
Soortee Bagan/Soorti Bagan, 50n53, 77, 85, 89, 99, 102, 104
Soorti Bagan Scheme, 85
South Calcutta Defence Force, 140
South-Suburban School, 174
sprawling avenues, of Calcutta, 208
Standard Oil Company, 47

Star Theatre, 49
state–capital complex, 207
Statesman, The, 110, 191, 223
state–society–capital relations, 21n49
Strand Road, 39–40, 64, 77, 80–82, 85, 114
street
    in Bombay, 55
    Canning Street, 73, 113, 120, 224
    city streets, 56
    College Street, 44, 61, , 60, 77, 80–82, 89, 93, 98n53, 114, 121, 142, 148, 152, 208, 224, 231
    commoning the, 54–59
    Cornwallis Street, 39, 60, 64, 89, 131, 133–134, 142, 198, 223
    Cotton Street, 73, 79, 79–81, 120
    definition of, 8
    Dharmatala Street, 65–66, 68
    discrete zones, 51
    Halliday Street, 52, 73, 76, 85, 93–94, 96, 98, 104, 113, 120
    macro-segregation of, 51
    organized street agitation, 59–63
    as public space, 55
street-as-commons, 59
street-building
    in Calcutta, 46
    objectives and implications of, 12
street construction. *See* road construction
street culture
    in Bombay, 55
    in Calcutta, 72
street economy, 214, 242
street hawkers
    ability to retain the footpaths, 213
    in Bombay, 54
    claim to entrepreneurialism, 231
    consensus-building exercise, 234
    eviction of
        by Calcutta Municipal Corporation, 222
    conflict with police, 224
    by CPI(M) cadres, 222
    in Dalhousie area, 223
    Operation Hawker, 216–218
    Operation Sunshine, 222–225
    resistance against, 225
    at Turkman Gate, Old Delhi, 215
    family enterprise, 243
    Left Front government's stand regarding, 221
    mass suicide of, 227
    media attack on, 237
    obstructionism in Calcutta, 246
    proposals of resettlement, 216
    rehabilitation of, 220
    rights of, 234
        legal 'formalization' of, 234
street protest, in Calcutta, 61n81
street schemes, in Calcutta, 11
street vendors, 186n85
Street Vendors (Protection of Livelihood and Regulation of Street Vending) Act, 2014 (SVA), 234–235, 244, 257
'striking defects' of Calcutta, 38
subterranean drainage network, 50
Sudhir Kumar Banerjee v. The Commissioner, 184n79
Supreme Court of India, 220
Surtee Bagan Lane, 99
Swadeshi era (1905–1911), 60
    protest marches during, 61
Swadeshi Movement, 11, 60–61

Tagore, Rabindranath, 49
    plan for *rakhibandhan*, 60
Tagore, Surendranath, 168, 168n32
Tahrir Square protests, in Cairo, 267
taktaposh (wooden platforms with four legs), 184
Talukdar, Tushar, 207, 227
Tanzeem-ul-Mussalman, 140
Tarit Kanti Biswas, Printer vs Unknown (1917), 84n23
tarmacadam, 45

Tata, Ratan, 212
Teachers' Movement (1953–54), 70n111
tea export, impact of Partition on tea export, 28
Tegart, Charles, 65
Tejani, Shabnum, 111n91
Telegraph, The, 226
tenants' lease and occupancy rights, 31
territoriality of property, 25
*thana*s, 122, 124, 131
    legal jurisdictions of, 137
Thika Tenancy Act of 1949, 31
thika (leasehold) tenants, 3n8
Thompson, E. P., 14, 254, 257
Tipoo Sultan Mosque, 89
town improvement, by recoupment, 77–86
Town Improvement Committee, 77
Town Vending Committee (TVC), 243
trade unionism, new strategy of, 229–233
trade unions, 216, 221
    creation of, 206
    modernizing of, 221
tramways workers' strike, 48
transfer of the capital, from Calcutta to Delhi, 7n13
trustee of public property, 56
Tsing, Anna, 16
Turkman Gate, Old Delhi, 215
twentieth-century street, 8–13

United Central Refugee Council (UCRC), 183
United Front, 214–216
United Provinces, 63n87
United States (US)
    oil companies in, 47
    Standard Oil Company, 47
universal adult franchise, 4n10
University Law College, 93
University of Calcutta, 90
urban capital, 59
urban civilization, 36
urban civil war, 127–139

urban commons, idea of, 56
urban craftsmen, 254
urban culture, 206
urban development, 21
    and 'stabilization' of the insurgent cities, 32
urban dialectics, of motion and obstruction, 13–18
urban improvement schemes, 21
urban insurrections, in Europe, 2
urbanization
    phenomenon of, 26
    process of, 26, 77
urban life, 9
urban mobility, 36
urban planning, 9, 21n48, 31, 118, 159
urban poetry, 244
urban property historiography, 21
urban renewal
    effects of, 119
    violence of, 93, 114
urban rent, 21n49
urban revolution, 4
urban sanitization, 215
urban space
    automobiles in, 51
    capital accumulation in, 222
    decolonizing of, 30
    in Delhi and Lucknow, 11
    Hinduization of, 256
    mono-functionality of, 51
    negative appropriation of, 26
    production of, 21
    recycling of, 11
    specialization of, 51
urban warfare, 119

van Doorn, Niels, 259n15
Vanaik, Anish, 11n22, 20n48, 23n56
vernacular motorbuses, 48
Vidler, Anthony, 9
village masses, empowerment to, 70
volunteer corps, 141

Index

Wallace, Rob, 264n28
Ward Institution Lane, 106
war-induced commercial and industrial boom, 109
wastelands, conversion into habitable properties, 160
　case of Russa Road, 160–165
water supply pipelines, 44
wealth accumulation, 110
welfare programmes, 230
Wellington Square, 60, 67, 68
West Bengal Hawkers Association, 184, 215–216
West Bengal Pradesh Congress Committee-R, 217
'white spaces' of the city, decolonization of, 63–68
White Town
　breaching of, 63–68
　of Chowringhee, 59, 160
wholesale markets, proliferation of, 184
women's control of property, 23n56
Workers' and Peasants' Party (WPP), 62
Workers Party of India (WPI), 184, 213, 215

working-class city builders, 56n69
working-class dwellers (*bharatiya*s), 3n8
working-class Muslims, 114
World War I, 27, 47, 173, 204
　hike in defence expenditure due to, 107
　land boom during and after, 85
　renewal and suburbanization during, 159
World War II, 7, 22, 28, 182, 205

Youth Congress, 214

Zakaria, Haji, 73
*zamindar*s, 3n8, 181
　of Bengal, 162
　of Gobardanga, 163
　investment in Calcutta's bazaars and real estate, 163n9
　of Midnapore, 172
zoning of city, 87, 246
　principle of, 26
　vending and non-vending, 235